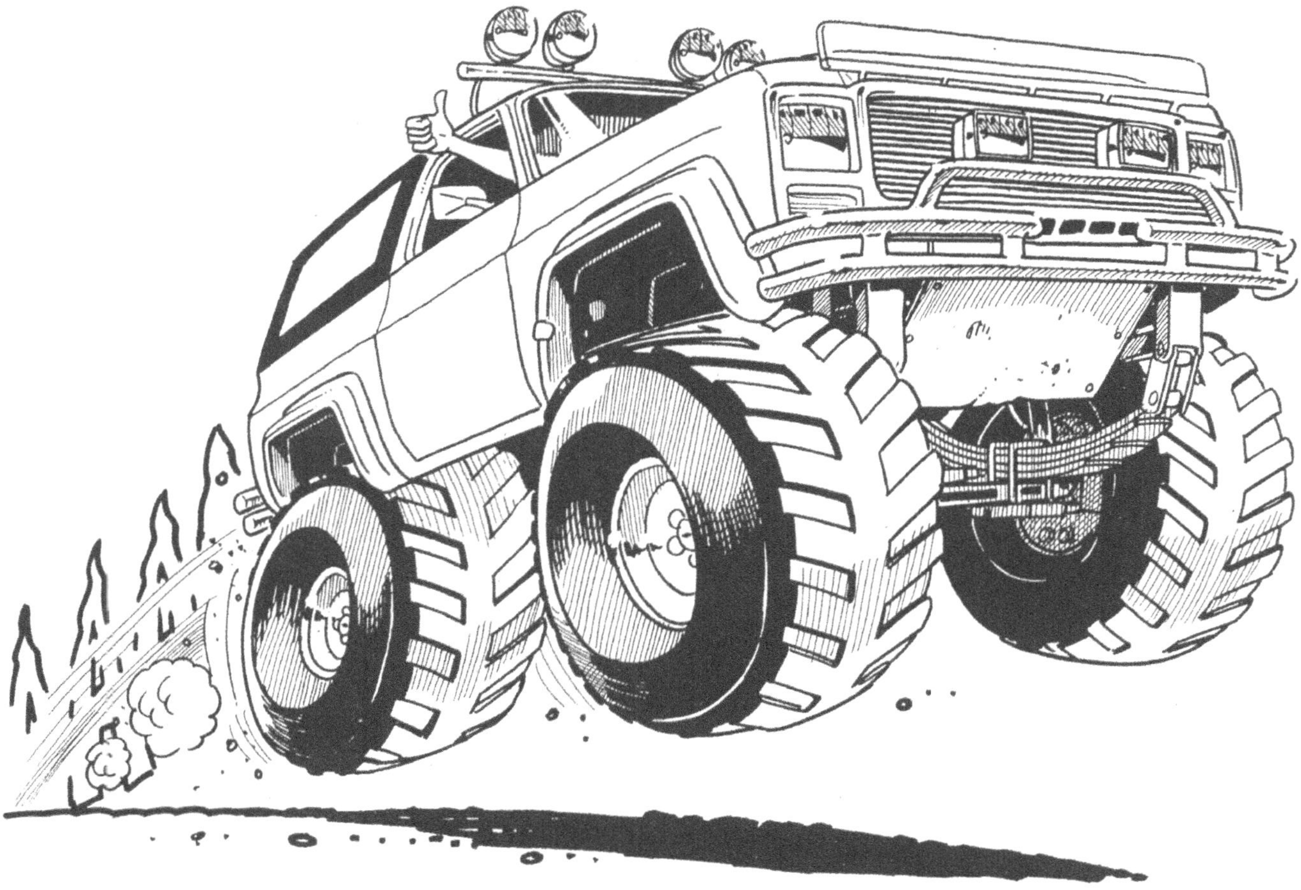

For limited-edition artwork, wall signs,
T-shirts, and other crazy Trosley stuff, visit
WWW.GEORGETROSLEY.COM

Trosley's HOW TO DRAW

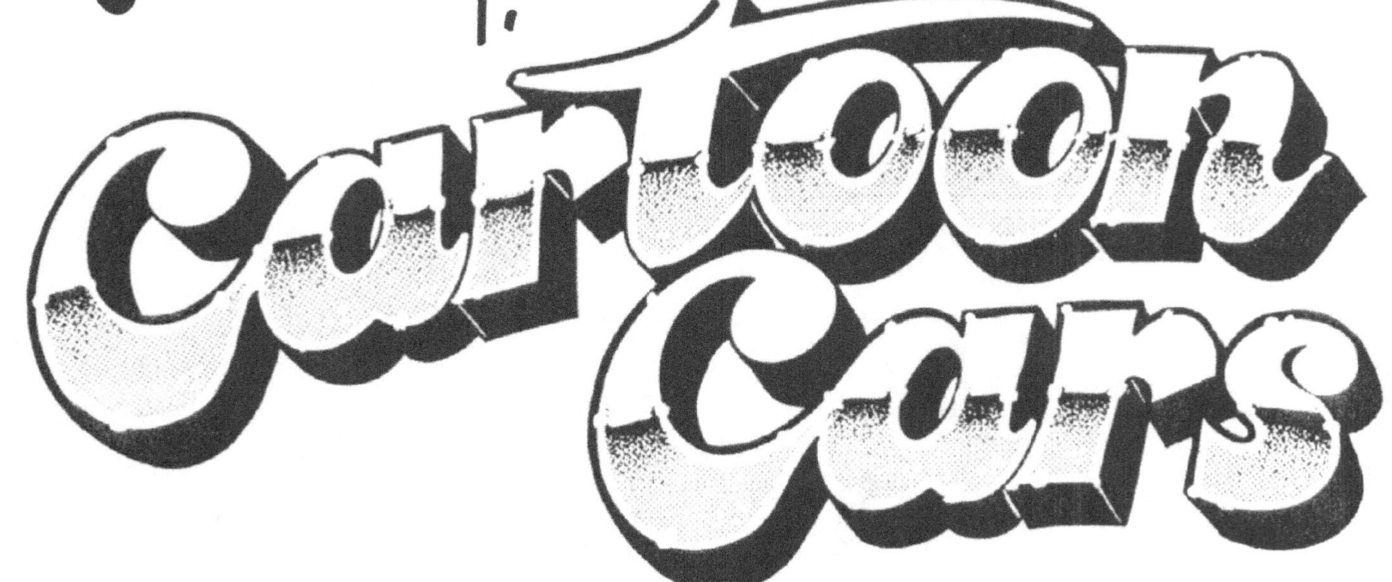

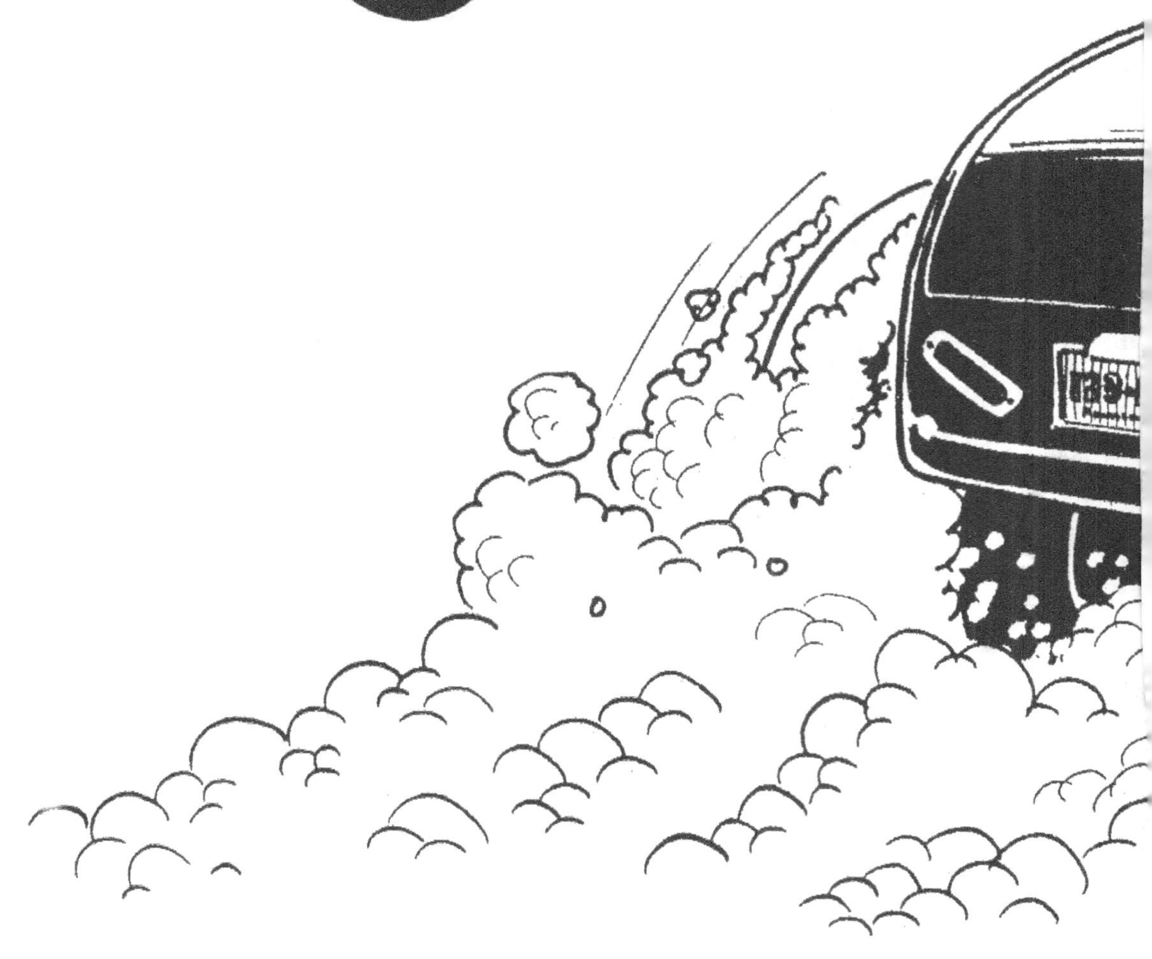

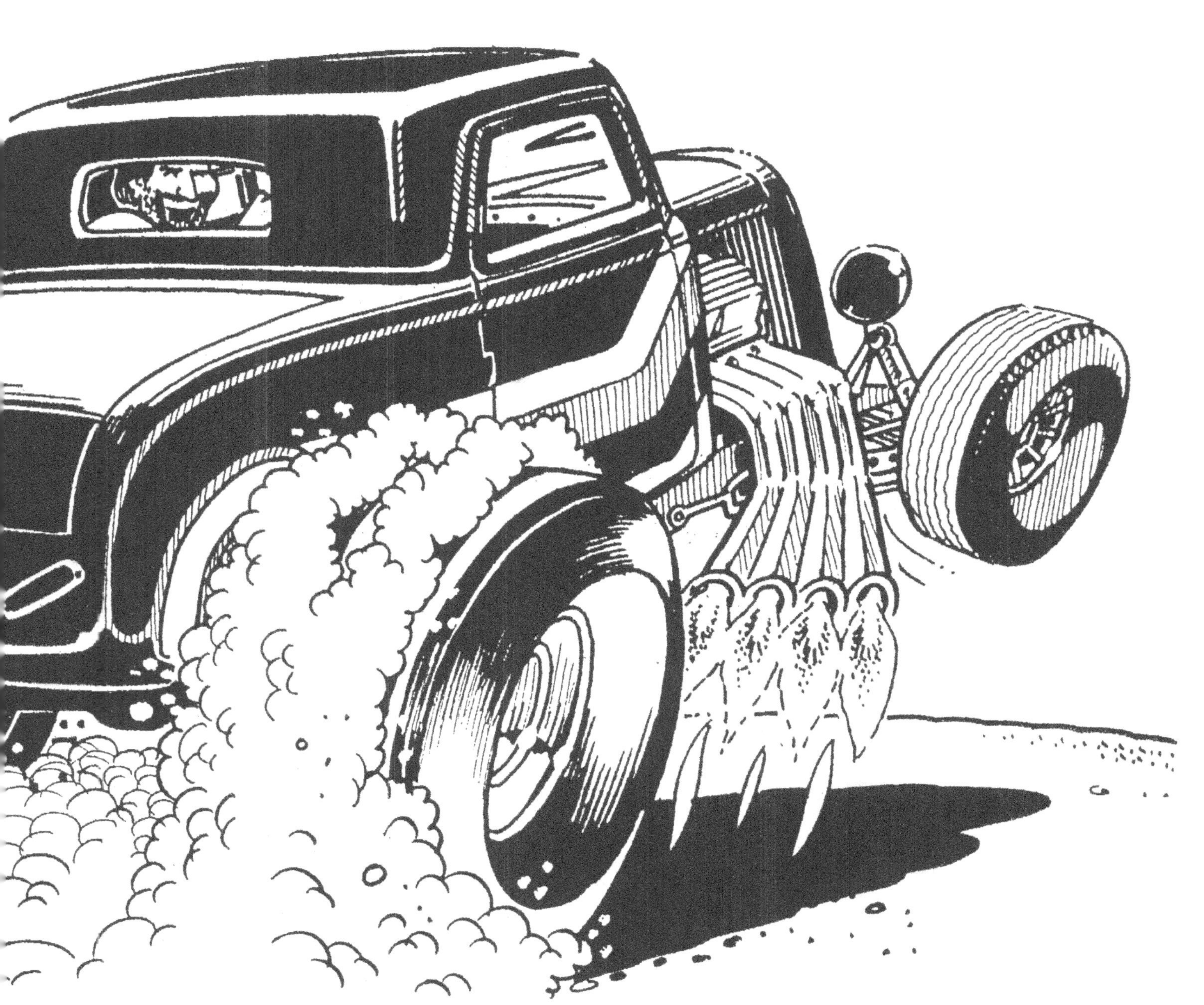

CarTech®

CarTech®, Inc.
838 Lake Street S
Forest Lake, MN 55025
Phone: 651-277-1200 or 800-551-4754
Fax: 651-277-1203
www.cartechbooks.com

Edit by Bob Wilson
Cover design by George Trosley
Page design by Connie DeFlorin
Layout by Monica Seiberlich

ISBN 978-1-61325-548-3
Item No. CT557P

Library of Congress Cataloging-in-Publication Data

Trosley, George
 Trosley›s how to draw cartoon cars / by George Trosley.
    pages cm
 ISBN 978-1-61325-235-2
1. Motor vehicles in art–Technique. 2. Comic books, strips,
etc.–Technique. 3. Cartooning–Technique. I. Title. II. Title: How to
draw cartoon cars.

 NC1764.8.M67T76 2015
 741.5›1–dc23

2014048717

Written, edited, and designed in the U.S.A.
Printed in the U.S.A.

TABLE OF CONTENTS

DEDICATION

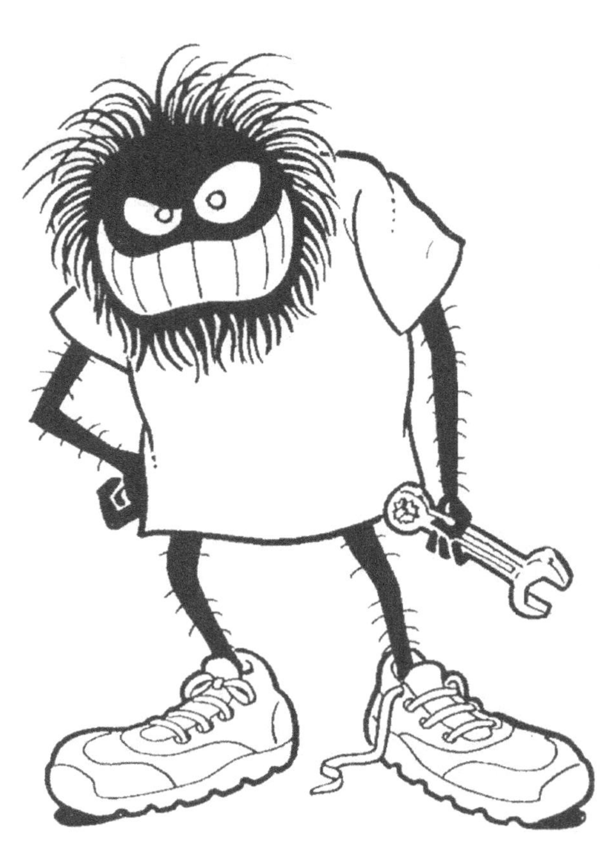

To my good buddy Paul Makowski
who makes it all happen!

ABOUT THE ARTIST

George Trosley began drawing cartoons at the tender age of five. Professional cartooning came 17 years later. After more than 30 years, Trosley's humorous automotive renderings are an illustrated slice of Auto-Americana. He's recognized as one of the major contributing artists in *CARtoons*, *Hot Rod Cartoons*, and *CYCLEtoons* magazines. However, many other national magazines and newspapers have bought and published Trosley's humorous art including *Street Rodder, Car Craft, Popular Hotrodding, Super Chevy* as well as commercial clients including Demon Carburetor and Powermaster Performance.

A free-flowing style and right-on appreciation of the human condition is what attracts automobile magazine editors to George's work. A master at composition and line quality, Troz, as his friends call him, has his finger on the pulse of the car-crazy community in all its rabid devotion and peculiarities. It's most likely due to the fact that George often illustrates his personal passion for automobilia. He can instantly relate what's funny about his own unusual habits, as well as those of other car nuts.

Here's what George has to say about himself and his profession:

"I'm told I was drawing from the time I could hold a crayon. Mom claimed she could always keep me quiet with a pencil and a piece of paper.

"Cars were always a major interest for my brother and me and I drew our 'dream machines' all the time. We built model cars while growing up; I could come up with wild customizing ideas and my brother, Harold, had the patience and body-working talent to turn them into prize-winning creations. Before long we had our driver's licenses and real cars to fool around with. My first car was a '47 Plymouth sedan that leaked a quart of oil a day and smoked two more out the tailpipe. That was followed by a '55 Ford Tudor with a 312-ci T-Bird engine and a severe rake. I lettered 'Village Vandal' on the trunk lid, much to my mom's grief. After I graduated from high school I attended the Hussian School of Art in Philadelphia and commuted in my recently acquired '39 Ford Deluxe Tudor. I spent the next four years learning about commercial art by day, and the workings of a prewar Ford by night.

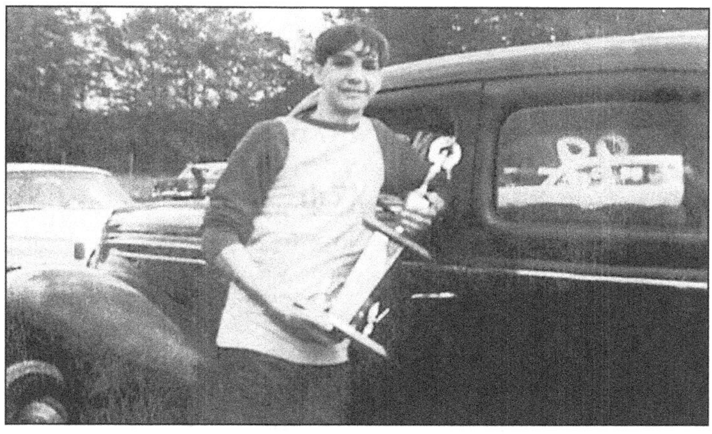

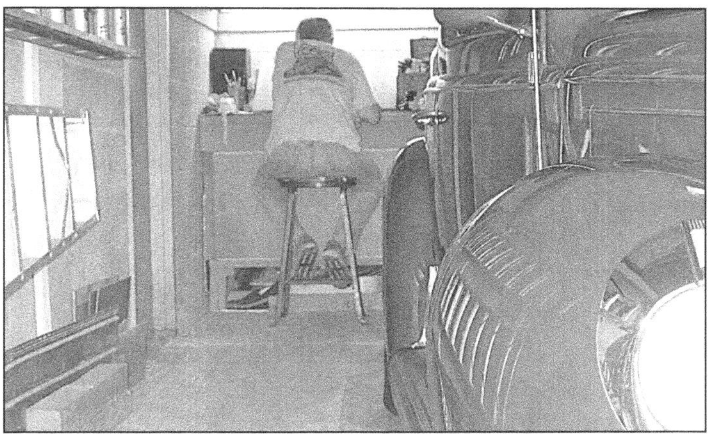

"After art school, I landed a job in a Philadelphia art studio but in the evenings I worked on some comic pages to send to Petersen Publications' *CARtoons* and . . . *they bought them!* That's all I needed. I quit my big city art studio job, moved into a small apartment, and started selling pages to *CARtoons* and *CYCLEtoons*. I eventually created two characters, Krass & Bernie, largely patterned after my brother and me. They chopped, rebuilt, ripped apart, and smoked their tires through the pages of *CARtoons* for decades . . . and I loved it! K&B presently does muscle car burnouts in *Car Craft* magazine and they are still building wild rods!"

Trosley's current passion is another really nice '39 Ford Deluxe Tudor that resides in his garage in Pennsylvania and also creating custom art portraits of hot rods, rat rods, trucks—anything that moves. Troz also specializes in custom T-shirts, event posters, and logos. Visit George's website (georgetrosley.com) for more of his zany visual insanity!

INTRODUCTION

End of summer . . . late Fifties . . . the sun is going down on another balmy day. It'll be dark soon and I'm heading home on my bike. I'd sprayed it baby blue, running whitewalls on chrome rims, no fenders. Unlike most of my friends I kept the chain guard on so I could flame it with my model car paint and brushes: traditional style, yellow to orange with cool blue tips. Every evening on my way home I'd roll my hot rod bike behind the local gas station where they threw old parts and burned trash in a huge oil drum. I'd find voltage regulators, a smoldering distributor cap, sometimes even a carb if I was lucky. I'd drag them home and take them apart marveling at the way they worked inside . . . little springs . . . contact points . . . valves and stuff. I had no idea what I was looking at but it all fascinated me. Eventually the smell of fire and gasoline would bring my mother to the top of the cellar steps telling me to take the junk outside.

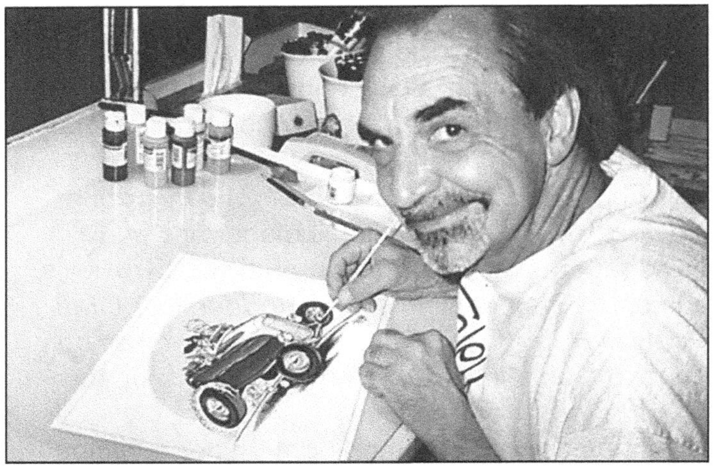

One evening was a little different. As I checked the smoking oil drum I didn't see a fuel pump or a melted coil. I found a copy of *Hot Rod* magazine with only the edges singed. Totally excited I rode to a nearby street light to peruse my treasure. Wow! Hot rods, souped-up engines, dragsters. And then I saw it, in the "Shop Talk" section: my first Pete Millar drawing! It was of a guy who'd shaved down his flywheel so much he was looking at us through it. It totally blew me away; it was so cool!

Everyone has had a moment or two in their life when all the lights and buzzers start going off in their head like a pinball machine when you hit for a free game. This was mine. There I was, my bike leaning against that pole and I'm sitting on the curb under that street light oogling those drawings. That moment changed my life forever.

After that night I'd hit all the local drug stores and news shops going through all the car magazines I could before the clerk would give me that old "This ain't a library, kid!" stuff. I'd always buy a few with my lawn-cutting money so I could have more Pete Millar, Don Jolley, Karl Kohler, Tom Daniels, Roth, and Mouse stuff to sit down and try to copy. I couldn't get enough. Then I found my first copy of the digest-size *CARtoons*. And that was it. The die was cast!

High school art classes, four years of Hussian School of Art, and then jobs in art studios in Philadelphia taught me how to produce commercial art but all those car magazines taught me how to draw cartoon cars. I draw a little like this guy, a touch of that guy, a bit like those guys. Actually, my style is sort of a stew made up of all the car artists I've loved over the years.

When I got a chance to do some pages for *CARtoons* in the Seventies I was thrilled. And when the editor asked if I could come up with a new reoccurring feature for the magazine there was no question in my mind. It had to be all the stuff I'd learned over the years, a "How to Draw Cars" feature. These are those pages.

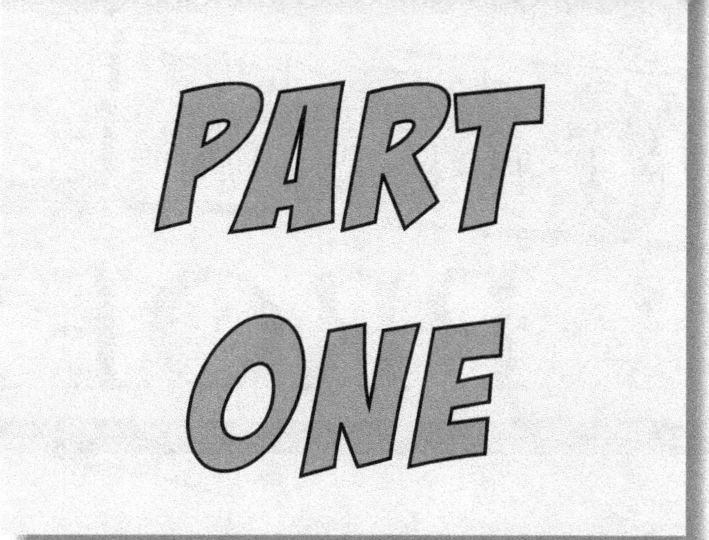

CAR DRAWING BASICS

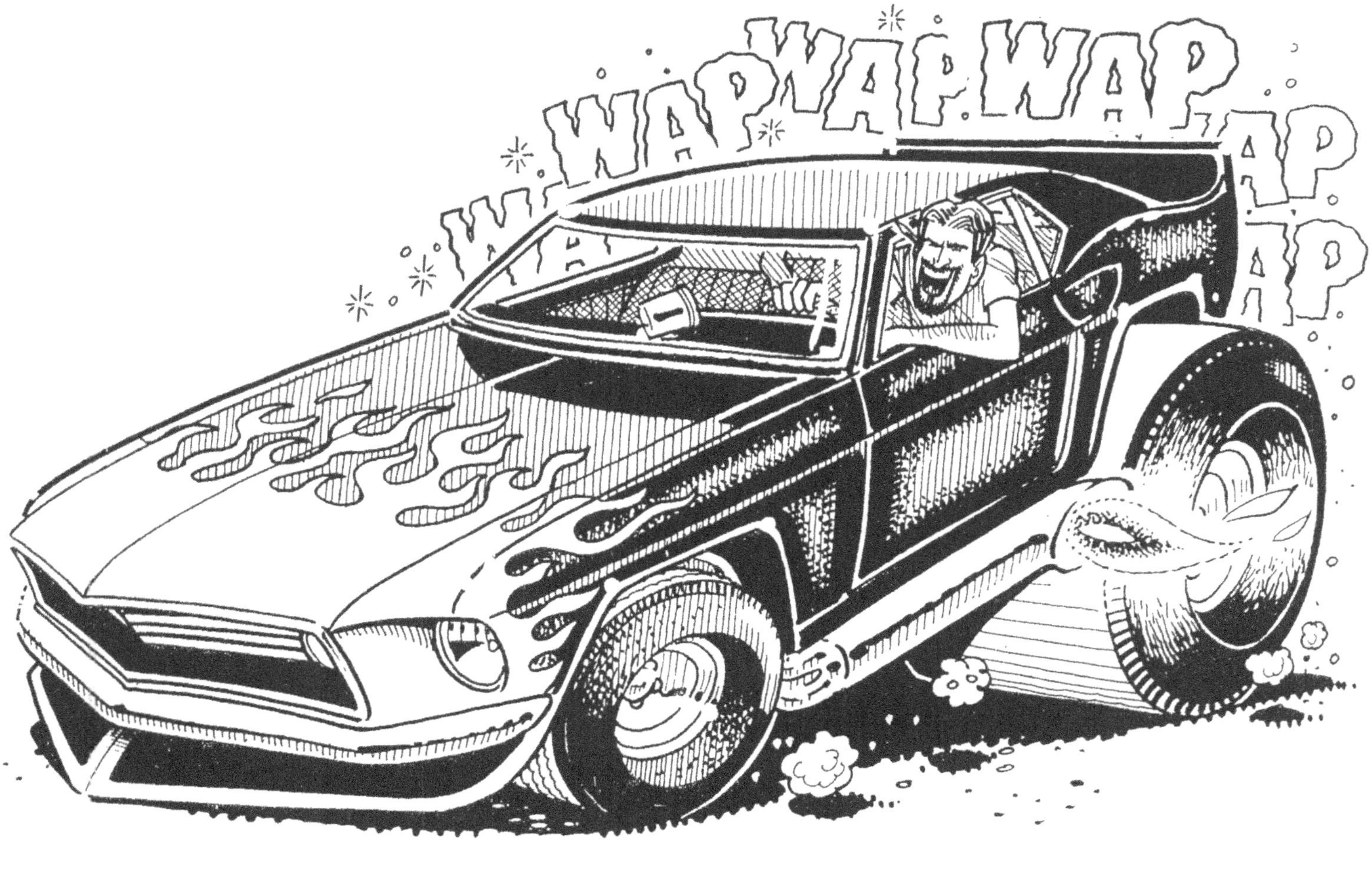

PROFILES

I thought a "how-to" on cars in profile would be a good way to begin. Let's start a Deuce couple with the basic shapes you see here. Some kind of straight edge for the boxes and a compass for the wheels will help a bunch. Take your time on this step. . . . It's important.

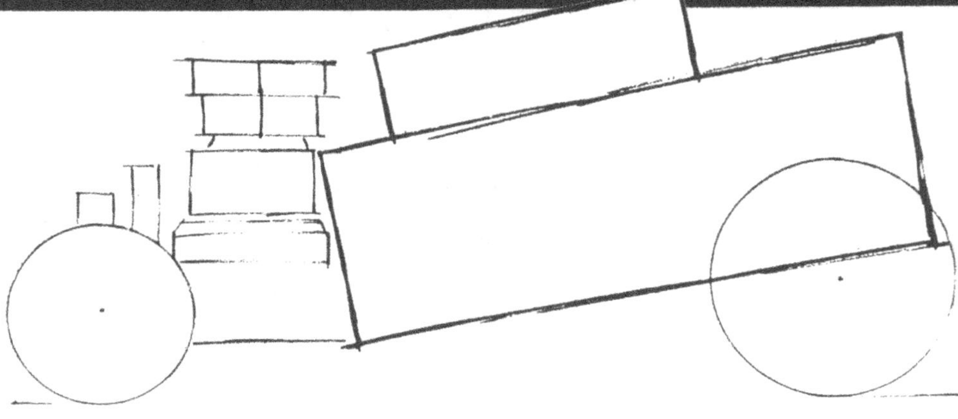

Start up front by carving the boxes into a blown Ford power plant. Air cleaners get tops and bottoms with carbs underneath. Vertical lines and the front pulley system help the blower. Rough in the exhaust as shown. Carve the roofline and trunk out of the box. The body line, door, and windows give the coupe an authentic look. Rough in the tires and rims.

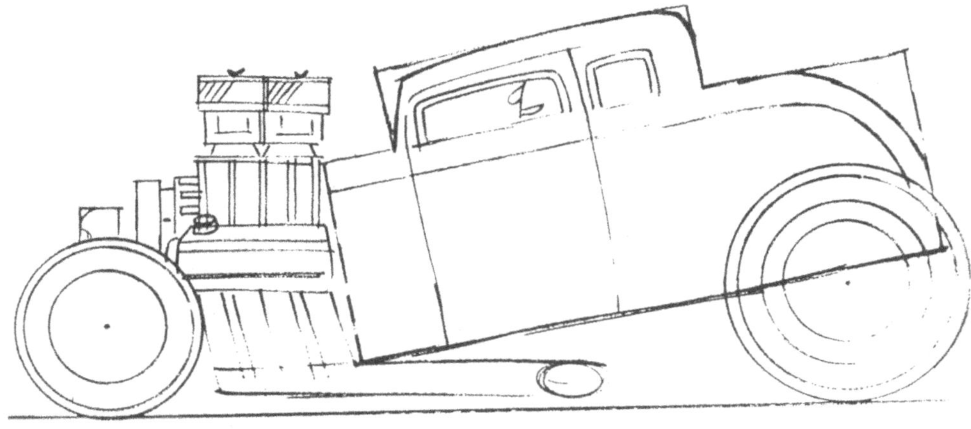

Okay, time to detail 'er out with engine fuel lines and plug wires. Don't forget chrome highlights. Flames and body lines snap up the coup a bit as does wheel detail and a full body shadow. Check over everything one more time then ink it in. Inking can be lotsa' fun. I like to use a fine-tipped felt-tip pen and a regular one for the black areas so I don't ruin the tip of the fine one. A ball-point pen is okay too.

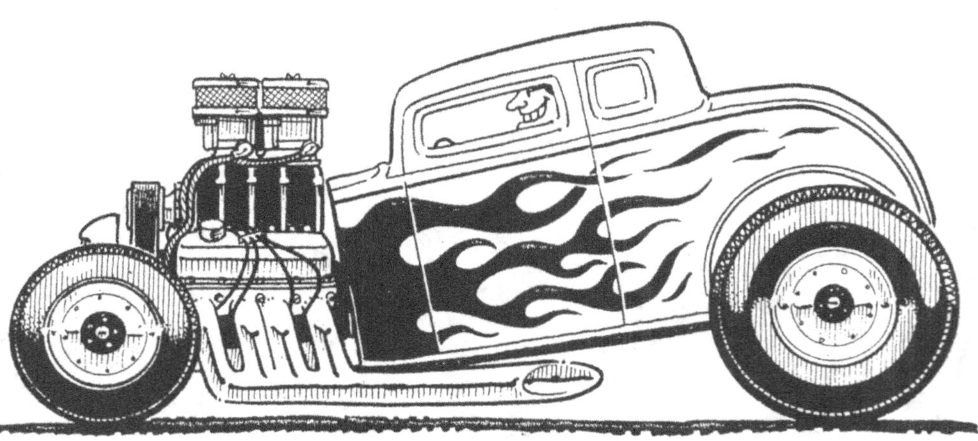

Let's apply some of those same principals to a **'69 Chevy Nova**. Start with the two basic boxes as shown here. Notice how the back roofline runs down into the body and meets the body line. Cut out some wheel wells and add the tires, an oversize one in the rear. Indicate an exhaust header and flame. The hood line slopes down in front and angles to the body line.

Puff up the rear fender and begin adding the shape to the roofline. Indicate windshields, center posts, and wind window. Rough in a driver too. Down below, add a rear bumper and angle the bottom to the wheel well. Rough in wheel flares, door lines, and a front bumper; then work out the header. More detail to the wheel gets it goin'.

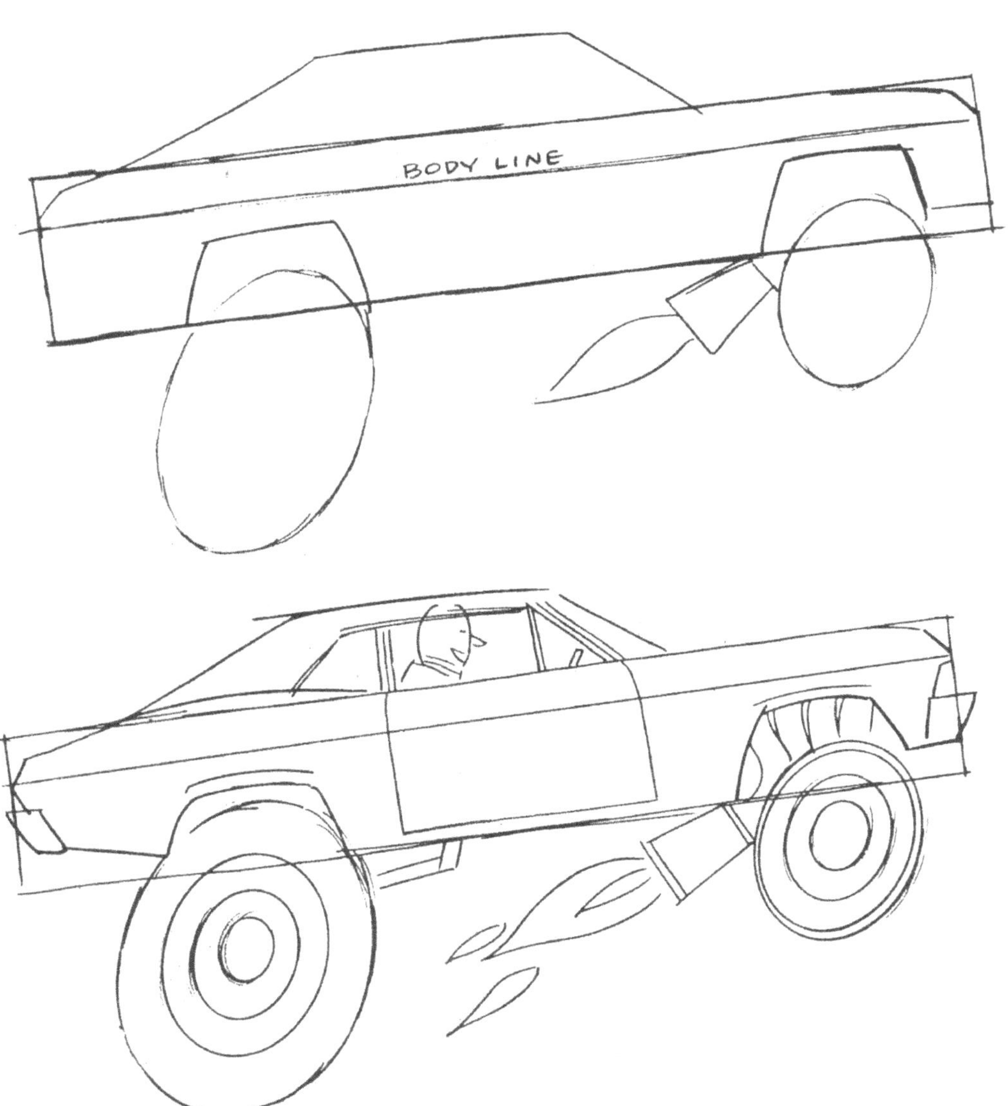

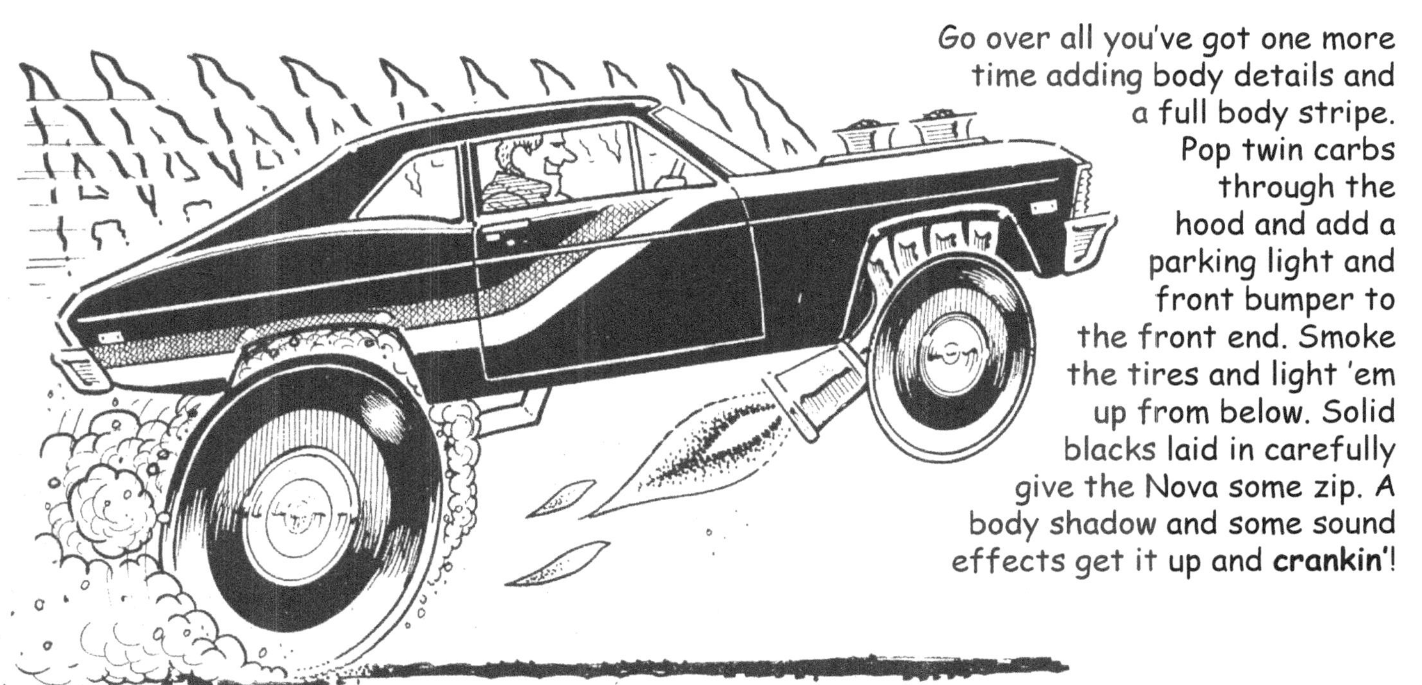

Go over all you've got one more time adding body details and a full body stripe. Pop twin carbs through the hood and add a parking light and front bumper to the front end. Smoke the tires and light 'em up from below. Solid blacks laid in carefully give the Nova some zip. A body shadow and some sound effects get it up and **crankin'**!

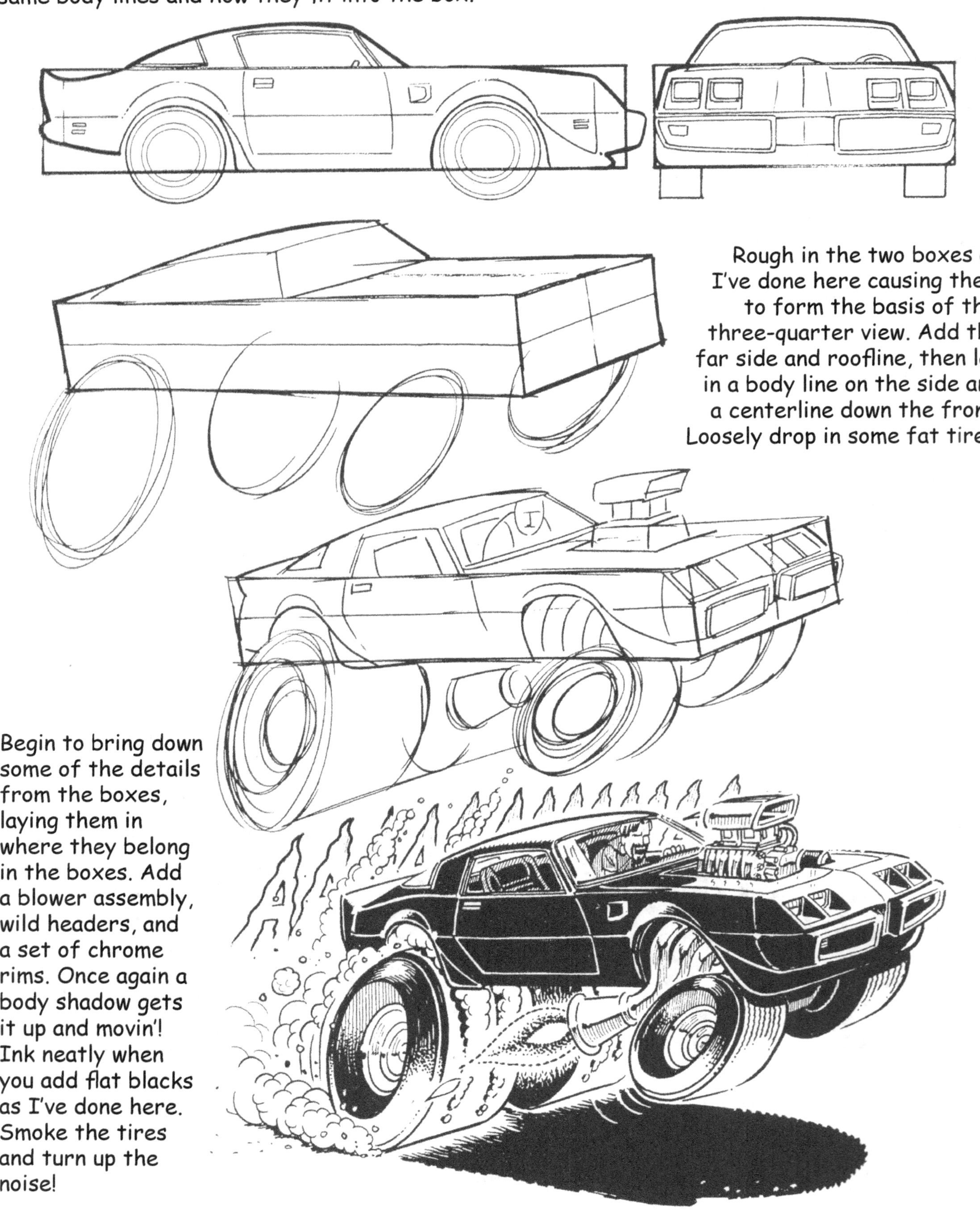

A good profile along with a good front view can give you the information you need to rough out a three-quarter view. Study the two examples below. Notice how many parts **line up** on the same body lines and how they fit into the box.

Rough in the two boxes as I've done here causing them to form the basis of this three-quarter view. Add the far side and roofline, then lay in a body line on the side and a centerline down the front. Loosely drop in some fat tires.

Begin to bring down some of the details from the boxes, laying them in where they belong in the boxes. Add a blower assembly, wild headers, and a set of chrome rims. Once again a body shadow gets it up and movin'! Ink neatly when you add flat blacks as I've done here. Smoke the tires and turn up the noise!

HOW TO DRAW
POINT OF VIEW

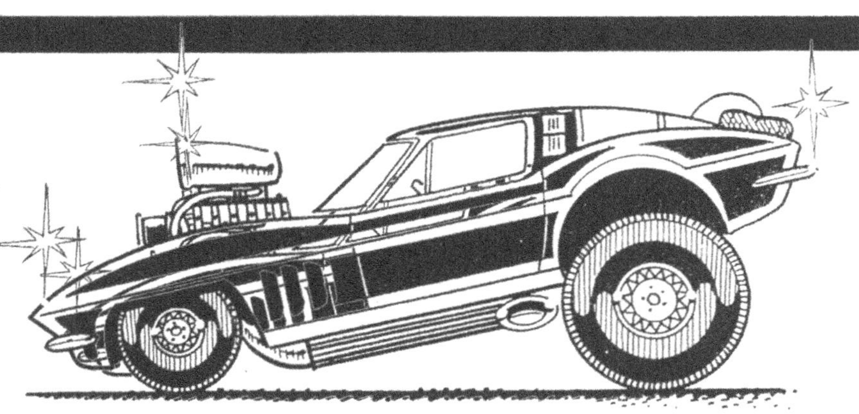

Take a look at the **'Vette** I've drawn here. Even with the custom paint, trick wheels, and engine modifications, it's still not a very exciting drawing. Why? Mainly because the side view I chose when I started is kinda' boring and static . . . It just sits there. I should have chosen a more exciting point of view.

I could've gone for a low point of view. It's much more dramatic and it highlights the sculptured body lines.

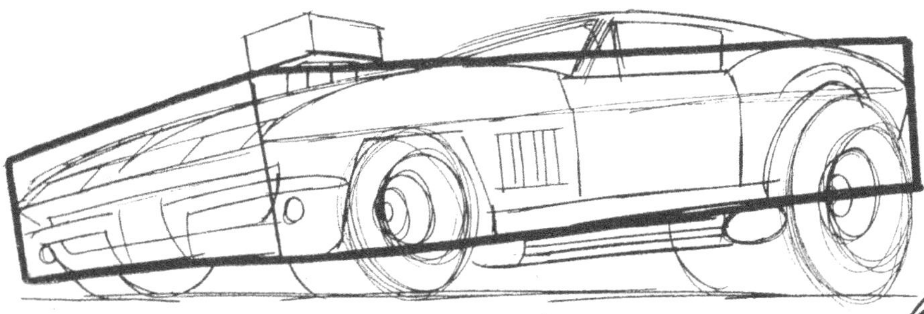

And what about an even lower point of view to put it up in the air . . .

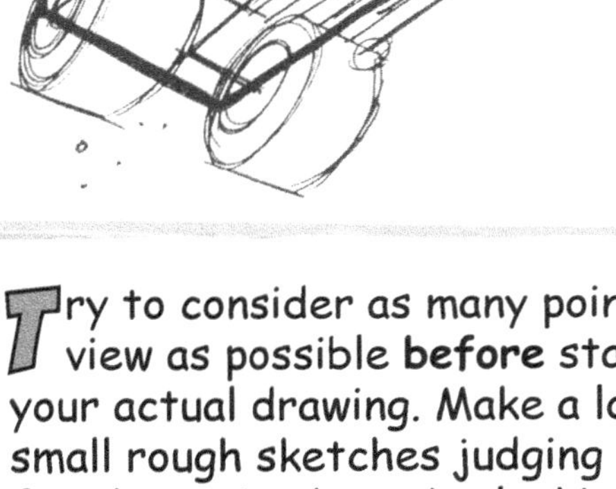

Or I could've chosen an aerial view to show movement and power . . .

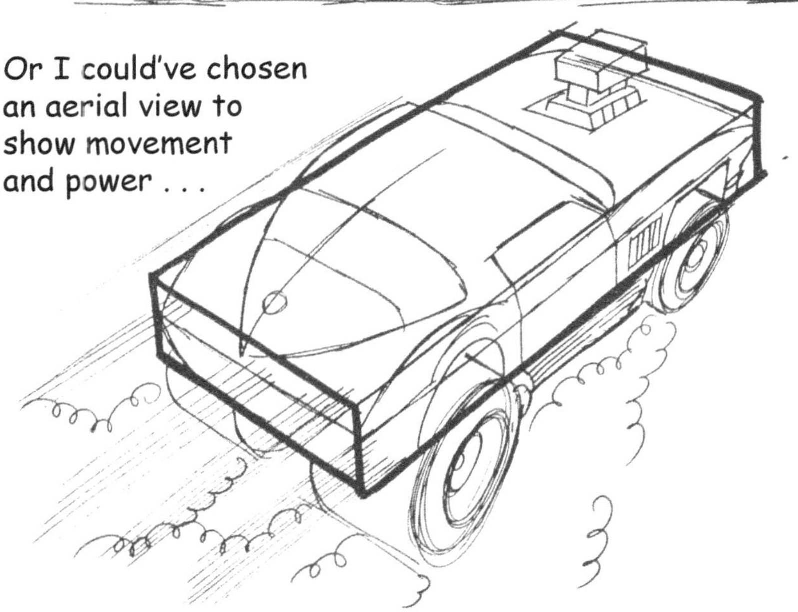

Try to consider as many points of view as possible **before** starting your actual drawing. Make a lot of small rough sketches judging each for the attitude you're looking for. Each view will say something different to your eye.

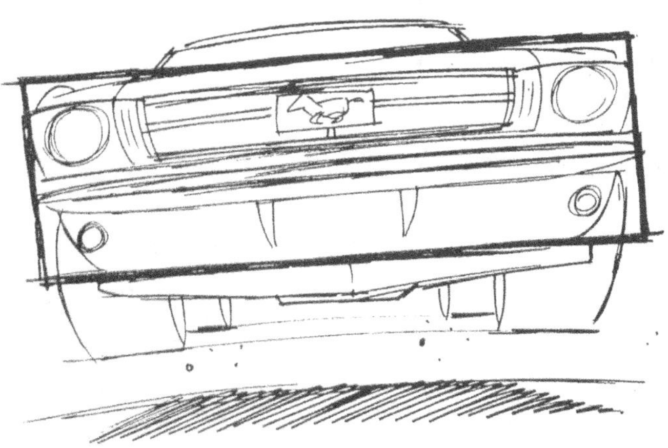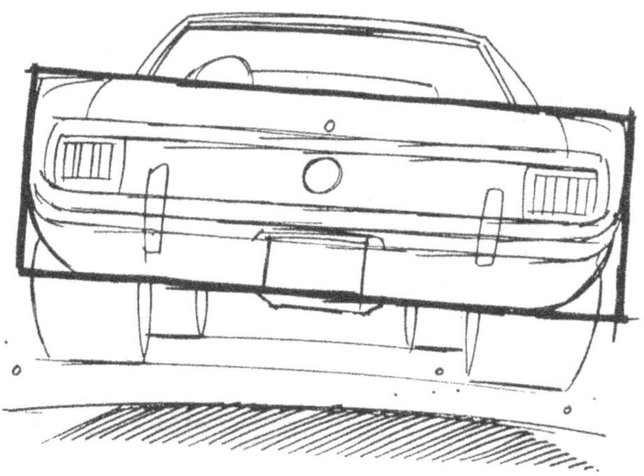

For instance, a head-on front view makes you feel like you're about to be run over.

A head-on rear view makes you feel like you have just **been** run over.

Another good thing to consider at this stage of the game is how the suspension works in relation to the body weight. Ever felt a car tilt a little as you go around a corner? Try to add that feeling to your action shots.

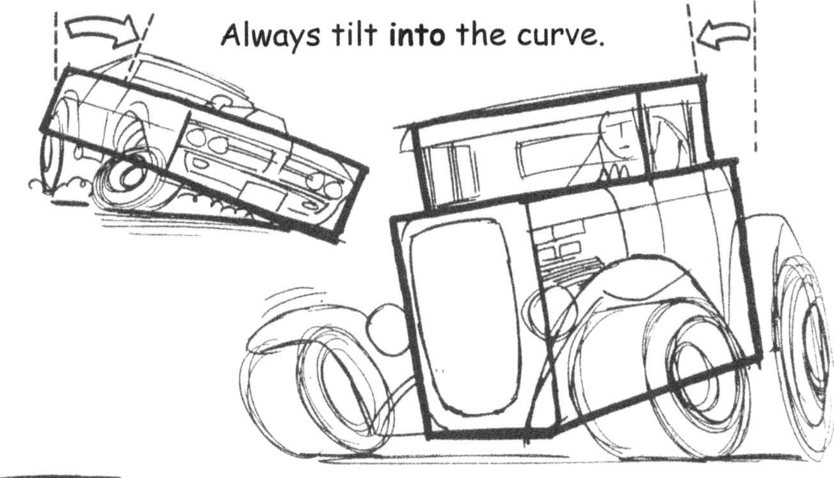

Always tilt **into** the curve.

Notice how the right point of view helps sell the action.

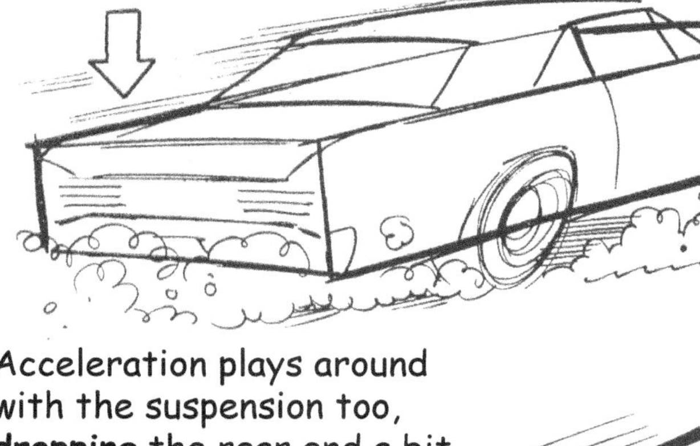

Acceleration plays around with the suspension too, **dropping** the rear end a bit.

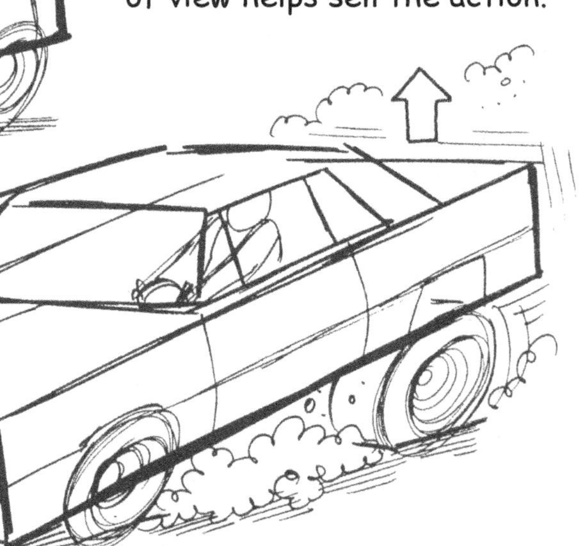

Braking does just the opposite: dropping the front end and **raising** the rear.

Okay . . . Let's try that 'Vette again, this time with a three-quarter rear view. Copy the basic box you see here along with the side body line. Locate the wheel wells then loosely rough in the wheels. Build up the roofline tapering it back to the center point of the rear. Work carefully.

Box in the blower assembly keeping your angles consistent with the basic boxes. Add side and rear windows, roughing in a steering wheel and bucket seats. Lay in the side pipe then add some dimension to the wheels. Check your art against mine closely.

Start detailing the blower, connecting fuel lines to carbs. Clean up the wheels and side pipes then drop in some taillights. A flame paint job adds some excitement while real flames bring the pipes to life. Ink it all in neatly then add solid blacks as I've done here. **Take your time.**

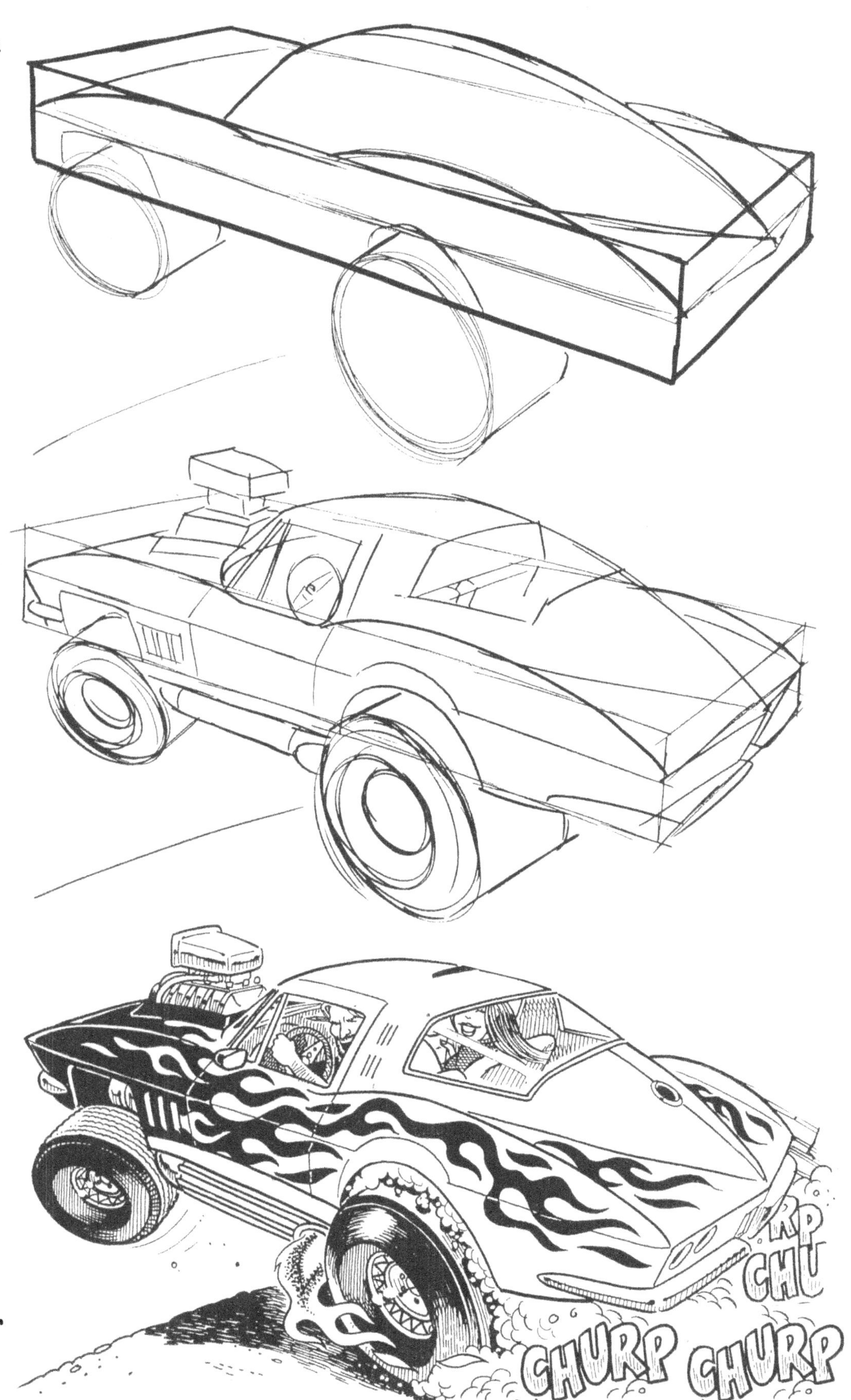

HOW TO DRAW SPEED

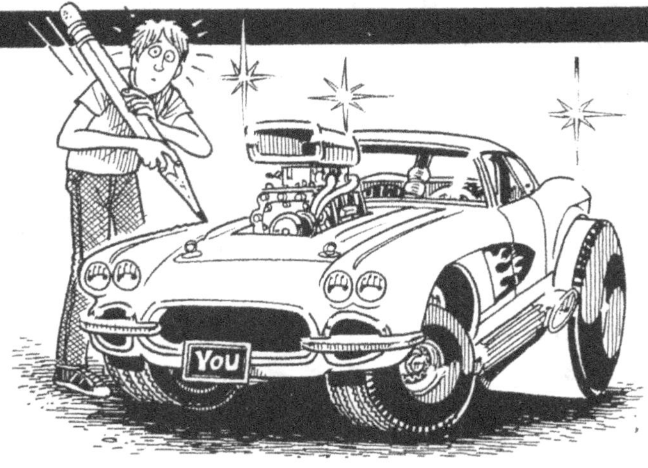

S o you've just finished a choice drawing of your favorite car equipped with all your favorite goodies when you realize something is missing . . . something exciting: movement! Cars move and are fun to draw that way, preferably moving really, really fast!

There are many ways to give the illusion of movement to a drawing; one of the easiest is by crankin' up the tires. Let's explore a few of the basic ways you can get this feeling across on paper.

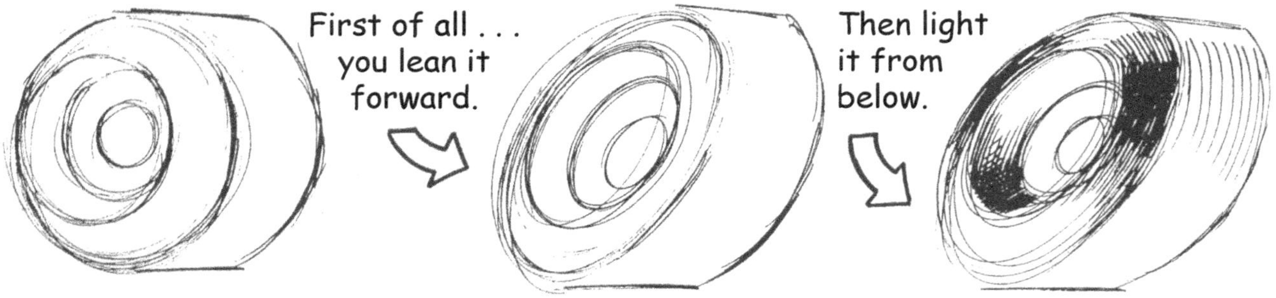

First of all . . . you lean it forward.

Then light it from below.

Then you have your choice of a few accent touches to help build the feeling of speed:

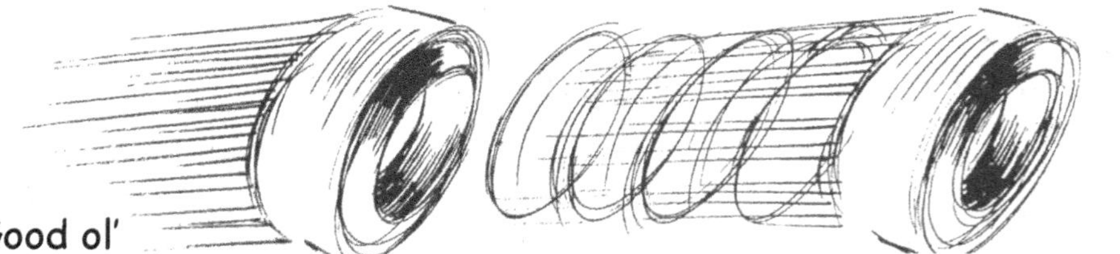

Smoke and cinders

Good ol' "speed lines"

Repetitive ellipses with speed lines

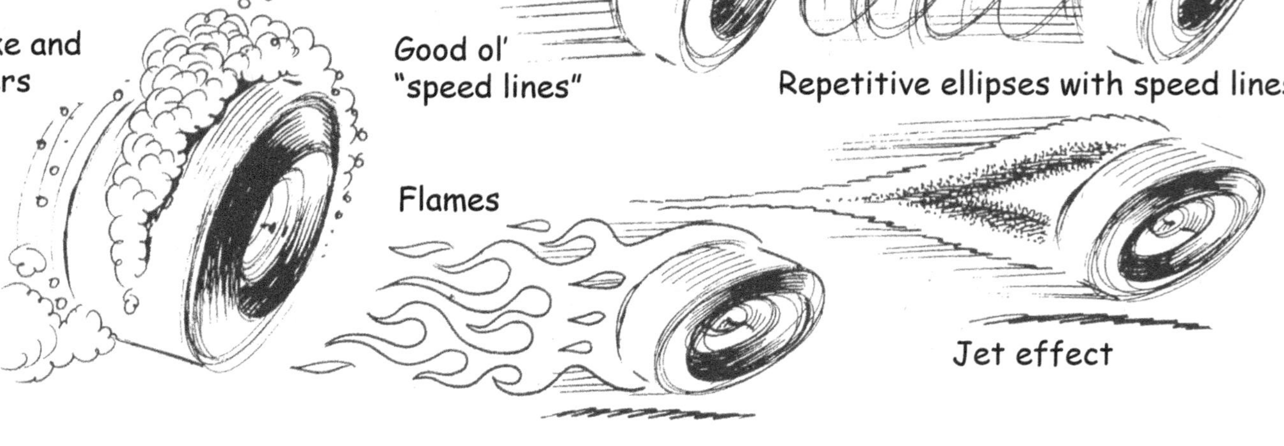

Flames

Jet effect

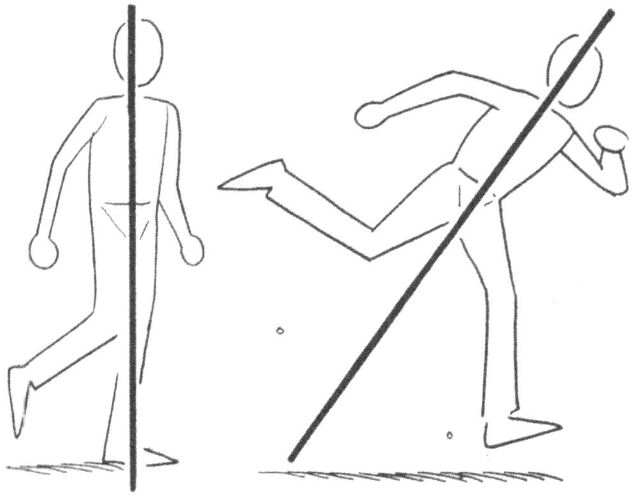

The nice thing about cartoons is that you can draw the way things **feel** rather than the way they really are. Check out these examples. When you walk, your body is upright but when you run, your body leans forward at an angle. Cars aren't flesh and bones so when they move quickly they don't actually lean but adding that feeling to them helps give the illusion of speed. It **looks** right.

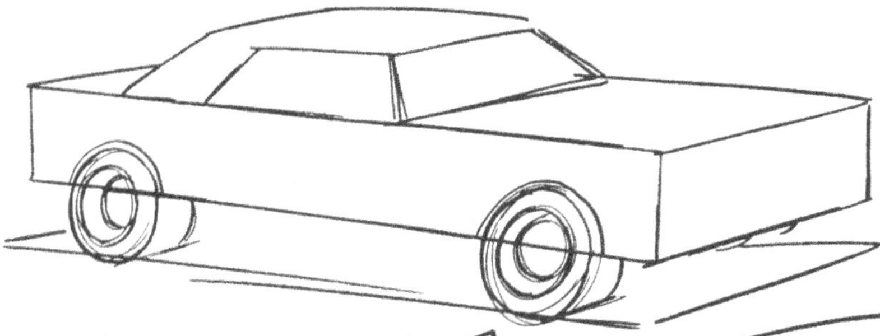

Angle everything and suddenly you've added some movement. Give the tires the same angle then pick it up by puttin' some space between the car and shadow.

With the basic car boxed out squarely, it sits solid and still. A tight shadow keeps it there.

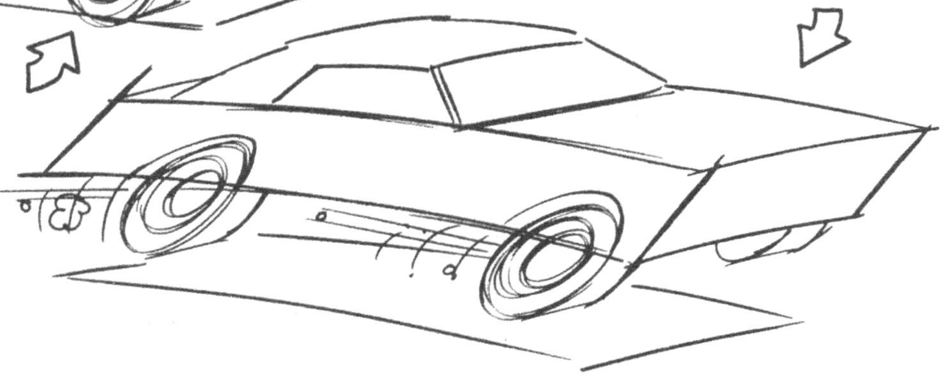

Another little trick is to remember that in this part of the world we read from left to right so things moving in that direction flow nicely with the normal movement of your eyes. This phenomenon makes things moving from left to right appear to move quicker than things moving from right to left, having to fight that eye movement.

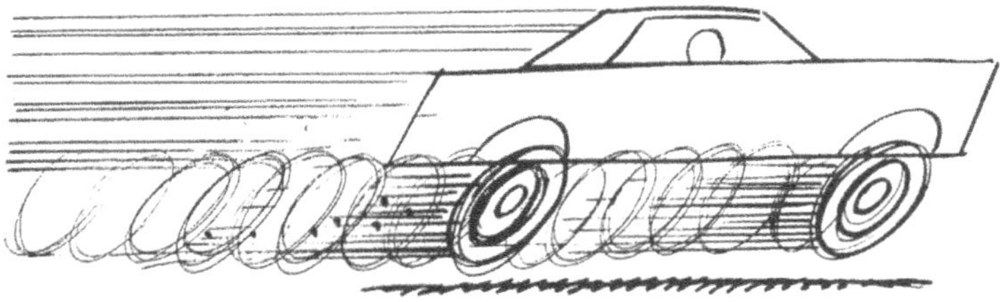

This angle seems to be "going . . ."

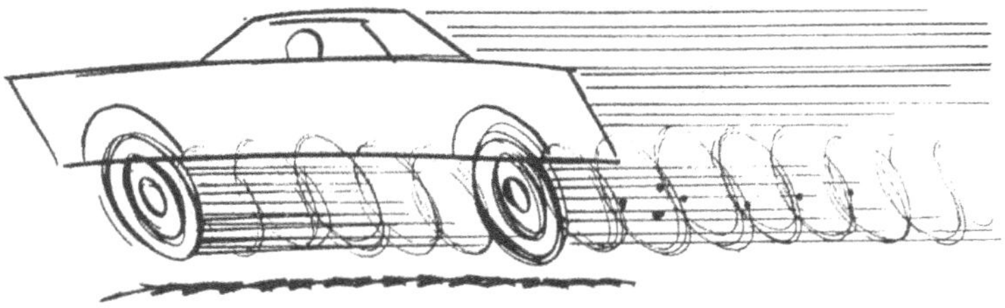

This angle seems to be "coming back . . ."

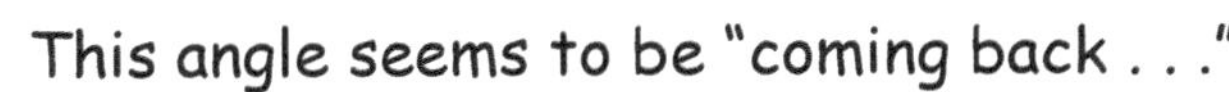

Let's see if you can put a little of what I just talked about together with a **'57 Chevy** and come up with some **speed!** Start with the basic box, angling the ends. Loosely rough in the tires angling them the same way. Starting at the right rear corner, curve the roofline up and over to the windshield. Add door lines.

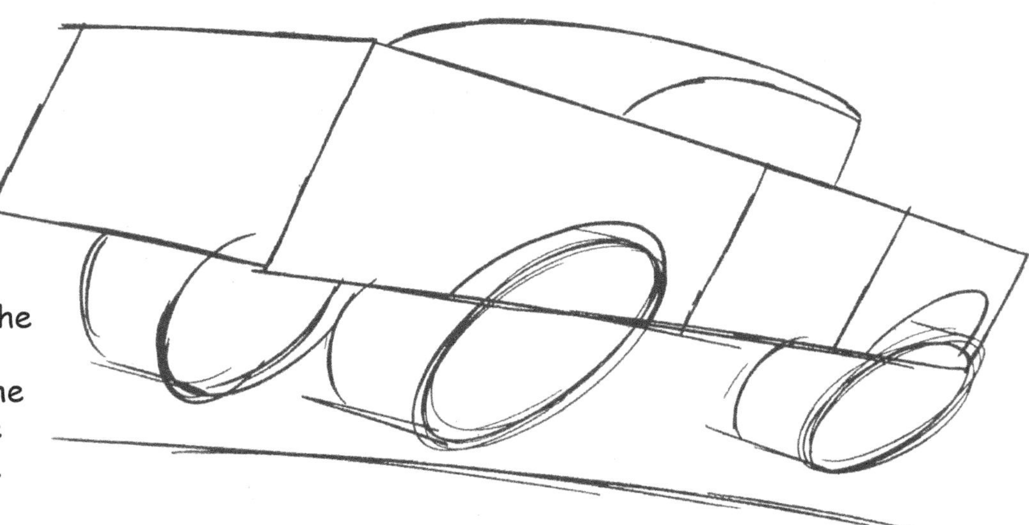

Start the rear fin area with the basic angle then build out from there. Add the vertical oval taillight housings and the center extended areas. Drop down a trunk line and rough in a license plate frame respecting that same back angle. Detail the roof and windshield then add side chrome. Give the tires some dimension and rims.

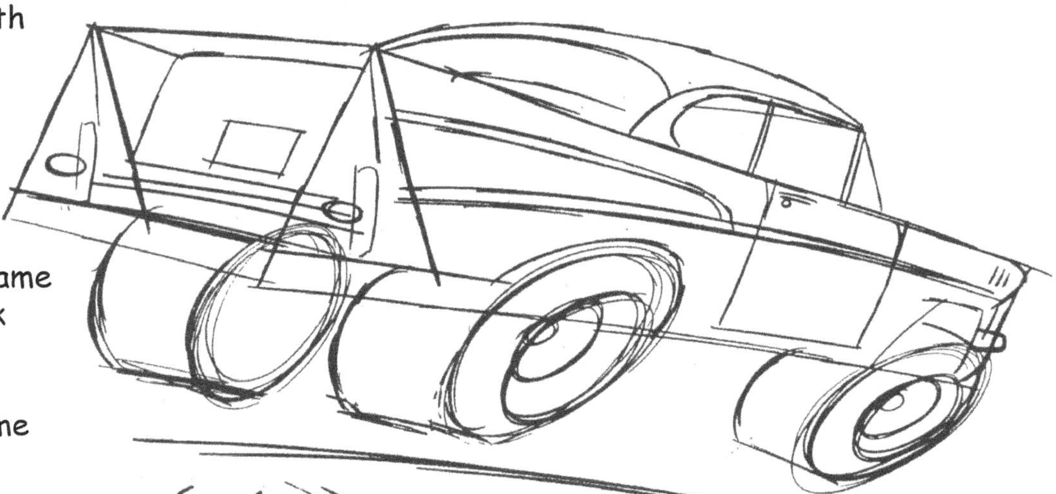

Check over your pencil sketch and compare it to mine. Detail it out until it's ready for inking then begin outlining with a ball-point or felt-tip pen. Add solid blacks as shown then get to work on speed accents to really get it up an' rollin'! A ruler helps keep the speed lines true.

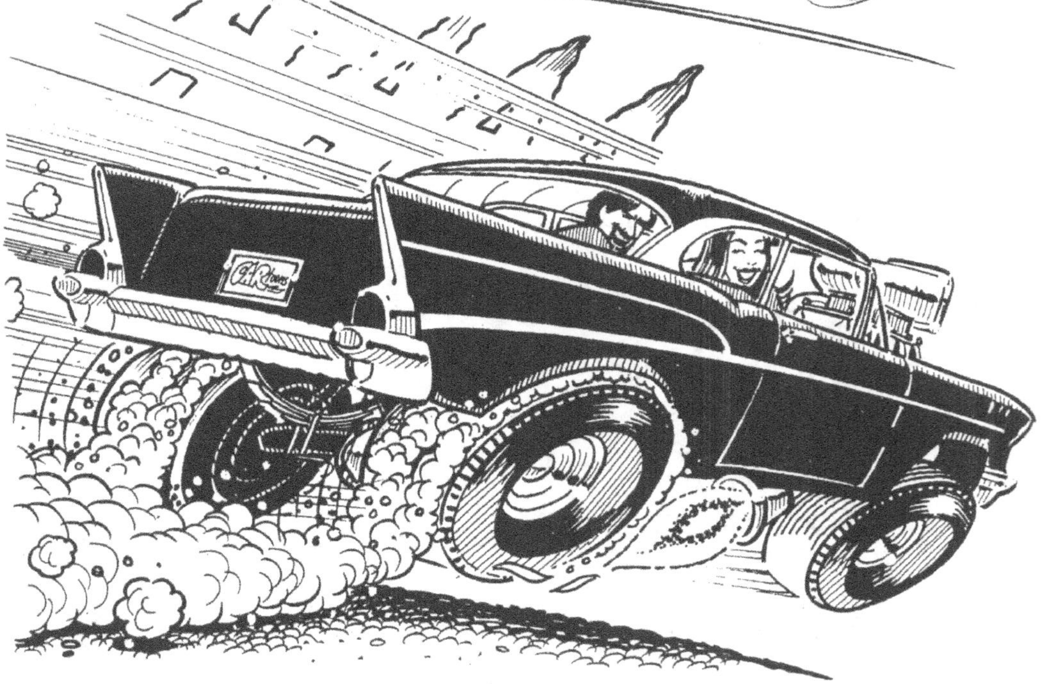

HOW TO DRAW
ATTITUDE

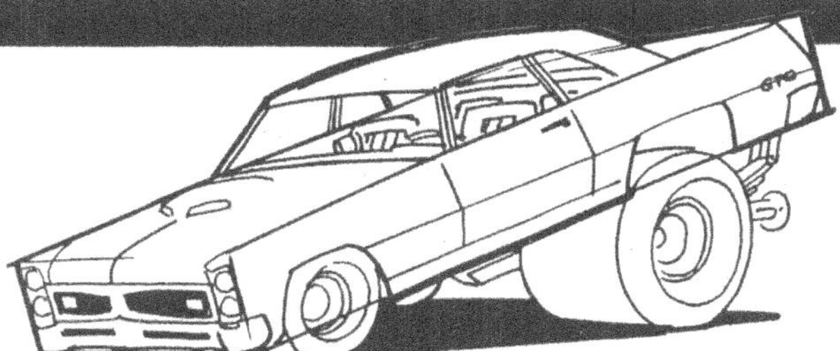

Up in the back looks **competitive**.

L et's get back to basics and work with attitude a bit. What's attitude, you say? Ever notice the way a car sits . . . its stance? Well that's got a lot to do with its attitude and as an artist, it's something you control from the moment you begin to box in the car. Getting this basic idea down will help a lot later . . .

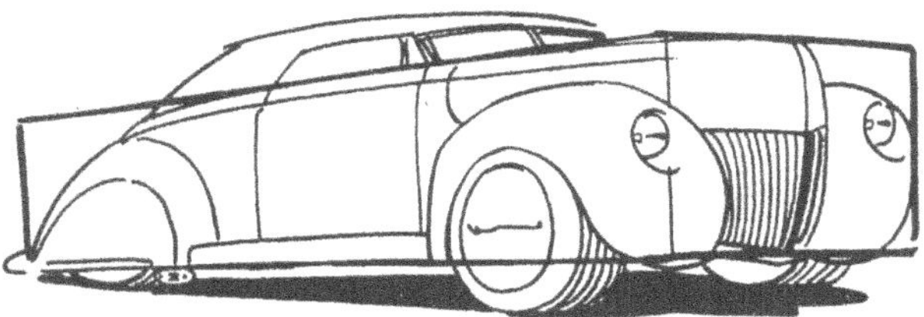

Down in the back looks **custom**.

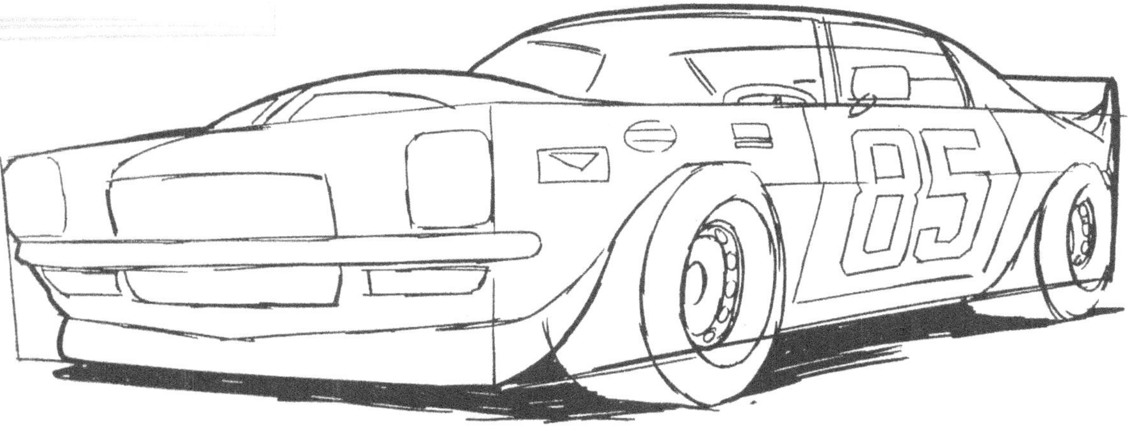

Down all the way around looks **aerodynamic**.

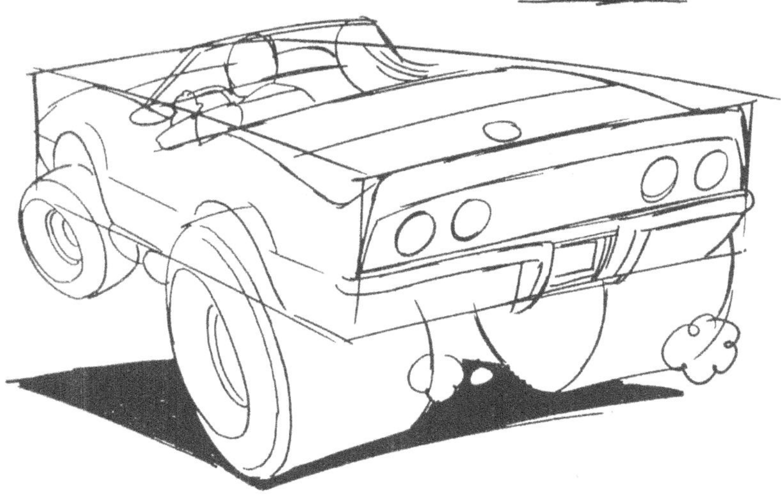

P oint of view has a lot to do with attitude too. Top view. Side view. Rear view. Low angles. Each shows the car in a different way. Decide what attitude you want then find the point of view that shows it the best.

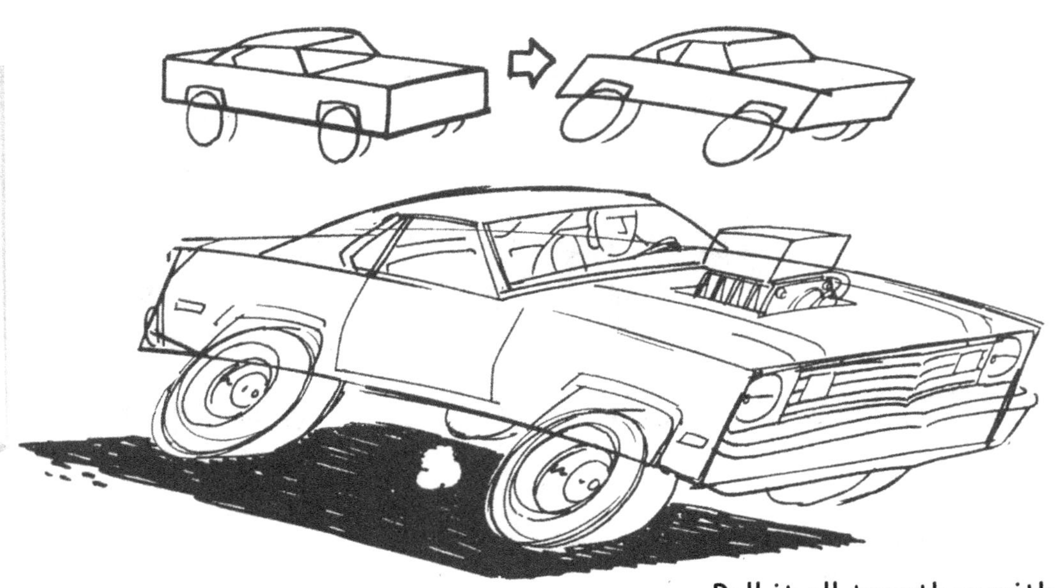

Imagine a pickup in a hard turn and lay in the basic body box, curving it as shown. Showing the centerline will help later.

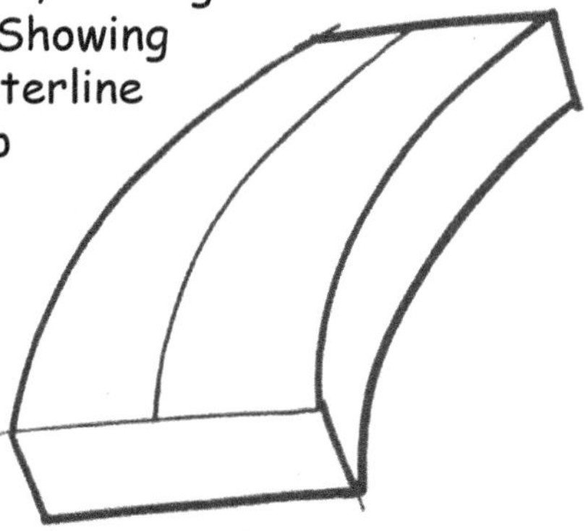

Add the roof and windshield keeping things very basic. The grill and bumper bend to point at the centerline. Rough in some street tires.

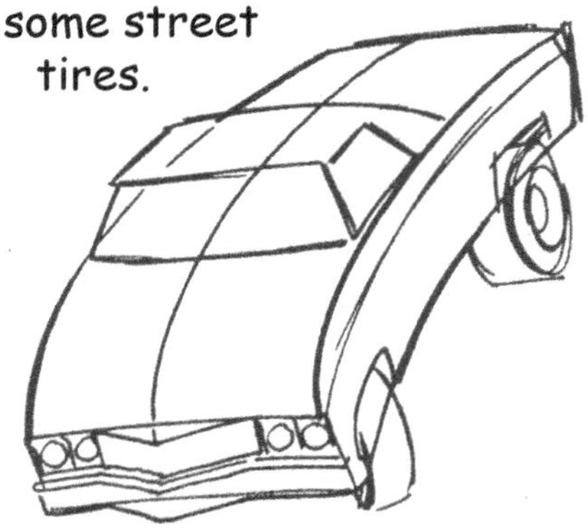

Pull it all together with some interior detail and a driver. Body lines follow the same curves as the basic box.

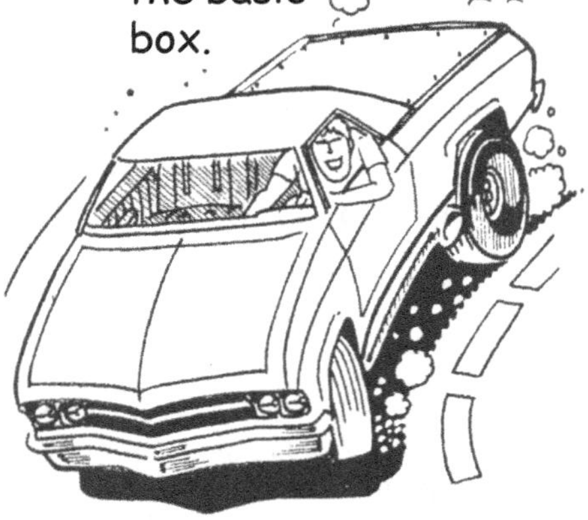

Acceleration can lift and twist a car but let's take it a step further and **bend** one. First, the basic box . . .

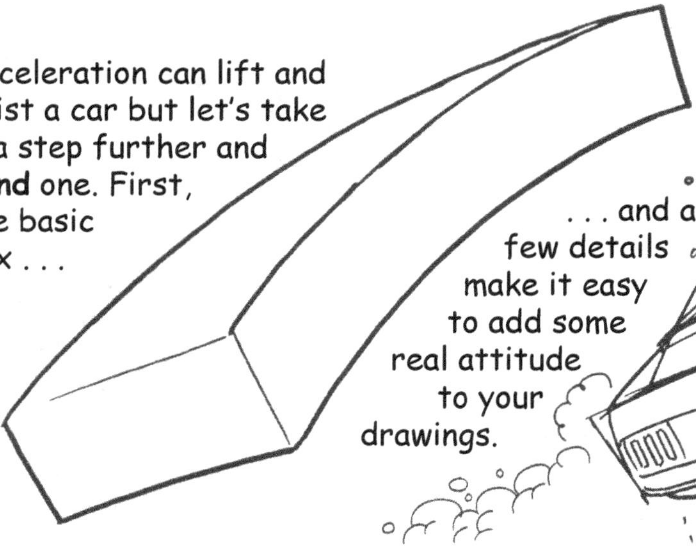

. . . and a few details make it easy to add some real attitude to your drawings.

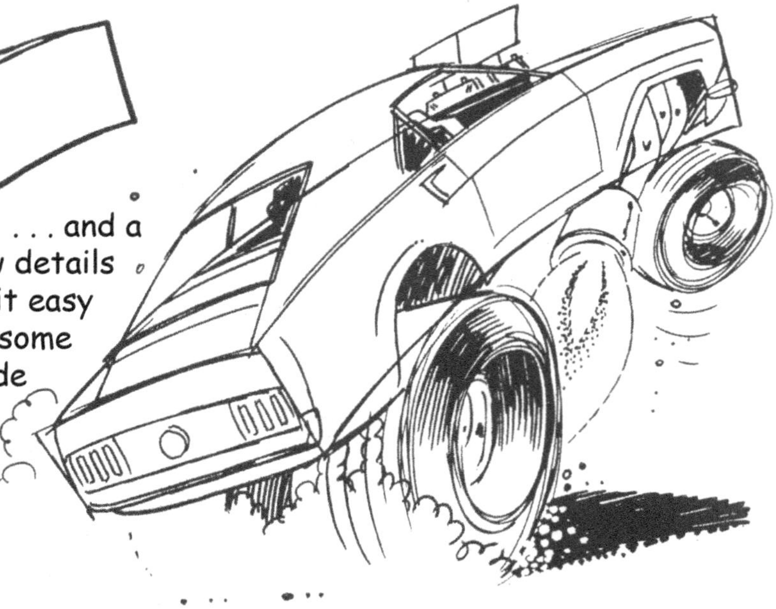

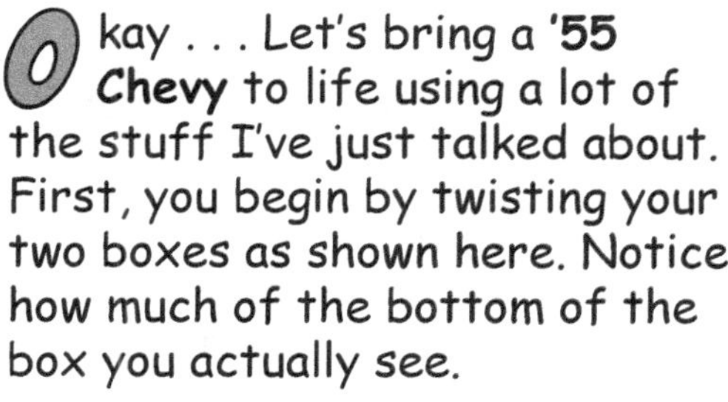

*O*kay . . . Let's bring a **'55 Chevy** to life using a lot of the stuff I've just talked about. First, you begin by twisting your two boxes as shown here. Notice how much of the bottom of the box you actually see.

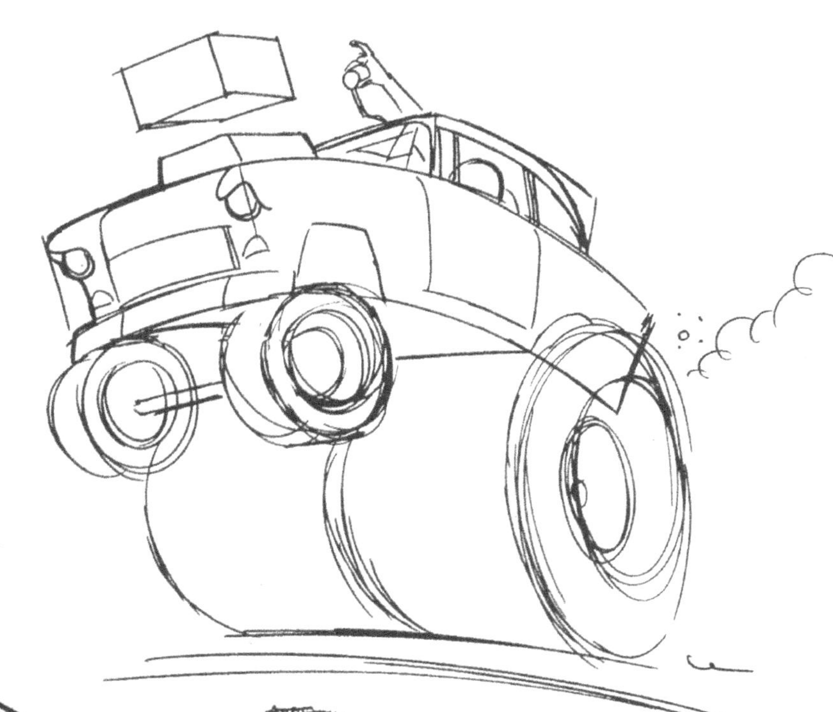

Build the body starting at the front with the headlights and grill, angling them for a "mean face." The bumper also follows the frown attitude. Box in the blower and the bug catcher then add some detail to the roofline. Add a hot rod crazie and a door for him to get in and out. Rough in a small set of street tires up front with monster (and I do mean **MONSTER**) slicks out back.

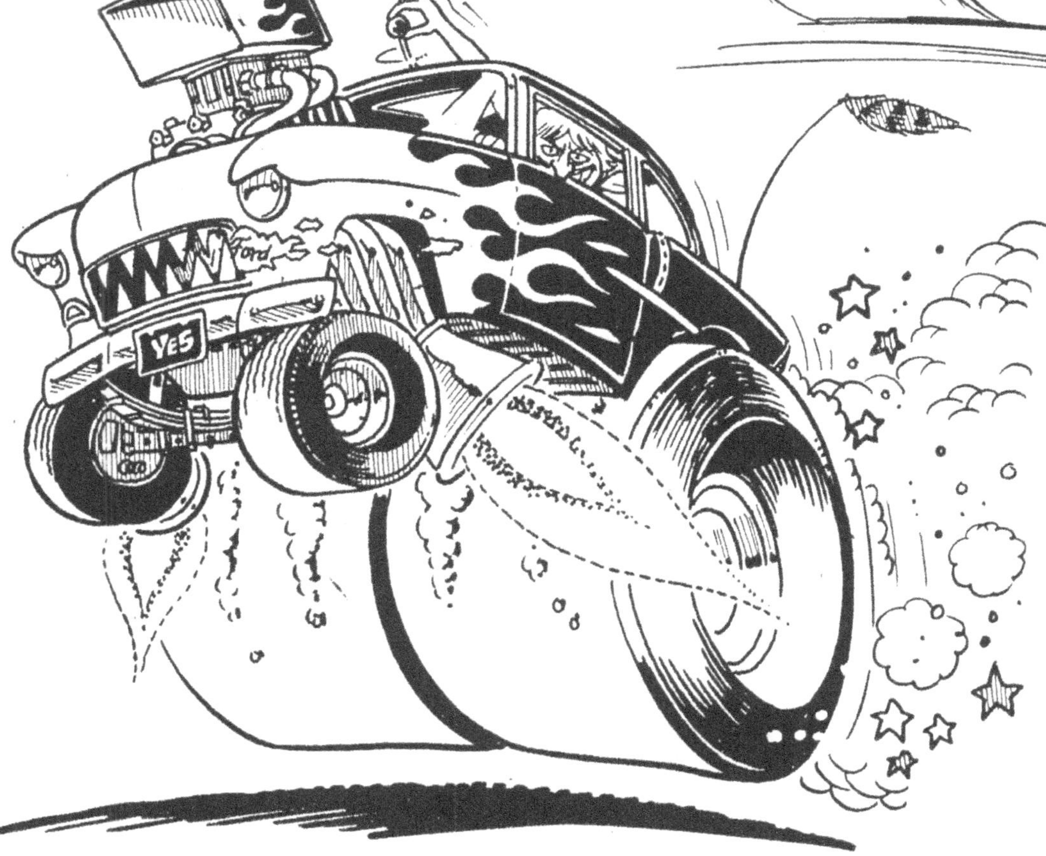

Finish 'er up with more blower detail and a wild set of pipes. The grill gets some teeth and pieces of its last "victim." Some suspension and a little more definition to the wheels help the look as well as some flames in the pipes. Speakin' of flames . . . Let's add some to the paint along with some body chrome. Ink all this in with your favorite felt-tip or ball-point pen and don't be afraid to use solid blacks here and there.

HOW TO DRAW
CAR & TRUCK BODIES

The first thing to do here is reduce things to their basic shapes so that you can keep your proportions correct from the start. **Keep it simple!**

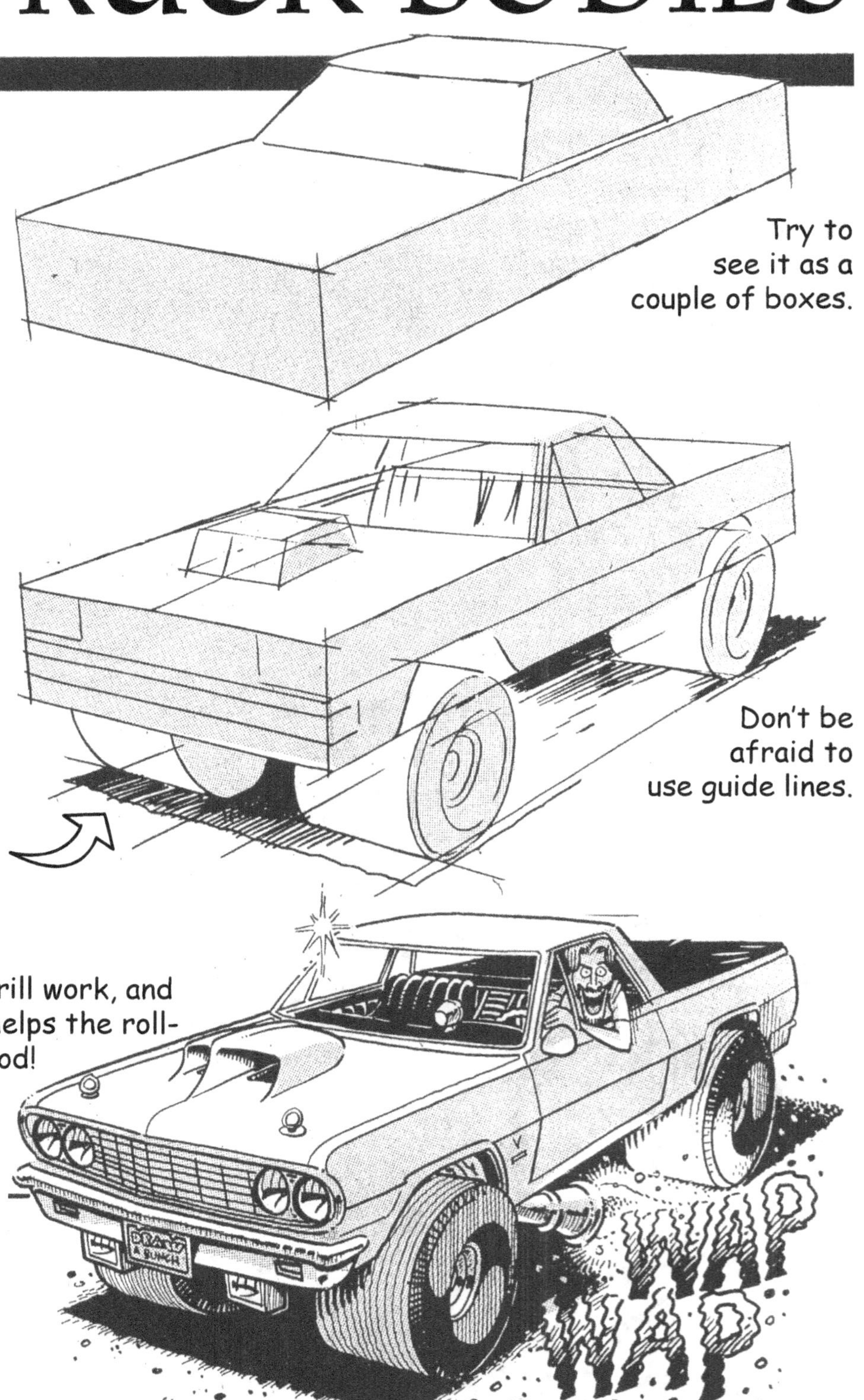

Try to see it as a couple of boxes.

Next, begin breaking up the body into sections, defining the windows, grill, an' bumper. Also blocked in are the wheels, keeping them in proper alignment with the perspective of the truck.

Don't be afraid to use guide lines.

Add a full-body shadow under the truck to help pick it offa' the pavement and give it some weight.

Finally, add details such as light, grill work, and accessories. Careful use of black helps the roll-and-pleat interior and tarp look good!

'TOONER TIP

Always try to get yerself a photo of whatever you're tryin' to draw. I had a good one of this Chevelle! Cut 'em outa' yer magazines before you chuck 'em out!

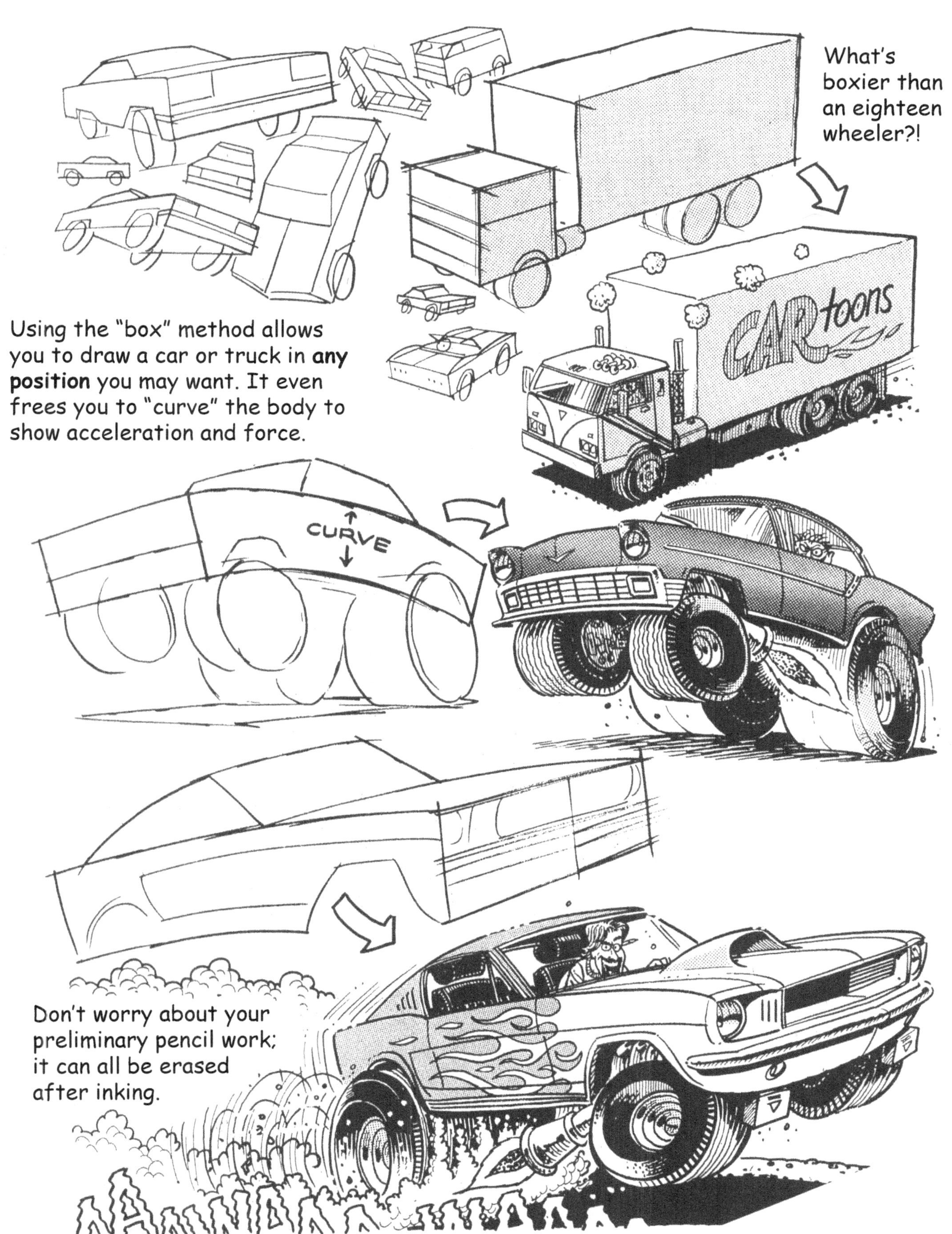

Using the "box" method allows you to draw a car or truck in **any position** you may want. It even frees you to "curve" the body to show acceleration and force.

Don't worry about your preliminary pencil work; it can all be erased after inking.

HOW TO DRAW OLD CAR BODIES

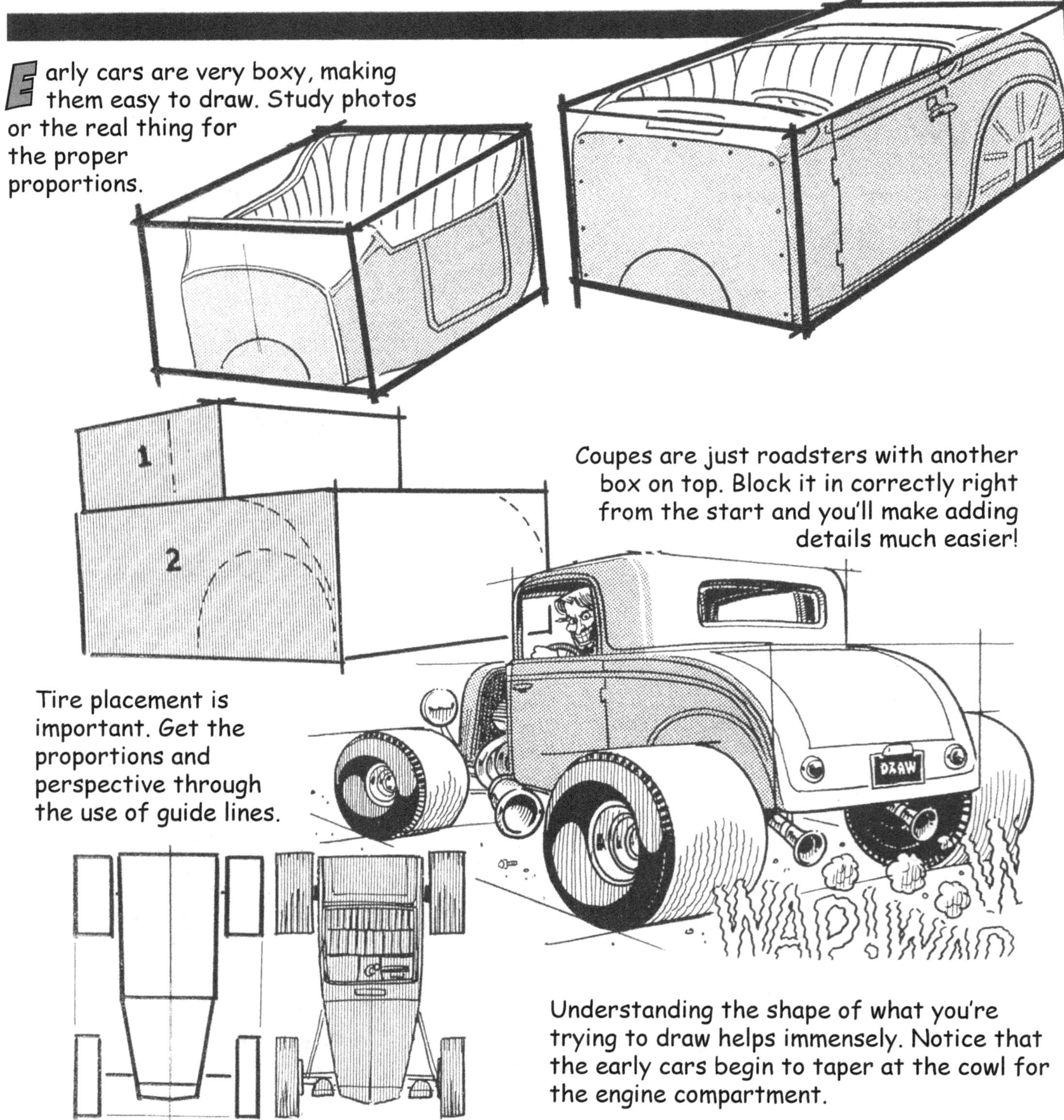

Early cars are very boxy, making them easy to draw. Study photos or the real thing for the proper proportions.

Coupes are just roadsters with another box on top. Block it in correctly right from the start and you'll make adding details much easier!

Tire placement is important. Get the proportions and perspective through the use of guide lines.

Understanding the shape of what you're trying to draw helps immensely. Notice that the early cars begin to taper at the cowl for the engine compartment.

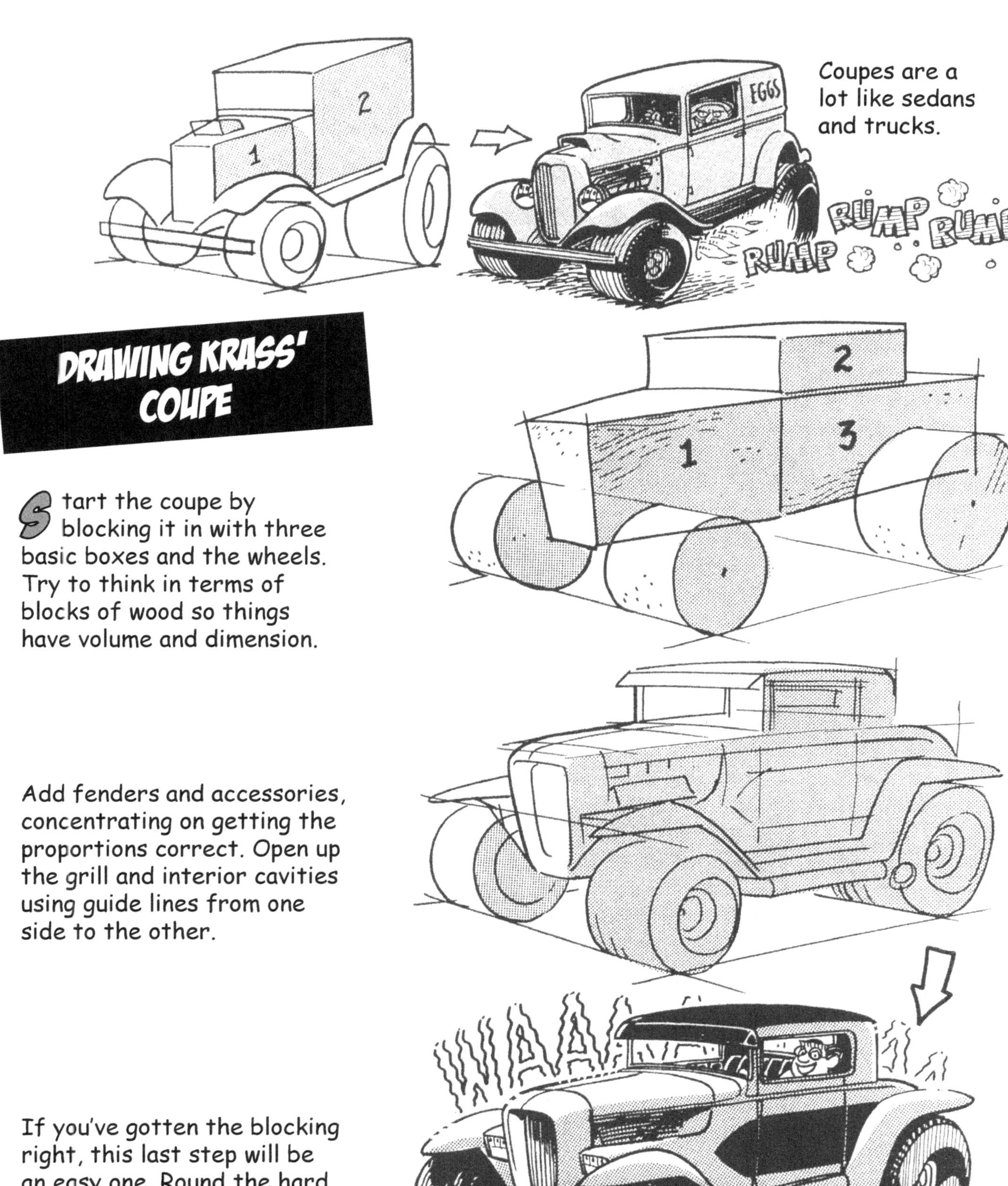

Coupes are a lot like sedans and trucks.

DRAWING KRASS' COUPE

Start the coupe by blocking it in with three basic boxes and the wheels. Try to think in terms of blocks of wood so things have volume and dimension.

Add fenders and accessories, concentrating on getting the proportions correct. Open up the grill and interior cavities using guide lines from one side to the other.

If you've gotten the blocking right, this last step will be an easy one. Round the hard edges, add blacks to the body an' tires with a few highlights, and ya' got it!

PRO STREET

Pro Street cars are real hot so let's take a close look at 'em. Basically, they're cars set up for the strip but with all the proper doodads to make them street legal. Full interior roll cages, giant slicks, and a wild rake are just the beginning. Cars from the Forties are naturals for the Pro Street treatment.

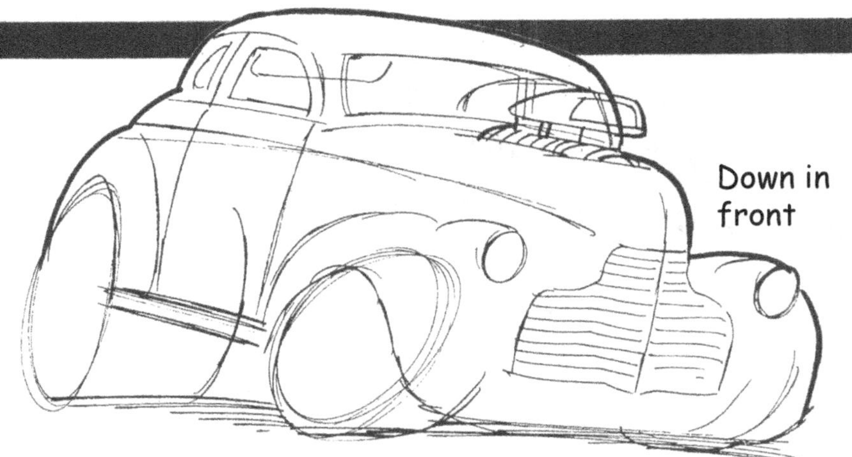

Down in front

Big cubic-inch blown engine with an aerodynamic "bug catcher"

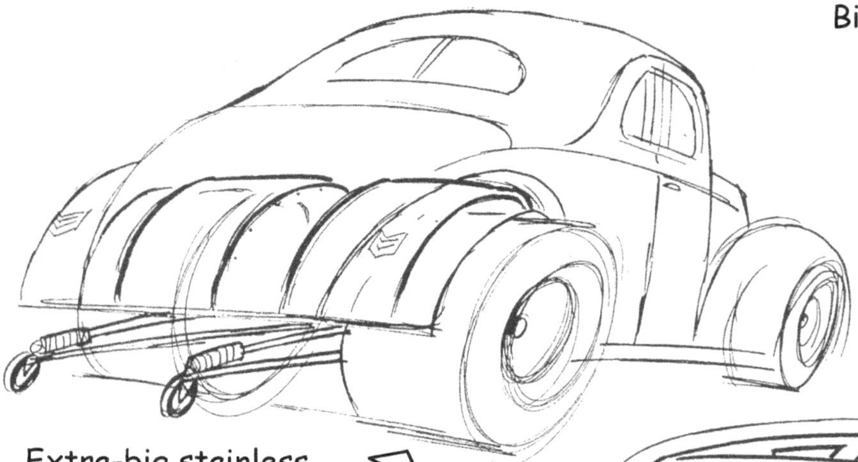

Wheelie bars

Extra-big stainless steel wheel tubs to accommodate the extra-big slicks

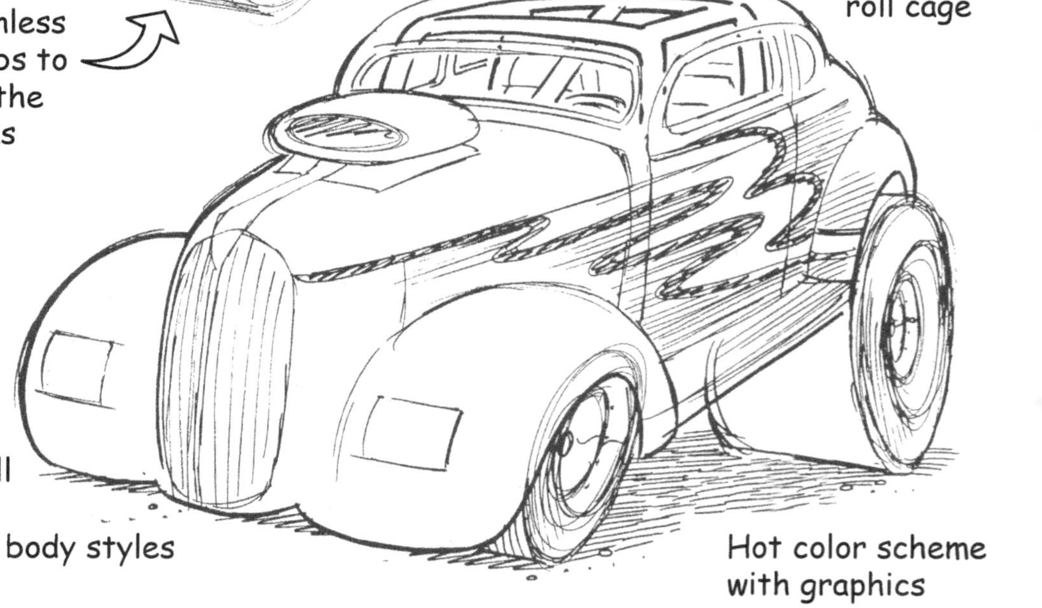

Full interior roll cage

"Smoothie" look with custom headlights

Aerodynamic color-coated grill

Off-beat body styles

Hot color scheme with graphics

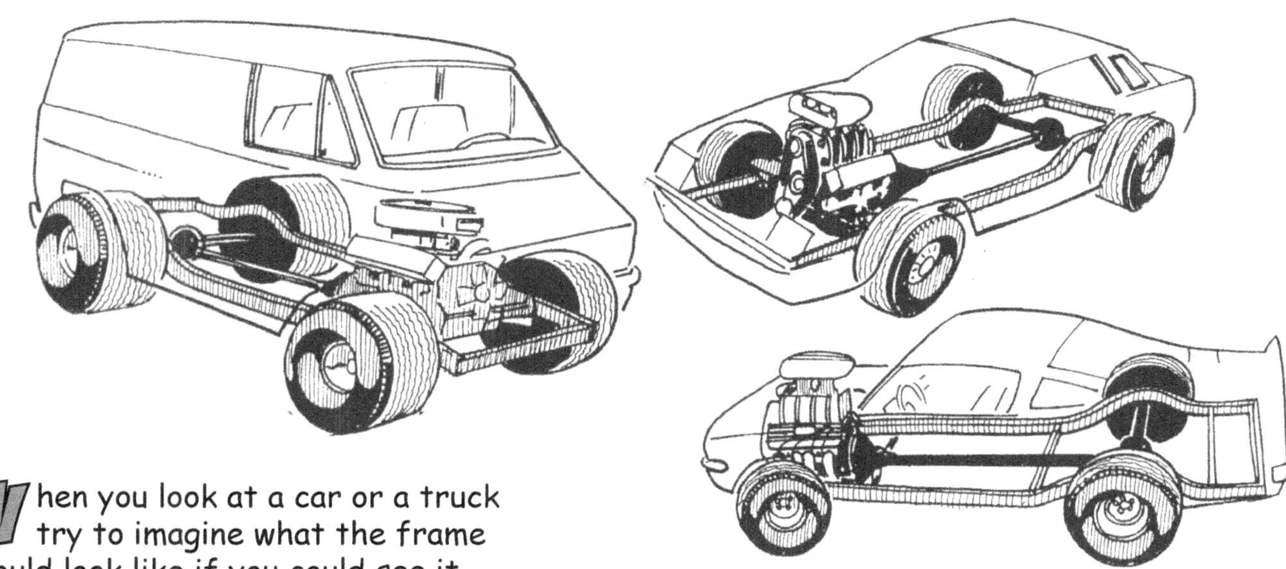

When you look at a car or a truck try to imagine what the frame would look like if you could see it.

Let's try a funny car with its very basic frame. Begin with the bottom rectangle building up to the top set. Notice how it angles up in back. Rough in tires as shown.

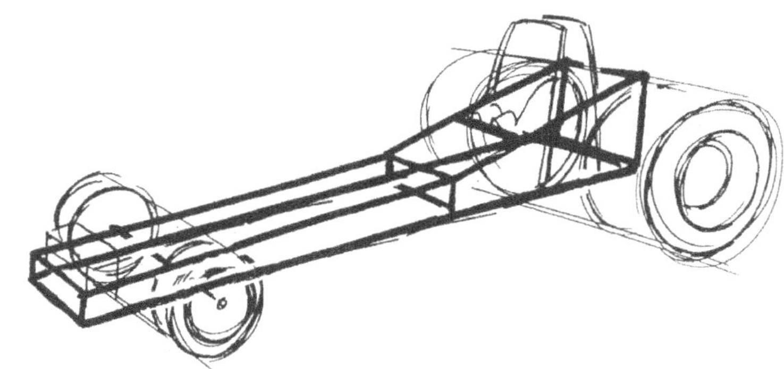

Rough in the engine with detail to the blower area. Then block out the body as I've done here. Note the windshield and roof angle as well as the rear spoiler.

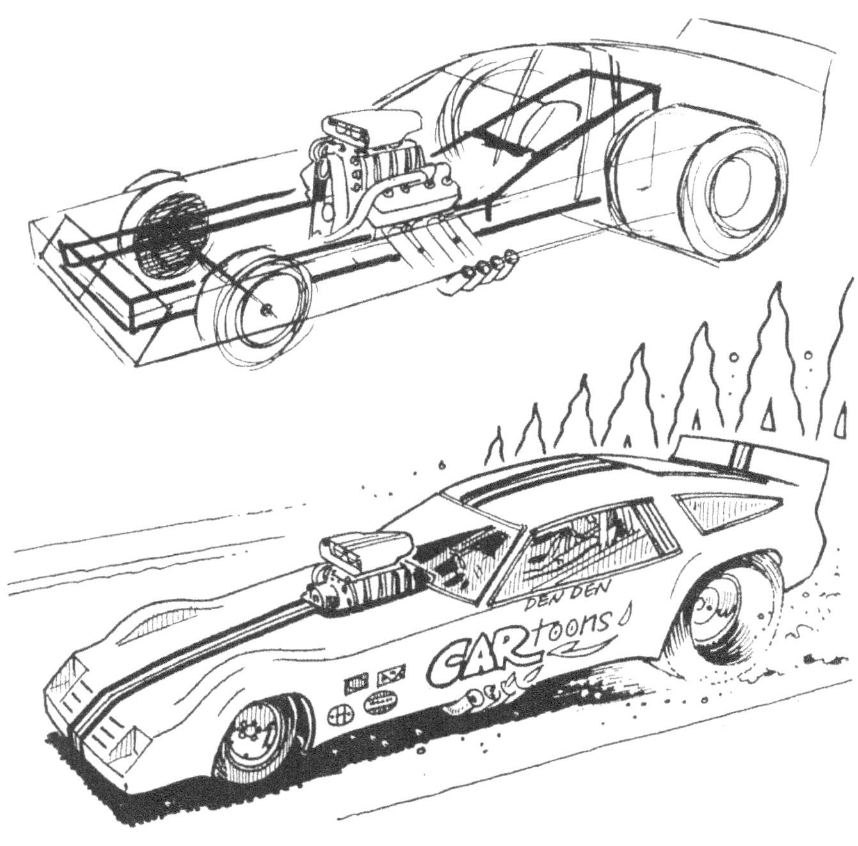

Detail the body a bit more. The front grill area gets lights and vents. The stripe flows back to the blower opening then over the roof to the spoiler. Smoke an' tire spin help. Ink . . . erase . . . and enjoy!

HOW TO DRAW BODY GRAPHICS

et's say you've just finished a really neat drawing of your favorite Corvette but it **needs** something . . . some snap and pizazz. How do you give it a little more excitement? Maybe body graphics are what you're looking for. You can add flames and scallops but contemporary paint jobs go way beyond them in terms of fresh originality. Once you get a few basics down, you can let your pen go wild!

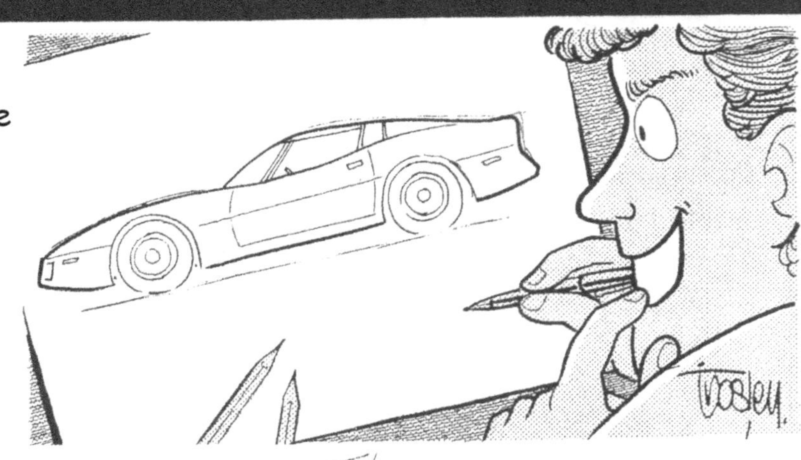

The basic zigzag can be treated in many different ways. The basic body stripe can be twisted, wiggled, or curved. Usually, the design flows with the existing body lines.

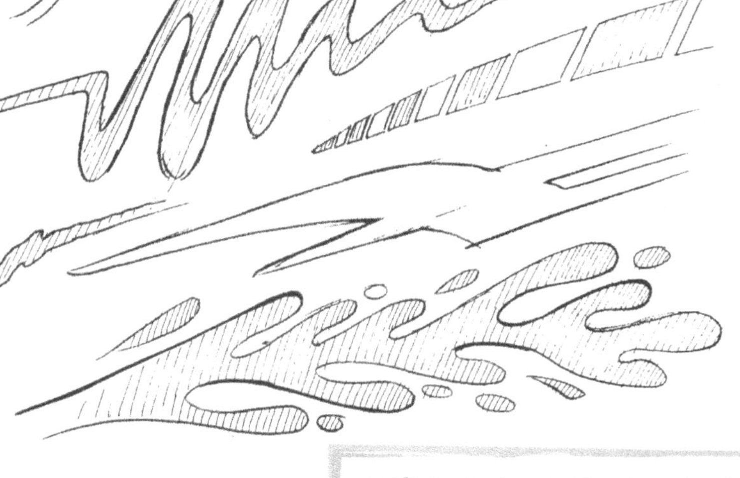

his is just the beginning. There are many more designs and plenty that haven't even been dreamed up yet. That's for you to do so sharpen those pencils an' get crankin'!

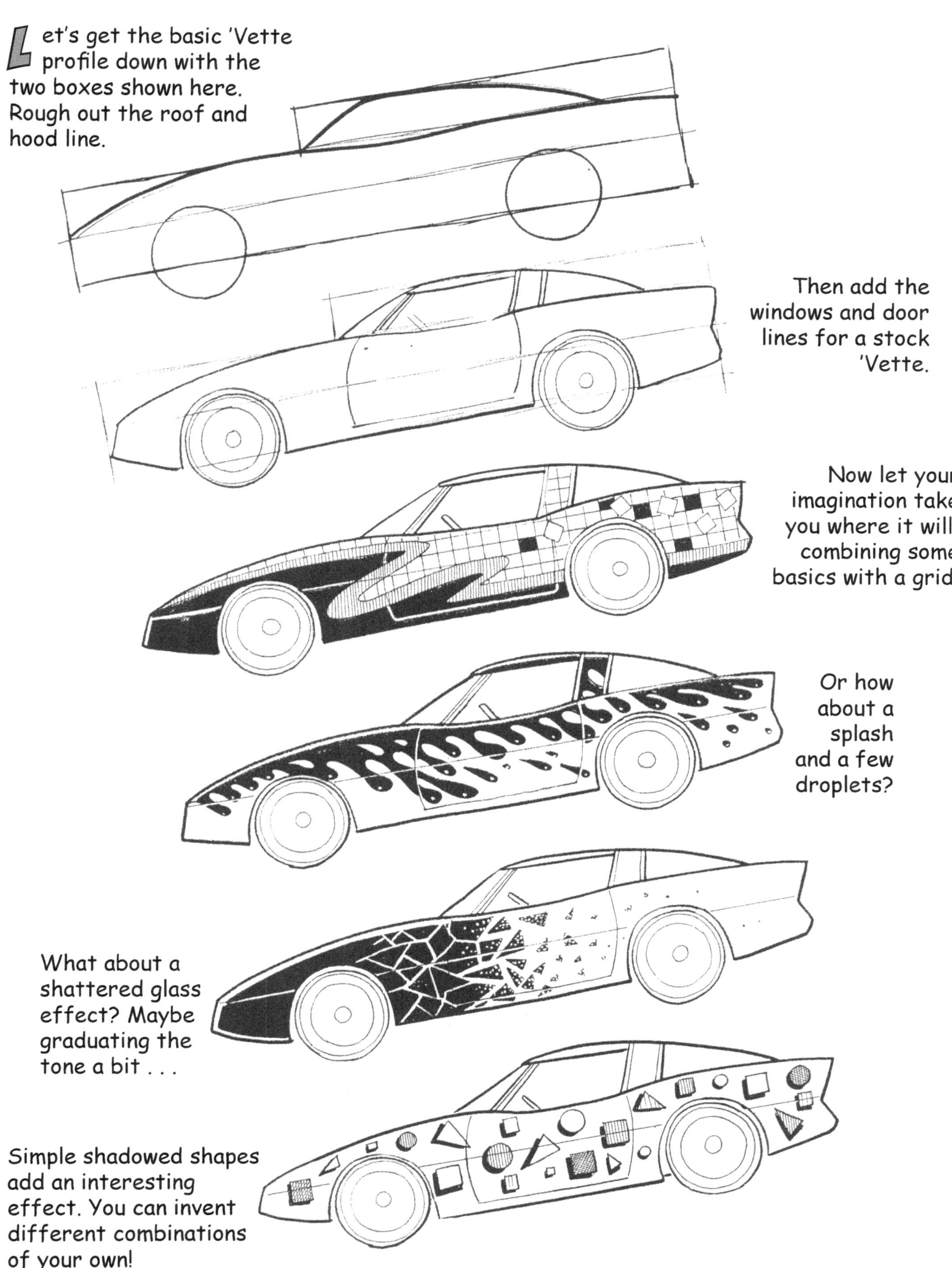

Let's get the basic 'Vette profile down with the two boxes shown here. Rough out the roof and hood line.

Then add the windows and door lines for a stock 'Vette.

Now let your imagination take you where it will, combining some basics with a grid.

Or how about a splash and a few droplets?

What about a shattered glass effect? Maybe graduating the tone a bit . . .

Simple shadowed shapes add an interesting effect. You can invent different combinations of your own!

Let's start a '69 Dodge Coronet R/T with this drawing. Photocopy it or draw your own. You're gonna learn how to do it up in full color with pencils, markers, or whatever you've got!

Lay on a coat of light orange leaving the hood and roof alone. On the side let the color get lighter near the middle and darker as you go down to the bottom of the door.

Time for a medium gray on the roof and hood; try to keep it even and flat. Also, give the tires, grill, interior, and that rear stripe a shot of gray too.

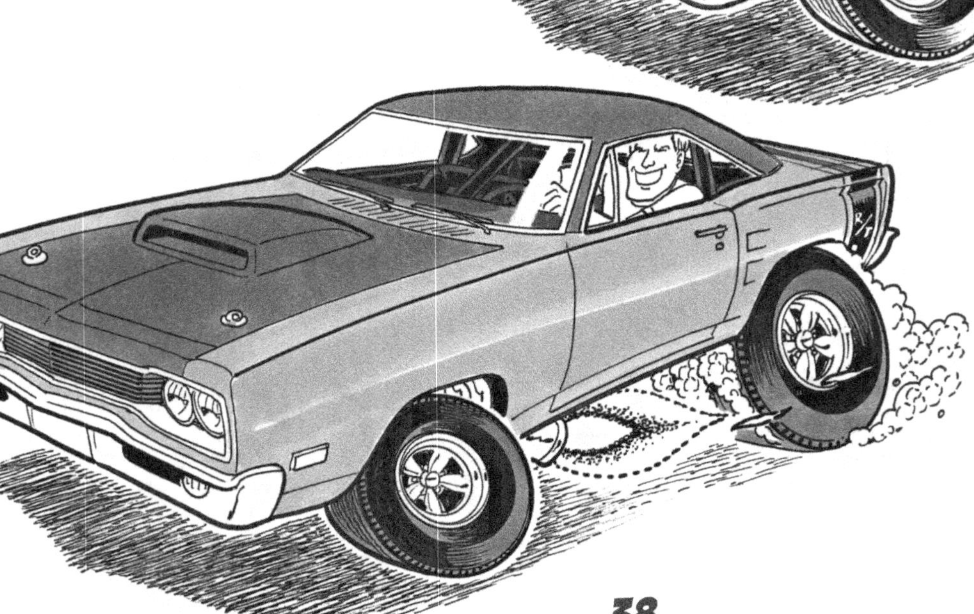

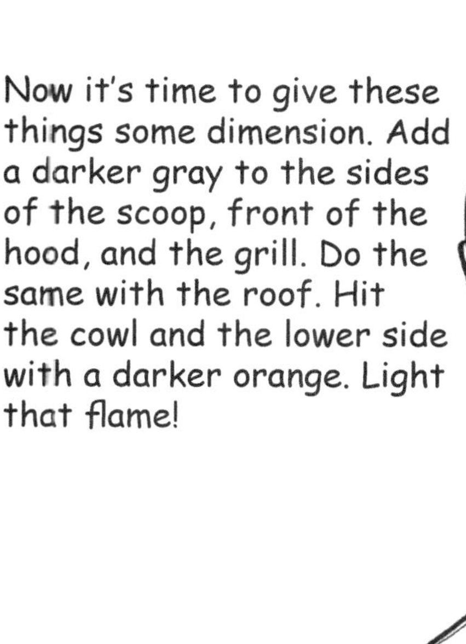
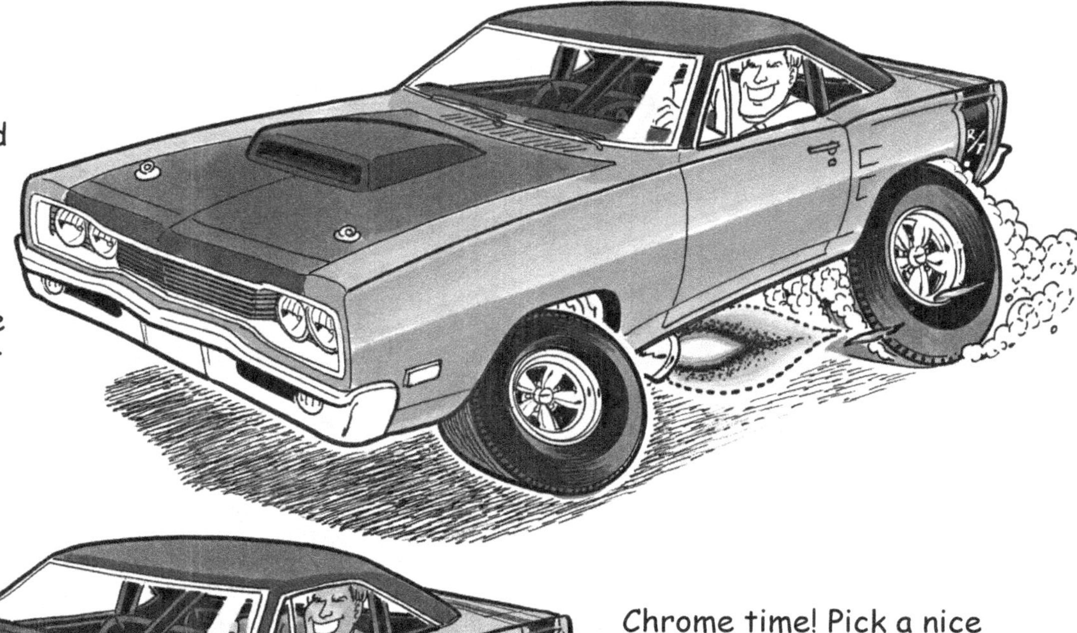

Now it's time to give these things some dimension. Add a darker gray to the sides of the scoop, front of the hood, and the grill. Do the same with the roof. Hit the cowl and the lower side with a darker orange. Light that flame!

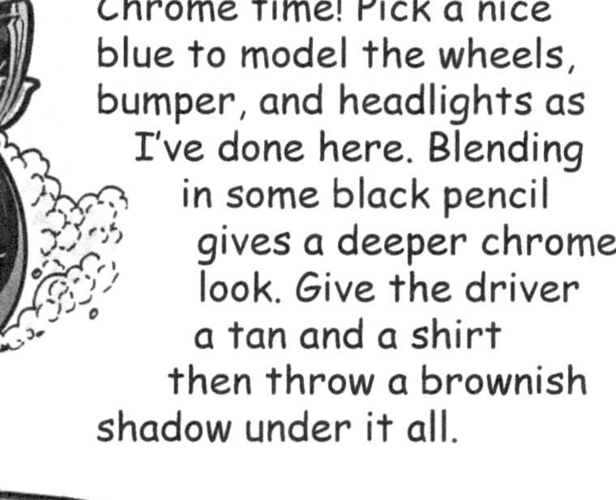

Chrome time! Pick a nice blue to model the wheels, bumper, and headlights as I've done here. Blending in some black pencil gives a deeper chrome look. Give the driver a tan and a shirt then throw a brownish shadow under it all.

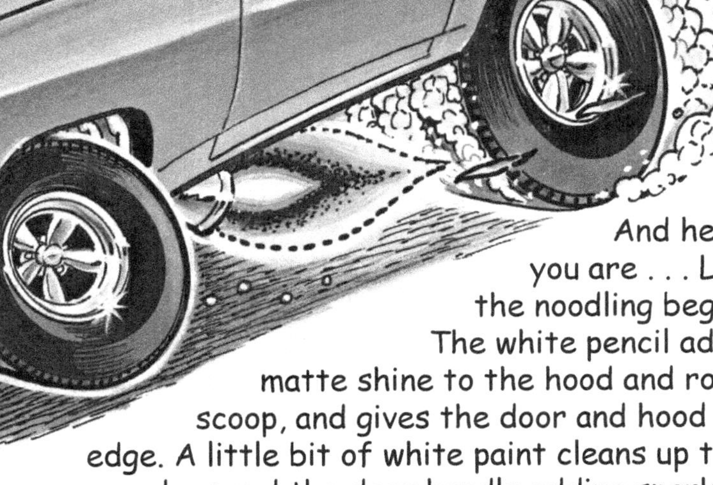

And here you are . . . Let the noodling begin! The white pencil adds matte shine to the hood and roof scoop, and gives the door and hood an edge. A little bit of white paint cleans up the edges and the door handle adding sparkle!

COLOR A HOT ROD

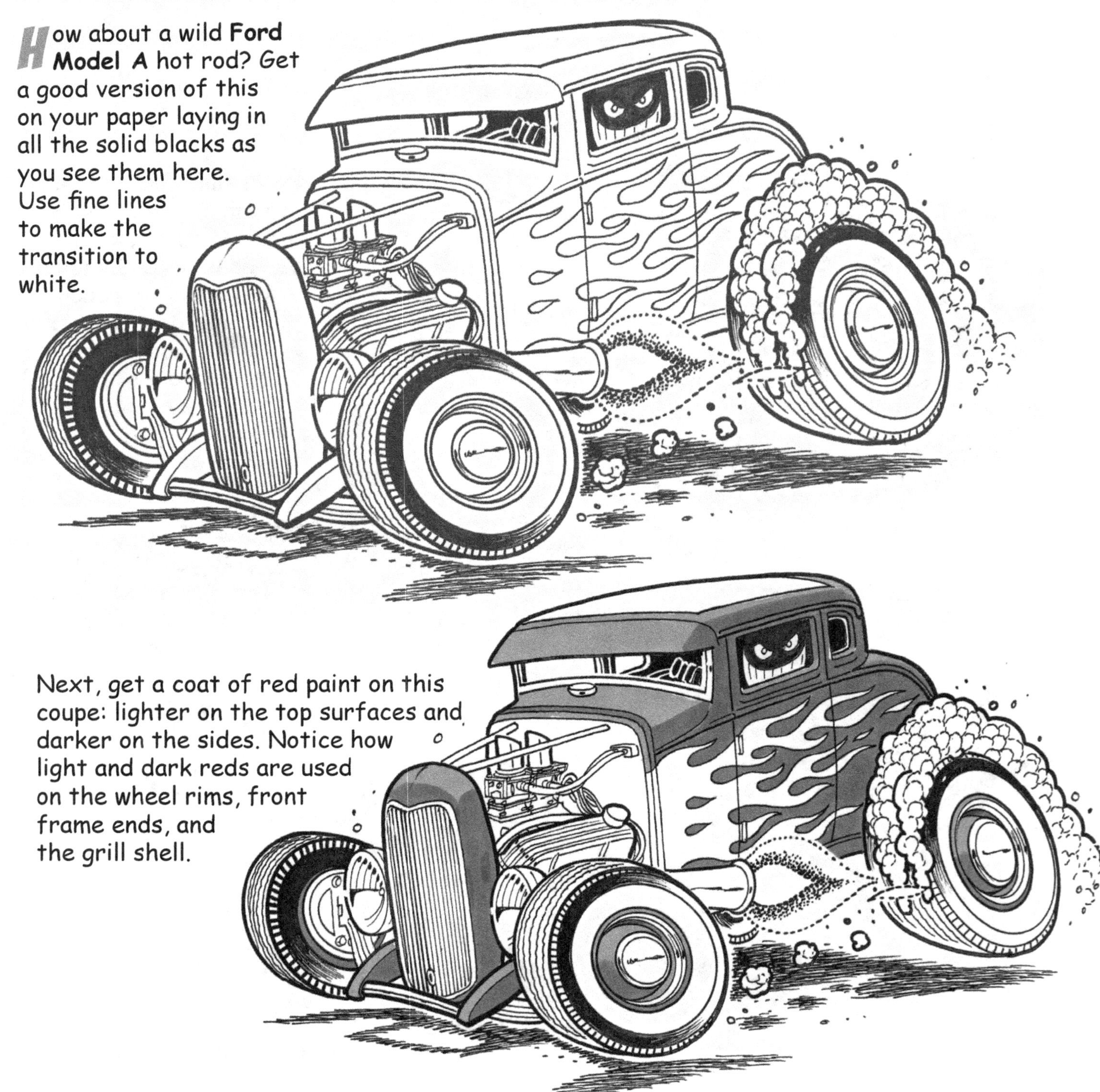

How about a wild **Ford Model A** hot rod? Get a good version of this on your paper laying in all the solid blacks as you see them here. Use fine lines to make the transition to white.

Next, get a coat of red paint on this coupe: lighter on the top surfaces and darker on the sides. Notice how light and dark reds are used on the wheel rims, front frame ends, and the grill shell.

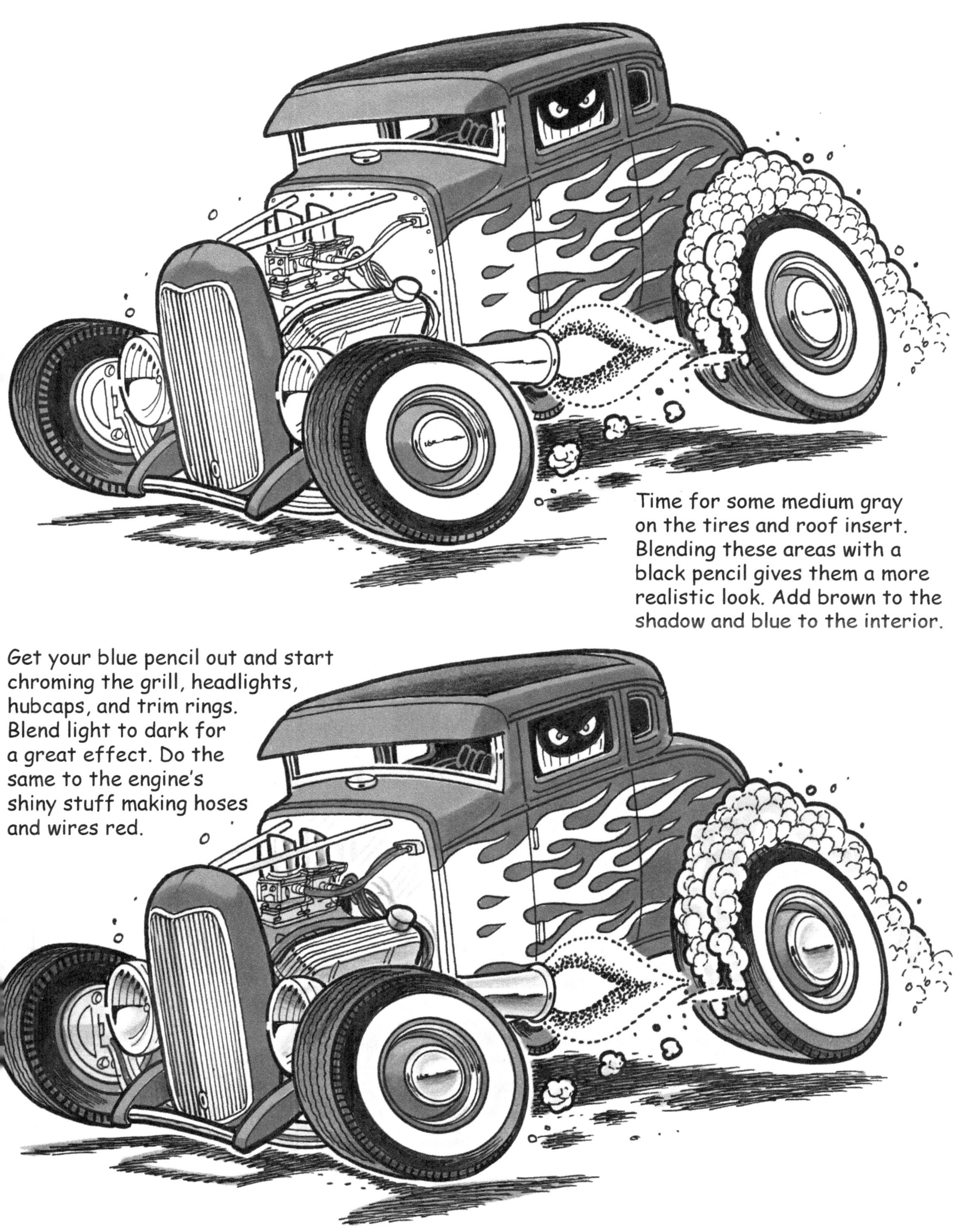

Time for some medium gray
on the tires and roof insert.
Blending these areas with a
black pencil gives them a more
realistic look. Add brown to the
shadow and blue to the interior.

Get your blue pencil out and start
chroming the grill, headlights,
hubcaps, and trim rings.
Blend light to dark for
a great effect. Do the
same to the engine's
shiny stuff making hoses
and wires red.

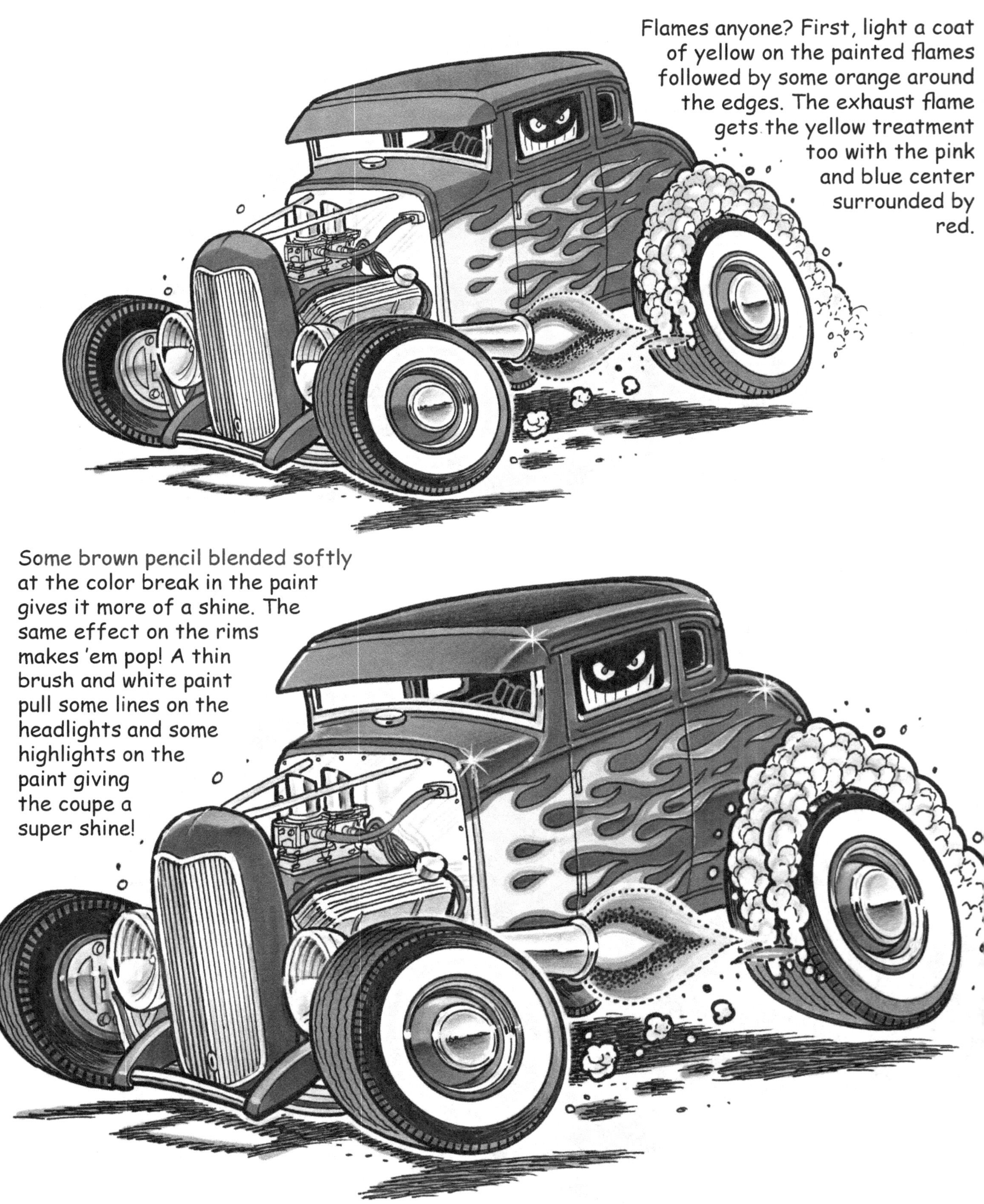

Flames anyone? First, light a coat of yellow on the painted flames followed by some orange around the edges. The exhaust flame gets the yellow treatment too with the pink and blue center surrounded by red.

Some brown pencil blended softly at the color break in the paint gives it more of a shine. The same effect on the rims makes 'em pop! A thin brush and white paint pull some lines on the headlights and some highlights on the paint giving the coupe a super shine!

Pickups are always popular so let's start with the **GMC** shown here. Once you get it down on paper, add the solid blacks then grab some color so you can put an awesome shine on this hauler!

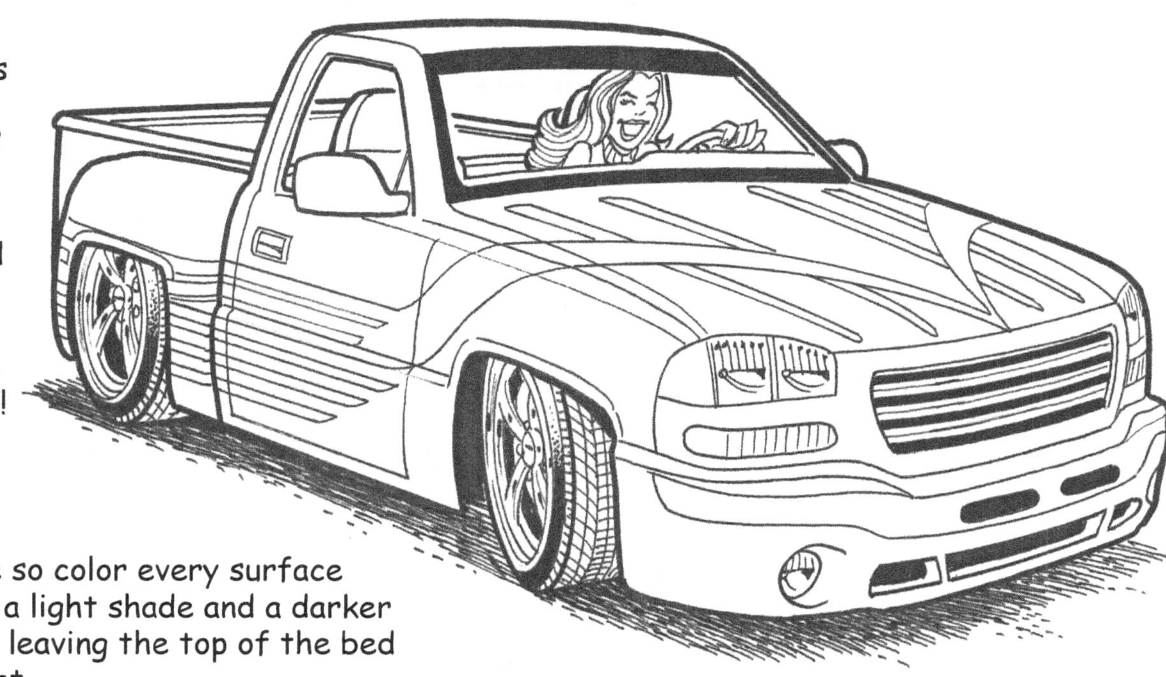

Yellow is the choice so color every surface facing the sky with a light shade and a darker version on the side, leaving the top of the bed and rear fender light. Add a roof shadow on the hood.

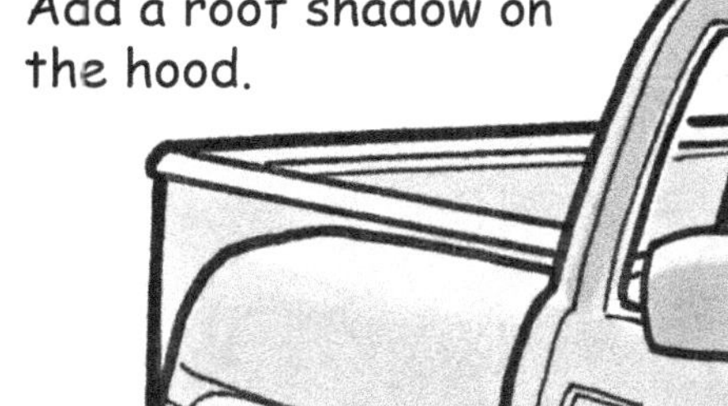

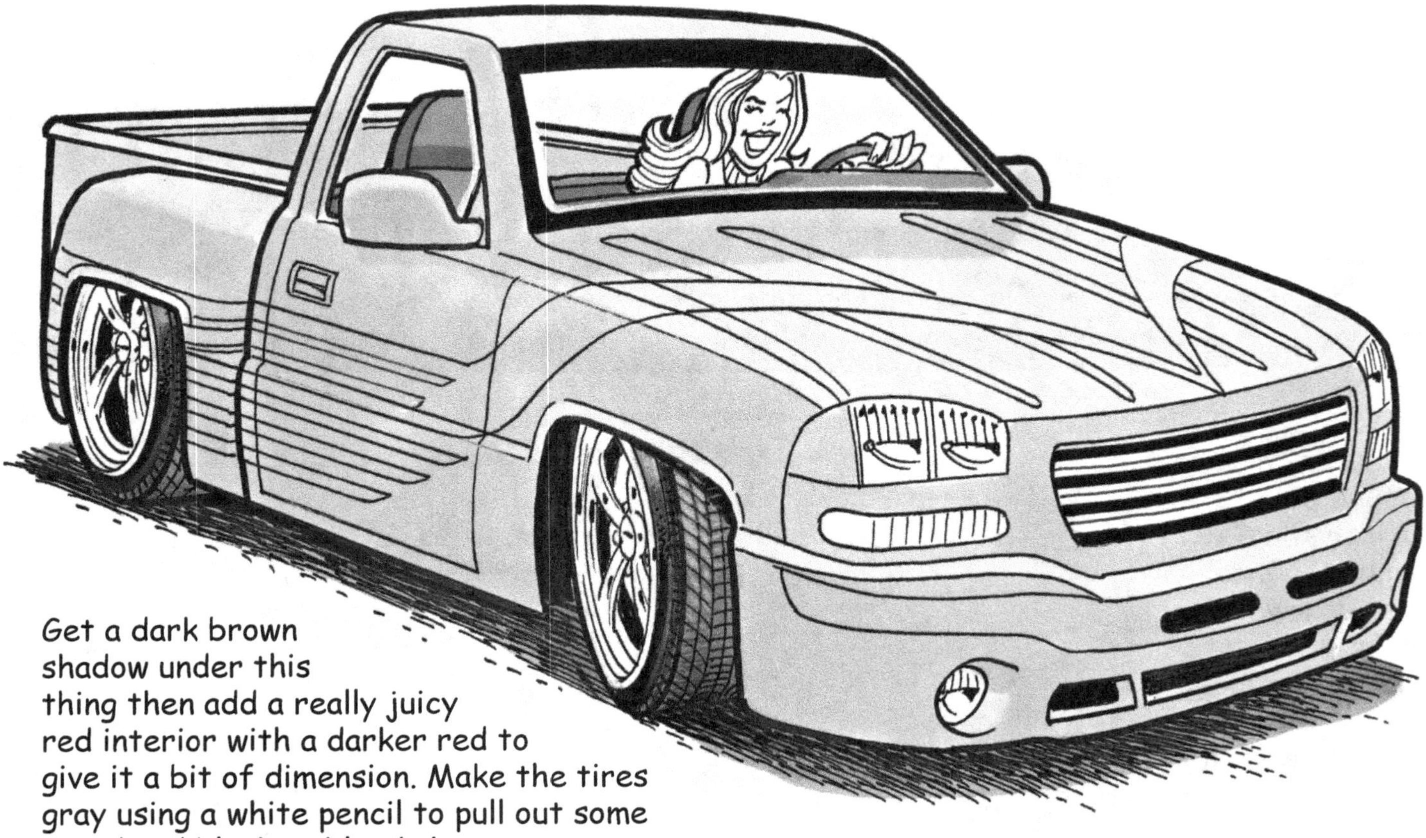

Get a dark brown
shadow under this
thing then add a really juicy
red interior with a darker red to
give it a bit of dimension. Make the tires
gray using a white pencil to pull out some
tread and black to blend the curves.

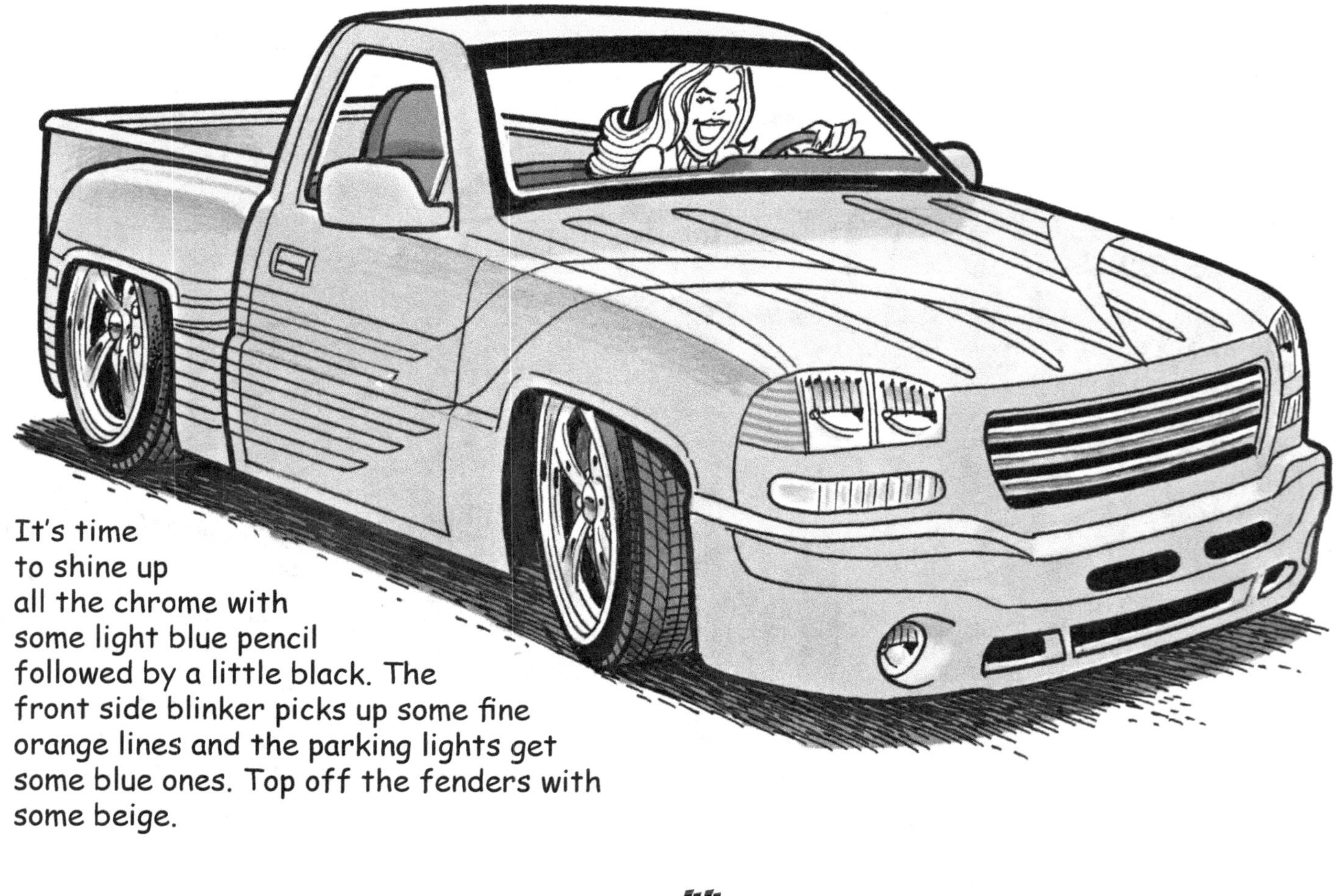

It's time
to shine up
all the chrome with
some light blue pencil
followed by a little black. The
front side blinker picks up some fine
orange lines and the parking lights get
some blue ones. Top off the fenders with
some beige.

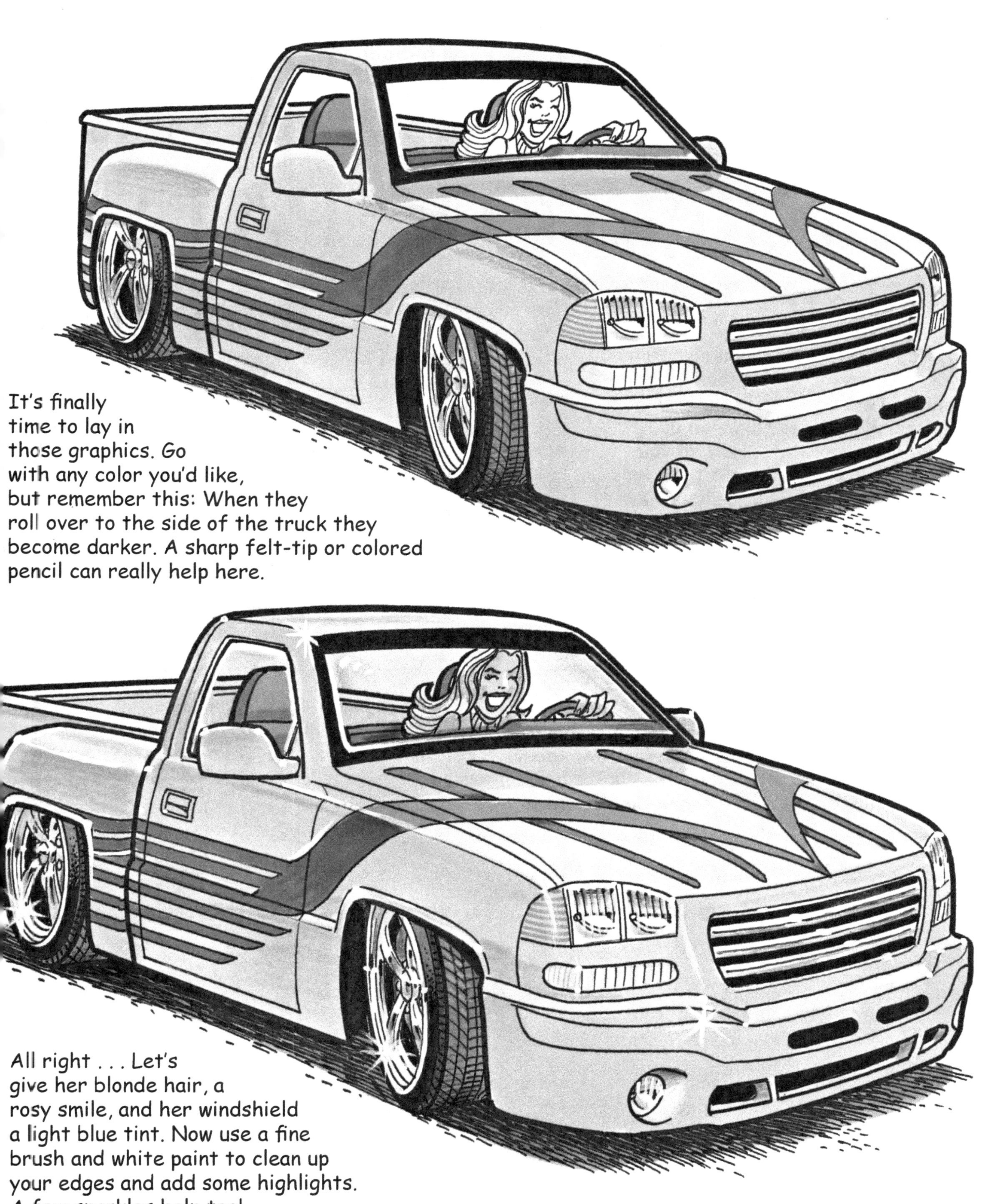

It's finally
time to lay in
those graphics. Go
with any color you'd like,
but remember this: When they
roll over to the side of the truck they
become darker. A sharp felt-tip or colored
pencil can really help here.

All right . . . Let's
give her blonde hair, a
rosy smile, and her windshield
a light blue tint. Now use a fine
brush and white paint to clean up
your edges and add some highlights.
A few sparkles help too!

HOW TO DRAW CUSTOM PAINT

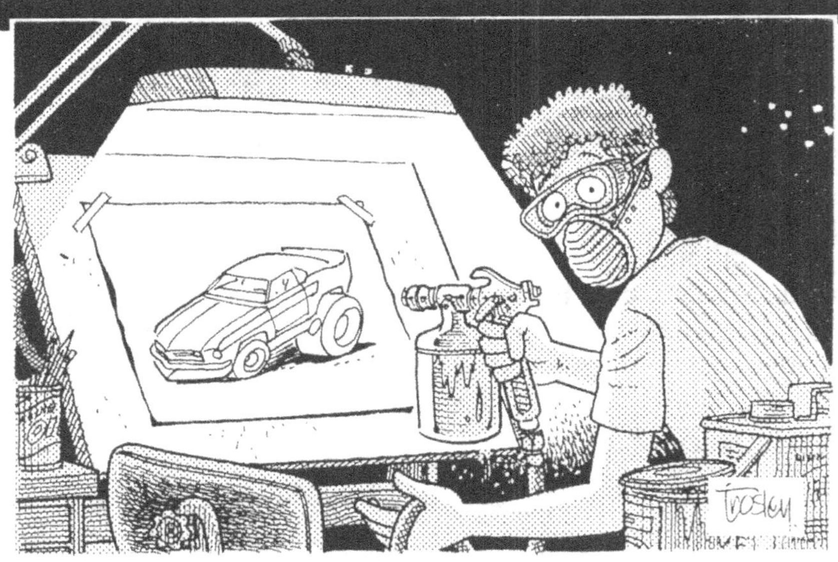

Say you've got a real nice outline drawing of a great lookin' rod and you want to give it the look of a super high-gloss paint job using only black and white. How do you do it? Using your pen and the white of the paper you can easily achieve a variety of tones and textures to give your art that finishing touch.

Let's start with some basic principles about why paint looks like it does. Look closely at something glossy or shiny. Notice how much **reflection** there is. The shinier something is, the more reflection there is. The smoother the surface, the more **mirror effect** you get. These reflections are distorted by the curves and contours of the body, a principle you can use to make your drawings look three-dimensional.

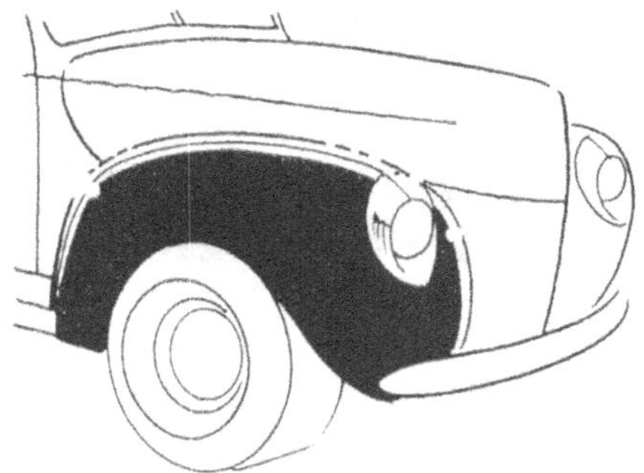

Add some solid black leaving a thin white edge. A fine line following that helps to indicate the way the fender rolls over.

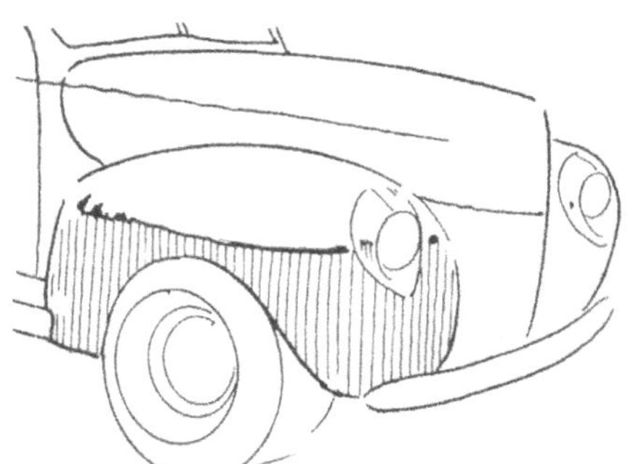

Lighter colors can be indicated in much the same way as chrome: a dark horizon line with a middle tone dropped in below it.

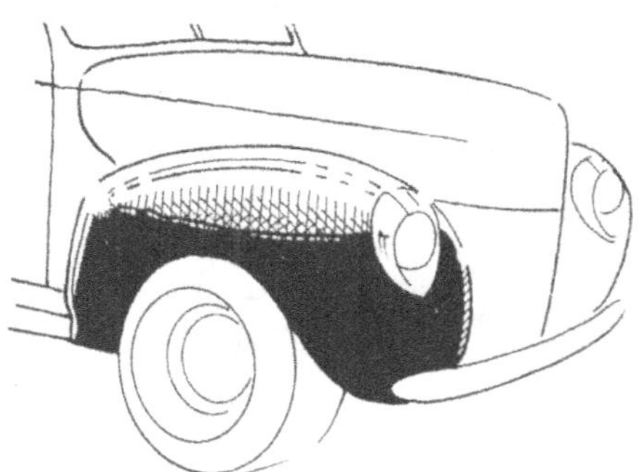

Other more imaginative effects can be found by experimenting with combinations of the last two techniques you've just picked up.

On this three-quarter view, the hood, roof, and truck reflect the sky. The hood also reflects the windshield.

Break your line at high-gloss spots.

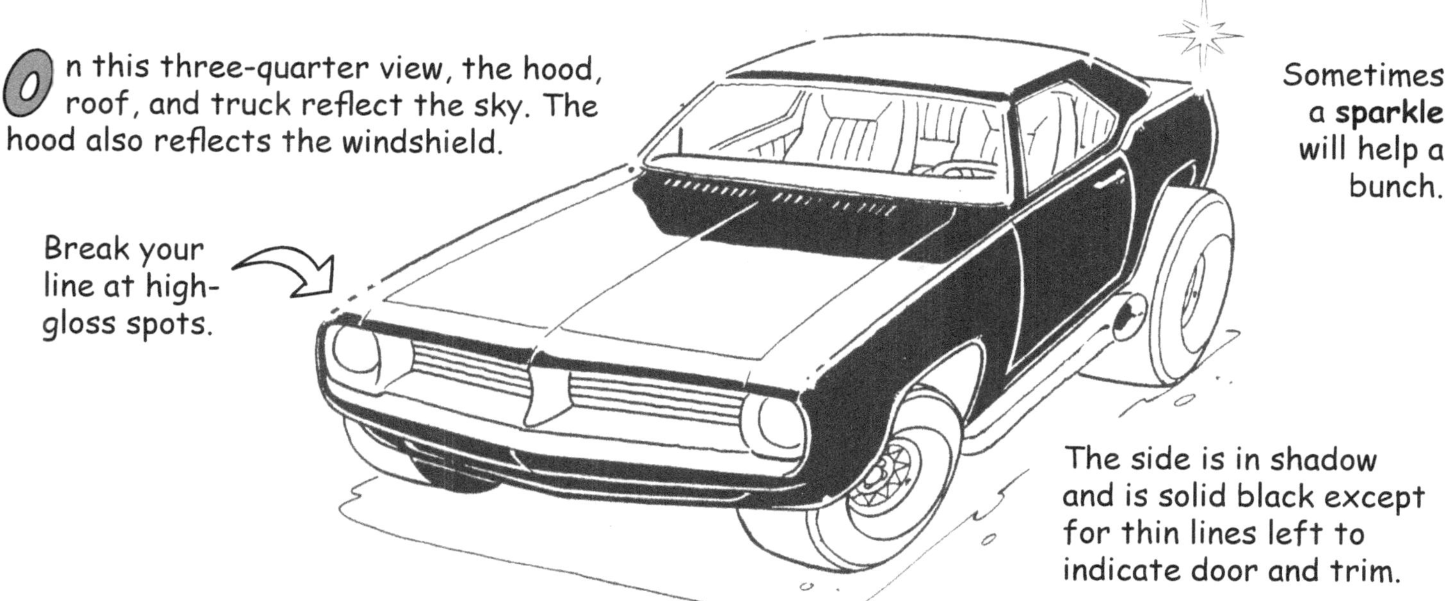

Sometimes a **sparkle** will help a bunch.

The side is in shadow and is solid black except for thin lines left to indicate door and trim.

Look at some custom paint in a magazine or at rod gatherings. There are many different styles especially with flames. Try to master the thicks and thins of this traditional style noting how the design flattens as it goes across the hood.

Paneling is another custom paint trick that's fairly easy to do. Outline areas leaving a similar-width margin throughout. Try to follow and work around existing body lines.

Blending colors can be handled by using many small dots graduating them from loose to tight, light to dark. Work carefully to achieve a smooth overall effect. This technique comes in handy when doing many other types of custom paint. Don't be afraid to **experiment**!

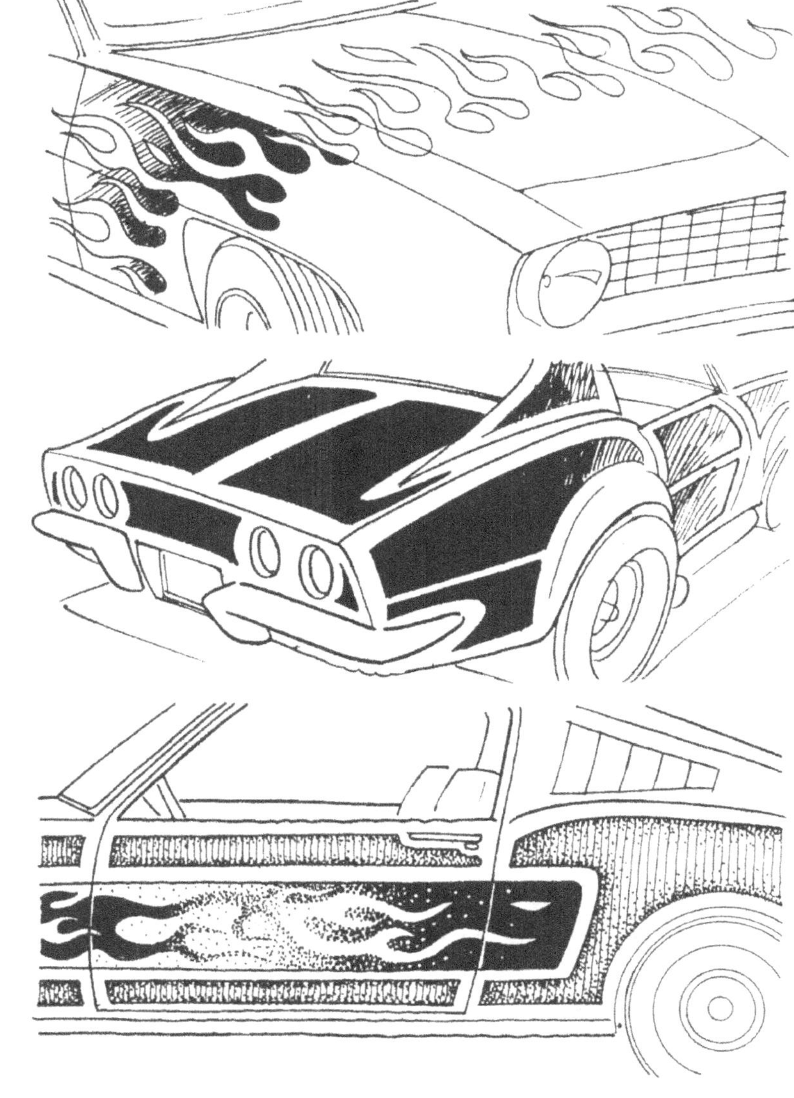

ot all that? Good, cause you're gonna put it to use on this **'69 'Stang**. Copy this box and roofline as closely as you can. Make sure you get the proportions right. Add a centerline then begin dropping and pointing the nose. Notice how much it drops. Roughly lay in some wheel wells and varying-size tread. Use all your guidelines.

Box out the grill and headlight area bending a bumper and air dam around the same angles. Detail the roofline adding side windows, rear fender curve, and fender scoop. Notice how the scoop keys off the side body line. Rough in an oversize side pipe then indicate dashboard, seats, and steering wheel. Check everything.

Hokay . . . Add details to the interior, lights and darks to the chrome, and dimension to the tires. Now it's finally time to give your 'Stang that super paint job I talked about earlier. Pencil in some flames and then detail the body adding blended panels inside the bigger ones. Ink everything carefully adding lights and darks as I've done here.

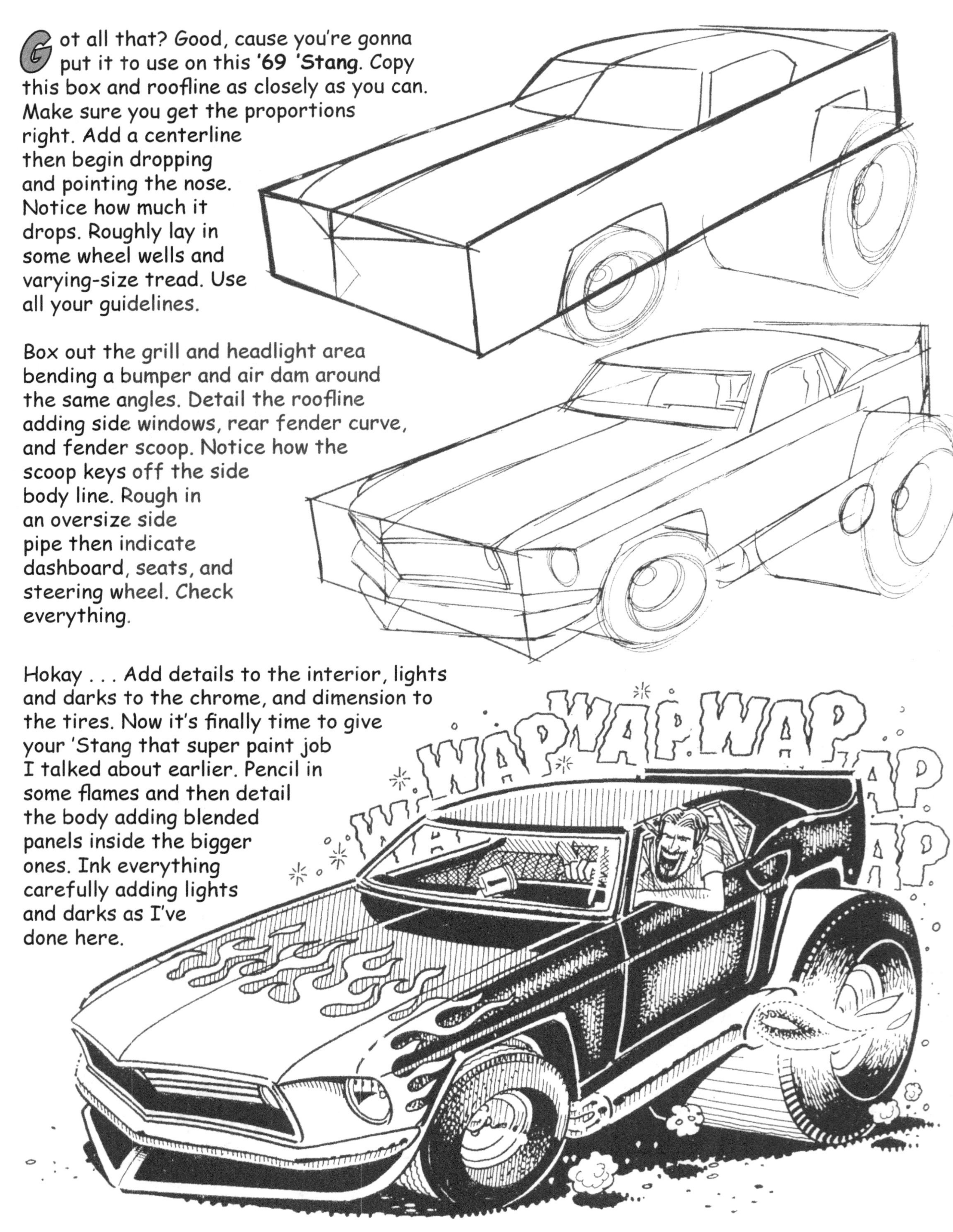

HOW TO DRAW TIRES *and* Chrome

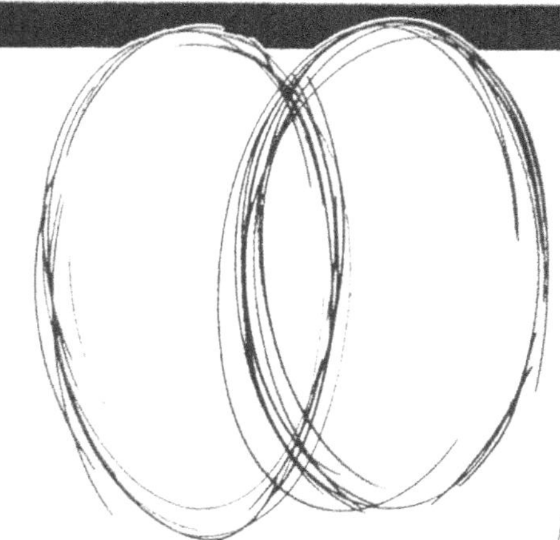

ow you're gonna work on a few basics such as tires and chrome (two of my **favorite** things). You begin any tire with two ellipses as I've done here, keepin' them exactly the same. Next add some depth and contour by laying in two more ellipses to the side along with a top and bottom to the tire. A slight lip at the edge of the tread area helps give it a **real** look.

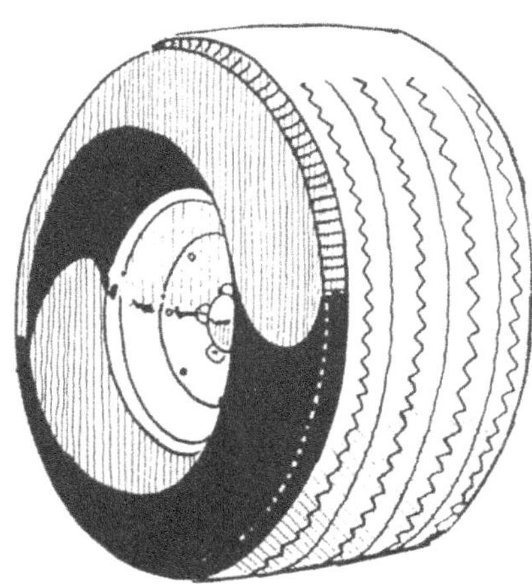

Last, check over all your ellipses for the proper alignment and spacing. Add a rolled edge to the outer part of the rim as well as an inner division and indicate screws and lug nuts. Carefully add some tread design leaving the top section white for highlighting. Note how blacks and halftones **chrome** the rim and finish up the tire.

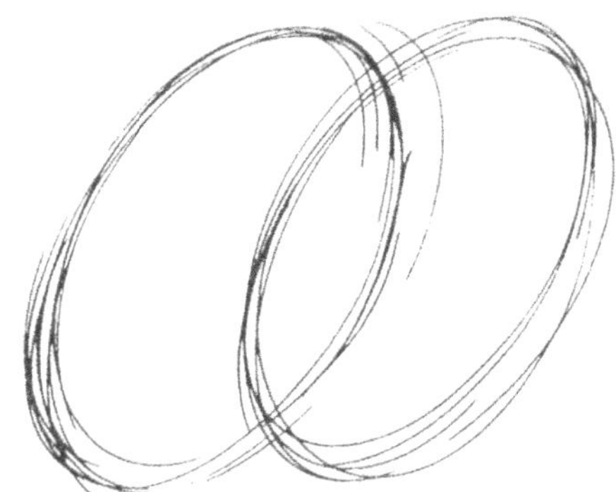

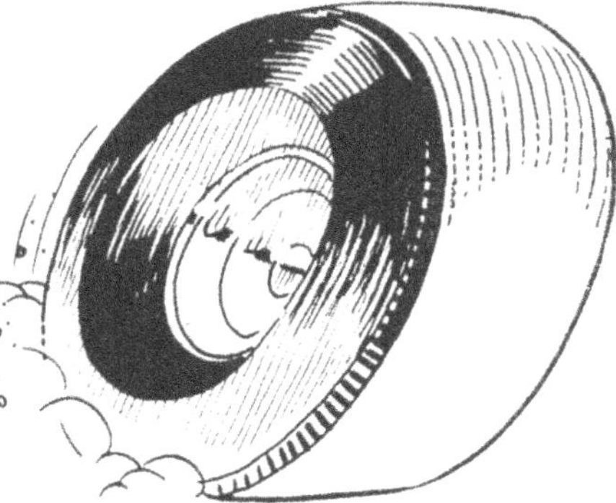

To give the tire a sense of motion you start with two angled ellipses. Try to keep them as identical as you possibly can.

Add two more ellipses to the side for contour. Add the lip to the rim along with the inner ring and hub.

Tighten everything up and add tread to the top, this time highlighting the bottom for action. Blacks are opposite here too.

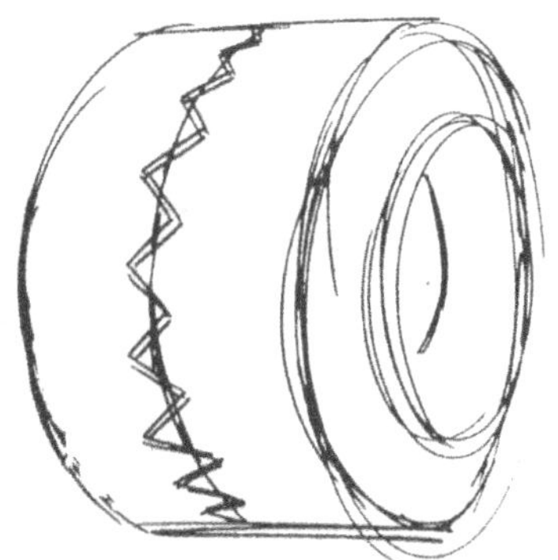
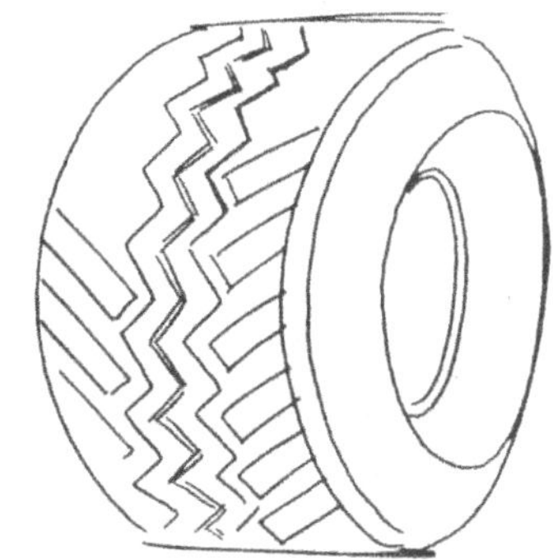
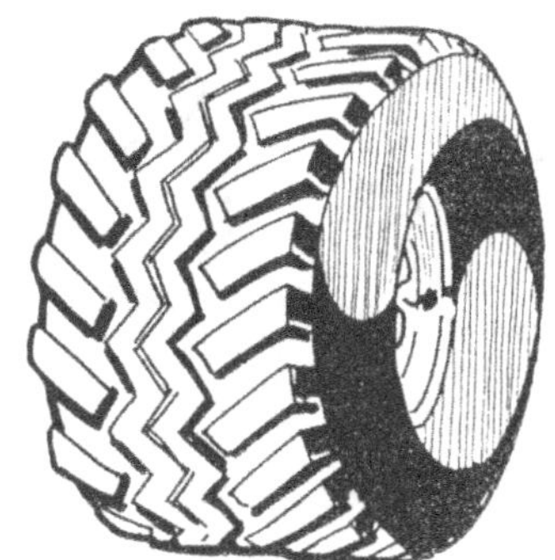

Off-road tires are a bit tricky but fun. Start the same as before and add a zigzagged centerline.

Add a line on either side of that to make a double-tread design. Carefully add side bars into the angled areas.

Give some detail to the rim then finish up by indicating tread thickness with shadows.

Once you get the basics down you can draw any tire. Look at real tires and notice how the tread designs vary.

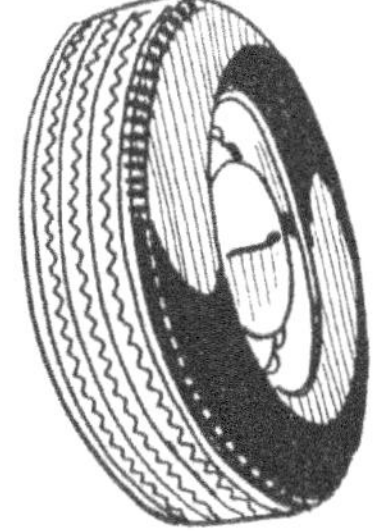

Racing slick

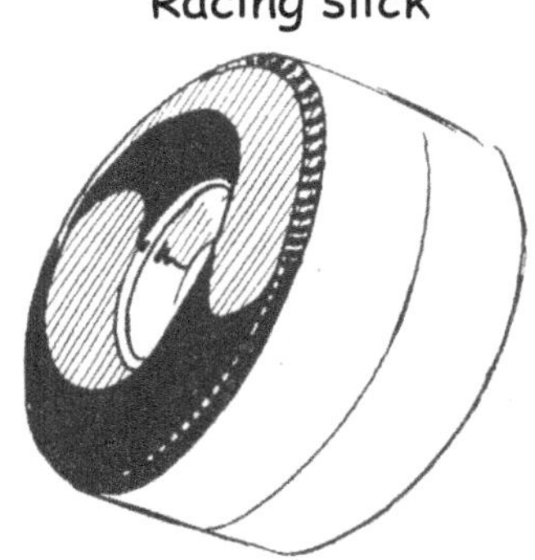

Stock tire

Cycle tire

Tires usually sit on rims. Hopefully **chromed!** Start with the same ellipses. Because chrome mirrors its surroundings you want to indicate a horizon line.

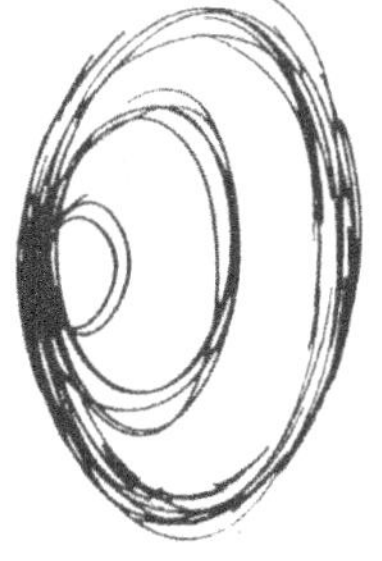
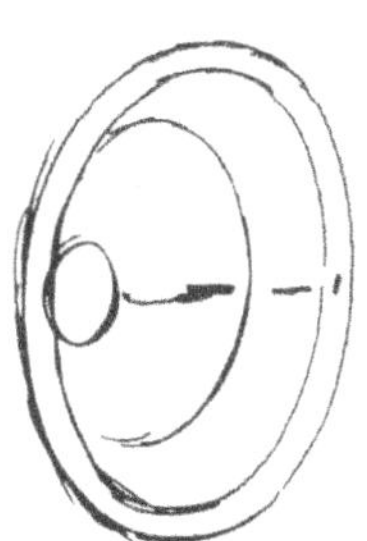
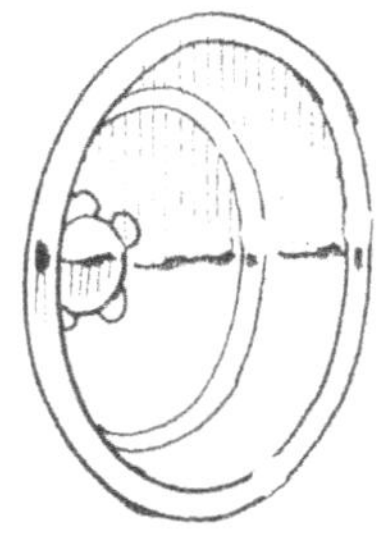

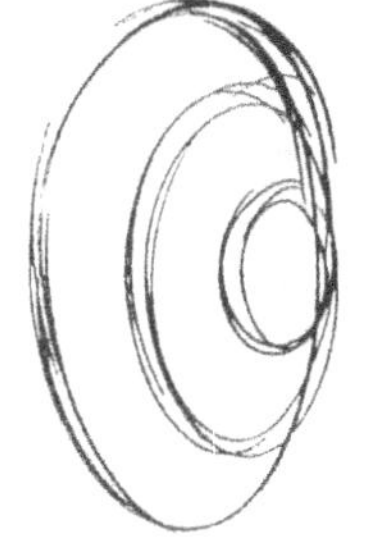
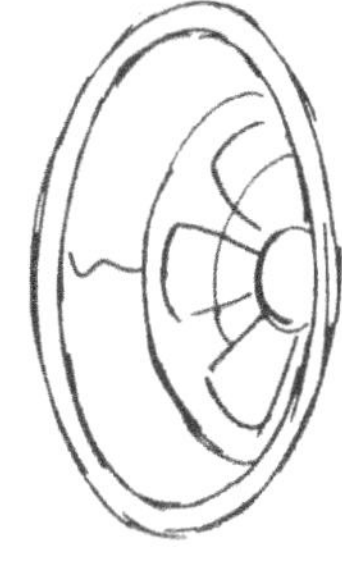
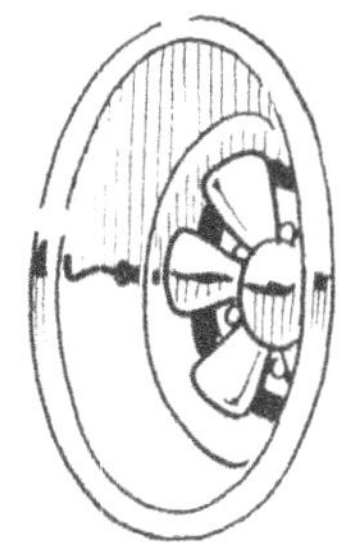

Another type of rim has a spoked design. Same beginning as before then rough in the center hub and a few spokes. The lug nut area and dark areas between spokes help a bunch.

Ellipses show up a lot in auto parts. Lots of 'em are chrome too so these basics will help you in many areas of car art!

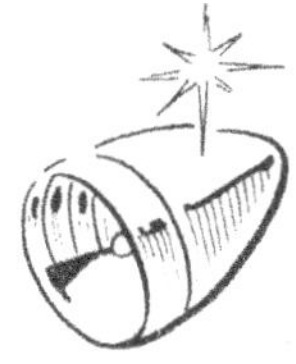
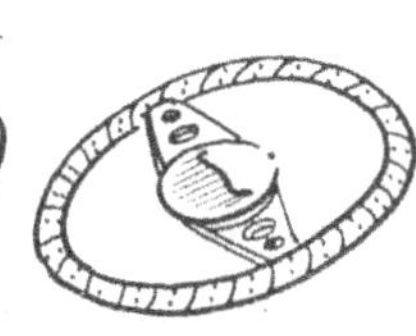
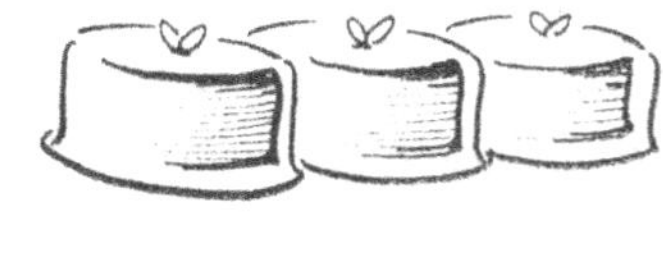

*L*et's see if you can put what you've just learned to use building this insane mini truck hot rod! Start with the two strange boxes shown here and add two huge slicks to either side. Block in the engine, valve covers, blower, and scoop carefully noting their position in relation to the rest of the car. Indicate the front cycle tire.

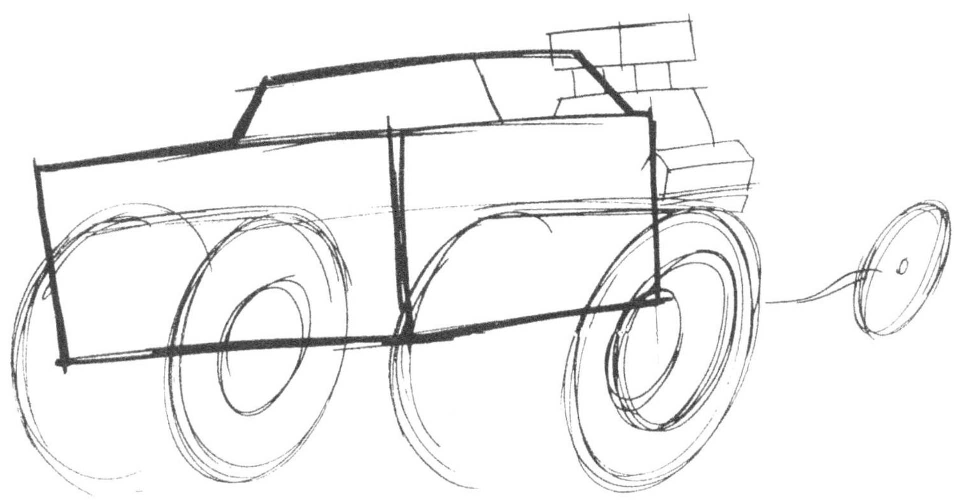

Begin detailin' the basics you've laid in. Divide the body from the bed adding a body line running along the top of both. Roof and rear window detail can be popped in along with a driver. The taillight section is divided off as is the tailgate. Detail the blower assembly and rough in some big pipes and a headlight.

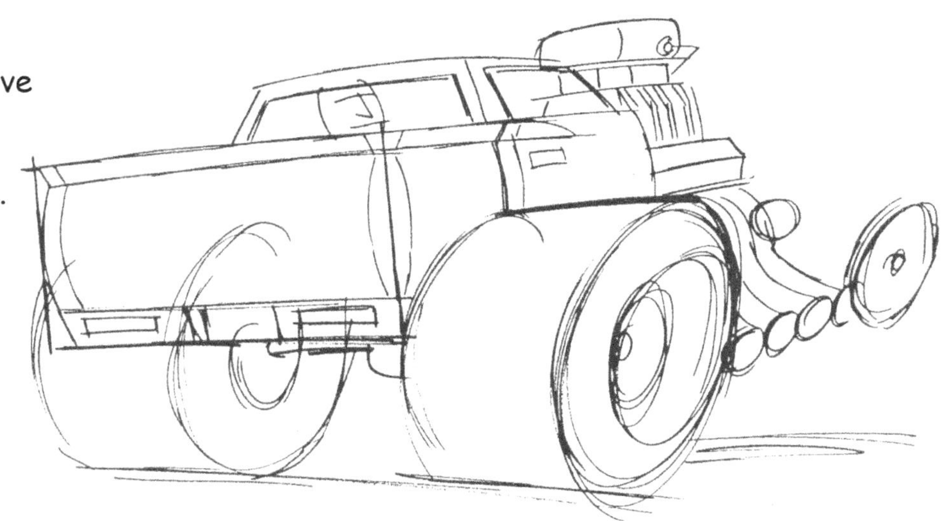

Here's where you find out how much you've learned. Go over everything once more adding a few details such as door handles, flames, smoke, and a license plate. Ink all this very neatly with a felt-tip or ball-point pen applying what you've studied about chrome and tires. Make 'em **sparkle!**

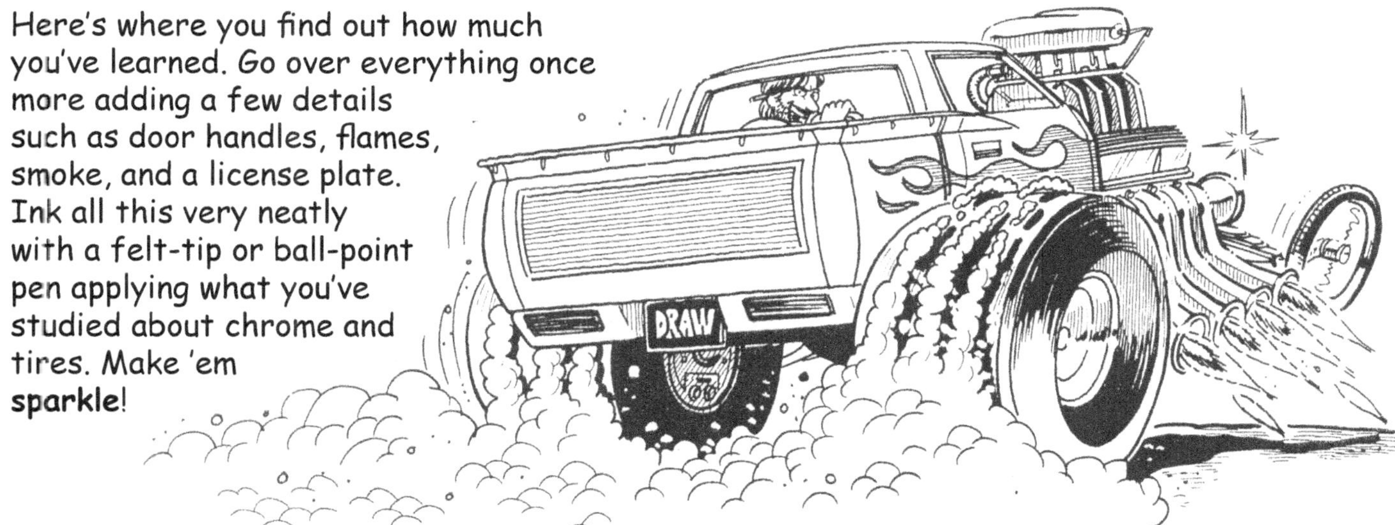

PART TWO

TRUCKS

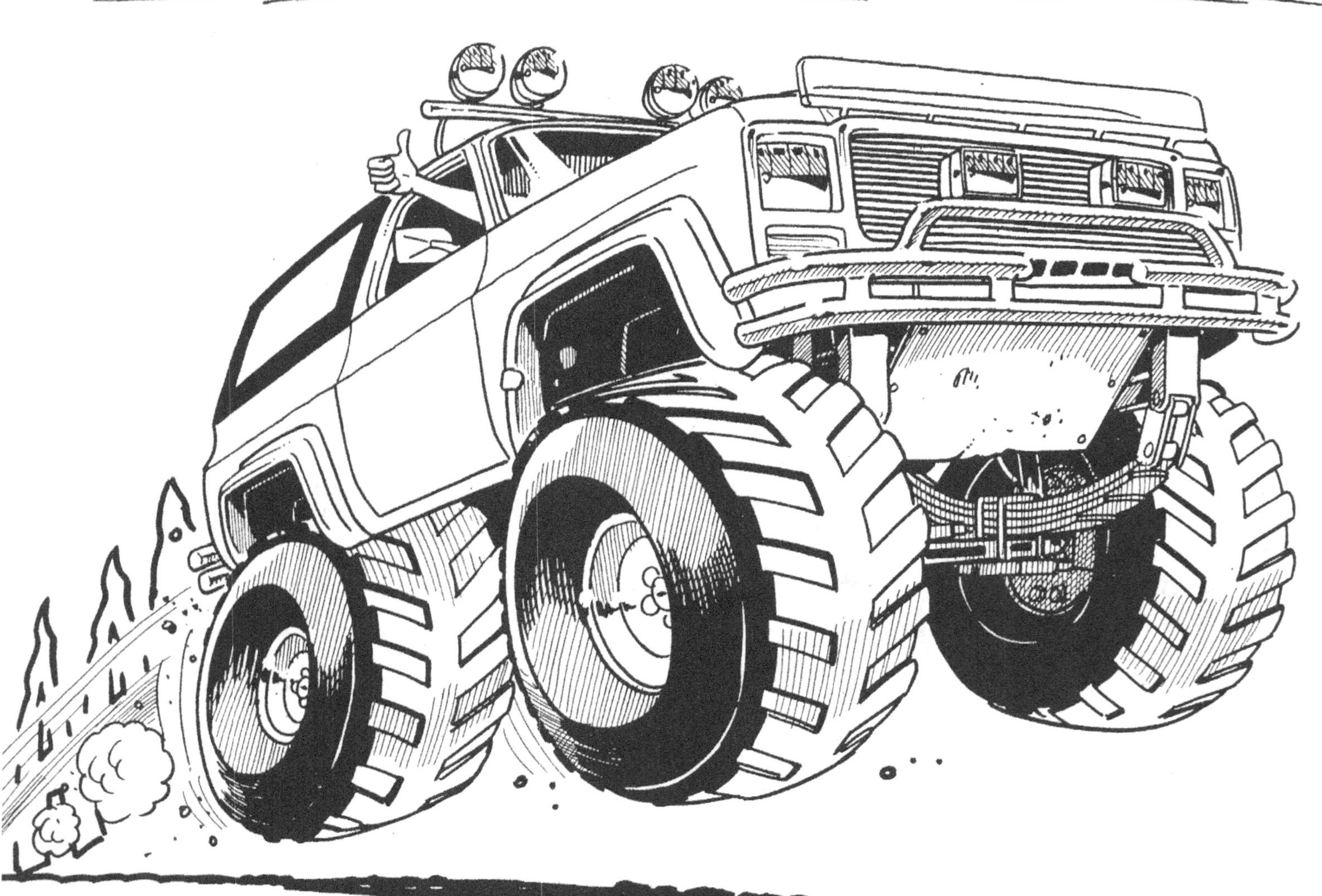

PICKUPS

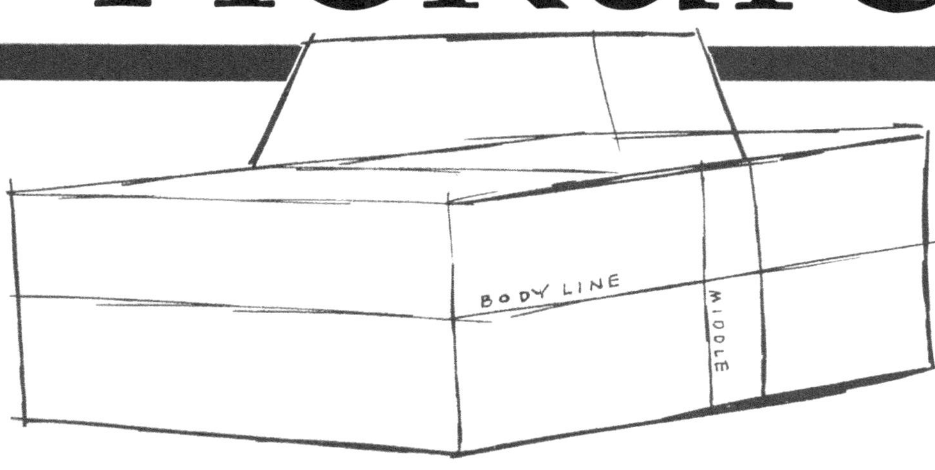

*L*otsa' custom pickups are poppin' up at car shows and lookin' decent. To get yours goin' copy my two boxes. Notice how the back of the cab hits just past the middle of the block and the way the roofline angles in. Wrap a body line around the bottom box.

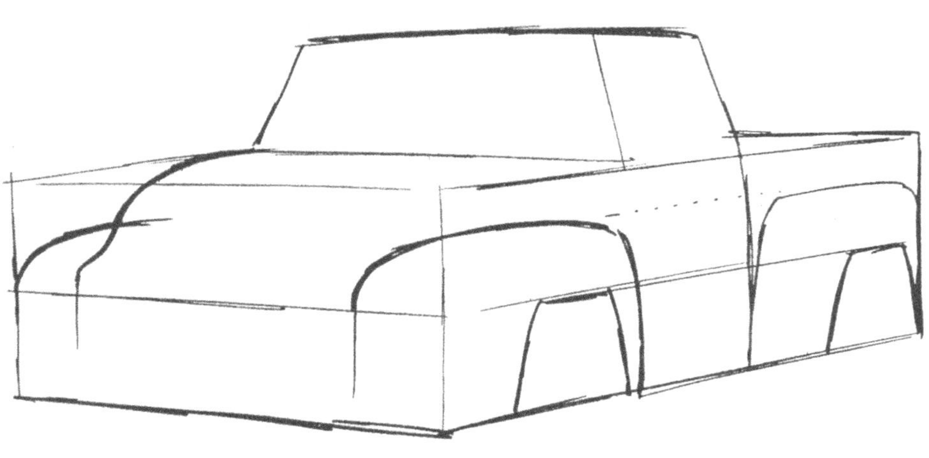

Carve the front fenders out of the box as shown adding wheel wells that key off the body line. The hood curves down to meet the grill area. Lay out the rear fender with guide lines from the front one. For a good look everything must **coordinate**.

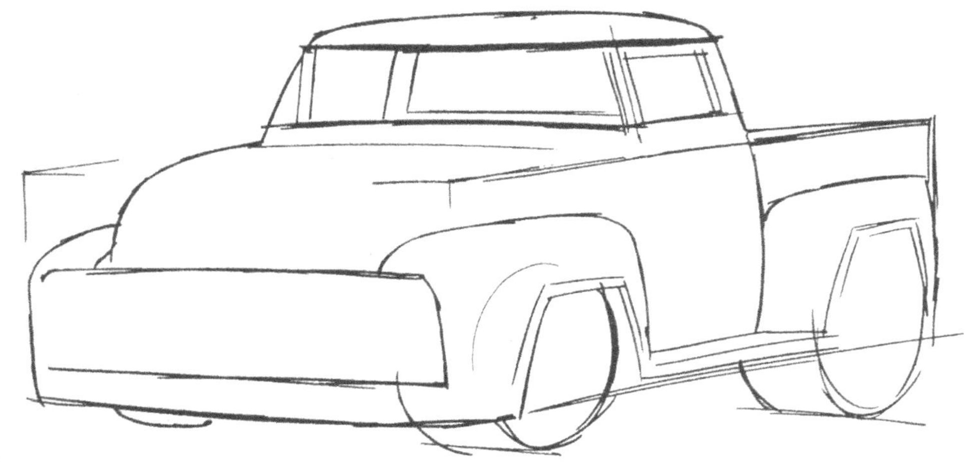

Next, block in the grill area curving the edges to align with the fenders. Roll the pan underneath it then loosely rough in the running board. For a really low look you can push the tires way up into the fenders. Chop the top and lay in the windshield an' window by using a slight lift at the bottom and a gutter line on top.

Now it's starting to look like a **'56 Ford F-100**, isn't it? Let's keep that feeling goin' by working out the grill and quad headlights. Rubber bumperettes protect the rolled pan. The hood line and the door line can now be added along with a little more detail to the cab and some rodders. Indicate some contour to the wheels and a full-body shadow.

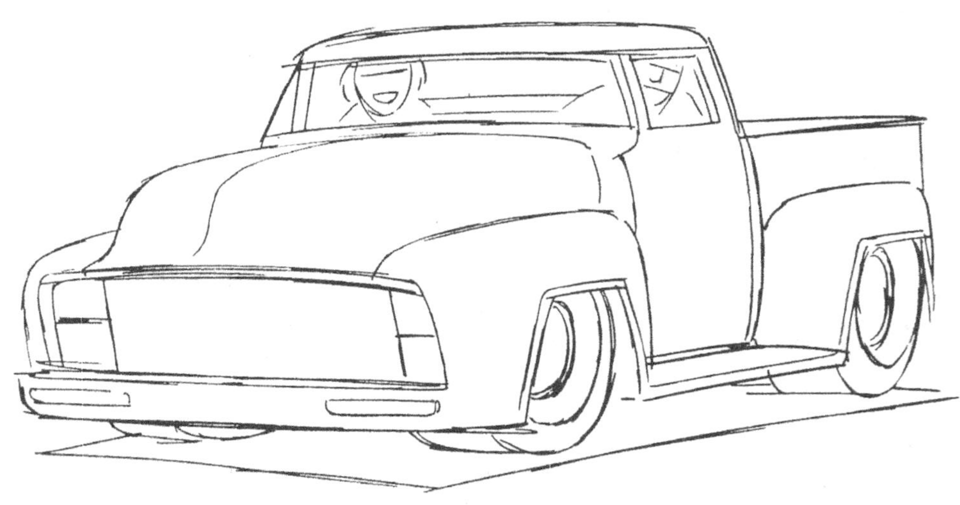

This is the step where you start to check it all over and refine it. Try to give the occupants a little personality and detail the windshield and side windows. The wheels can also use some final detailing. Add a full side pipe while you're there.

Ink all this in with your favorite ball-point or felt-tip pen as neatly as you can. A few solid blacks and some body graphics help give it a **now** look. A ruler helps with the straight bar grill.

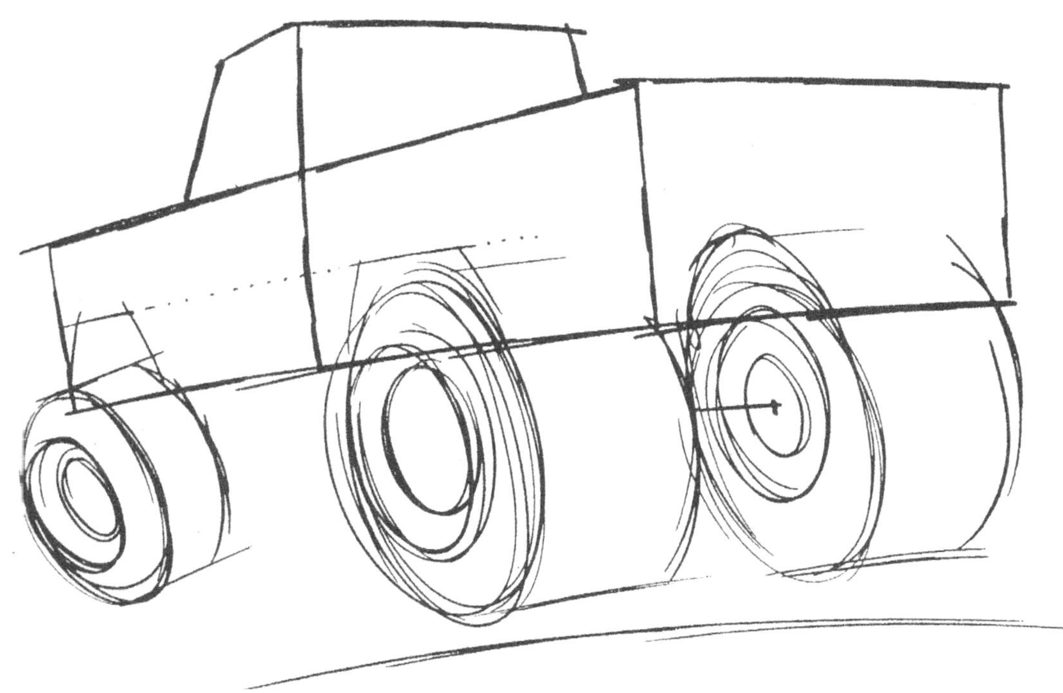

How about a **'56 Chevy**? Lay in the basics with the back of the cab falling midway through the bottom box. Position the wheel wells as shown lining 'em up with a guide line. Loosely rough in the tires with big oversize types out back. Indicate rims and a rear-end centerline.

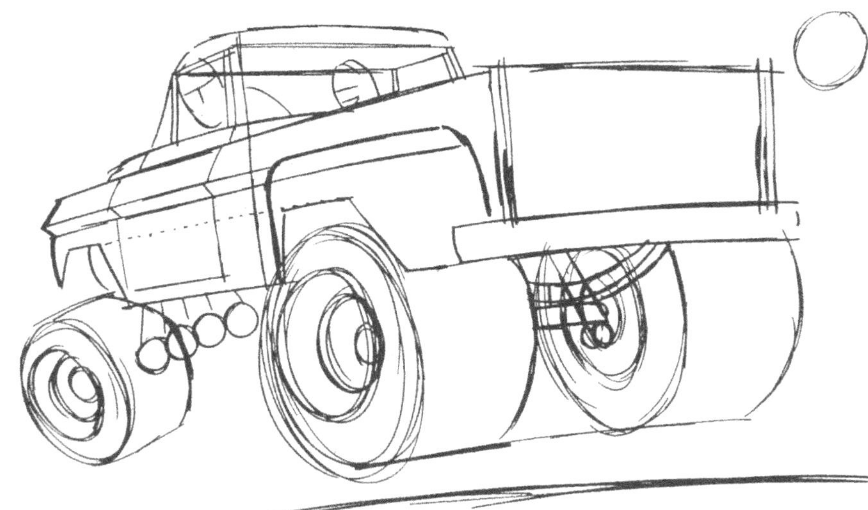

Lots to do here . . . Carve out the cab with the roofline and add a couple of rodders. To keep things true, draw right through areas of the sketch. Notice the front fender contour runnin' back to the rear fender. Door lines, rear bumper, and side pipes help as does rear-end suspension.

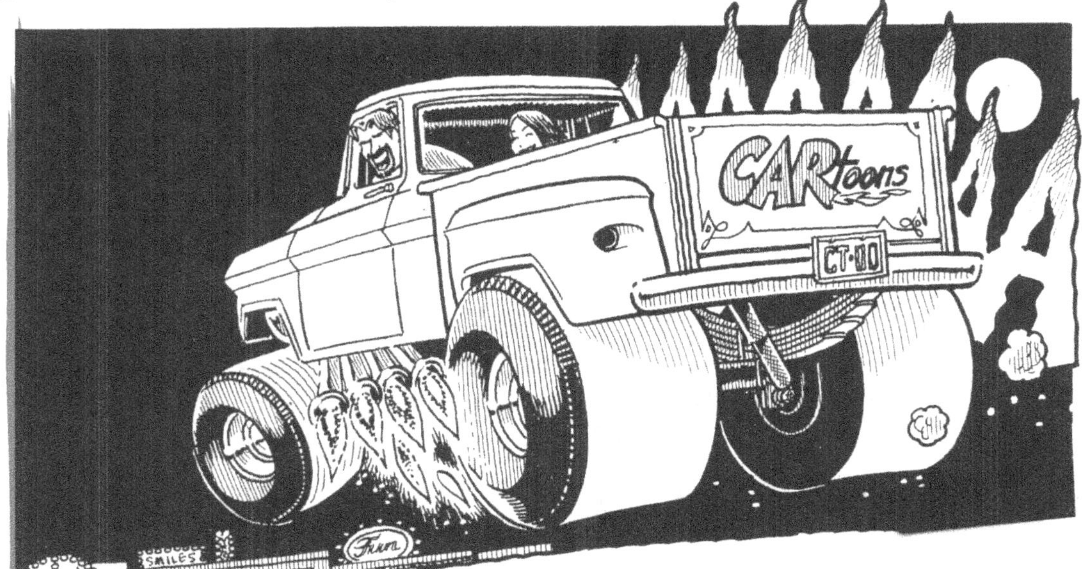

Check 'er over one more time before inking added detail along the way. Flames, sound, and the right lighting give the drawing some excitement. Add **your name** to the rear gate then ink yourself inside. Oh, yeah . . . Be neat!

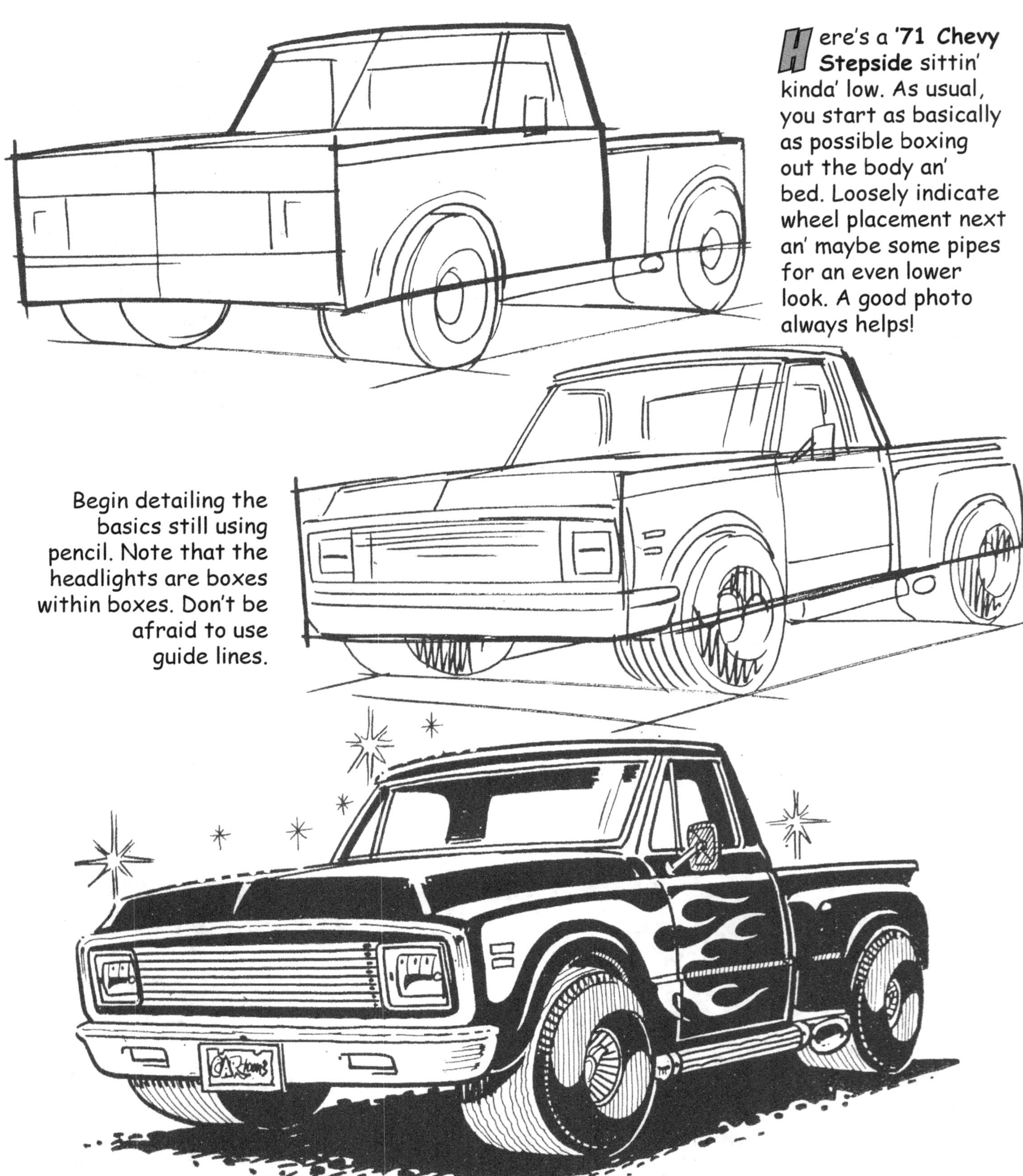

ere's a **'71 Chevy Stepside** sittin' kinda' low. As usual, you start as basically as possible boxing out the body an' bed. Loosely indicate wheel placement next an' maybe some pipes for an even lower look. A good photo always helps!

Begin detailing the basics still using pencil. Note that the headlights are boxes within boxes. Don't be afraid to use guide lines.

Now you finish it off an' tighten it up by adding the trim to the grill an' body. Selective use of blacks adds a look of color. If you plan to ink your pencil drawing with ball-point or felt-tip pen, outline everything first, add highlights, then solid blacks. Try to **build** your drawing like a car!

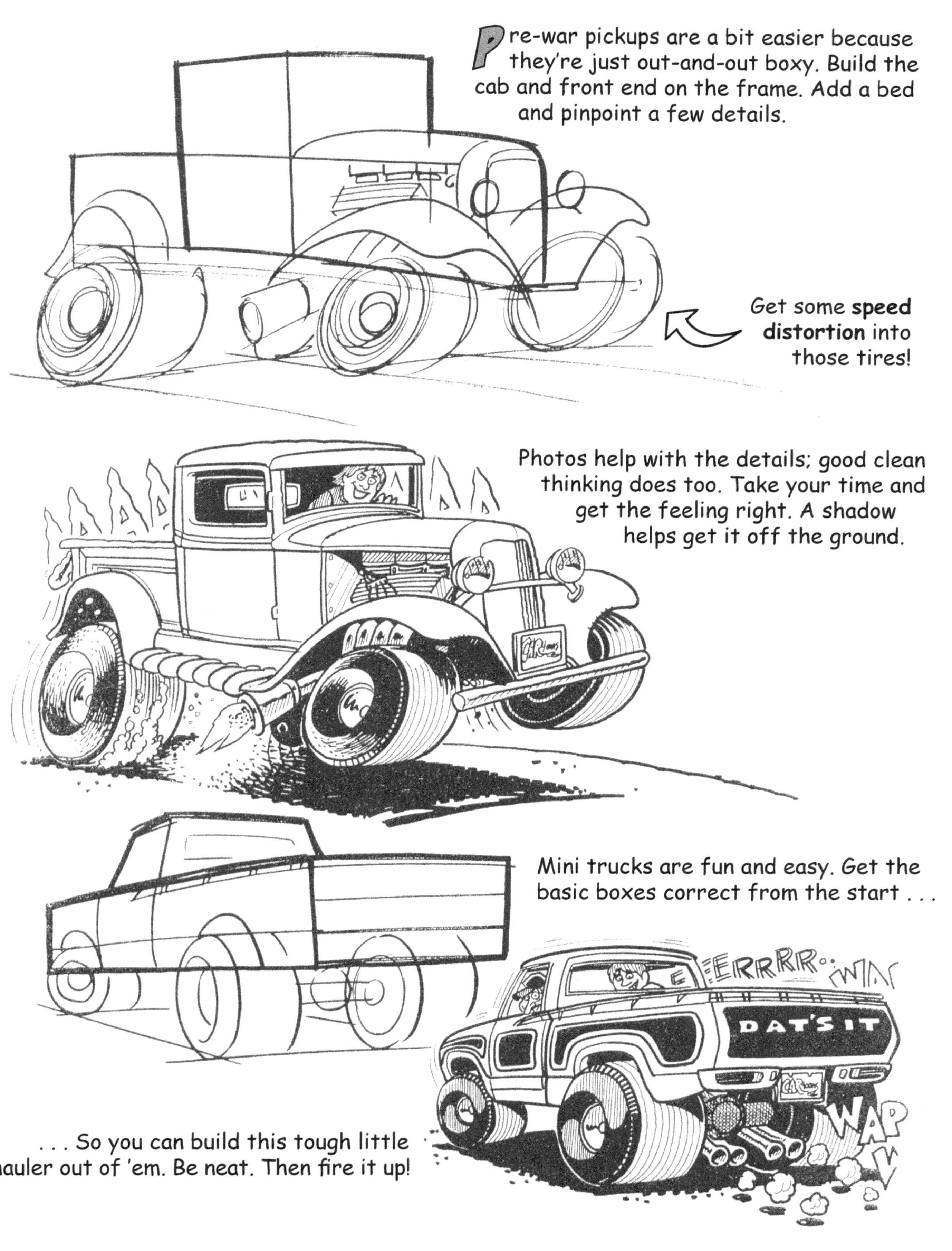

Pre-war pickups are a bit easier because they're just out-and-out boxy. Build the cab and front end on the frame. Add a bed and pinpoint a few details.

Get some **speed distortion** into those tires!

Photos help with the details; good clean thinking does too. Take your time and get the feeling right. A shadow helps get it off the ground.

Mini trucks are fun and easy. Get the basic boxes correct from the start . . .

. . . So you can build this tough little hauler out of 'em. Be neat. Then fire it up!

H ot trucks are just trucks . . . hot rodded! You can start an **'88 Chevy 1500** with the box you see here. Add wheels and openings, a windshield, then divide and bump out the front end.

Build a hot engine with boxes stacked on top of one another. Add a driver then cut a dip in the side of the body. Up front, rough in some headlights and a bumper. Door lines and tire contour get you ready for . . .

. . . Inking with your favorite ball-point or felt-tip pens. Custom paint, lots of chrome, and wild pipes give this ride a **hot rod** look. Personal touches help make it yours!

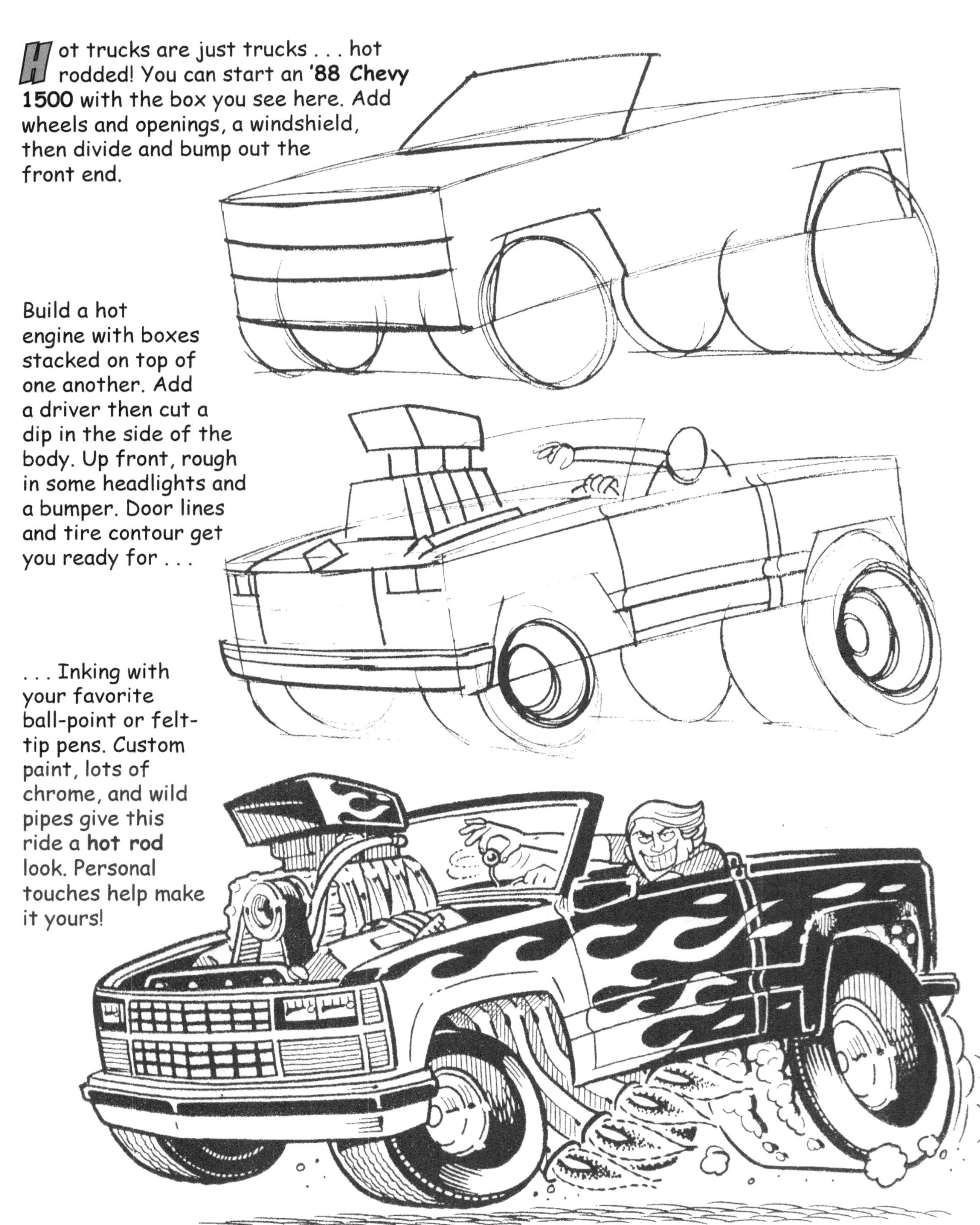

okay . . . Let's go a little hotter with a **Chevy Blazer**. Carefully copy these two boxes with the top one sitting just about midway on the bottom one. Also, indicate the wheel wells.

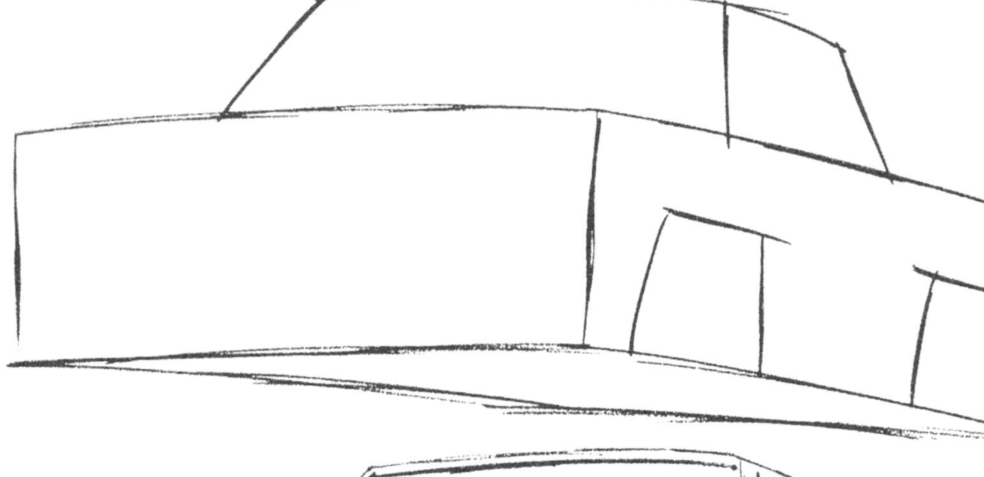

While you're at it, rough in some normal tires up front and a set of humongous slicks in the back. Keep things lined up and true with some guide lines. Add contour to the tires and indicate the rims. Now carve out the cab area, drawing right through things at this rough pencil stage.

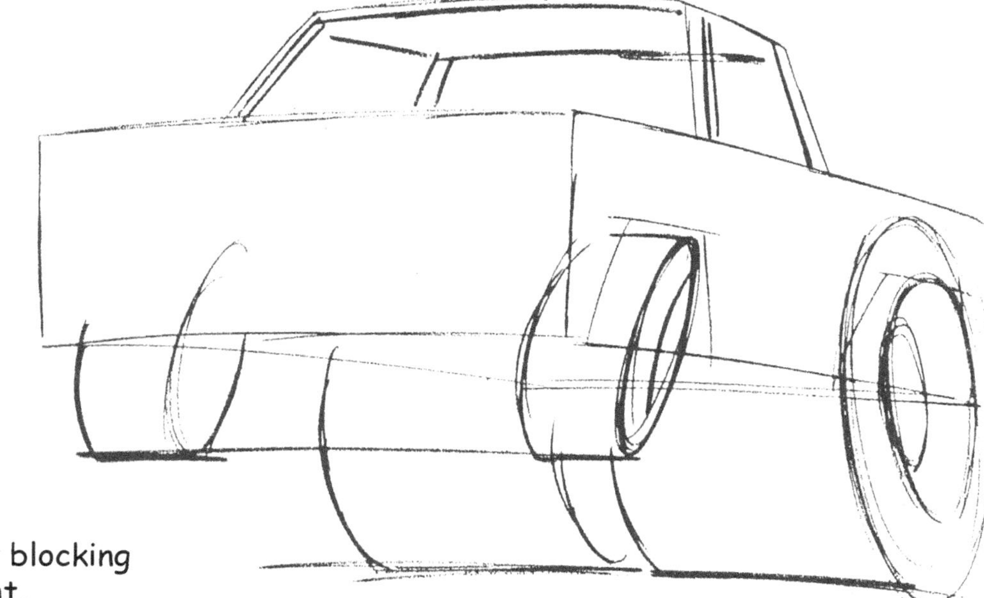

Next, tackle the front end by blocking out the headlight, parking light, and grill areas along with the front bumper. Then detail each of those areas with some round headlights, square parking lights, and a straight bar grill. Lay in the rubber strip across the bumper.

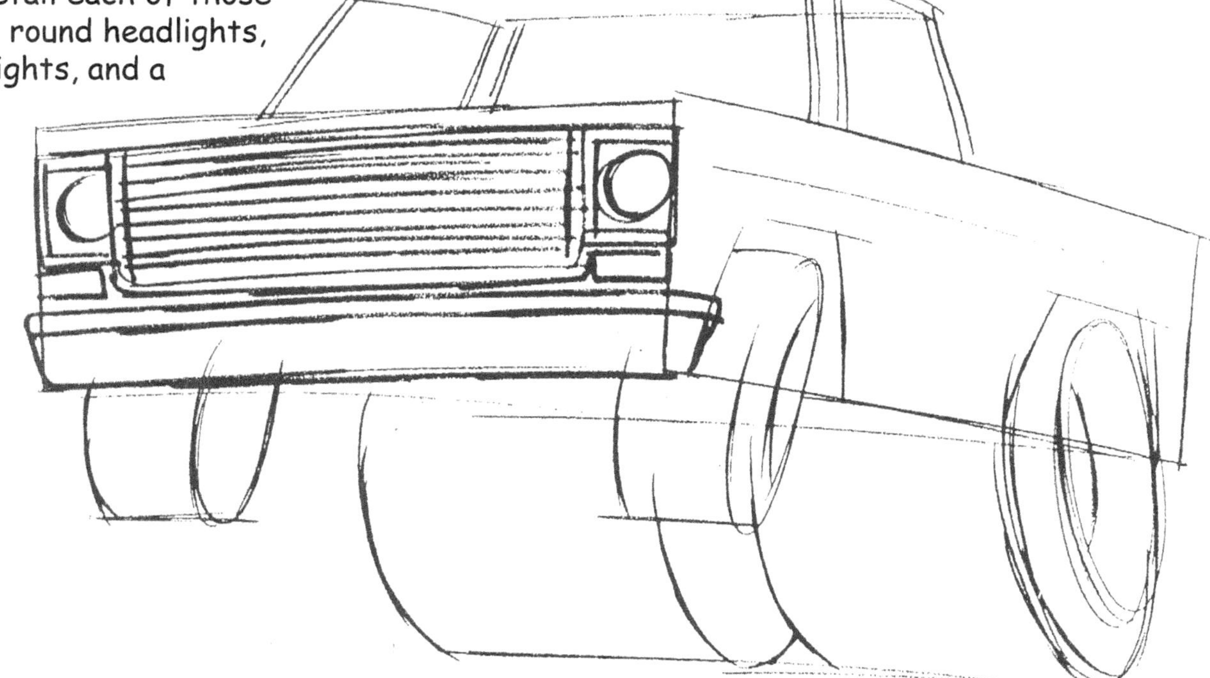

Time to drop in a monster engine starting with the basic boxes that are **stacked up here**. Then add things such as a curved bug catcher, fuel lines, and some blower details. It's also a good time to rough in some pipes, then drawing right through them to get the ellipses right.

This is your last chance to pencil in some goodies like a spoiler on the roof as well as one on the back. Rough in yourself as the driver then add details like the door lines, wheel well flares, and the characteristic side body line and side signal light.

It's that time again . . . inking! Neatly outline the basic shapes with a fat-tip pen adding the details with a fine-line tip. Solid areas help the overall look of your drawing. Highlights help add sparkle and shine. **Go magic fingers!**

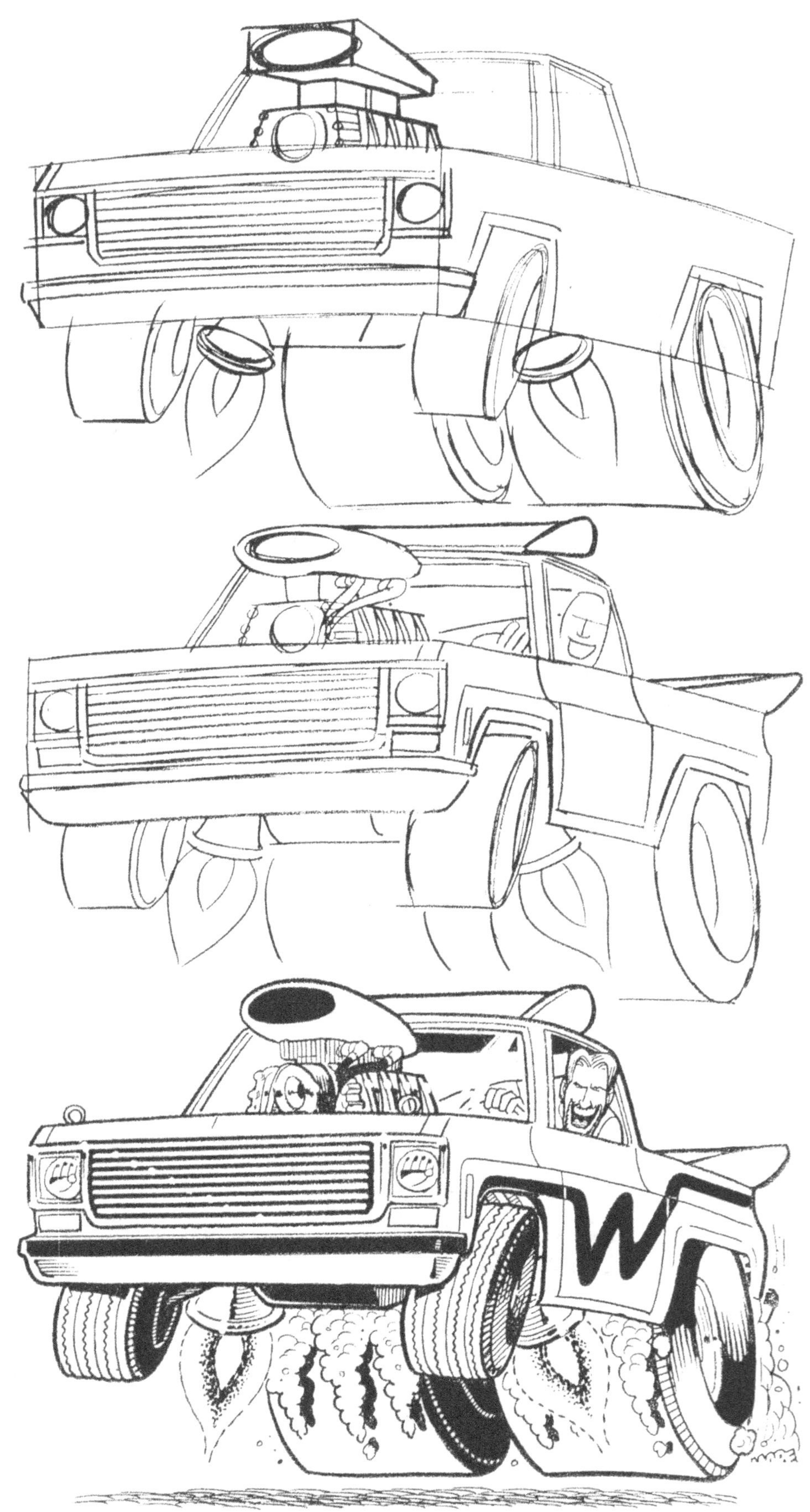

HOW TO DRAW

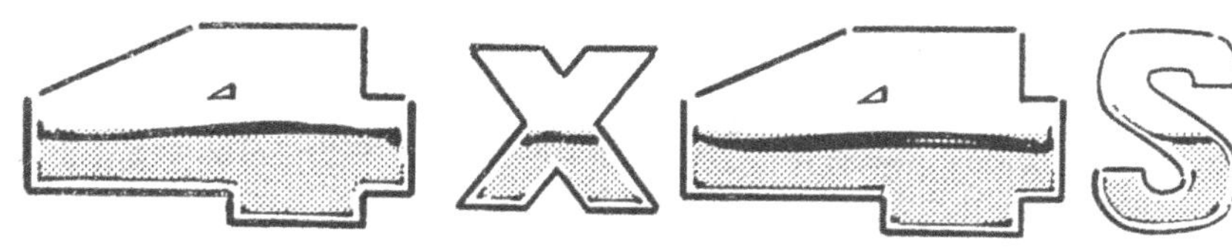

You see lots of rugged lookin' 4x4s on the street so let's build a real mean one. Start with the two basic boxes shown here. Break them down into a few of the basic body parts.

Loosely rough in some **big** feet using guide lines to keep the stance right. The front bumper and crank rack can be detailed out a little more as well as the cab area. Block in seats and a driver and then add a custom-formed roll bar mounted in the bed.

Here's where you can go crazy with **extras!**

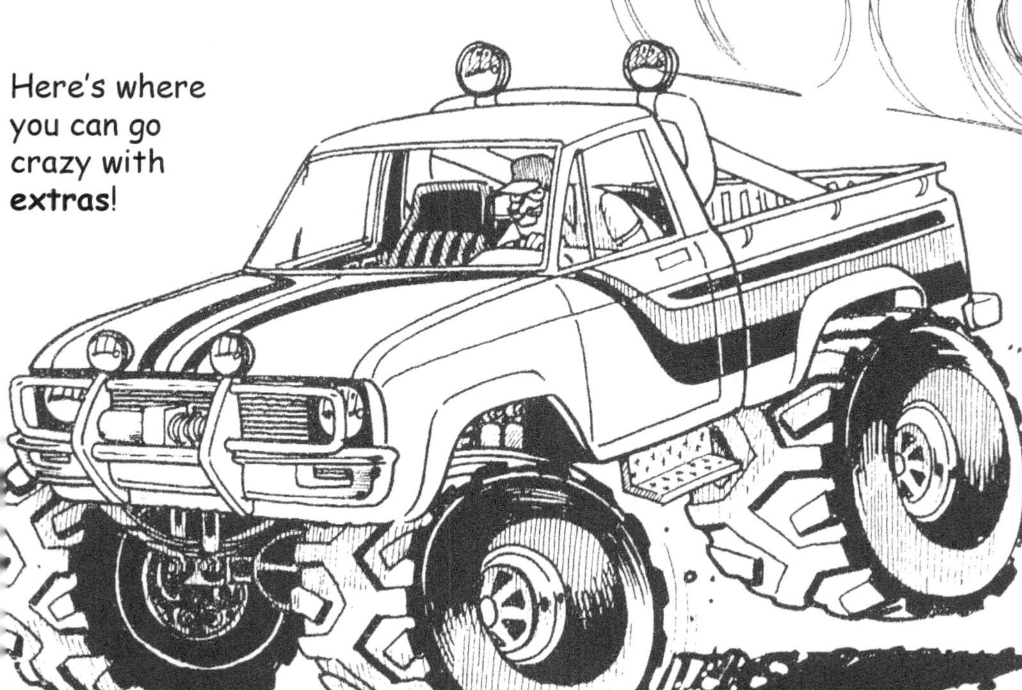

Clean up the body then add a stone guard and a crank to the grill area. Drop in front suspension and shocks along with a side step. Handle the lights atop the roll bar and the front rack the same as the headlights. Check the tire tread carefully and get it right. Then neatly ink everything and add solid blacks where shown.

Now let's see what you can do with a **Ford F-250**. The boxes are simple but make sure your proportions are right. Wheel openings and tires should be roughed in checking placement along the way. Once again, notice how a few guide lines keep everything true. The rear suspension and rear end can also be dropped in.

Some detail to the tailgate is in order. Note the special bumper made from chrome tubing with a trailer hitch in the center. Taillights and twin exhaust pipes finish up the rear; fender flares and a full-length body stripe accent the side. A roll bar and cab detail as well as the addition of a couple of rodders finish this step.

Now we're gettin' down to it; roll bar, lights, and window netting add authenticity while tire spin and smoke add action. Details like a front stone guard and a side step help too! Ink it neatly then . . . **Hit the dirt!**

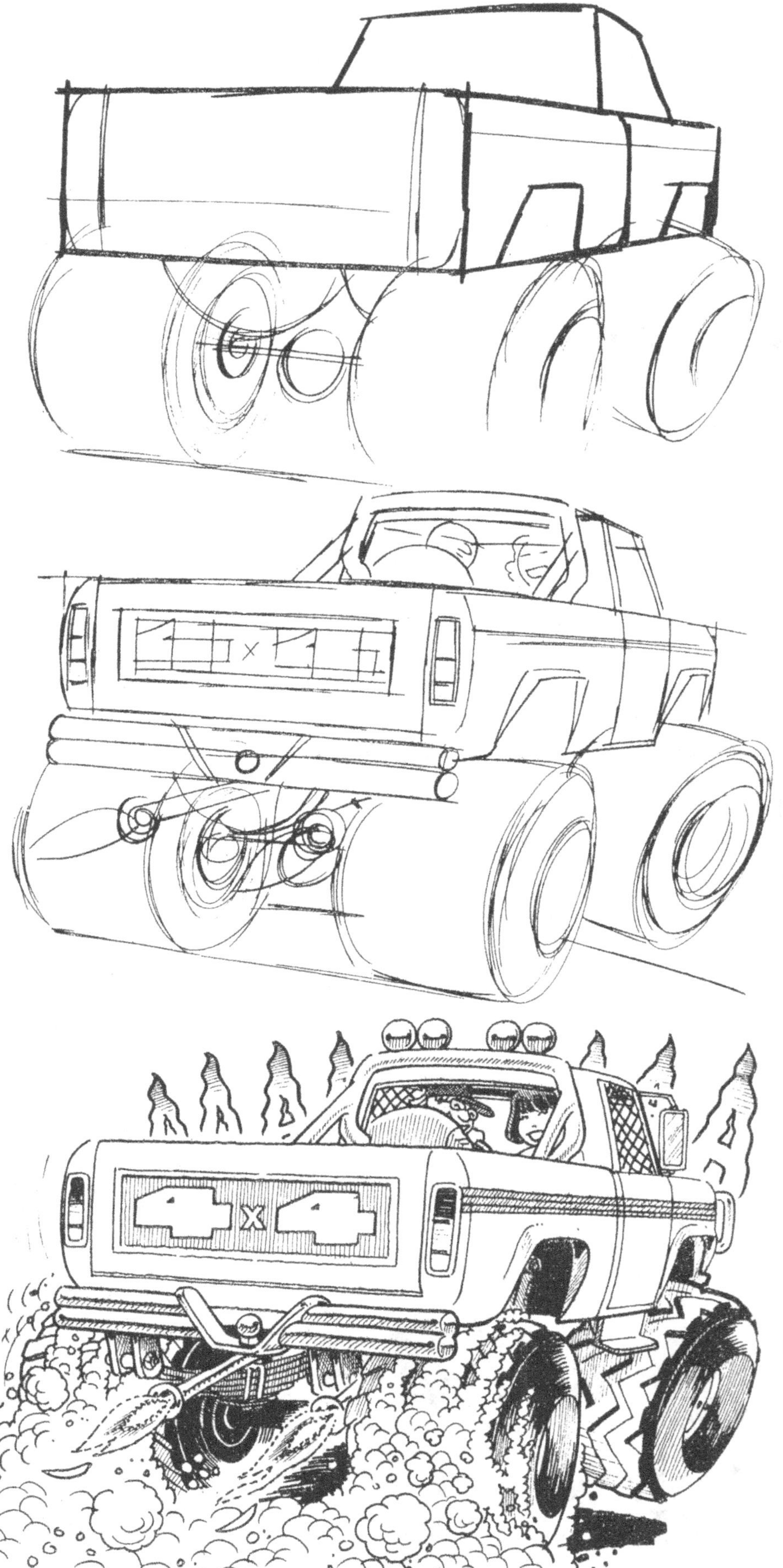

HOW TO DRAW 4X4 GOODIES

F our wheelin' has quickly grown into a very popular sport with sanctioned races, events, and rallies; even sand drags. Of course, the aftermarket goodies industry has grown too with more new products than ever before. Let's check out a few of 'em!

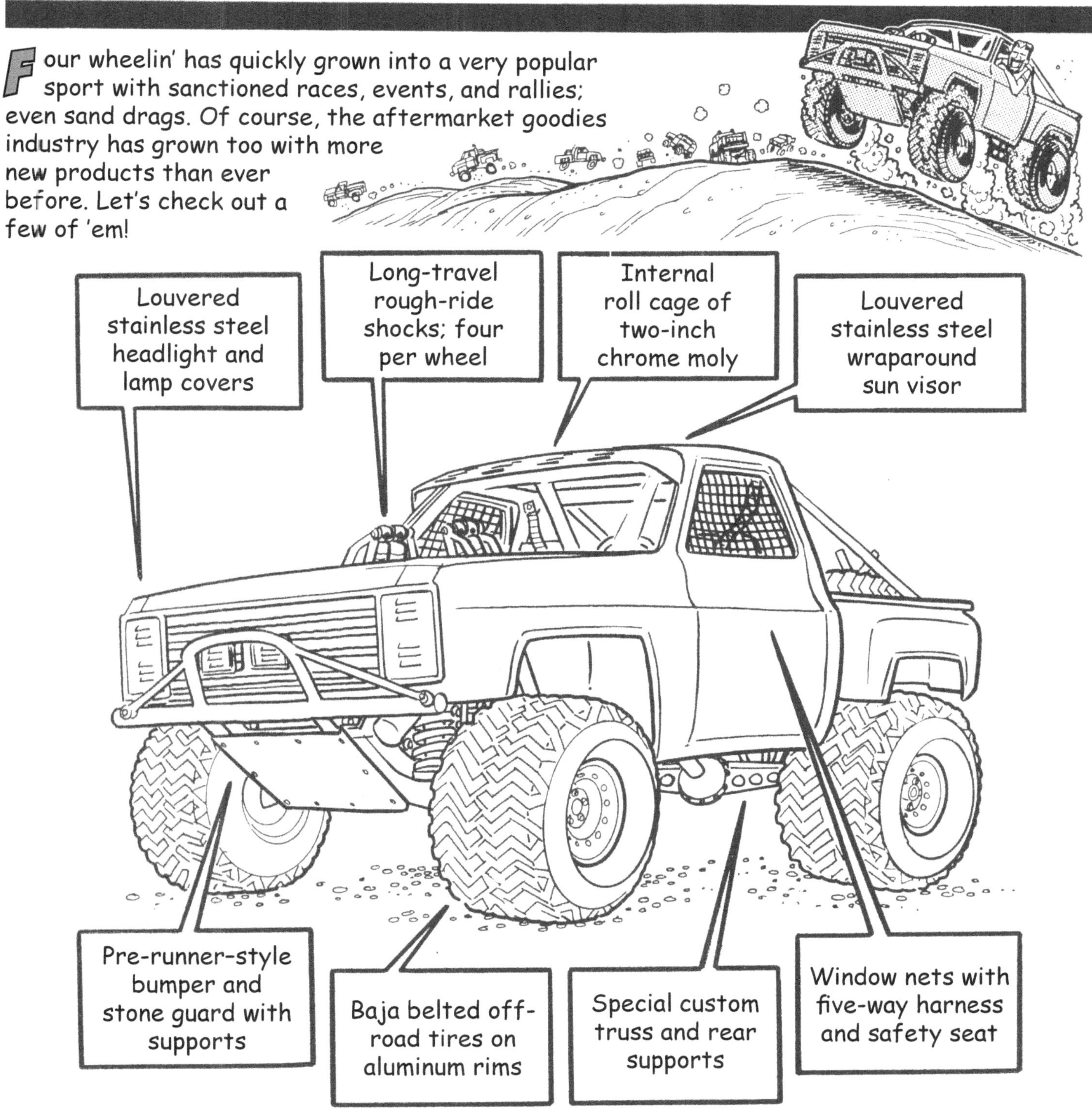

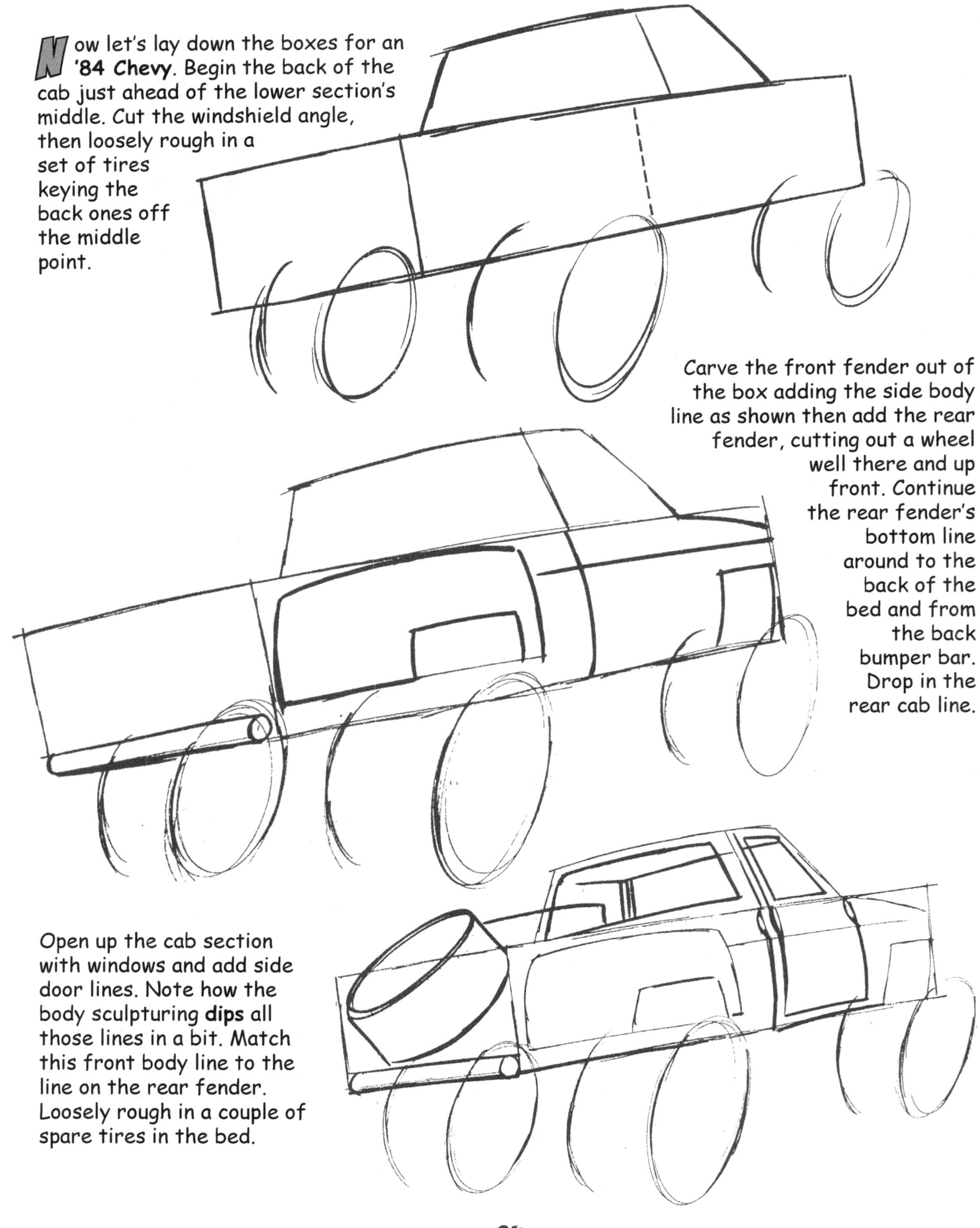

Now let's lay down the boxes for an **'84 Chevy**. Begin the back of the cab just ahead of the lower section's middle. Cut the windshield angle, then loosely rough in a set of tires keying the back ones off the middle point.

Carve the front fender out of the box adding the side body line as shown then add the rear fender, cutting out a wheel well there and up front. Continue the rear fender's bottom line around to the back of the bed and from the back bumper bar. Drop in the rear cab line.

Open up the cab section with windows and add side door lines. Note how the body sculpturing **dips** all those lines in a bit. Match this front body line to the line on the rear fender. Loosely rough in a couple of spare tires in the bed.

Carefully work out the tube cradle for the spare then add the rolled edge to the top of the bed. Drop in the internal roll cage and its supports along with the notch in the bottom of the can. Now work in the rear-end truss and add **dimension** to the tires.

Stickin' with the tires, let's add some tread keeping in mind that it's just a repetitious pattern. Some smoke gives them the **illusion** of speed. Square off the end of the bed. Rough in the rear springs, gas tank, and occupants.

A few more things such as tire hold-downs, rim detail, and some noise an' you're all set for inking! Outline everything with your favorite felt-tip or ball-point pen then add solid blacks as I've done here.

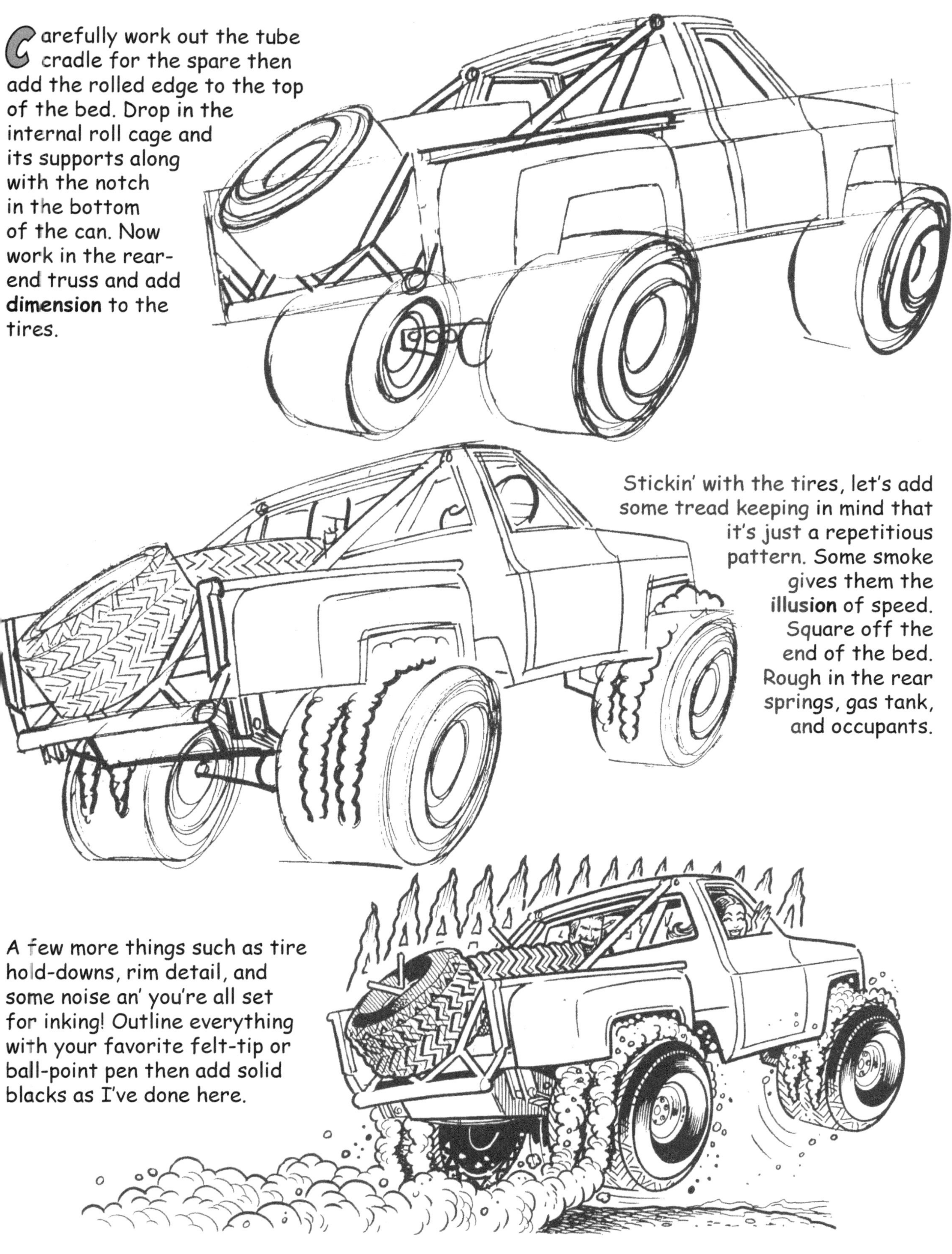

HOW TO DRAW

MONSTER TRUCKS

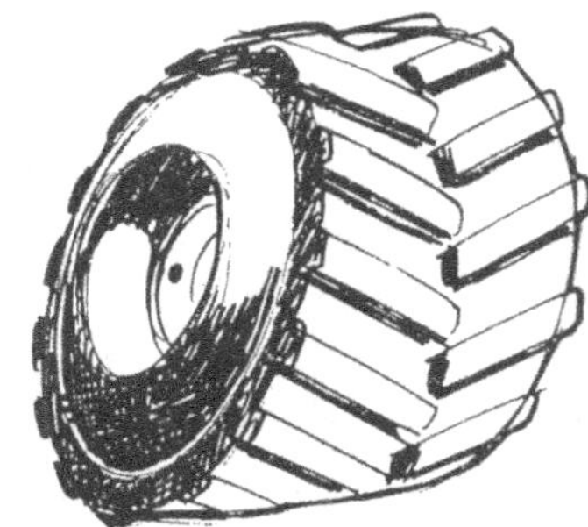

Monster trucks . . . What a concept! Four-wheel-drive trucks with humongous power plants and enough torque to pull down a building, suspended on heavy-duty springs and lots of tube shocks with a set of 8-feet-tall tires making all this **get up and go**.

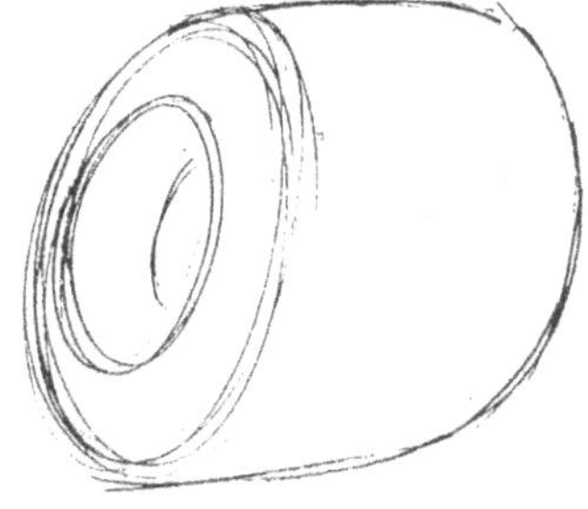

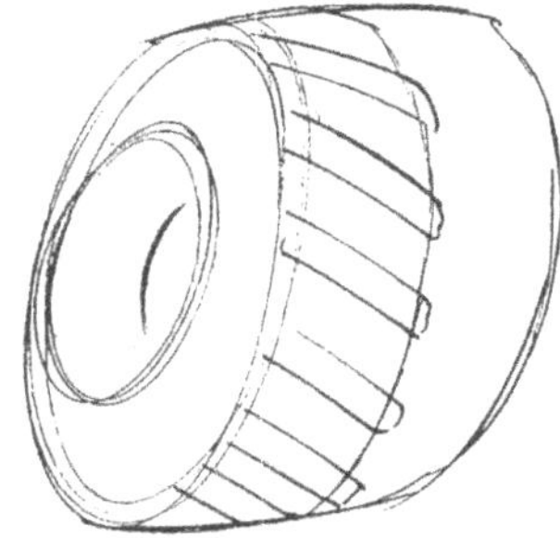

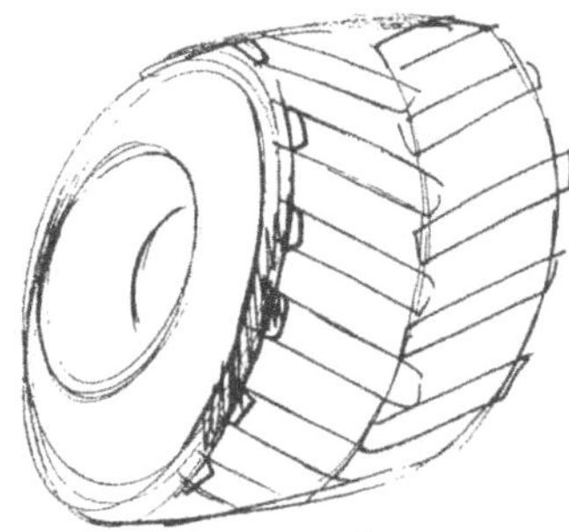

Before I get into the truck itself, let's take a minute to figure out how to draw monster tires. Begin with the basic tire shape. It's okay to be loose.

After dropping a centerline around the middle of the tire, start laying in the individual tread, first on the left side . . .

. . . Then on the right side, between the others. Add a contoured edge and some height to the tread on both sides of the tires.

Here's where dark shadows help a lot! Give one to each tread, then add some solid black to the sides for depth and definition.

Another thing to consider is **proportion**. At this point you can make it as wild as you want so go ahead and play with a few shapes.

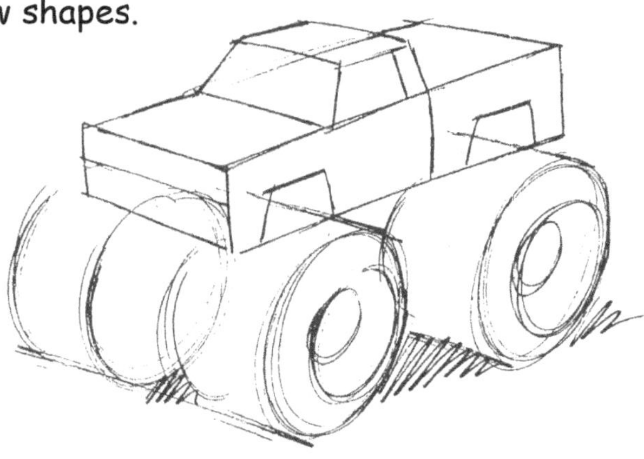

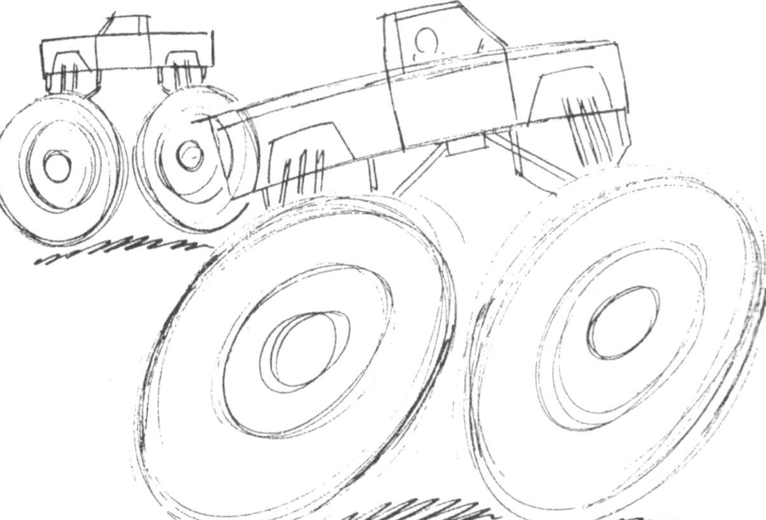

*I*f you're ready, try a **Ford F-350** beginning with the curved box for the body and bed. Locate the center then place the cab evenly on either side of it and add your roofline on the same angle as the hood line. Rough in a big set of monster tires keeping that same perspective in mind. Indicate some wheel wells.

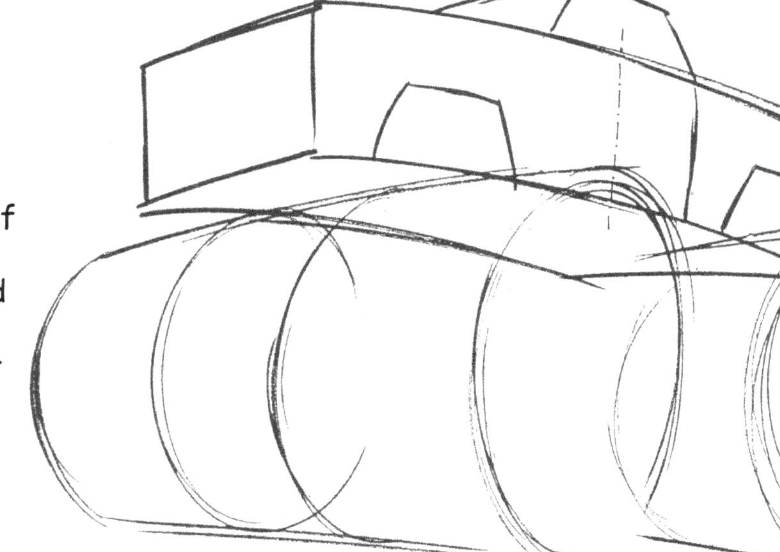

Detail the front end a bit more by first splitting the box in half then dividing the grill area as shown. Next, carefully rough in the bumper; it is divided into thirds and angles up on each side with parking lights above that. Add the body line, door line, and a windshield.

Rough in some carburetors and filters keeping the perspective right. Side lights can be roughed in now along with a peek at the engine and exhaust. Lay in the front spring supports with a 2x3-inch boxed frame running the length. Wheel well flares and some contour to the cab and door lines help finish this step.

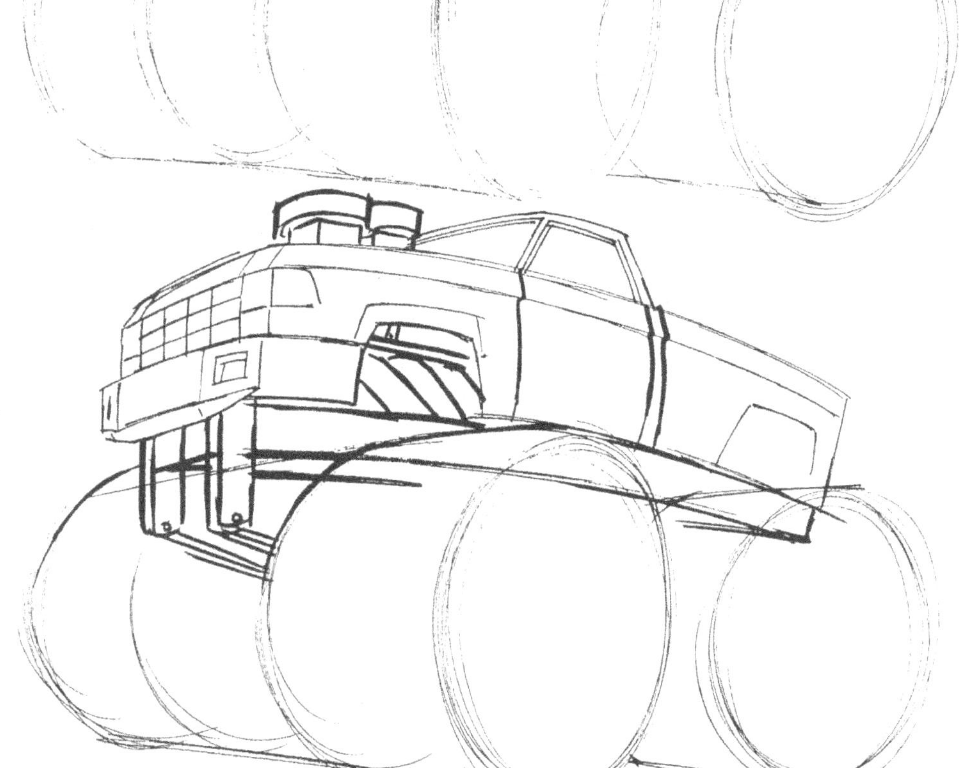

*T*ires are next so let's lay in the **heavy tread** beginning with the centerline to keep 'em even. Detail out the front suspension a bit more, adding shocks and some handsome axle detail. Back to the tires: Add some contour and a set of chrome rims.

You can now rough in some goodies: a roll bar, lights, and a driver as well as some flamed exhaust. Check over everything again and get it all ready for inking.

Outline everything with a good felt-tip or ball-point pen using a finer point for details. I tilted mine and couldn't resist goin' with some **bigger** tires. It's your monster truck; do it any way you like!

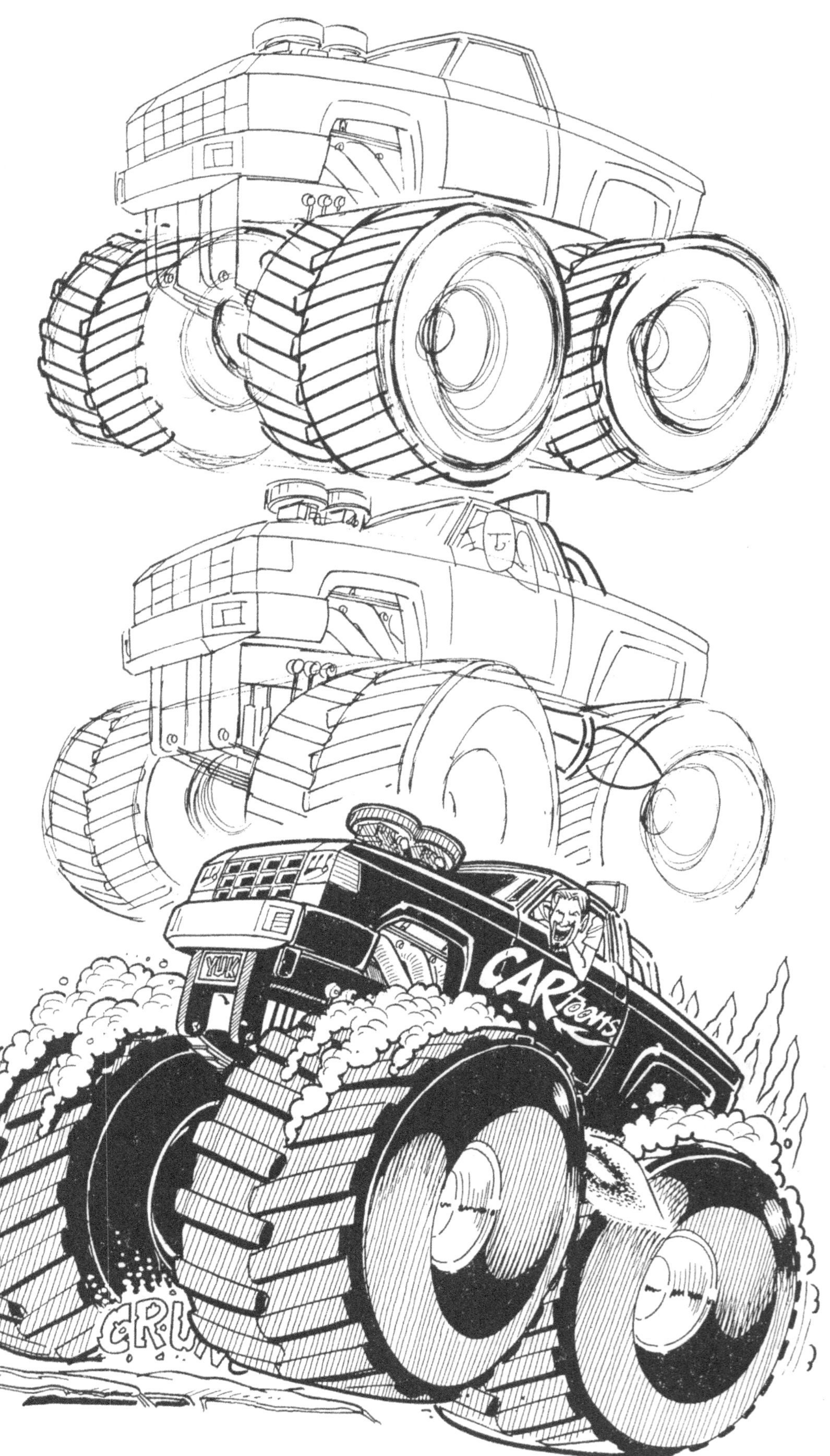

HOW TO DRAW OFF ROADIES

*O*ff roadies are fun to drive and they're fun to draw too, especially when you play around with your drawing style, instead of a straightforward realistic approach, try an exaggerated caricature. What's that, you ask?

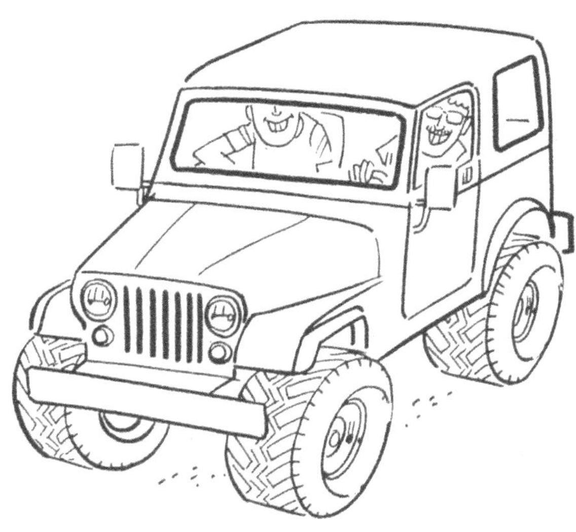

The drawing above keeps all the proportions and dimensions of a **CJ-7 Laredo** accurate and represents the way this vehicle really looks.

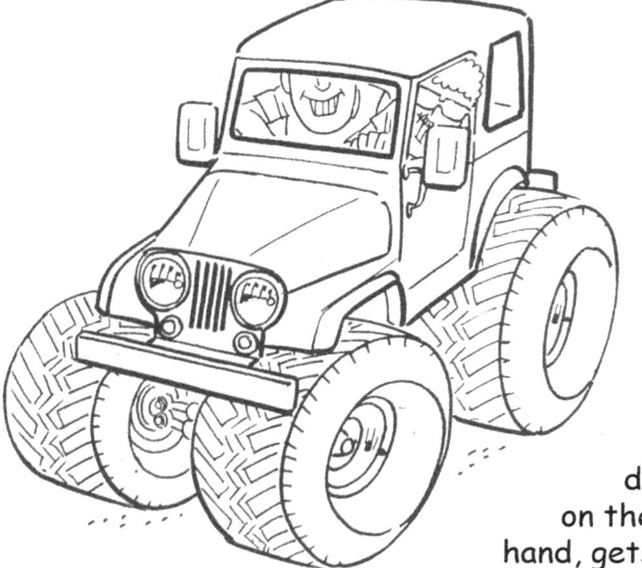

This drawing, on the other hand, gets crazy with the Laredo and is a caricature. Proportions and dimensions are exaggerated a bunch!

*T*ry a few rough sketches to get a "feel" for the distortions. Be free. Experiment.

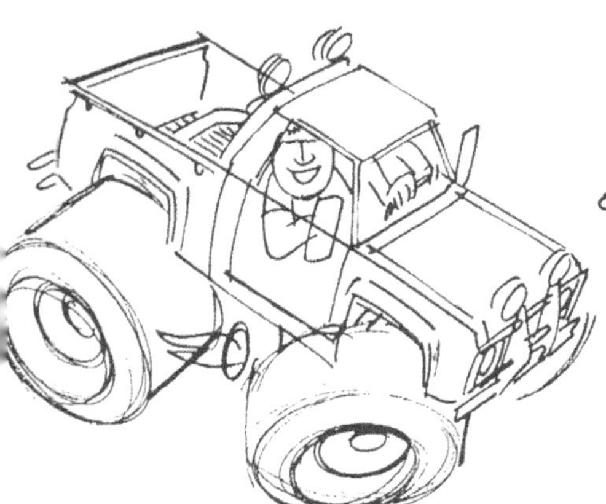

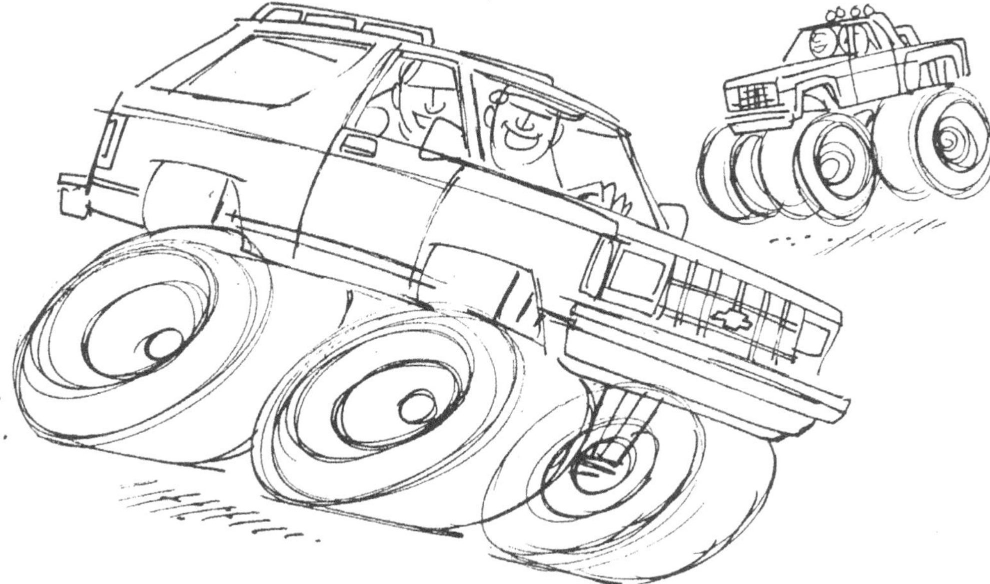

*L*et's see what kind
of wildness you can
whip on a **Toyota Mini**.
Begin with two boxes,
noting the low point of
view. You can see **under**
the truck. Loosely rough
in some giant tires well
below it. Copy this first
step carefully. You'll be
building a truck on it.

Add some dimension to the cab
then taper the hood down to the
grill. Rough in headlights and pan,
then wheel wells. Loosely
indicate springs and
shackles as well as tube
shocks. **Keep it simple.**
This is a good time to add
some contour to the tires
and rough in some
off-road tread.

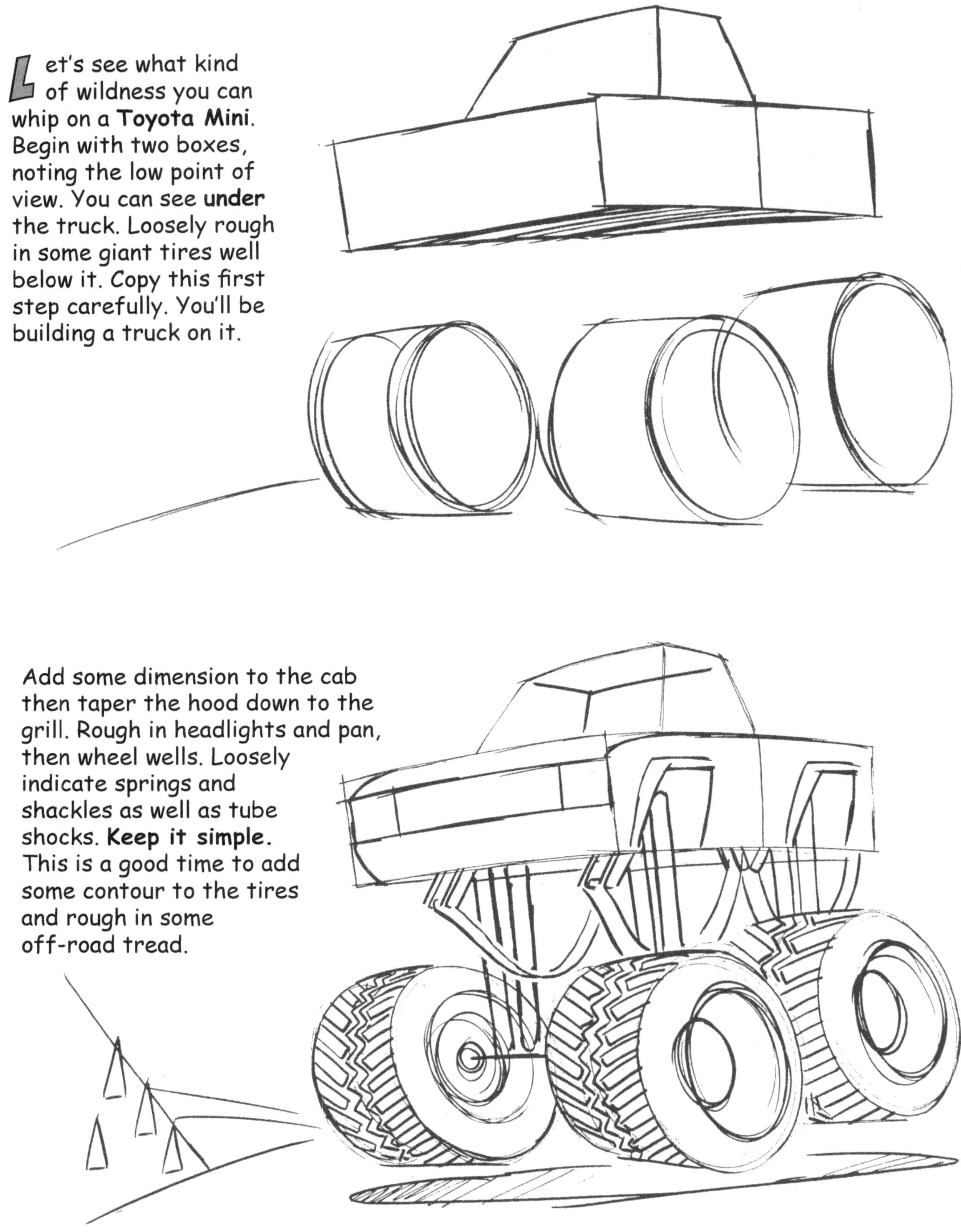

Lotsa' details to add so let's get busy . . . Up front, add a stone guard and bumper. A ruler helps a lot here as well as with the side body line. Carve out the bed then rough in a roll bar and lights. Side mirrors, pipes, people, and more suspension detail and tire smoke do it.

Go over all you've done, detailin' the grill, lights, and other accessories. Then ink 'er in with your favorite pen outlining the basics first then adding details. Chrome **generously** then add some solid blacks as I've done here. The scenic background makes it more than just another car drawing.

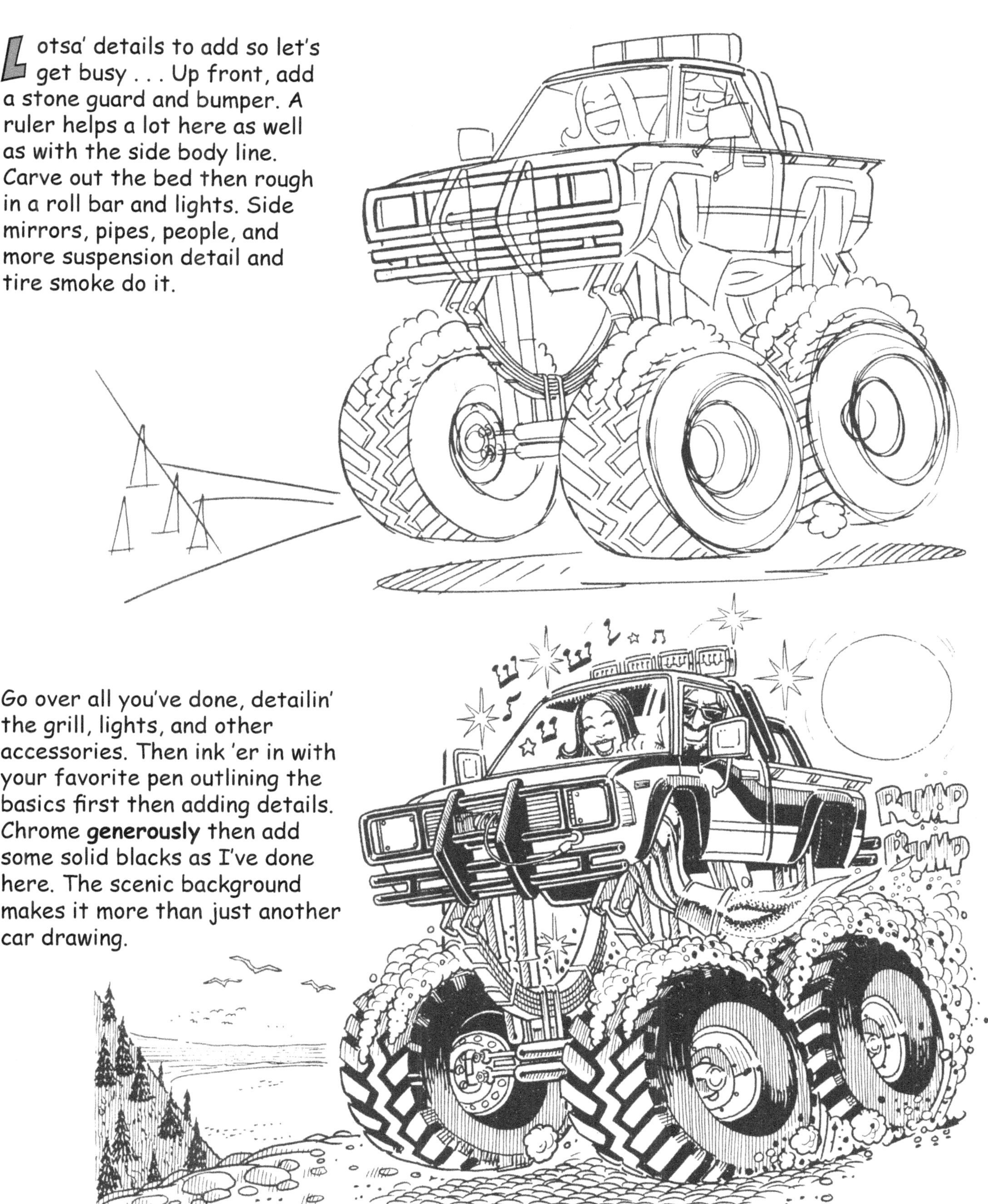

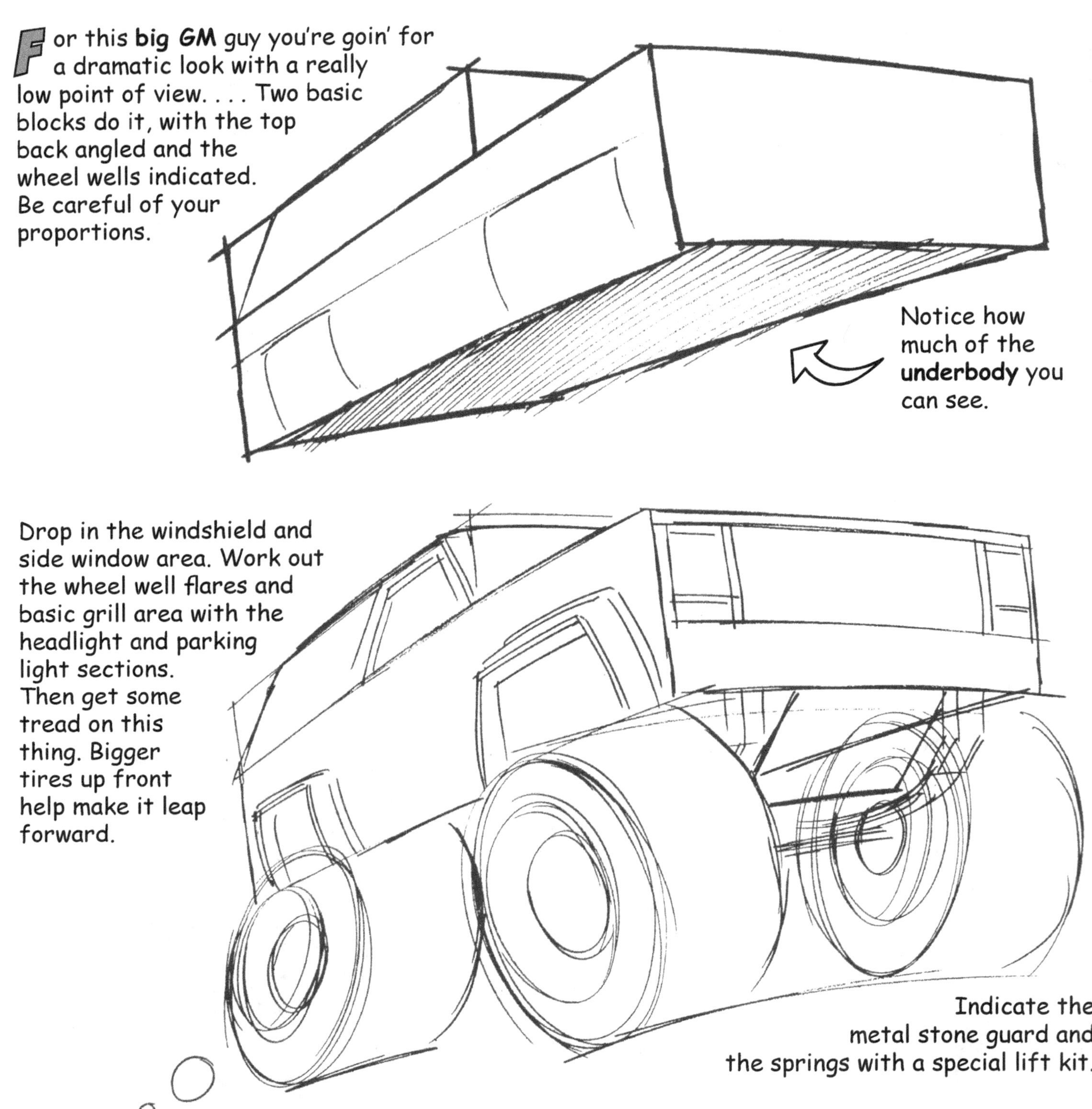

For this **big GM** guy you're goin' for a dramatic look with a really low point of view. . . . Two basic blocks do it, with the top back angled and the wheel wells indicated. Be careful of your proportions.

Notice how much of the **underbody** you can see.

Drop in the windshield and side window area. Work out the wheel well flares and basic grill area with the headlight and parking light sections. Then get some tread on this thing. Bigger tires up front help make it leap forward.

Indicate the metal stone guard and the springs with a special lift kit.

*T*ime to detail the body a bit more by adding accessory lights to the roof and a body line down the rise. The grill area could also use a little **more detail** so add headlights and a grill. The bar bumper is next, wrapping around the entire front end. A grill guard spans the separation.

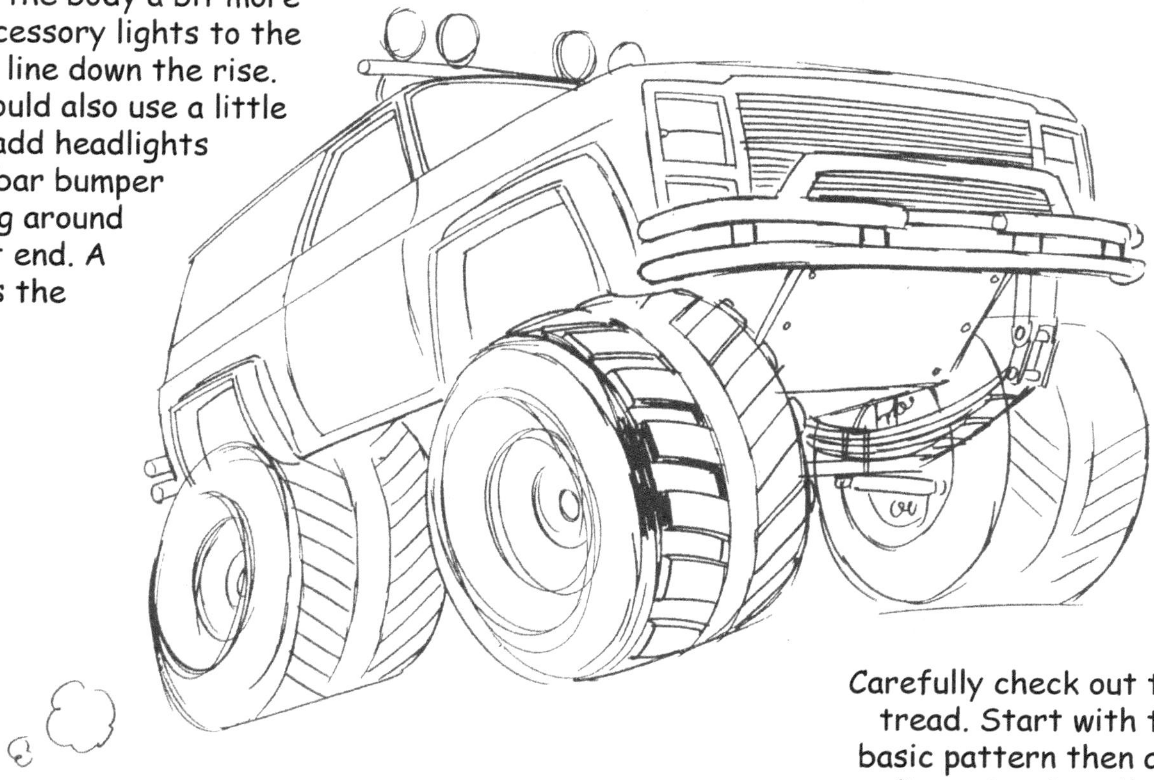

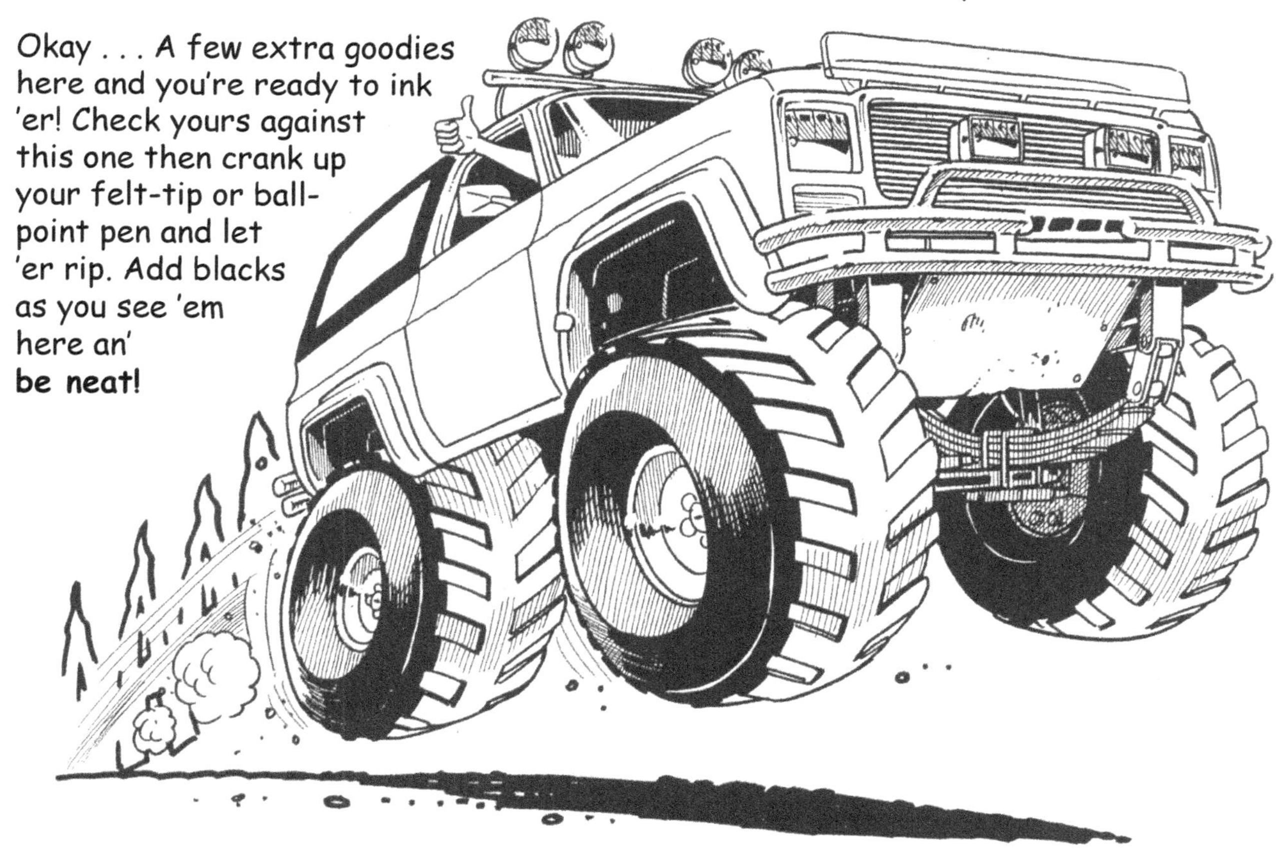

Carefully check out the tread. Start with the basic pattern then add some dimension. Detail the suspension as I've done here.

Okay . . . A few extra goodies here and you're ready to ink 'er! Check yours against this one then crank up your felt-tip or ball-point pen and let 'er rip. Add blacks as you see 'em here an' **be neat!**

Here you're going for a little more detail, especially in the suspension and accessory departments. Knowing **what** you're drawing is as important as knowing **how** to draw it so check over the diagram below to familiarize yourself with the names of the stuff you'll be drawing.

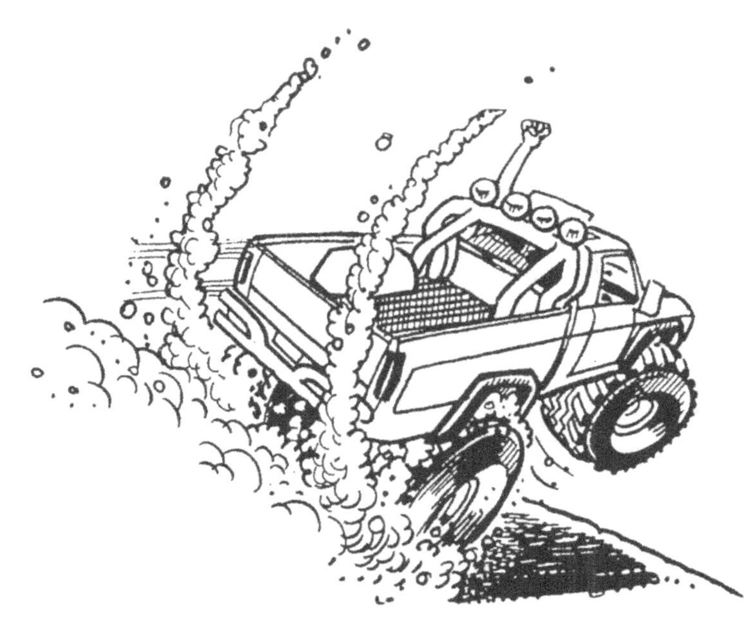

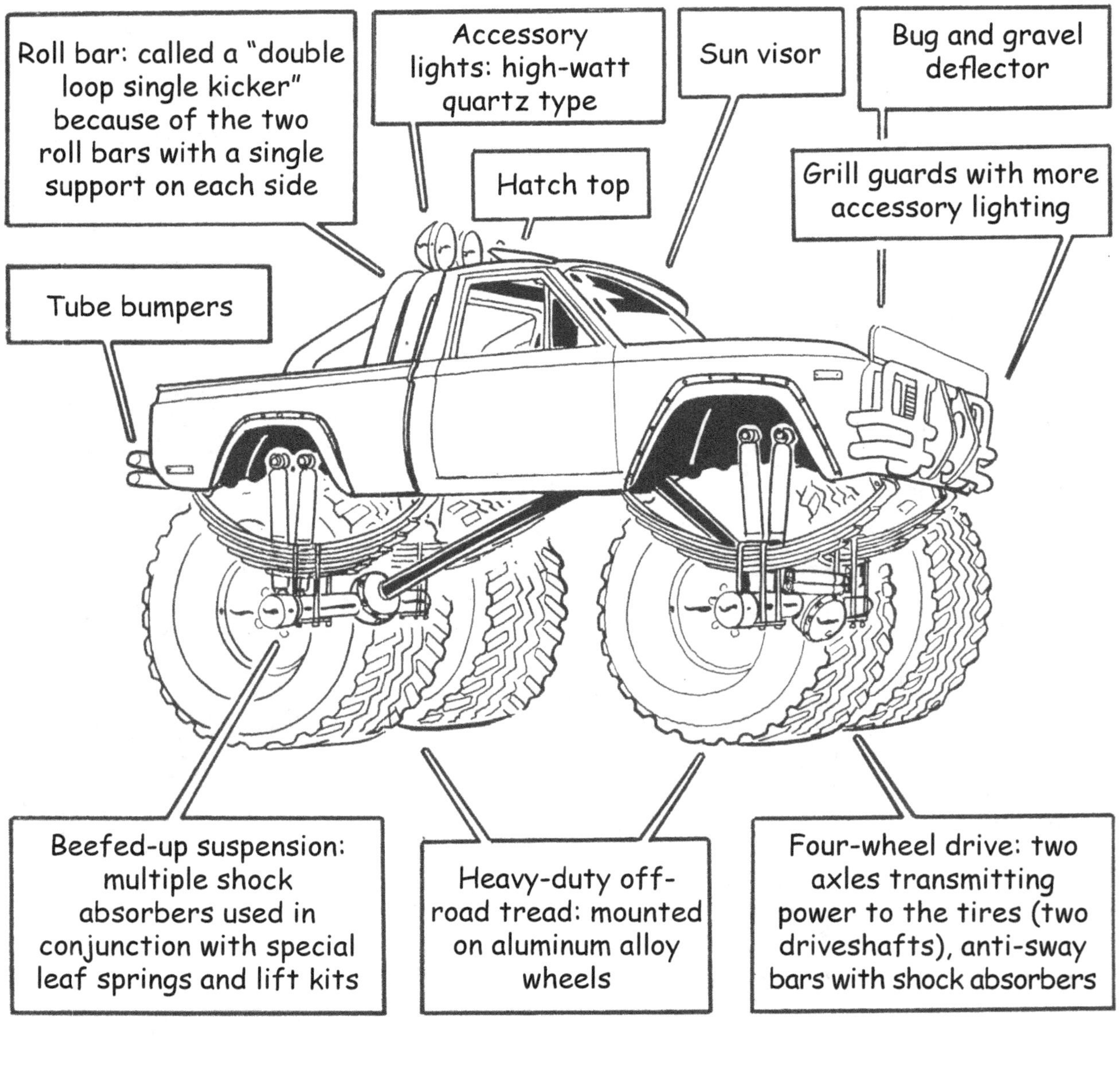

Roll bar: called a "double loop single kicker" because of the two roll bars with a single support on each side

Accessory lights: high-watt quartz type

Sun visor

Bug and gravel deflector

Hatch top

Grill guards with more accessory lighting

Tube bumpers

Beefed-up suspension: multiple shock absorbers used in conjunction with special leaf springs and lift kits

Heavy-duty off-road tread: mounted on aluminum alloy wheels

Four-wheel drive: two axles transmitting power to the tires (two driveshafts), anti-sway bars with shock absorbers ow let's give the off-roadie treatment to a new **Dodge pickup**. As always, start by copying the two boxes I've drawn here. When roughing in the top one be extra careful to transfer the roof angles correctly. Then loosely rough in some big tires and turn the front ones slightly.

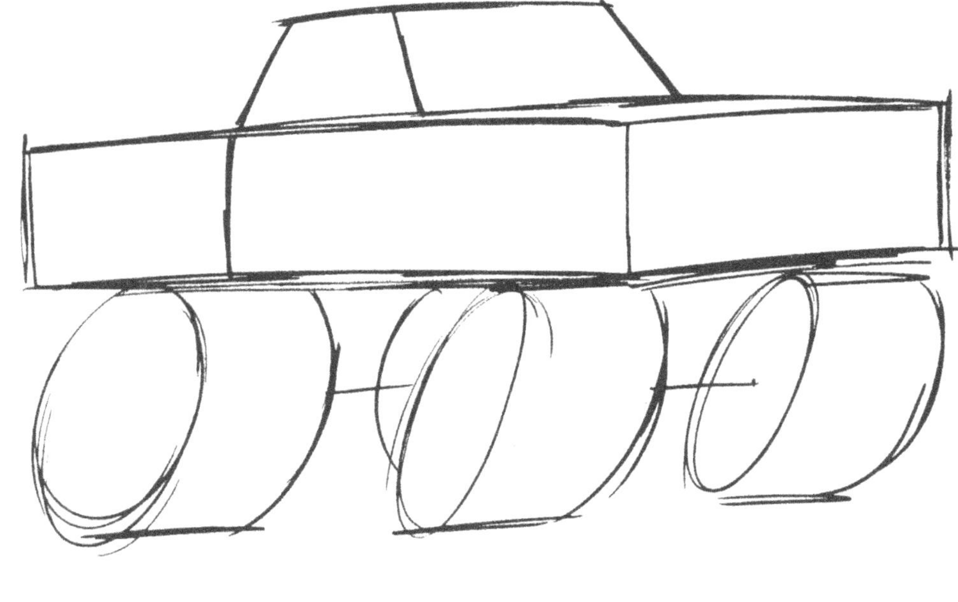

Remember those roof angles? Let's clean 'em up a bit then add some detail. Add wing windows along with the corresponding rear roof post. Square the headlights and shape the grill cavity with a pair of long, rectangular parking lights. Drop in a bar between the headlights as well as a pair of wheel wells over the tires.

Speaking of tires, you can give them some dimension by adding contour and a set of rims. Be careful to get your ellipses just right to achieve that **spinning** look. Locate the axles by drawing right through the tires to the inside of the rims. Add the driveshafts then some dimension to the wheel wells.

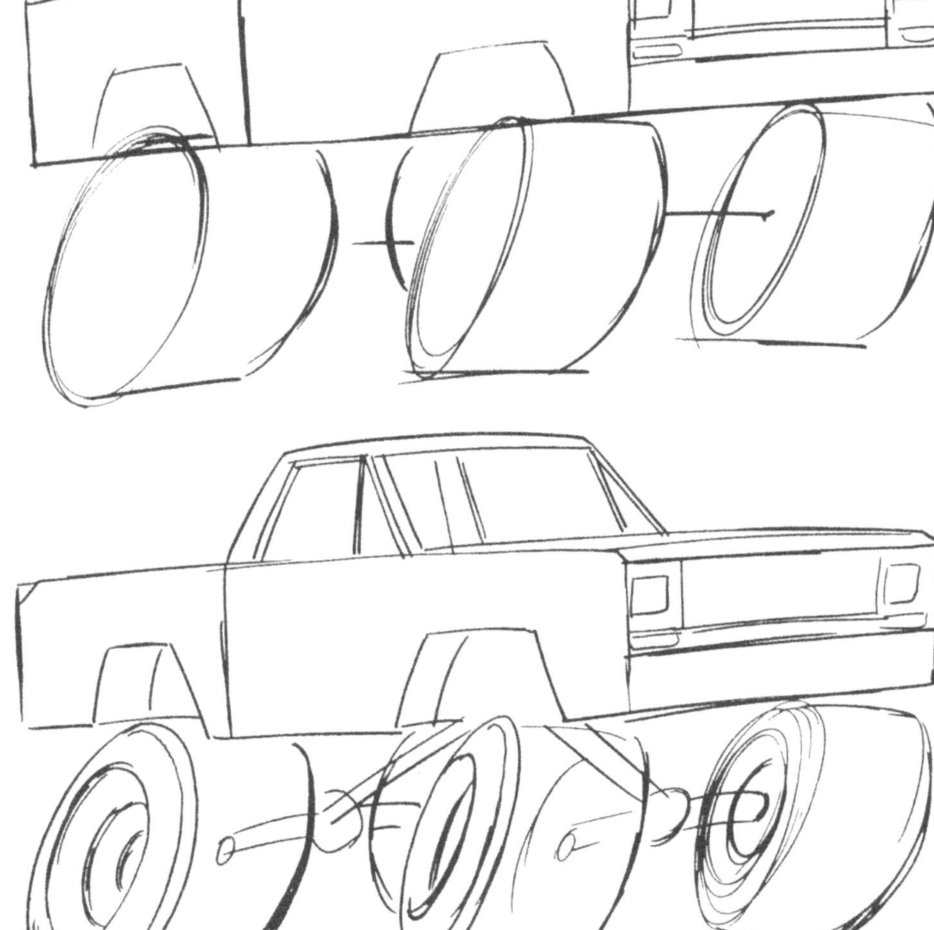

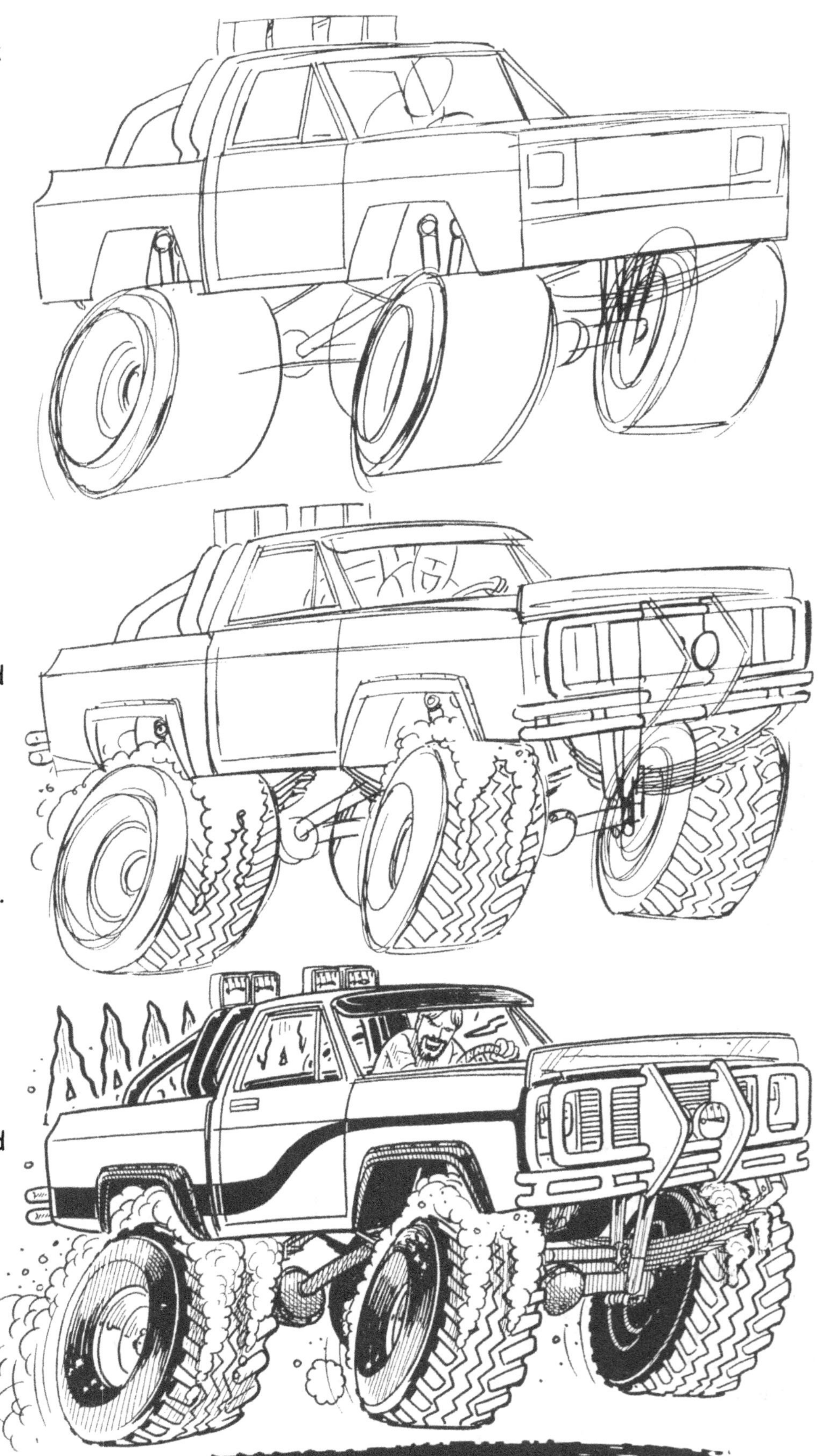

Now it's beginning to look like something! Start adding accessories such as a roll bar and quartz lights. Locate the shock absorbers in the wheel wells angled in toward the axles. Loosely indicate sets of leaf springs both in front and rear. Rough in some sort of driver too.

A few more **accessories** and you've got it. Some plastic wheel well flares as well as some tread design to the tires help. Work it out basically first, then add detail. Tube bumpers front and rear with a grill guard up front get you closer. Rough in a bug an' gravel guard then add more detail to the springs. Lay in a sun visor for the smiling driver.

Almost done . . . Check it over and tighten it up one more time. More accessory lights on the grill guard and some body graphics give it a **pro look**. Neatly ink it all in adding solid blacks as I've done here. Smoke and noise bring it to life!

PART THREE

CARS

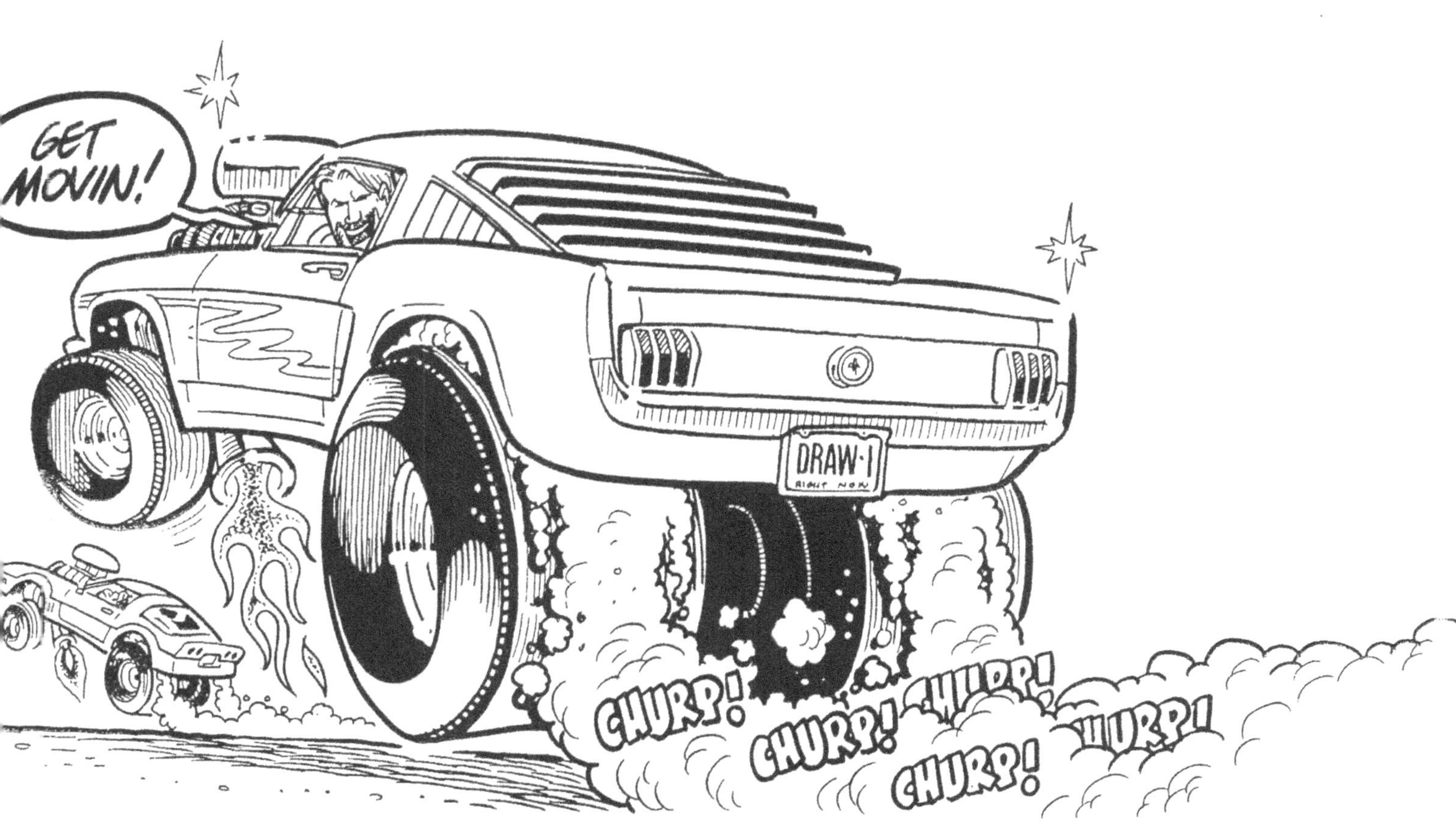

HOW TO DRAW *Corvettes*

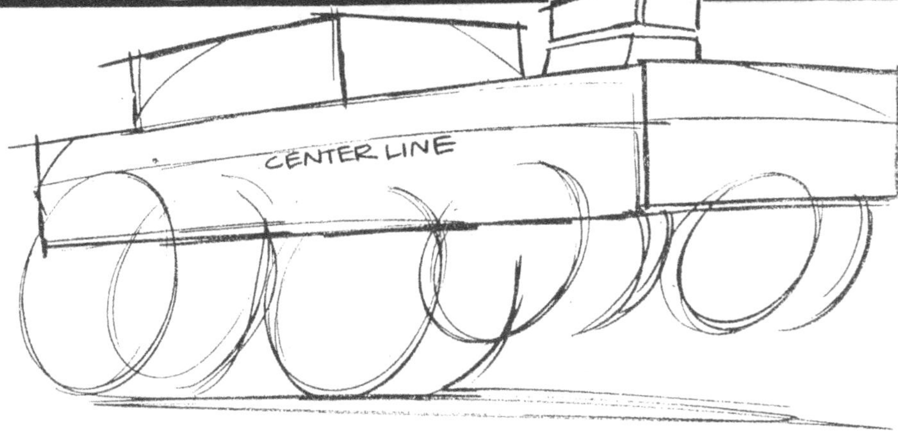

Hey . . . What hot rodder's heart doesn't pound at the sight of a well-done 'Vette? And they're not that hard to draw. Start boxing out the 'Vette with a long hood, small passenger area, and practically no trunk. Exaggerate the tread, especially those big rear ones!

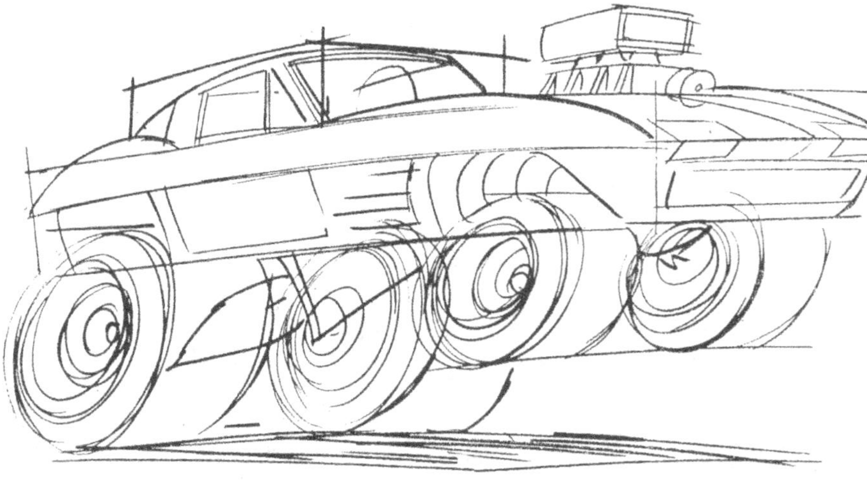

Begin forming the bubbled fenders, respecting the centerline on the side. Note how it divides the side panels and defines the wheel wells. It wraps around the entire car and plays a big part in the drawing. Check out the details in this example; you'll need 'em to be correct.

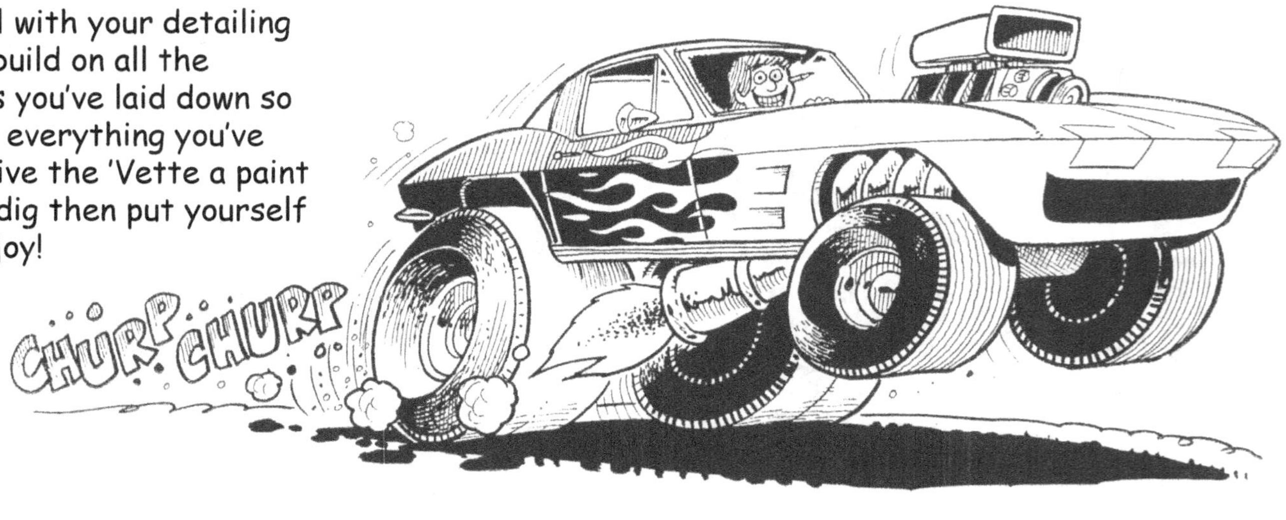

Be careful with your detailing here and build on all the guide lines you've laid down so far. Using everything you've learned, give the 'Vette a paint job **you'd** dig then put yourself inside! Enjoy!

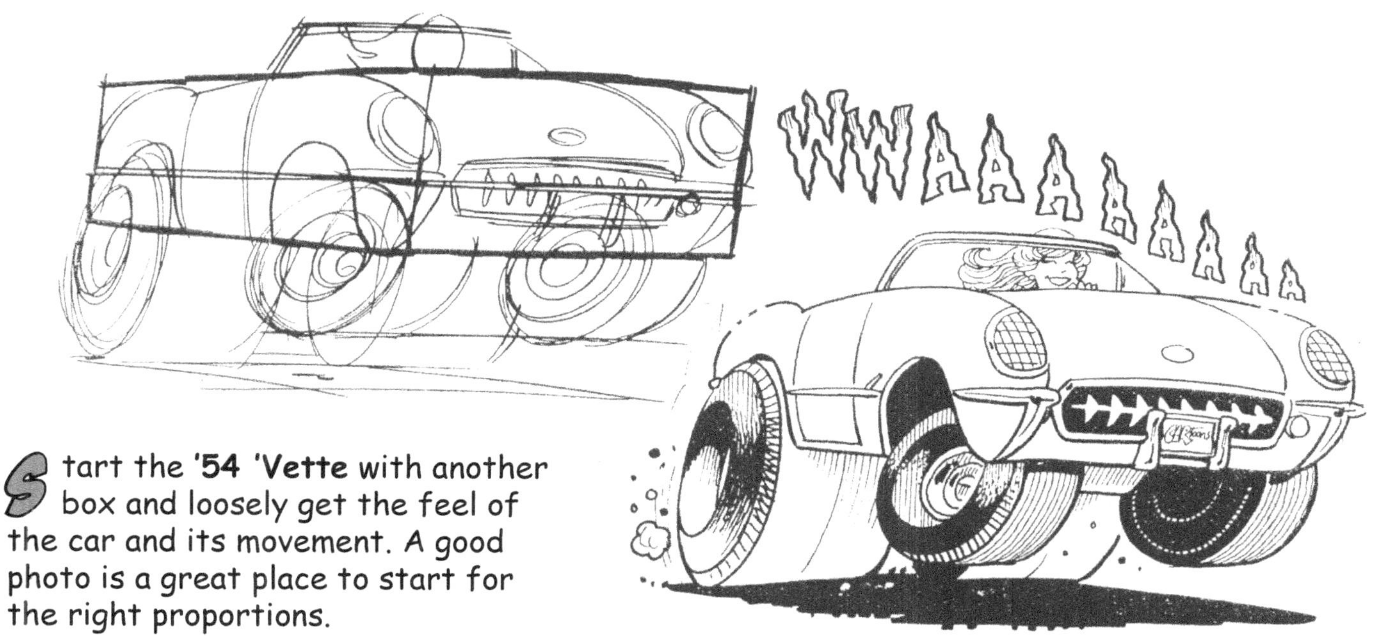

tart the **'54 'Vette** with another box and loosely get the feel of the car and its movement. A good photo is a great place to start for the right proportions.

ow 'bout a big muscle street freak like this ? No big deal. Block in the basic stance of the body adding oversized tires and an exhaust system. Rough in the blower an' scoop and the other details. Make good use of your guide lines.

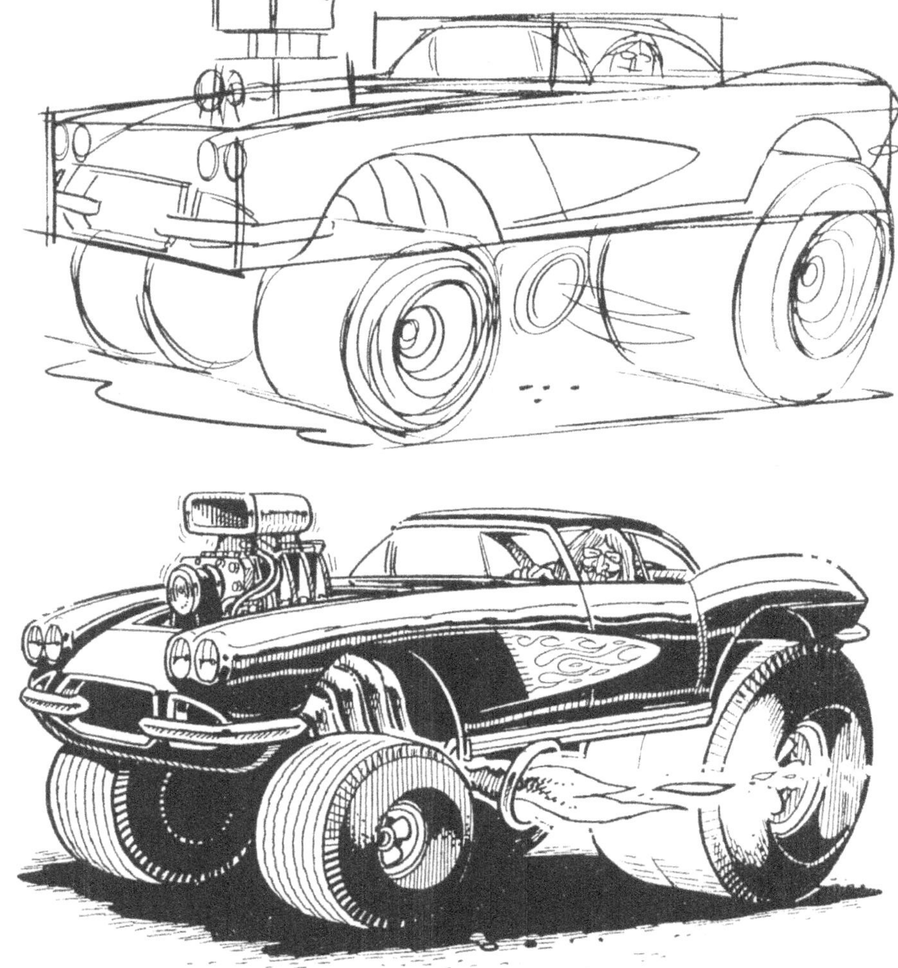

Correct and tighten up your loose pencil drawing making sure you've got most things the way you want 'em. Ink over your pencil with a good ball-point or felt-tip pen. Be neat and careful. Add darks to the tires and body where needed.

*T*his time let's work on a . Begin with the basic box shown here. Make sure you get your guide lines right!

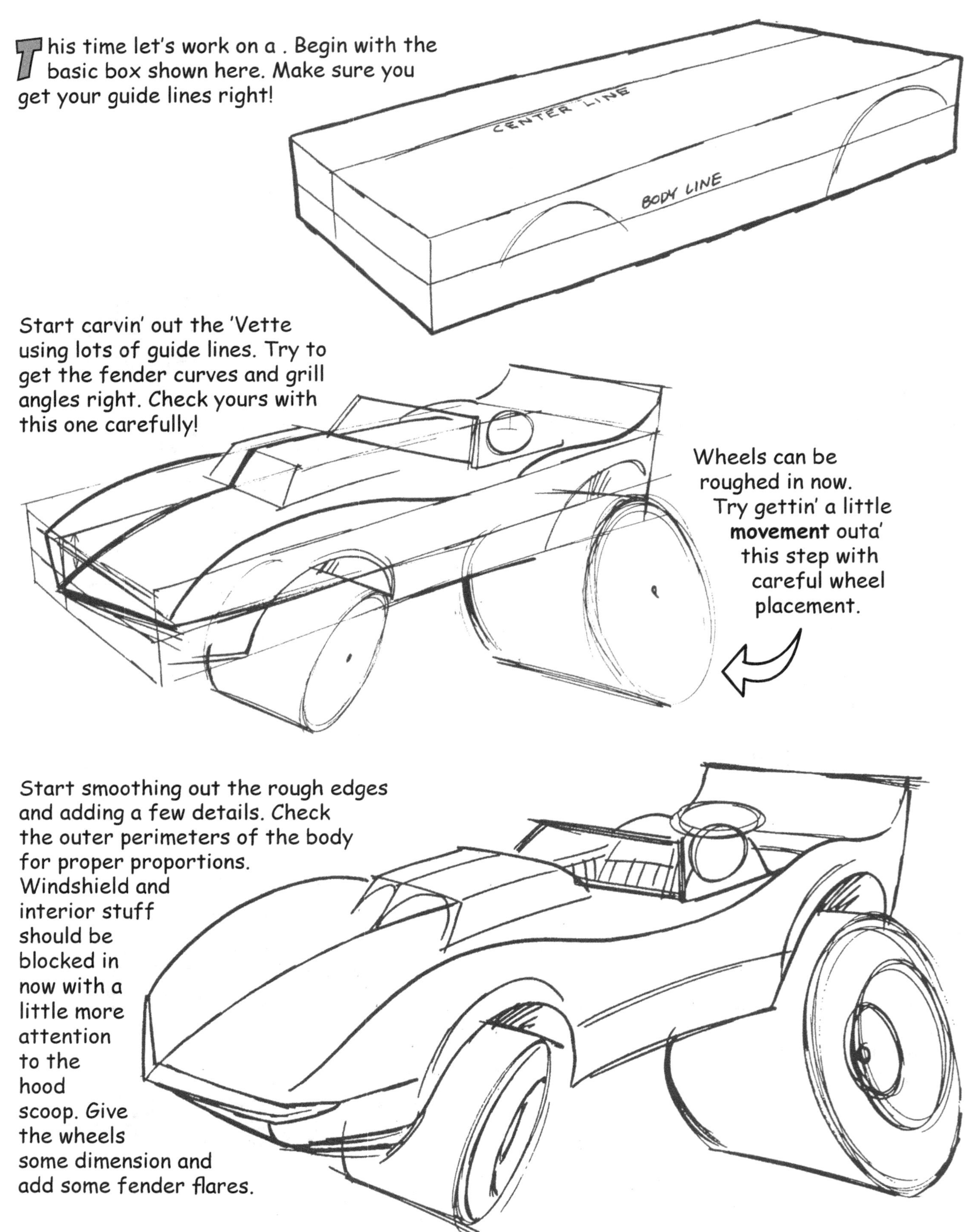

Start carvin' out the 'Vette using lots of guide lines. Try to get the fender curves and grill angles right. Check yours with this one carefully!

Wheels can be roughed in now. Try gettin' a little **movement** outa' this step with careful wheel placement.

Start smoothing out the rough edges and adding a few details. Check the outer perimeters of the body for proper proportions. Windshield and interior stuff should be blocked in now with a little more attention to the hood scoop. Give the wheels some dimension and add some fender flares.

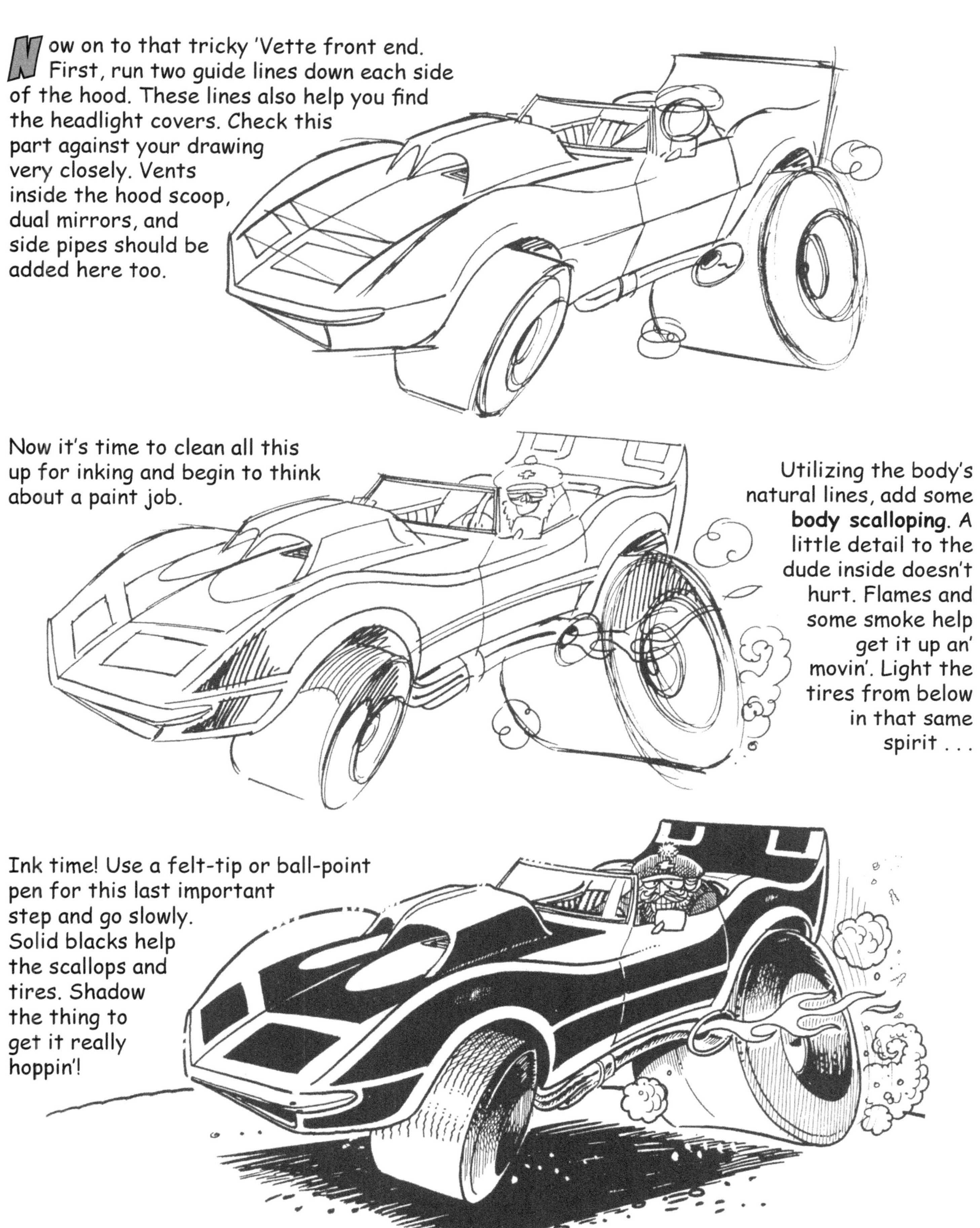

Now on to that tricky 'Vette front end. First, run two guide lines down each side of the hood. These lines also help you find the headlight covers. Check this part against your drawing very closely. Vents inside the hood scoop, dual mirrors, and side pipes should be added here too.

Now it's time to clean all this up for inking and begin to think about a paint job.

Utilizing the body's natural lines, add some **body scalloping**. A little detail to the dude inside doesn't hurt. Flames and some smoke help get it up an' movin'. Light the tires from below in that same spirit . . .

Ink time! Use a felt-tip or ball-point pen for this last important step and go slowly. Solid blacks help the scallops and tires. Shadow the thing to get it really hoppin'!

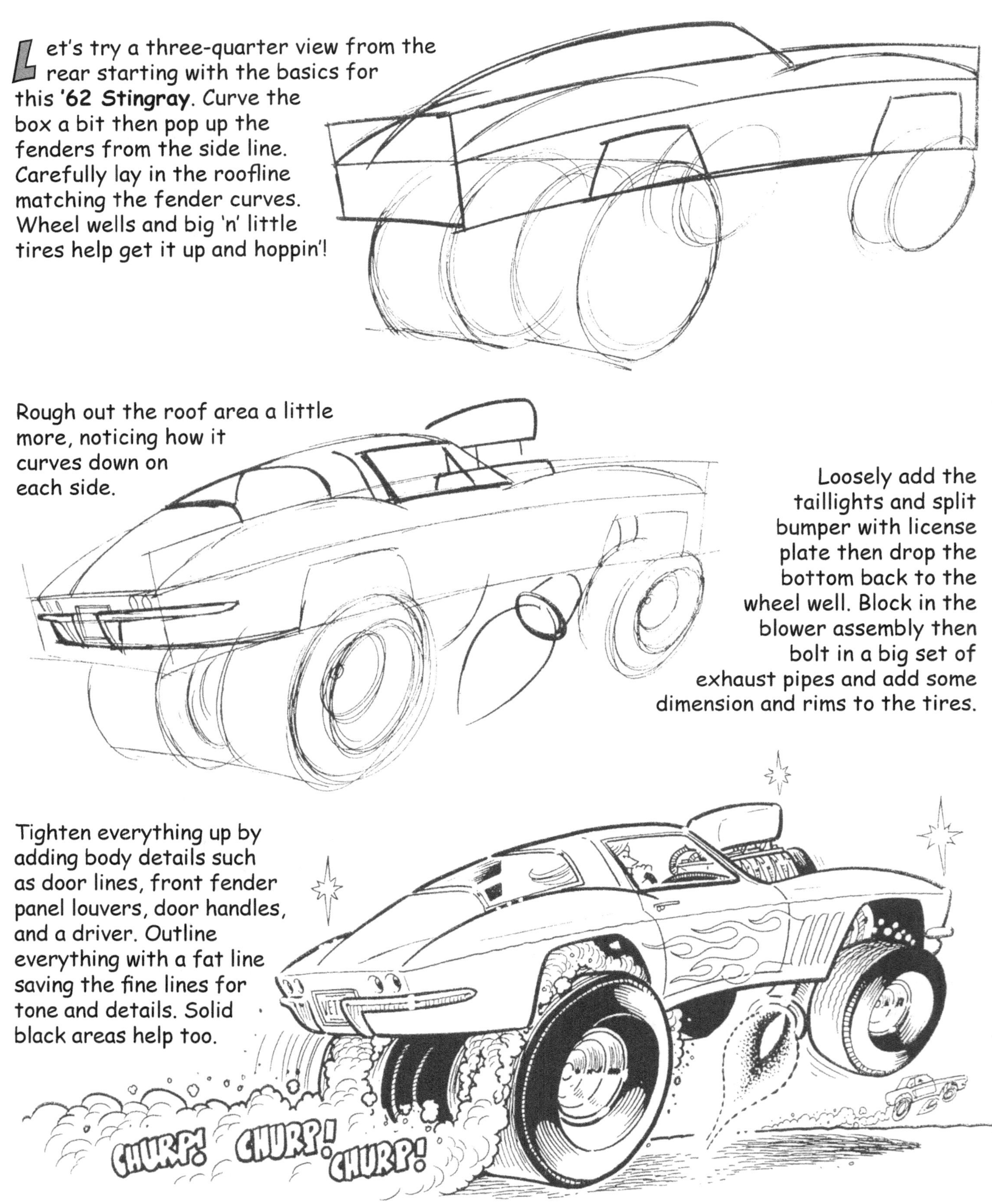

*L*et's try a three-quarter view from the rear starting with the basics for this **'62 Stingray**. Curve the box a bit then pop up the fenders from the side line. Carefully lay in the roofline matching the fender curves. Wheel wells and big 'n' little tires help get it up and hoppin'!

Rough out the roof area a little more, noticing how it curves down on each side.

Loosely add the taillights and split bumper with license plate then drop the bottom back to the wheel well. Block in the blower assembly then bolt in a big set of exhaust pipes and add some dimension and rims to the tires.

Tighten everything up by adding body details such as door lines, front fender panel louvers, door handles, and a driver. Outline everything with a fat line saving the fine lines for tone and details. Solid black areas help too.

HOW TO DRAW MUSTANGS

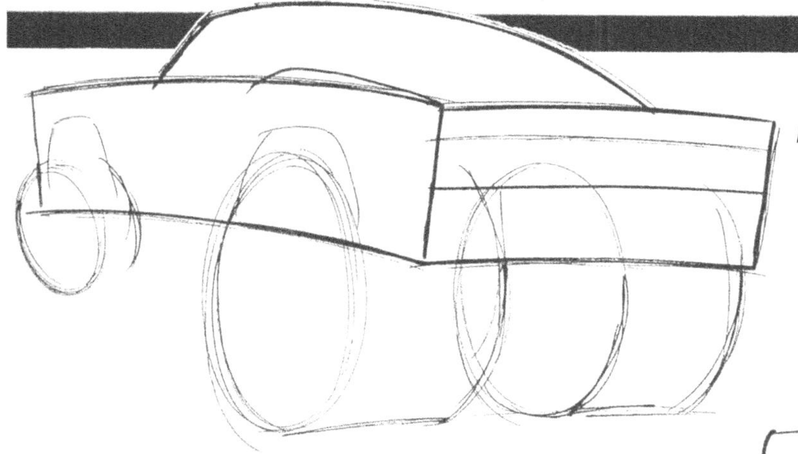

Here you can try another rear view. This time it's a Mustang! Get the basic box down then loosely lay in the roofline. Next, cut out some wheel wells and pop on some monster tread. Draw right through things at this point. Divide the rear panel in half then drop the trunk line a bit from the top. While you're back here **bump up** the rear fender line a bit.

Detail the roof area by adding the side window and louvered side trim then cutting open the back window and adding more louvers. Side sculpturing and door lines help as does the roughed-in engine stuff. Finish up the wheels then get busy on the taillights and bumper, checking the contours carefully. Gas cap and license plate finish 'er up!

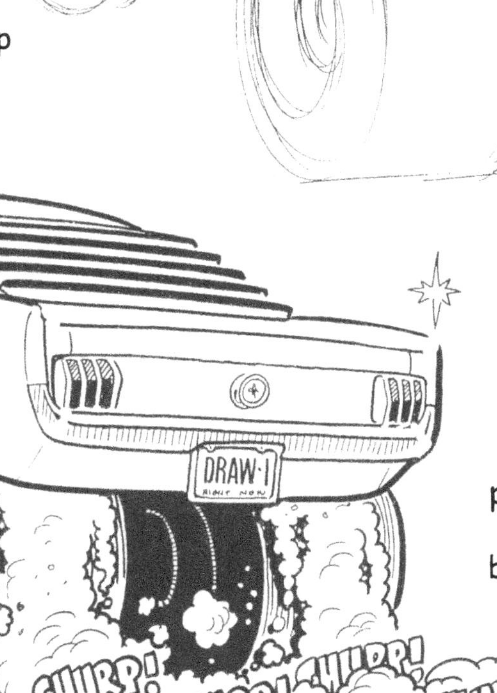

You're ready for ink after you check over everything once more. Body graphics can be added and a few well-placed highlights always help a bunch. Grab your pencils and breathe some life into one of these babies. **Go magic fingers!**

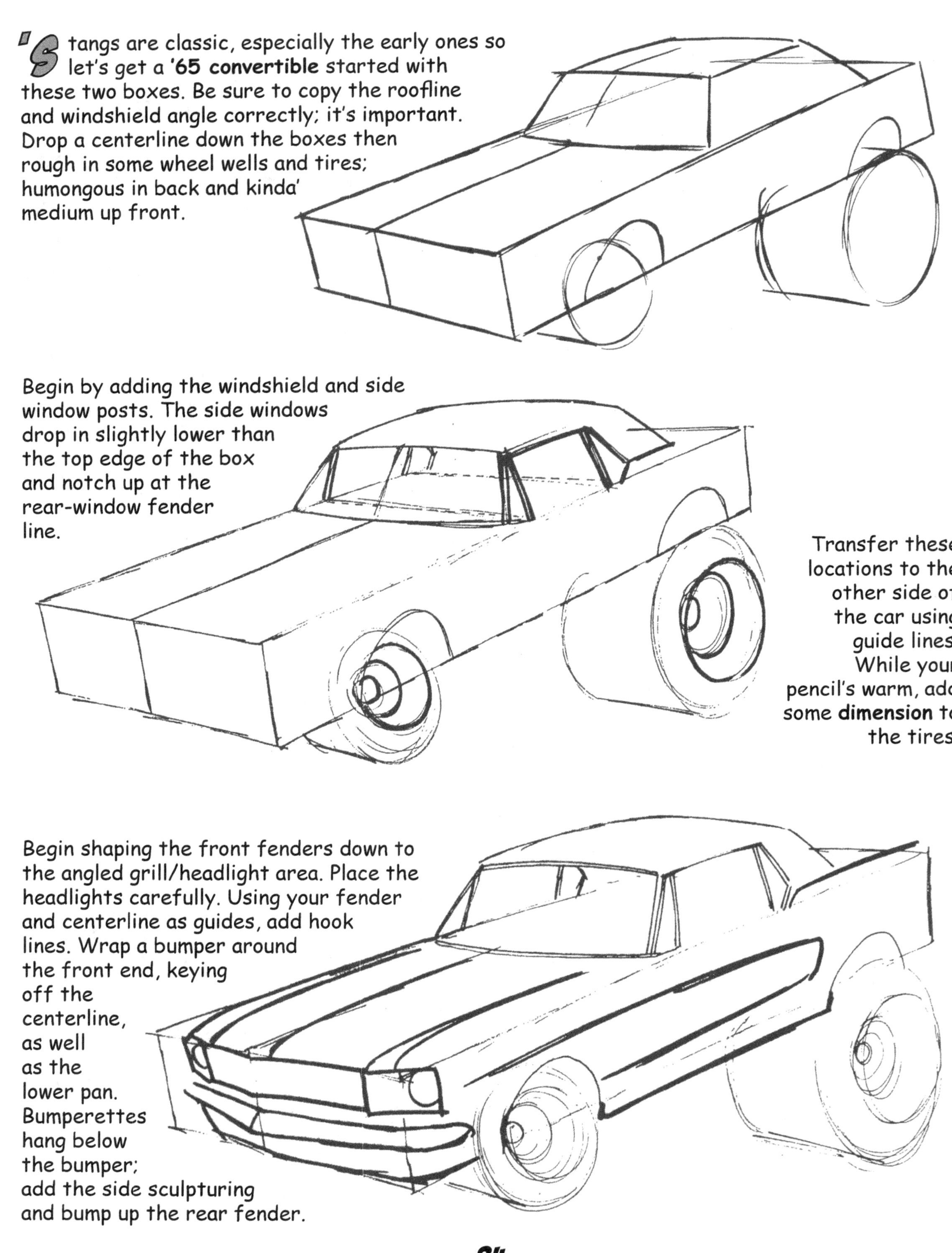

'**S**tangs are classic, especially the early ones so let's get a '**65 convertible** started with these two boxes. Be sure to copy the roofline and windshield angle correctly; it's important. Drop a centerline down the boxes then rough in some wheel wells and tires; humongous in back and kinda' medium up front.

Begin by adding the windshield and side window posts. The side windows drop in slightly lower than the top edge of the box and notch up at the rear-window fender line.

Transfer these locations to the other side of the car using guide lines. While your pencil's warm, add some **dimension** to the tires.

Begin shaping the front fenders down to the angled grill/headlight area. Place the headlights carefully. Using your fender and centerline as guides, add hook lines. Wrap a bumper around the front end, keying off the centerline, as well as the lower pan. Bumperettes hang below the bumper; add the side sculpturing and bump up the rear fender.

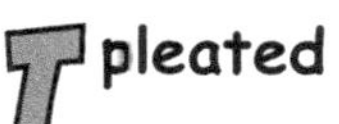

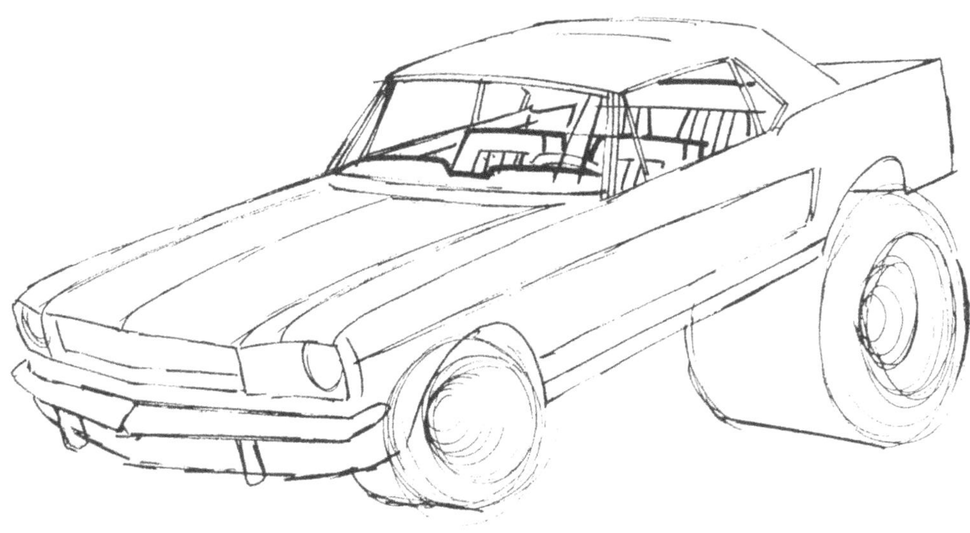

Add some typical Sixties-type goodies. First, rough in a big hood scoop and a racing stripe keying both off the centerline.

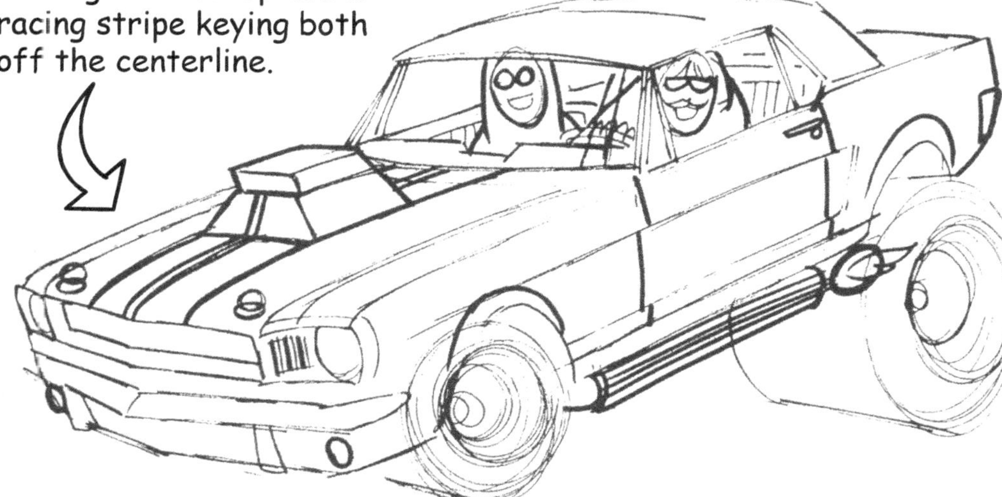

Then drop in a set of hood pins. While you're in that area add the louvers alongside the headlights and turn signals below that. Lay in some wheel well flares, a door handle, and a rear bumper. Side pipes and **hippies** complete this step.

Go over your sketch one more time checking against what I have here. Add flames or stripes to make yours just a little bit different. Ink all this in carefully with your favorite pen outlining the basics first then goin' for the details. Note how lights and darks are used to indicate chrome, glass, and so on. Try leaving a white edge to the line in the flat black areas. Add sound effects and body shadow, then erase and it's done!

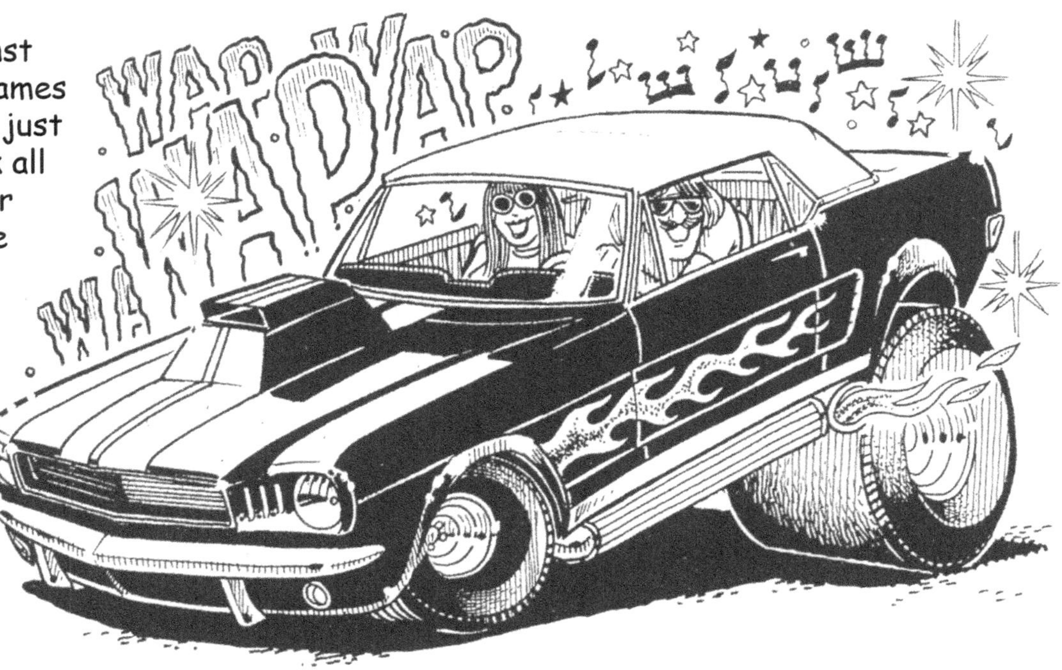

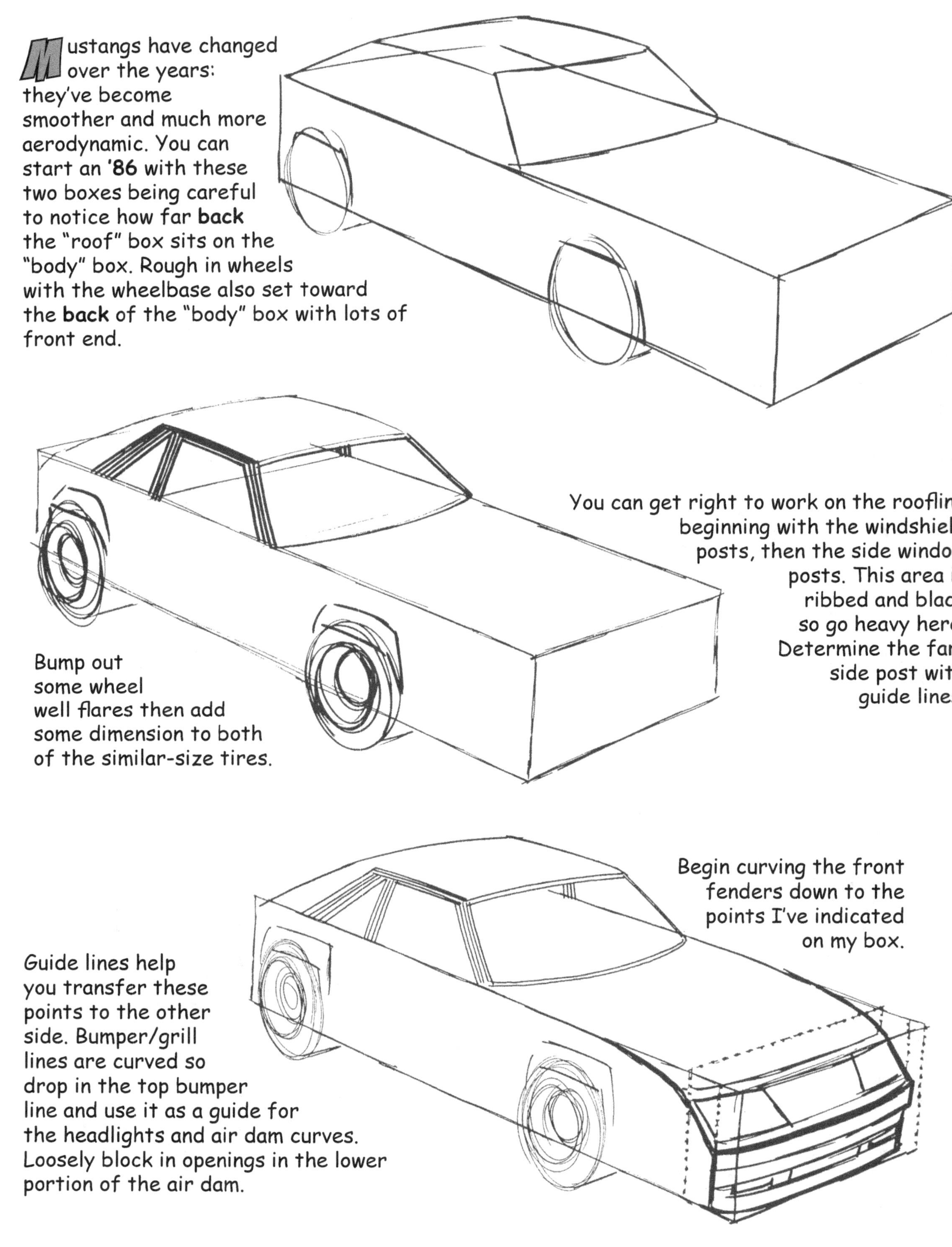

Mustangs have changed over the years: they've become smoother and much more aerodynamic. You can start an '86 with these two boxes being careful to notice how far **back** the "roof" box sits on the "body" box. Rough in wheels with the wheelbase also set toward the **back** of the "body" box with lots of front end.

You can get right to work on the roofline beginning with the windshield posts, then the side window posts. This area is ribbed and black so go heavy here. Determine the far-side post with guide lines.

Bump out some wheel well flares then add some dimension to both of the similar-size tires.

Begin curving the front fenders down to the points I've indicated on my box.

Guide lines help you transfer these points to the other side. Bumper/grill lines are curved so drop in the top bumper line and use it as a guide for the headlights and air dam curves. Loosely block in openings in the lower portion of the air dam.

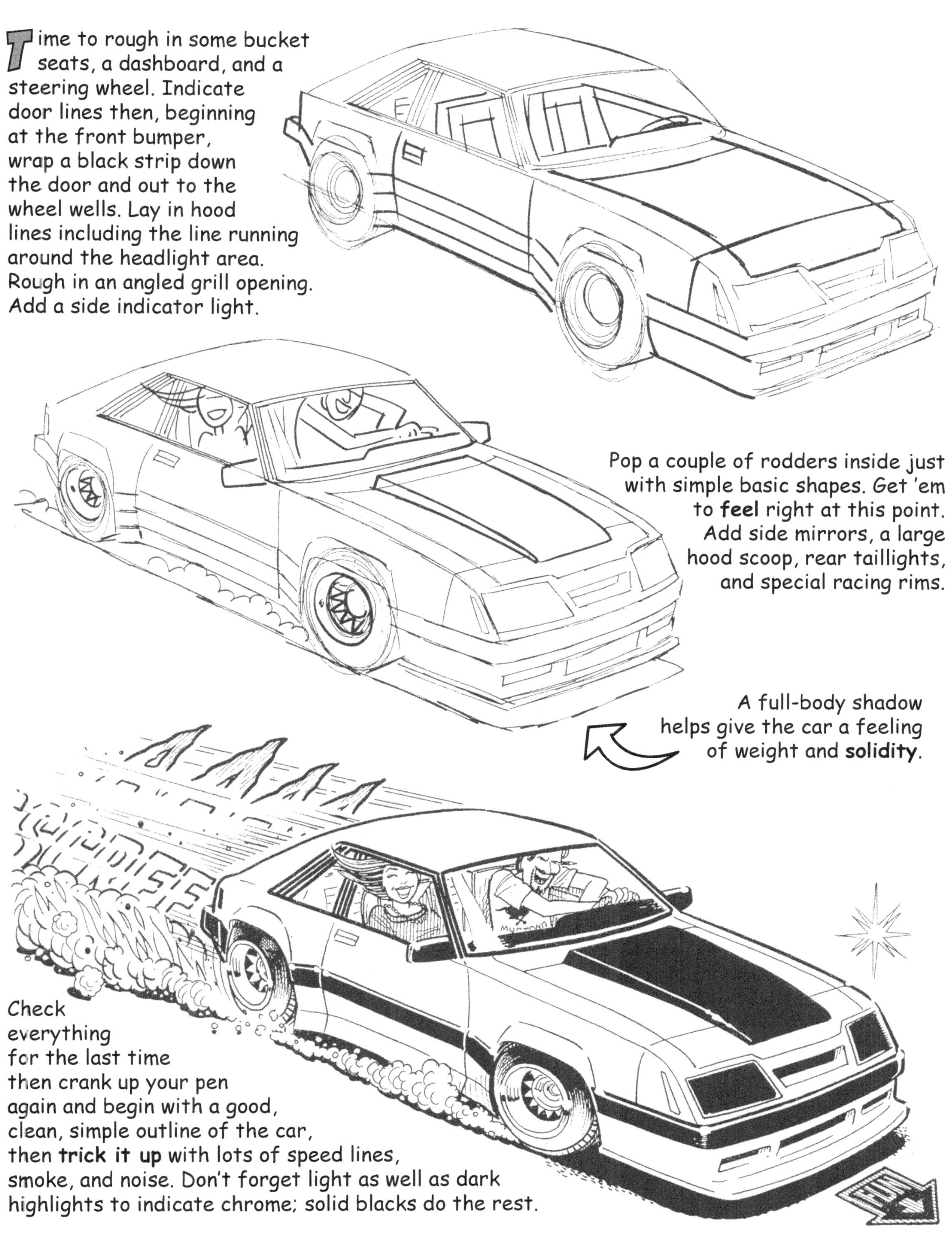

Time to rough in some bucket seats, a dashboard, and a steering wheel. Indicate door lines then, beginning at the front bumper, wrap a black strip down the door and out to the wheel wells. Lay in hood lines including the line running around the headlight area. Rough in an angled grill opening. Add a side indicator light.

Pop a couple of rodders inside just with simple basic shapes. Get 'em to **feel** right at this point. Add side mirrors, a large hood scoop, rear taillights, and special racing rims.

A full-body shadow helps give the car a feeling of weight and **solidity**.

Check everything for the last time then crank up your pen again and begin with a good, clean, simple outline of the car, then **trick it up** with lots of speed lines, smoke, and noise. Don't forget light as well as dark highlights to indicate chrome; solid blacks do the rest.

Mustangs are a real good lookin' car to draw including this '65. You start with the two basic boxes. A centerline will help you lay things in properly. Begin roughing in the roof and fender lines as you see here. Add wheel openings checking their position against other body lines.

Detail the roof and interior section a bit and loosely drop in the tires. The grill an' headlight section is a bit tricky so **take it slow**.

First, box out the grill in the center arching back on each side to the headlights. Rough in the bumper and belly pan adding details as done here.

Go over what you've done an' check it closely. Then add a hood scoop, some hood pins, and a tube grill. A side body line and flared wheel openings help as well as the full-length pipes. Check your pencil work carefully then ink it all in with a good ball-point or felt-tip pen adding solid blacks to the tires, shadow, interior, and so on. A good photo of what you're trying to draw always helps. **Be neat!**

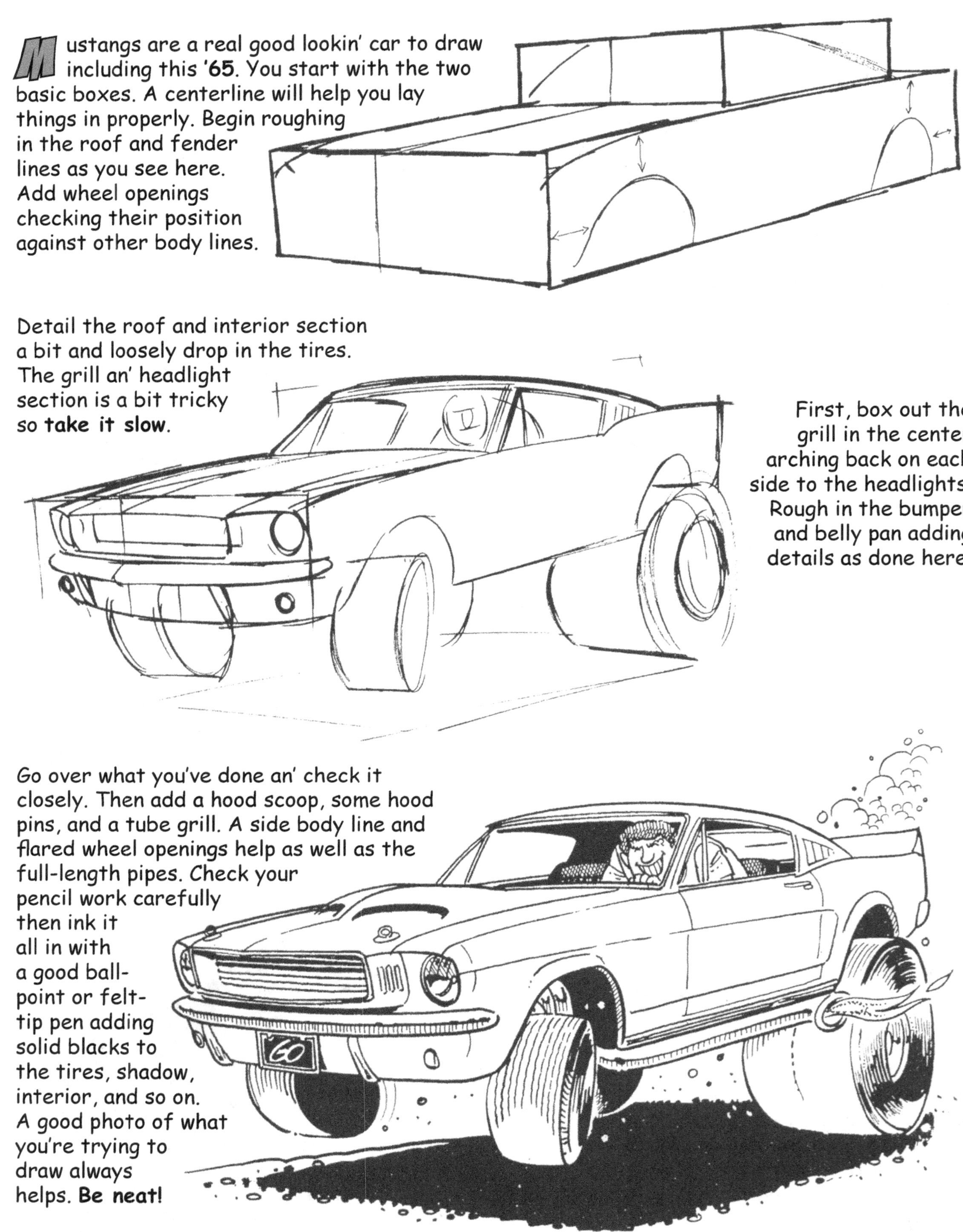

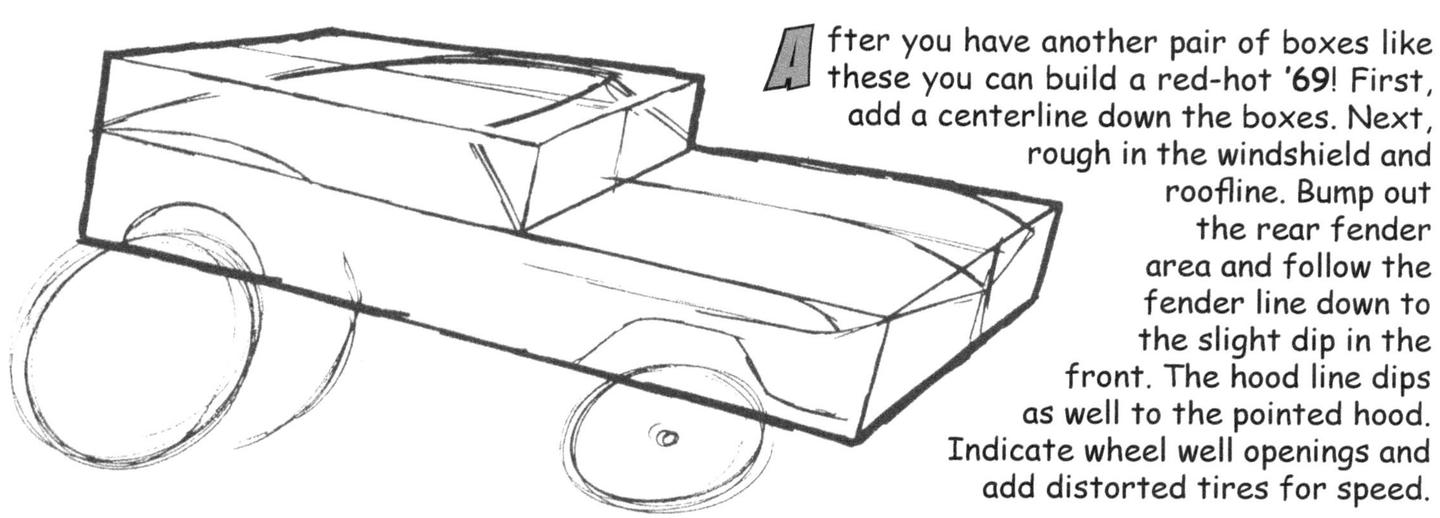

After you have another pair of boxes like these you can build a red-hot **'69**! First, add a centerline down the boxes. Next, rough in the windshield and roofline. Bump out the rear fender area and follow the fender line down to the slight dip in the front. The hood line dips as well to the pointed hood. Indicate wheel well openings and add distorted tires for speed.

You can add a bit more detail to the interior by placing a few **hot rod crazies**! The fender scoop and body line lead you back to the grill area where you'll add headlights, bumper, and the grill itself. Develop the front wheel into a motorcycle wire with really fat pipes behind it. Detail to the rear slicks and rear fender help round out this step.

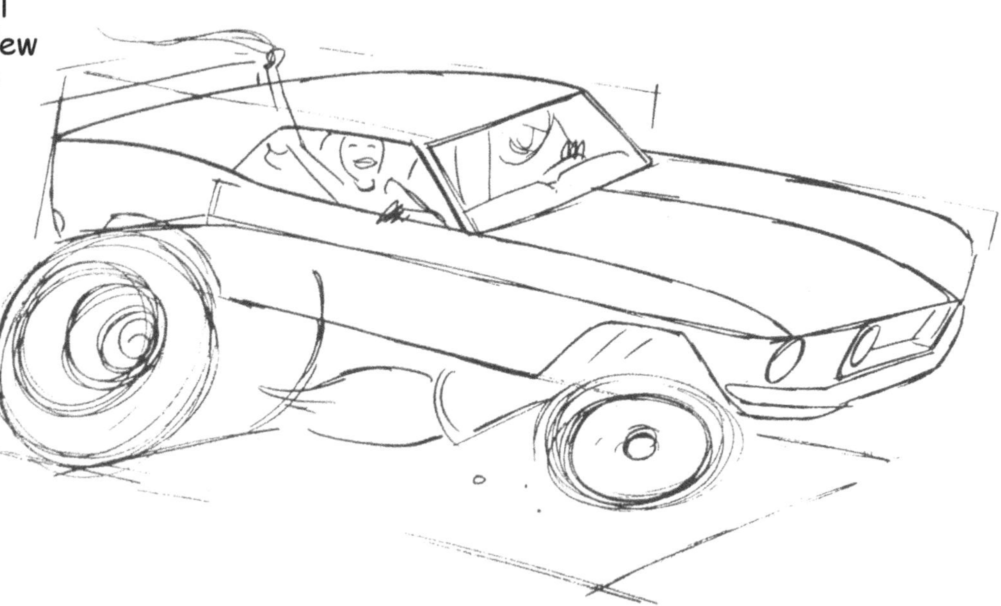

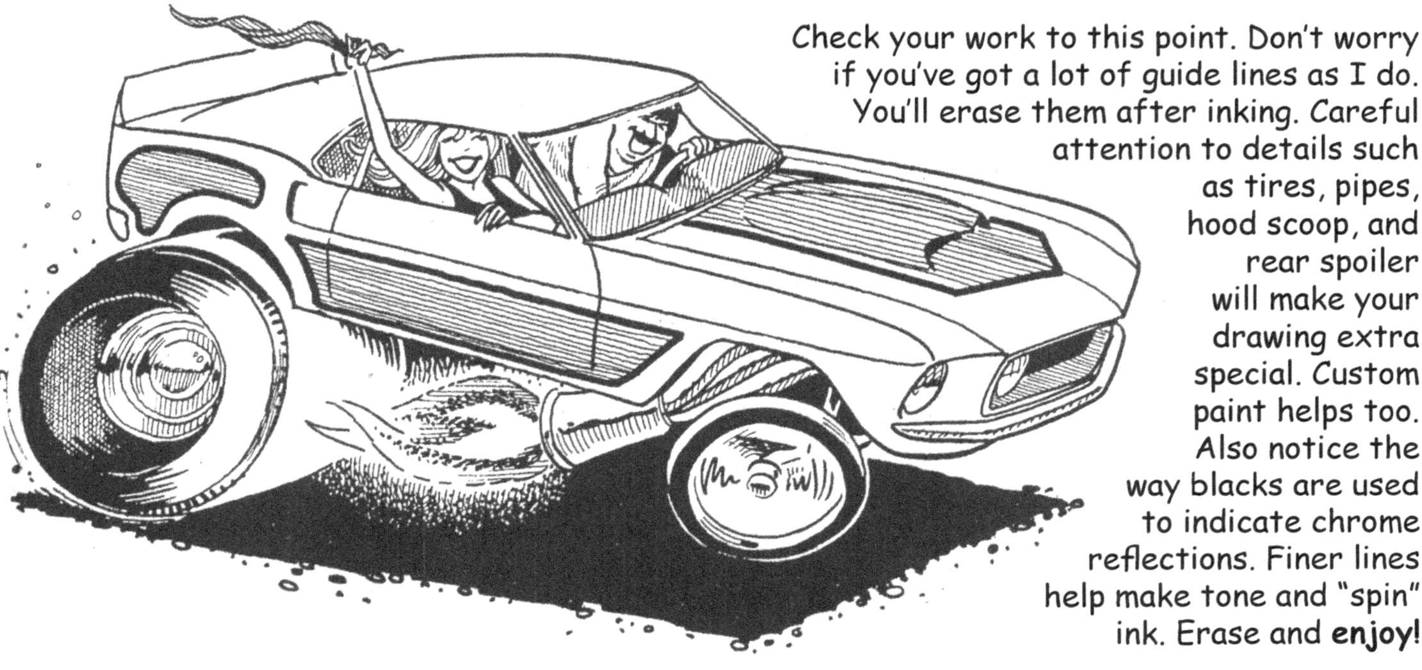

Check your work to this point. Don't worry if you've got a lot of guide lines as I do. You'll erase them after inking. Careful attention to details such as tires, pipes, hood scoop, and rear spoiler will make your drawing extra special. Custom paint helps too. Also notice the way blacks are used to indicate chrome reflections. Finer lines help make tone and "spin" ink. Erase and **enjoy!**

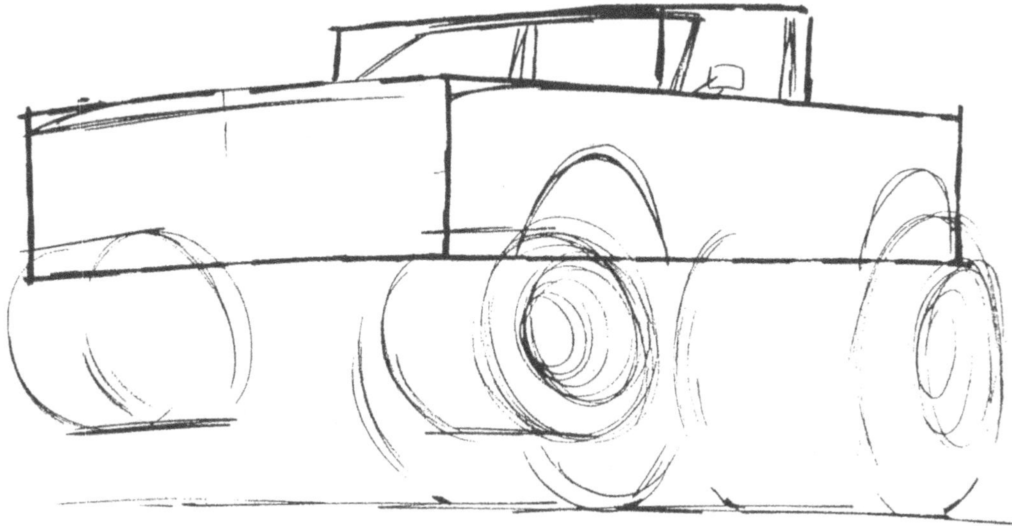

et's really get down to it with a **'70 GT 500 convertible**. Lay out your boxes as you see 'em here adding wheel openings in the proper places. Then throw on some smaller fatties up front. Since this is a convertible, work out the windshield and the Shelby rubber-encased roll bar.

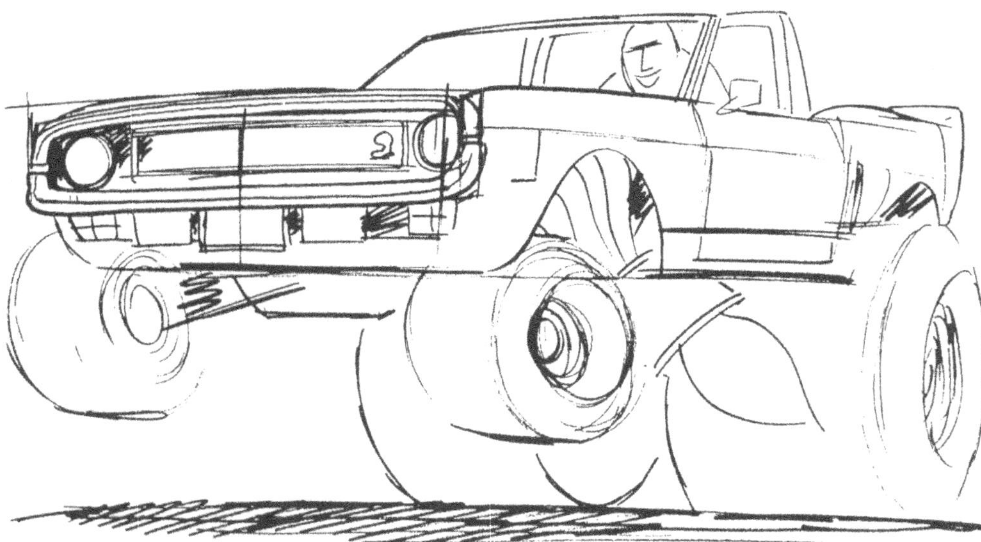

The grill section is boxy with chrome trim and bumper. The front splash pan has parking lights and accessory lights. The fender line curves up and back to the rear fender "bump" and spoiler. The body line begins at the grill going straight back to the scoop. Rough in door lines and the exhaust system. Flames and a shadow help too.

Details . . . details . . . details . . . First, check your pencil drawing adding the side stripe and front fender scoop. The grill and splash pan can be developed a bit further. Special V-shaped hood scoops, grill, and suspension all go black when inked. **Go to it!**

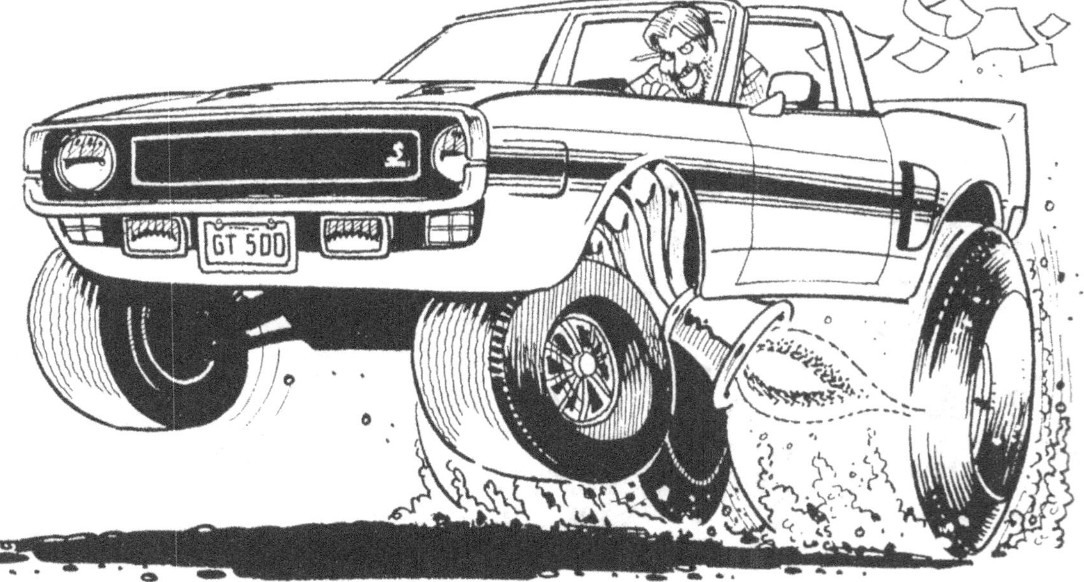

HOW TO DRAW '55 CHEVYS 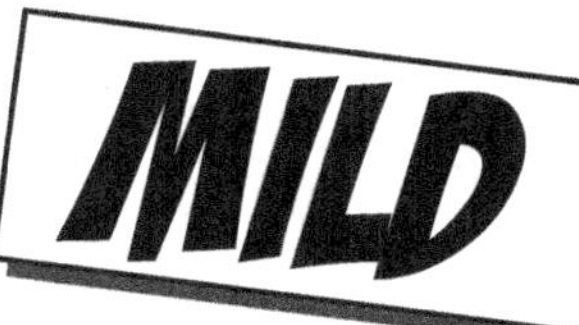 MILD

Some people feel the '55 is Chevy's classic hot rod body style and I do too. Let's get yours started with the two boxes shown here. Get your perspective right placing the front of the "roof" box **just forward** of the body's middle.

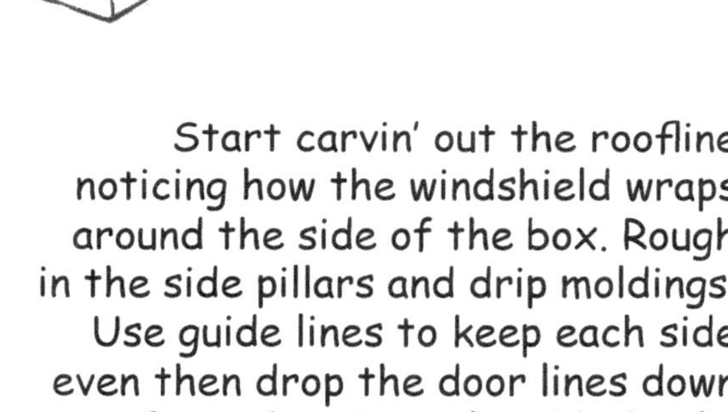

Start carvin' out the roofline noticing how the windshield wraps around the side of the box. Rough in the side pillars and drip moldings. Use guide lines to keep each side even then drop the door lines down from that. Loosely add wheels.

Drop in headlights and rough in chrome bezels around 'em. The hood line rolls down to the rectangle grill shell flanked by parking lights on each side. Block out the basic bumper then add a bump out on each side and a centerline.

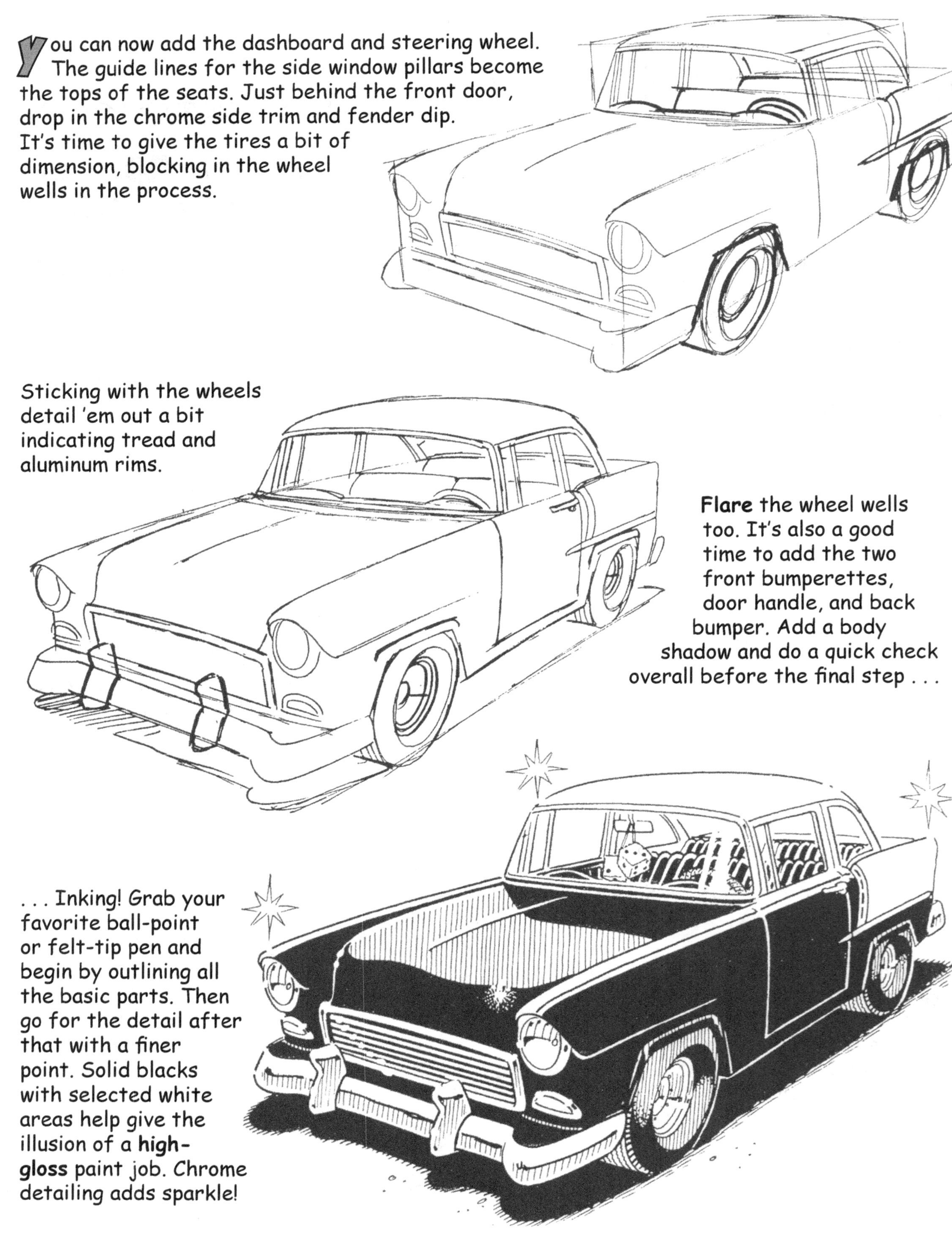

You can now add the dashboard and steering wheel. The guide lines for the side window pillars become the tops of the seats. Just behind the front door, drop in the chrome side trim and fender dip. It's time to give the tires a bit of dimension, blocking in the wheel wells in the process.

Sticking with the wheels detail 'em out a bit indicating tread and aluminum rims.

Flare the wheel wells too. It's also a good time to add the two front bumperettes, door handle, and back bumper. Add a body shadow and do a quick check overall before the final step . . .

. . . Inking! Grab your favorite ball-point or felt-tip pen and begin by outlining all the basic parts. Then go for the detail after that with a finer point. Solid blacks with selected white areas help give the illusion of a **high-gloss** paint job. Chrome detailing adds sparkle!

HOW TO DRAW '55 CHEVYS 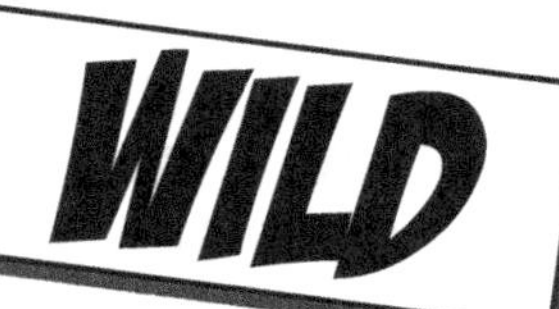

_I_f you've completed the mild '55 you've gotten the feel of this body style and you're gonna need it. To start the wild '55 begin with the curved boxes you see here.

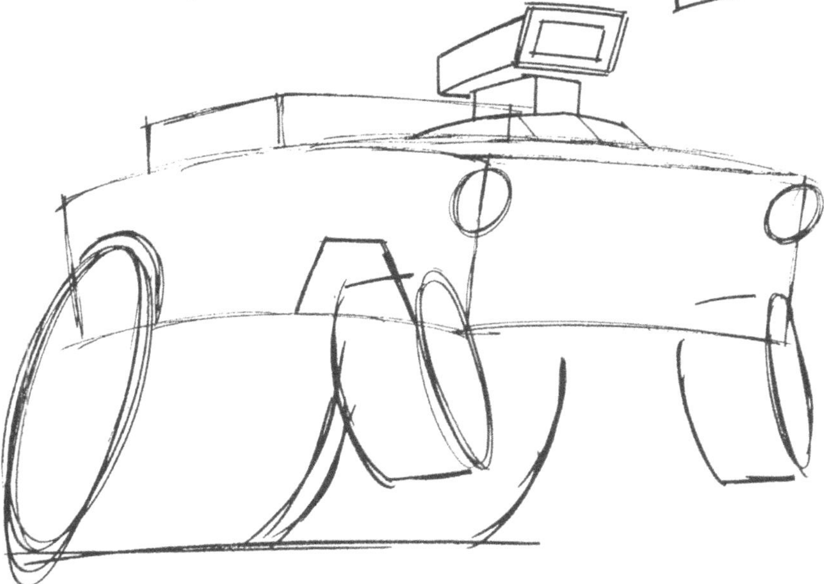

Box out the hood bubble then the carbs and the bug catcher above it. Rough in the headlights then drop down and bolt on some **humongous** rear slicks with a pair of twisted street tread up front. It's a good time to rough in some wheel wells too.

Add some headlight chrome then some angry "eyebrows" to the front end. Rough in an "angry" grill with the parking lights on either side. Curve the bumper to match and indicate the bump outs. A Chevy hood logo and curved hood line complete this step.

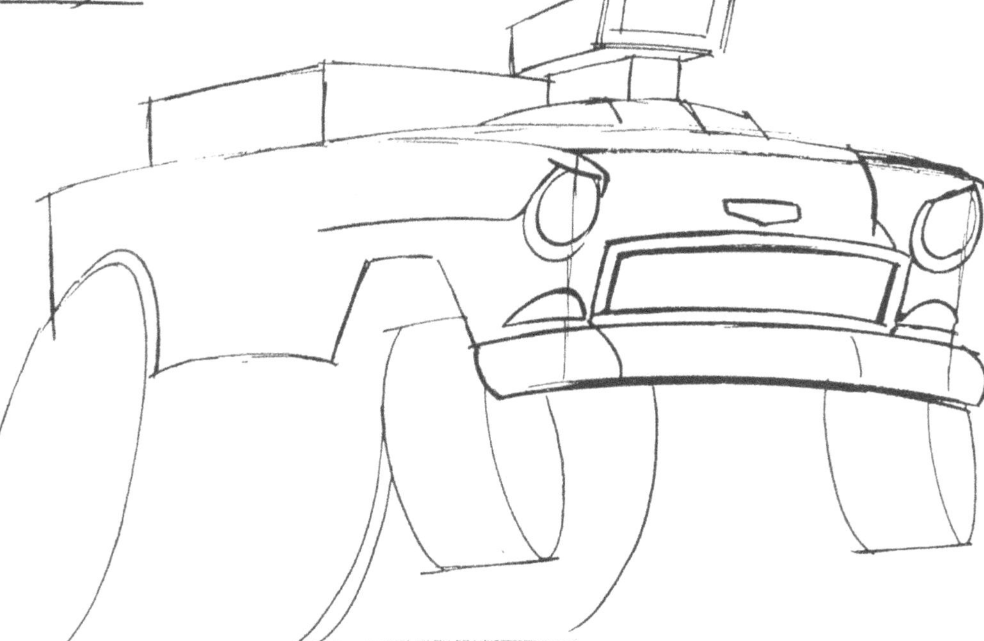

The roofline is next so get started carving out its curves. Check your sketch closely to mine. Indicate the **headliner** inside then give the tires some dimension as well as some suspension up front. The engine's oil pan is behind that. Add that well-known dip in the rear fender.

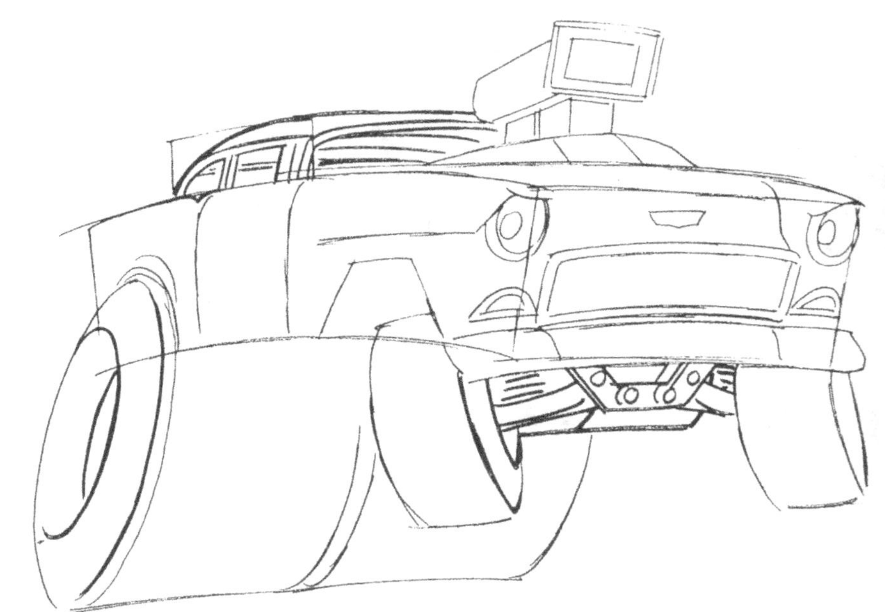

It's time to add some details like the taillights, fuel line, and carb particulars.

The side pipes may now be positioned with lots of flame. Smoke the tires then carefully rough in the flame paint job. **Jagged teeth** help finish the facial illusion of this nasty ol' '55.

Get out those pens again and outline everything before adding details and solid blacks. Well-placed darks and simple shading gives the chrome the right look. You can add a rear bumper and such in the teeth to indicate a recent conquest being chewed up by 'er. Remember . . . Be neat!

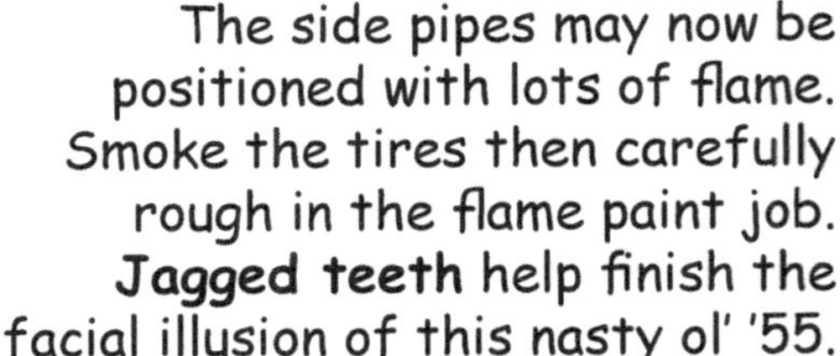

HOW TO DRAW '57 CHEVYS

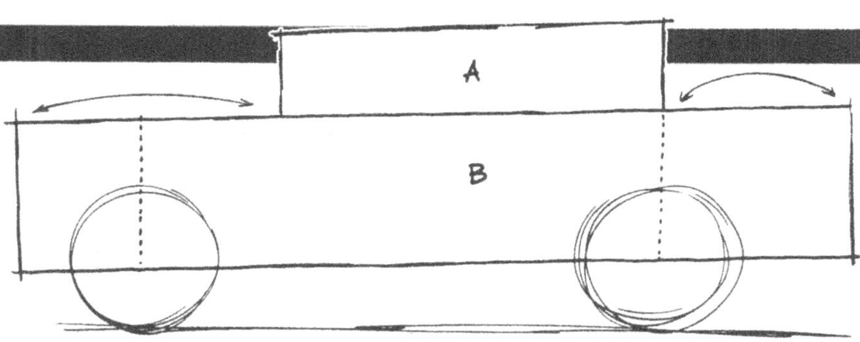

Everybody digs the classic '57 Chevy so let's give 'er a try. For a standard side view, start with two basic boxes placing "A" back on the body "B" a bit, giving more hood than trunk. Key in the wheels on the other guide lines as shown.

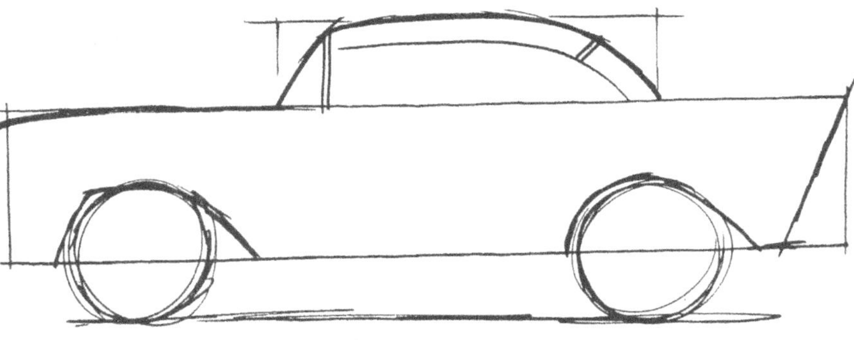

Next, work out the roofline using double lines to indicate window moldings. Wheel wells should now be roughed in around the tires.

Note that the front and back shapes differ. Add an angle to the rear fender.

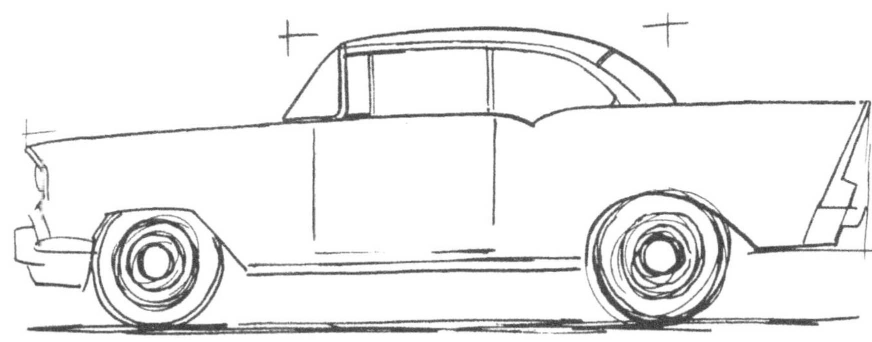

You can now add the headlights and grill section. Plus more detail for the wheels. And don't forget the **dip** in the fender line. The chrome and rear bumper stuff are next. Check your drawing against this one.

Okay. A few more details and you got it. Add side trim, door handles, and wing windows. Ink all this in neatly with a felt-tip or ball-point pen then erase all your rough pencil lines. Blacks for the tires an' shadow help too.

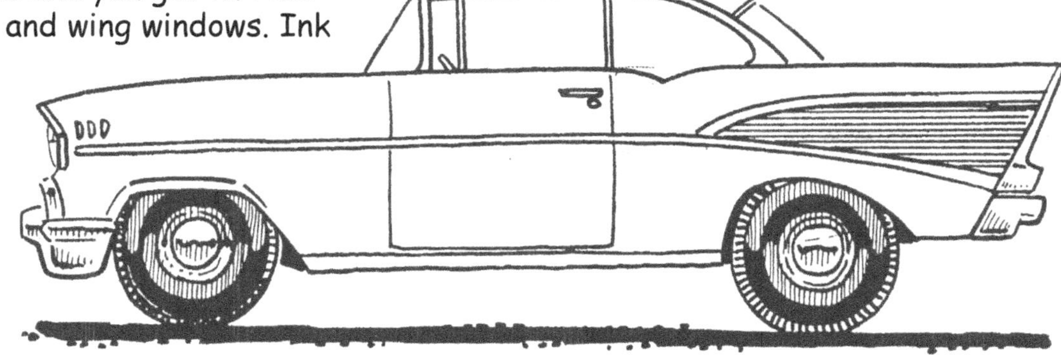

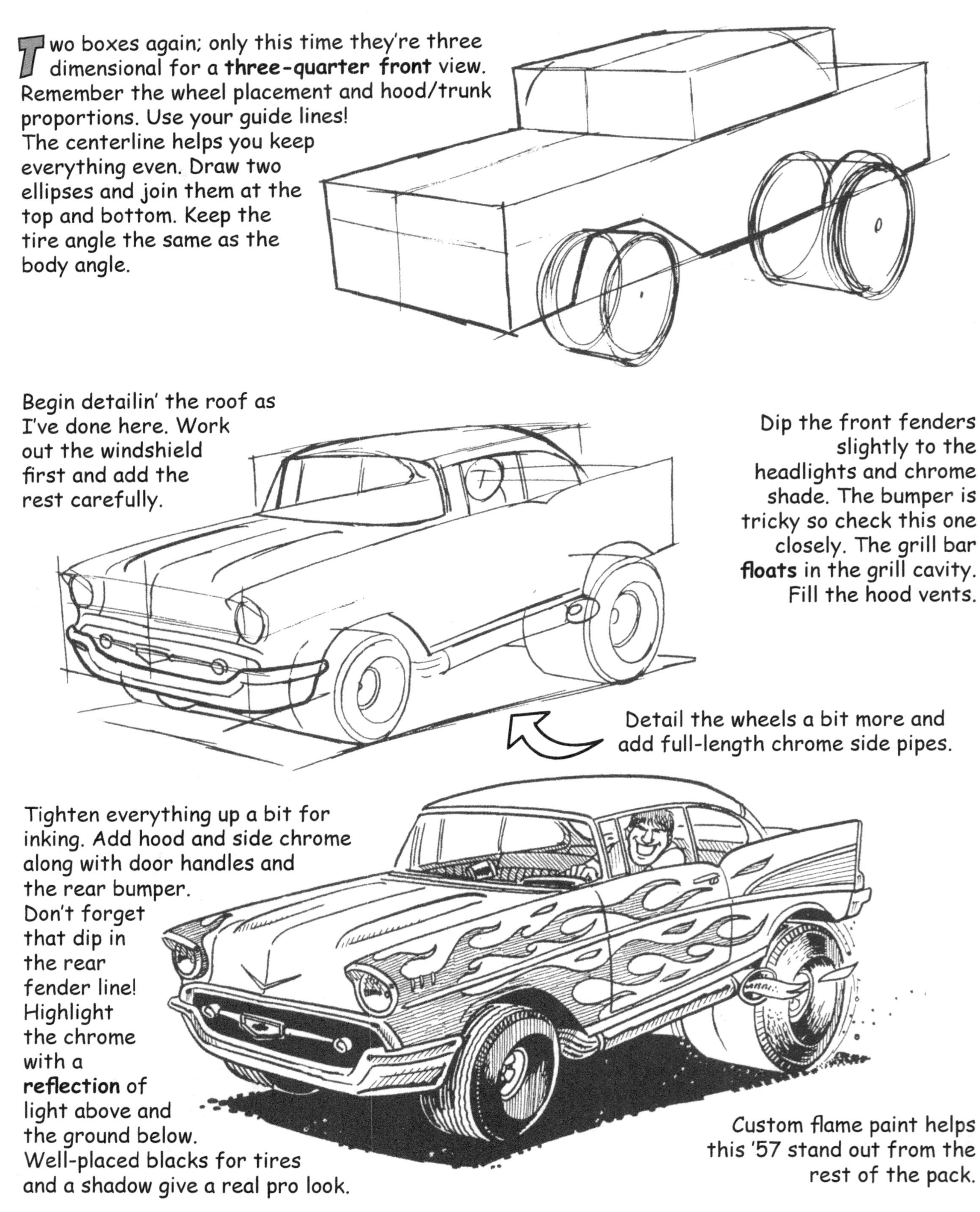

Two boxes again; only this time they're three dimensional for a **three-quarter front** view. Remember the wheel placement and hood/trunk proportions. Use your guide lines! The centerline helps you keep everything even. Draw two ellipses and join them at the top and bottom. Keep the tire angle the same as the body angle.

Begin detailin' the roof as I've done here. Work out the windshield first and add the rest carefully.

Dip the front fenders slightly to the headlights and chrome shade. The bumper is tricky so check this one closely. The grill bar **floats** in the grill cavity. Fill the hood vents.

Detail the wheels a bit more and add full-length chrome side pipes.

Tighten everything up a bit for inking. Add hood and side chrome along with door handles and the rear bumper. Don't forget that dip in the rear fender line! Highlight the chrome with a **reflection** of light above and the ground below. Well-placed blacks for tires and a shadow give a real pro look.

Custom flame paint helps this '57 stand out from the rest of the pack.

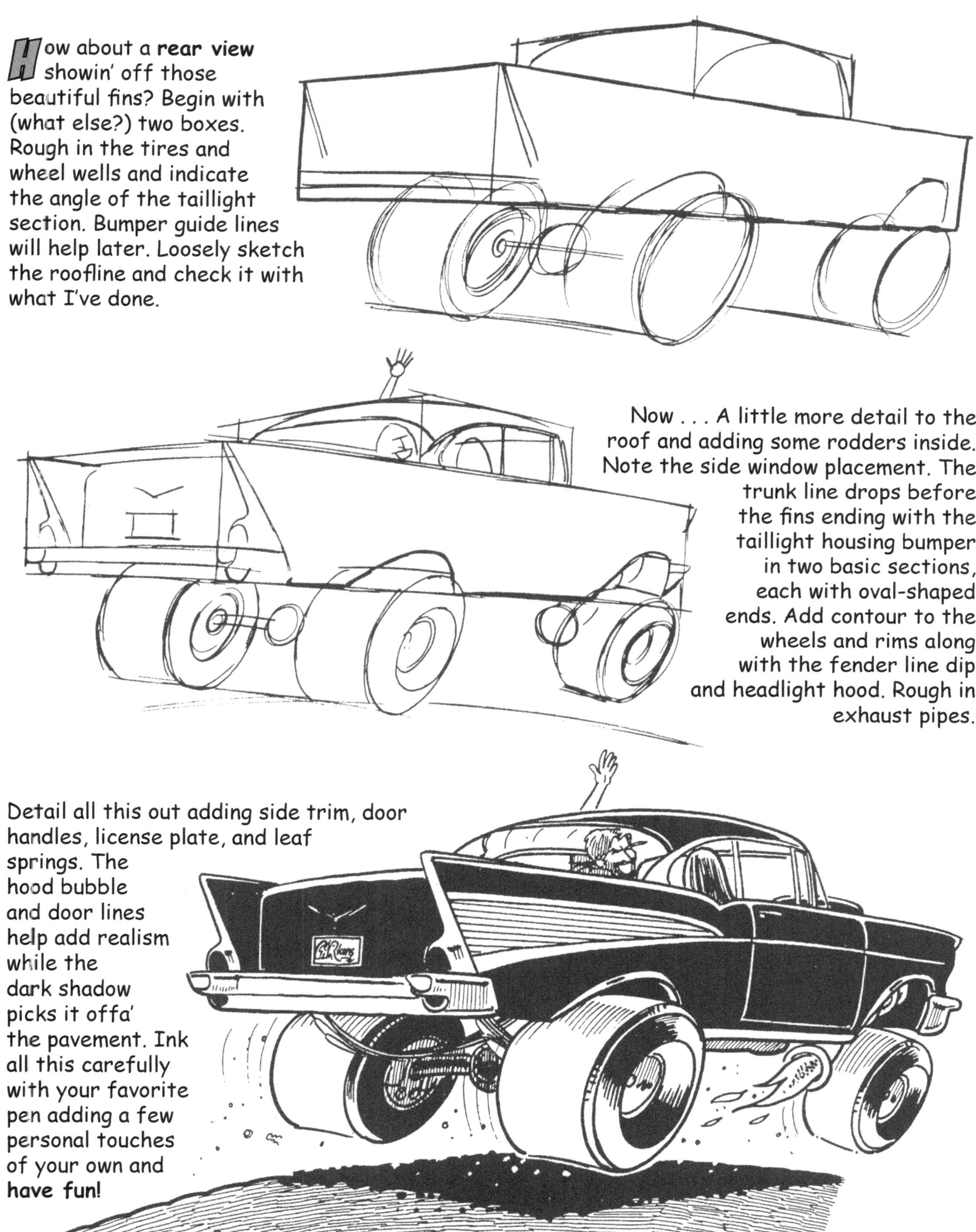

How about a **rear view** showin' off those beautiful fins? Begin with (what else?) two boxes. Rough in the tires and wheel wells and indicate the angle of the taillight section. Bumper guide lines will help later. Loosely sketch the roofline and check it with what I've done.

Now . . . A little more detail to the roof and adding some rodders inside. Note the side window placement. The trunk line drops before the fins ending with the taillight housing bumper in two basic sections, each with oval-shaped ends. Add contour to the wheels and rims along with the fender line dip and headlight hood. Rough in exhaust pipes.

Detail all this out adding side trim, door handles, license plate, and leaf springs. The hood bubble and door lines help add realism while the dark shadow picks it offa' the pavement. Ink all this carefully with your favorite pen adding a few personal touches of your own and **have fun!**

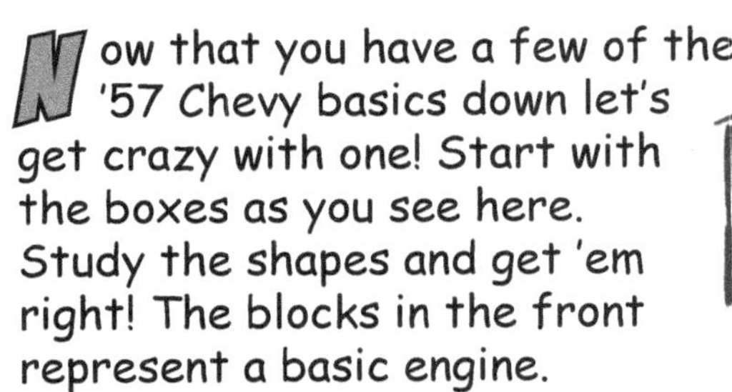

Now that you have a few of the '57 Chevy basics down let's get crazy with one! Start with the boxes as you see here. Study the shapes and get 'em right! The blocks in the front represent a basic engine.

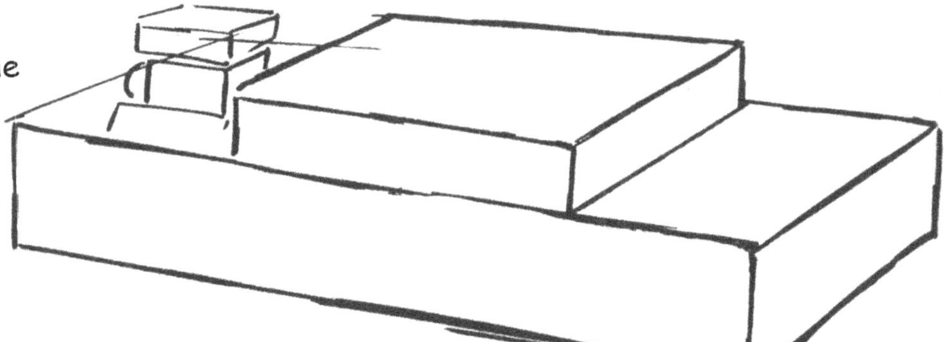

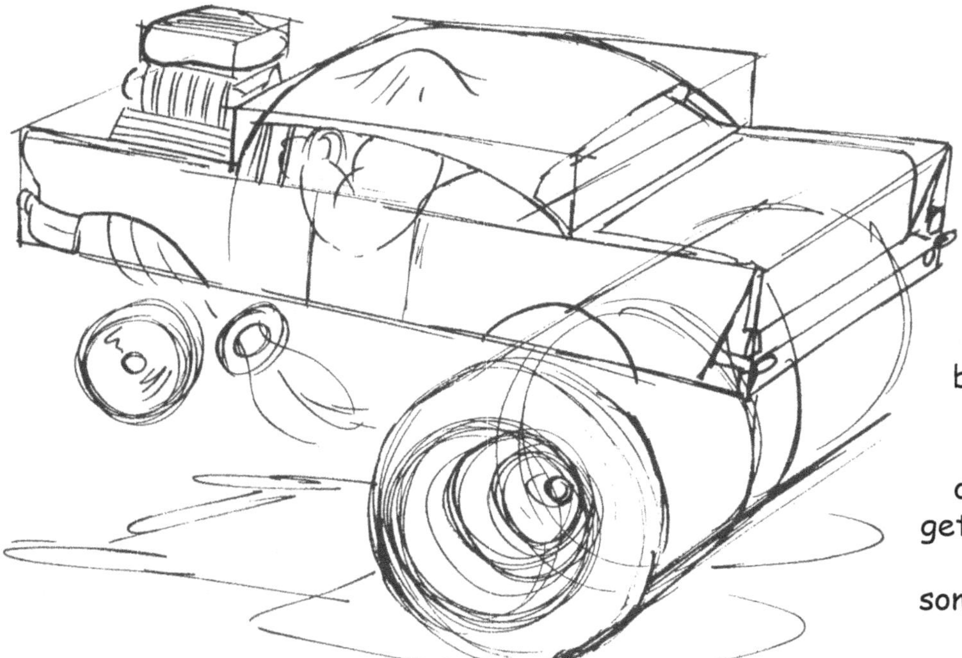

Okay . . . Let's get things hoppin' by adding small motorcycle tires in front with monster slicks in back. This is a good time to throw in an uncapped exhaust system blazin' with fire! And how about a **muscled-up** dude to drive 'er. Don't be afraid to use lots of pencil guide lines to help you get the feeling you're looking for. Work out the roofline and add some touches to the basic engine.

Pop a dent in the roof for the dude's head. Add a few finishing touches to the engine and wheels. Side chrome, door lines, and roof moldings should be added carefully. Detail the rear bumper area with blacks for taillights. A tuck-an'-roll interior and a pillow are easy. Fire it up and crank it on outa' here!

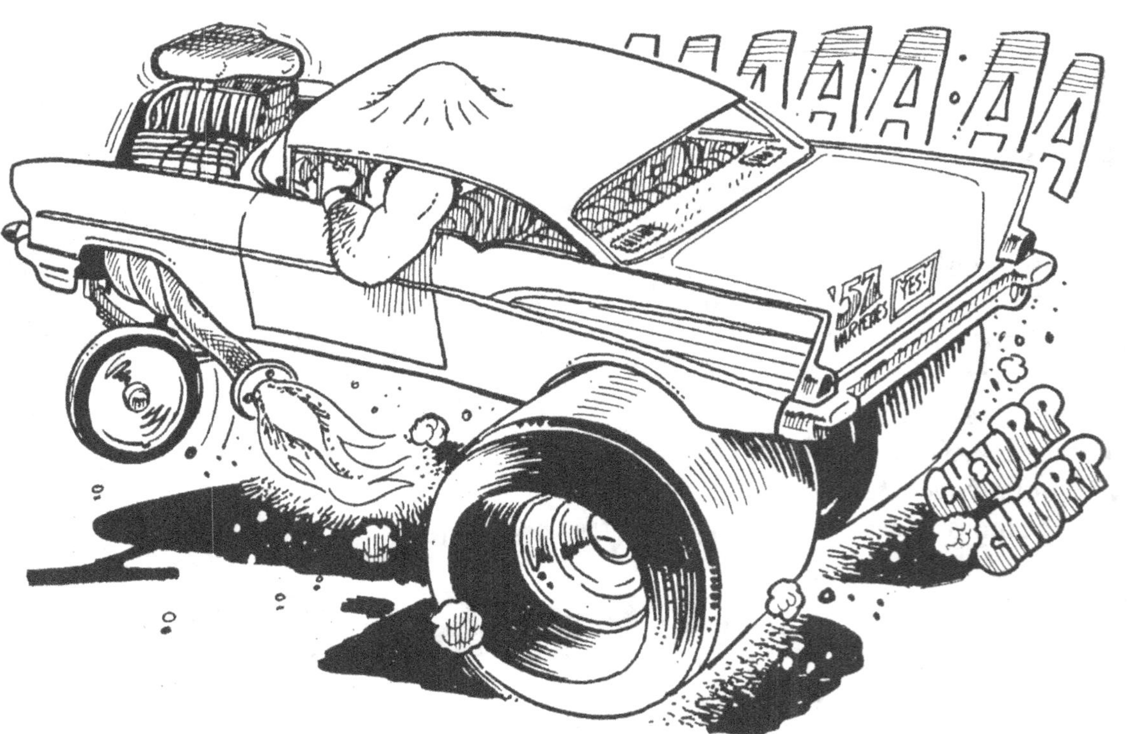

CAMAROS

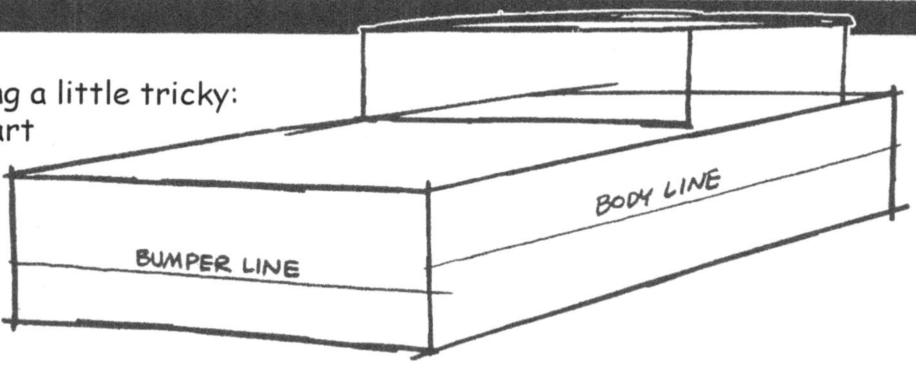

Okay, kids . . . Let's try something a little tricky: a **Camaro "Z."** As usual you start with two boxes. Note the body line on the side falls in the middle while the bumper line is a bit lower in front.

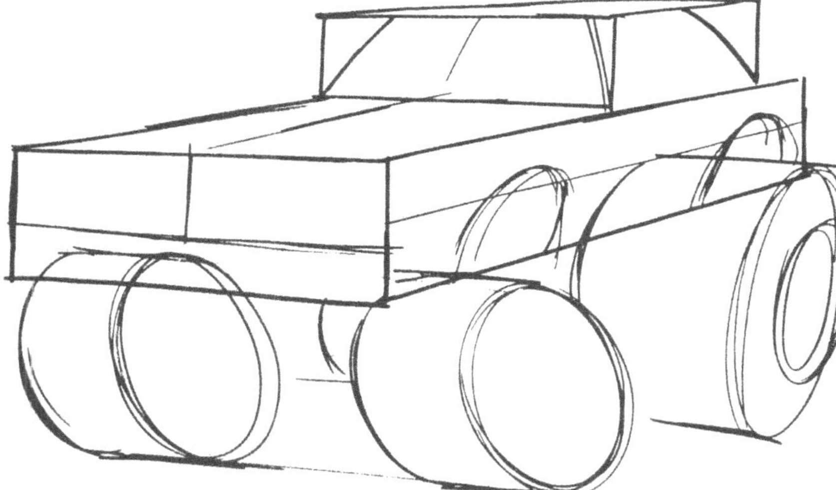

Now you loosely rough in the tires trying to give them a feeling of movement and speed. Guide lines help keep both sides uniform. You can also begin sketching the roof outa' the top block. You **already** have the look of the Camaro workin' and moving.

The front end is kinda' tough so get this part down good. Angle off the front of the Z and rough in the grill and headlight cavities. Note how they help to sculpt the hood area. Work to and through the bumper line.

The roof an' windshield can now be cut out of the box too. Rough it in carefully adding the door and the rear spoiler. You can work up the tires too. Loosely rough in contour and rims.

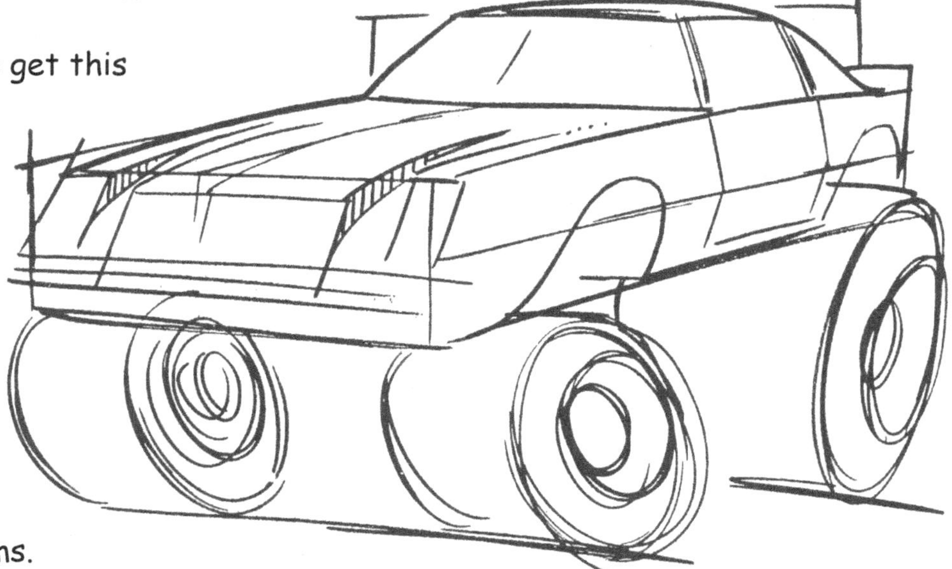

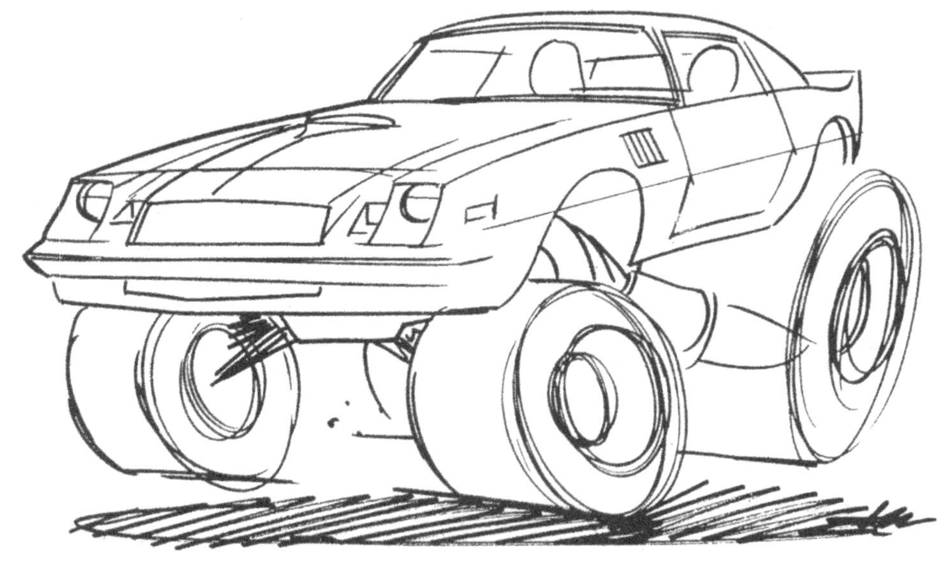

Add headlights an' bumper to the front. Mold everything into the body. Rough in the big headers with a **big flame** to match. Position the passengers and interior windows. Body stuff, such as the hood scoop and side louvers, can be blocked in. Rough in the suspension and oil pan underneath too. Indicate some kind of shadow under the Camaro to get it hoppin'.

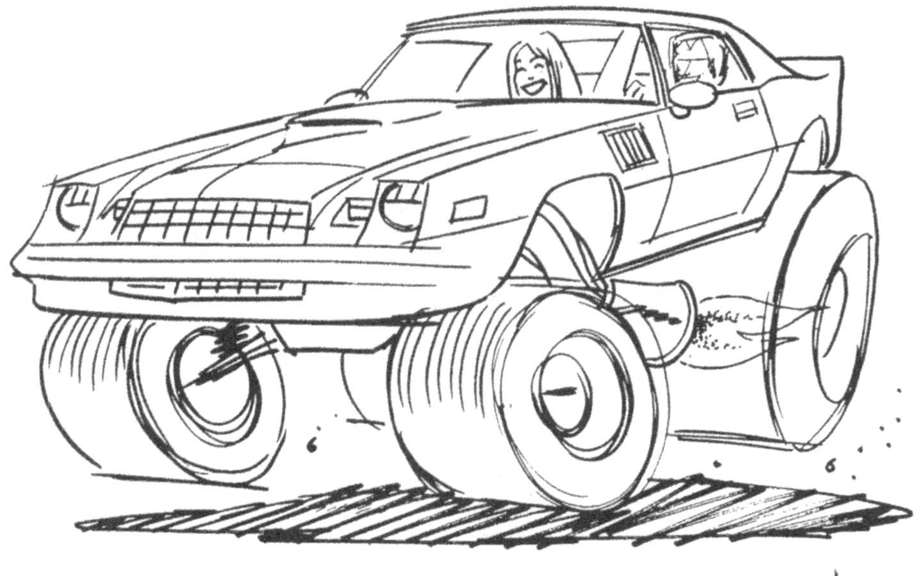

Okay, this is it: the final pencil work. Tighten up all you've done and check it for correct proportions, size, and so on. Just make sure it looks right **to you!** Add grillwork, parking lights, and details like door handles, side mirrors, and chrome stuff. Check your art against mine.

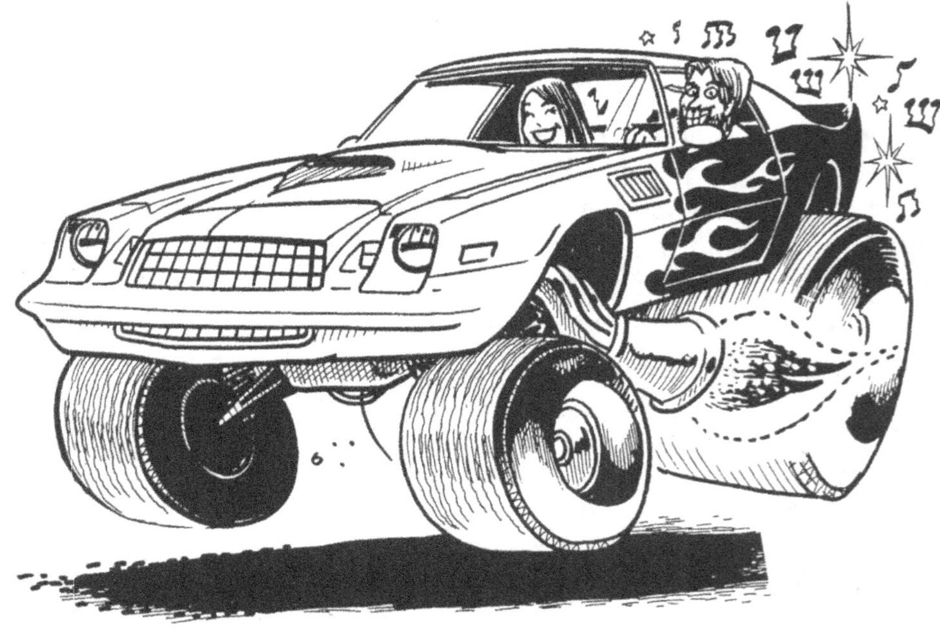

Carefully outline the body and tires leaving the heavy darks for last. I kinda' like flame paint jobs so my Z's got one. Darks on tires can be used to get that spinning look. Also, light areas around the exhaust and bottom of the tires help a bunch.

The '82 **Camaro** is super sleek. Start with a basic block shape. Add the centerline and the body line. You'll build on them later so get 'em positioned properly.

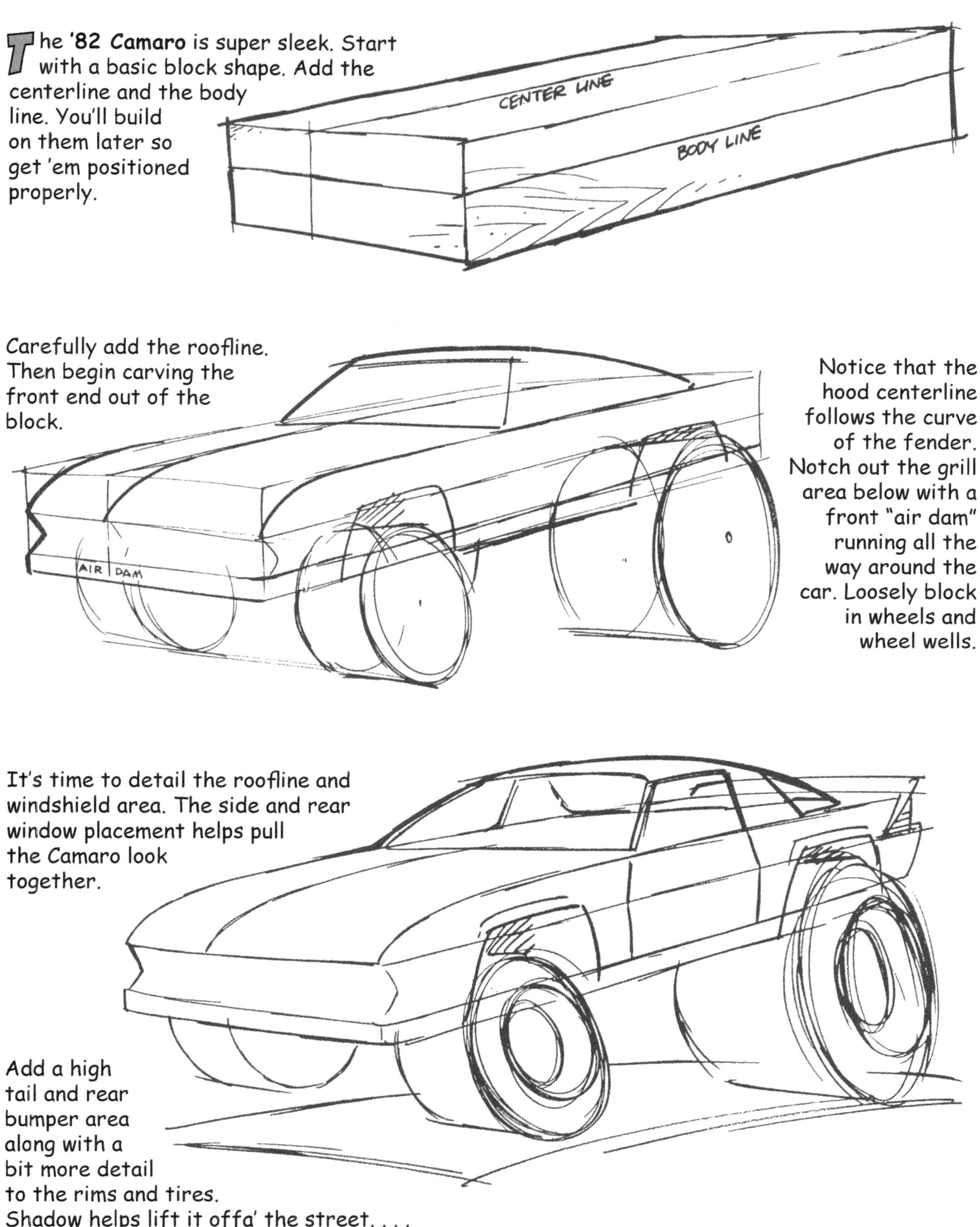

Carefully add the roofline. Then begin carving the front end out of the block.

Notice that the hood centerline follows the curve of the fender. Notch out the grill area below with a front "air dam" running all the way around the car. Loosely block in wheels and wheel wells.

It's time to detail the roofline and windshield area. The side and rear window placement helps pull the Camaro look together.

Add a high tail and rear bumper area along with a bit more detail to the rims and tires. Shadow helps lift it offa' the street. . . .

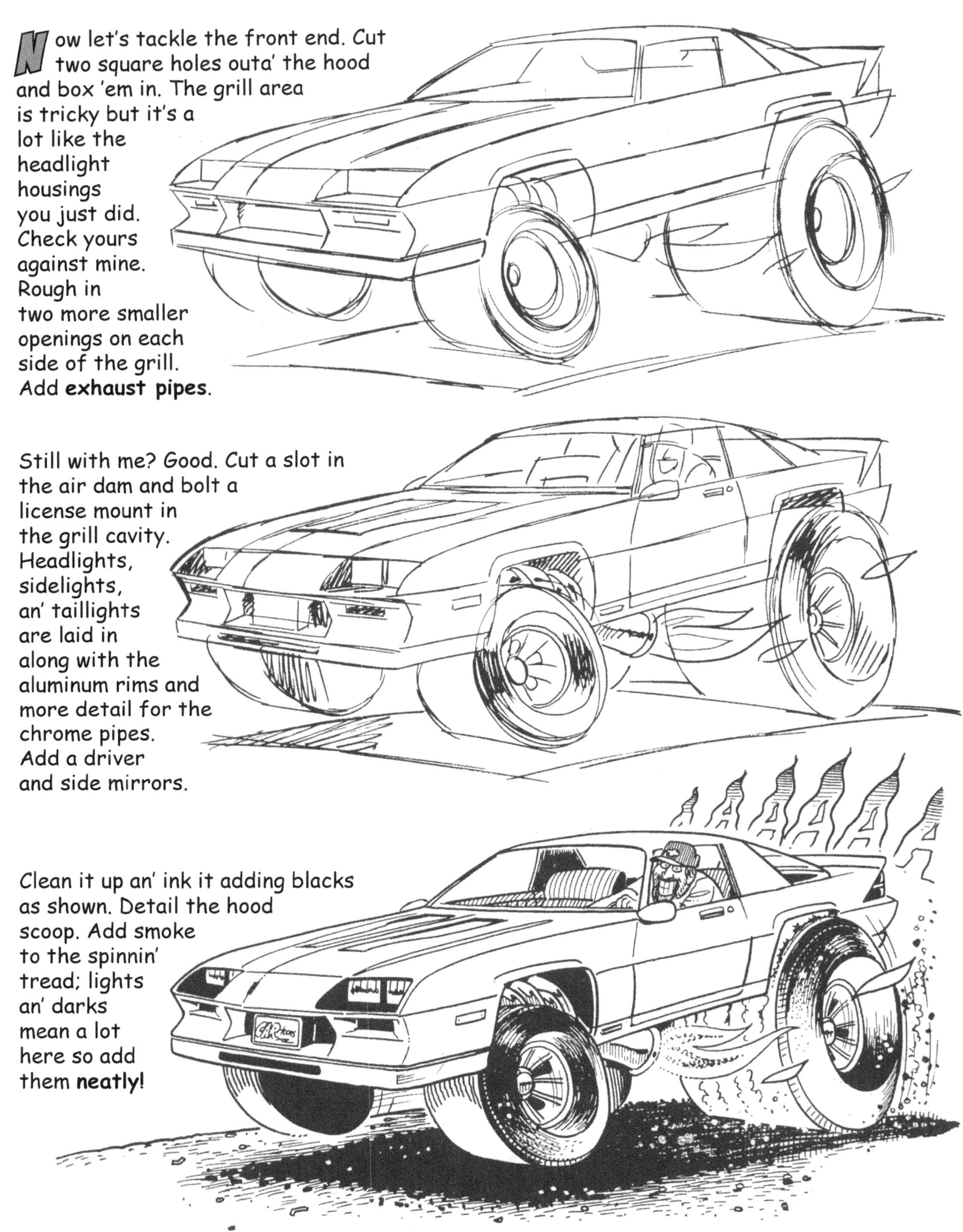

Now let's tackle the front end. Cut two square holes outa' the hood and box 'em in. The grill area is tricky but it's a lot like the headlight housings you just did. Check yours against mine. Rough in two more smaller openings on each side of the grill. Add **exhaust pipes**.

Still with me? Good. Cut a slot in the air dam and bolt a license mount in the grill cavity. Headlights, sidelights, an' taillights are laid in along with the aluminum rims and more detail for the chrome pipes. Add a driver and side mirrors.

Clean it up an' ink it adding blacks as shown. Detail the hood scoop. Add smoke to the spinnin' tread; lights an' darks mean a lot here so add them **neatly!**

HOW TO DRAW
LITTLE CHEVYS

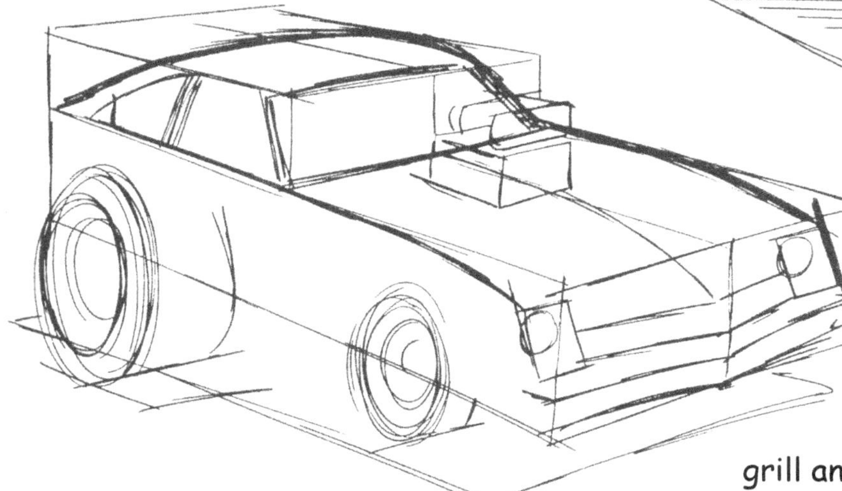

Chevrolet has lots of big muscle cars but you can't forget the little Chevys such as this Vega. Start with a two-box setup like this. A centerline up the middle help a bunch so lay one in. Rough in a shadow under 'em.

Start carving out the roofline and get the windshield tilt right as well as side window pillars. Box in a blower assembly through the hood. Note how the fender line dips down to the headlights. The hood centerline dips even more. Box in the grill and bumper and loosely detail the wheels.

A little more detail to the blower, grill, and tires is needed as well as a roll bar and driver inside. Work out some **body graphics** then neatly ink all this in using a ball-point or felt-tip pen adding blacks to the tires and shadow. Smoke an' sound help too!

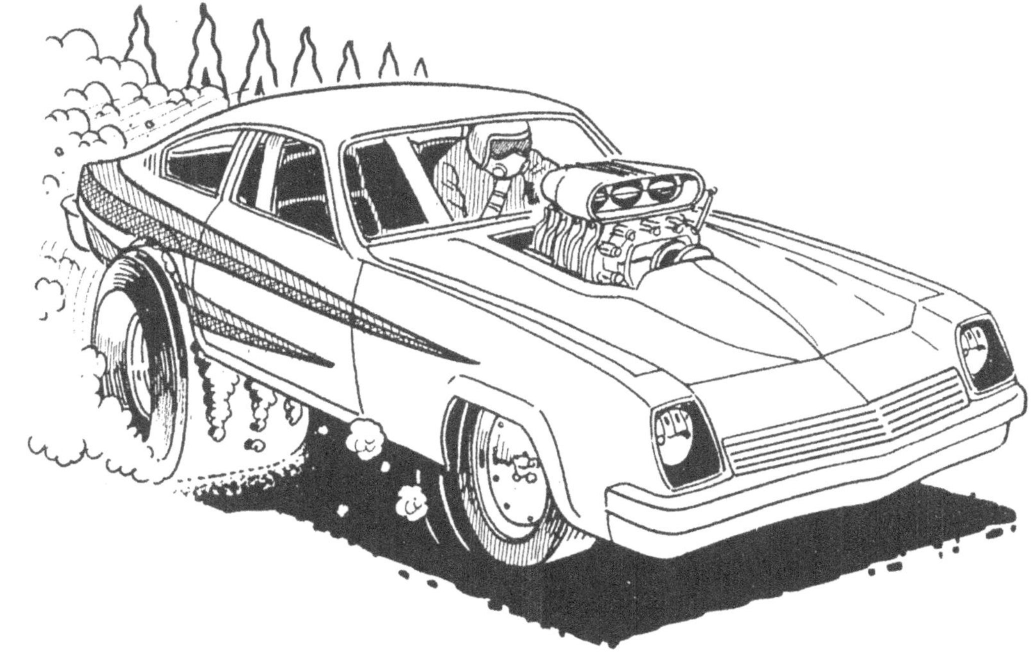

HOW TO DRAW DEUCE COUPES

For many years the '32 **Ford** has been almost synonymous with the term *hot rod*. Every rodder should be able to draw one. You start with these two basic boxes. Go carefully and make sure you get the proportions right!

Tackle the roof area first by roughing out the basic roof outline. Then add the windshield and side windows. Note that the side windows are divided by the door line. Work your way back to the **trunk line** curving it down to the rear end.

Carve out the famous Deuce grill shell paying close attention to the way the curves work. Notice the way the two front fenders pass by the grill at its middle. The front tips curve back and down. You can now rough in the rear fenders along with a big set of **slicks**. A pair of street tires up front help too. Be sure to indicate a shadow.

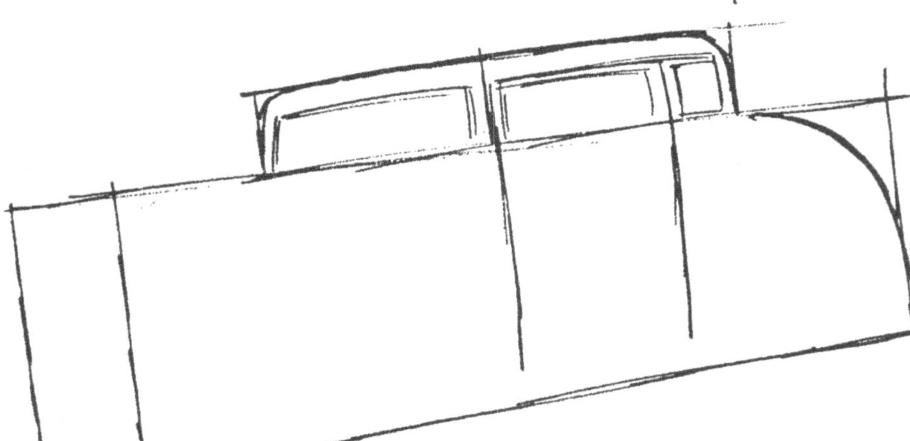

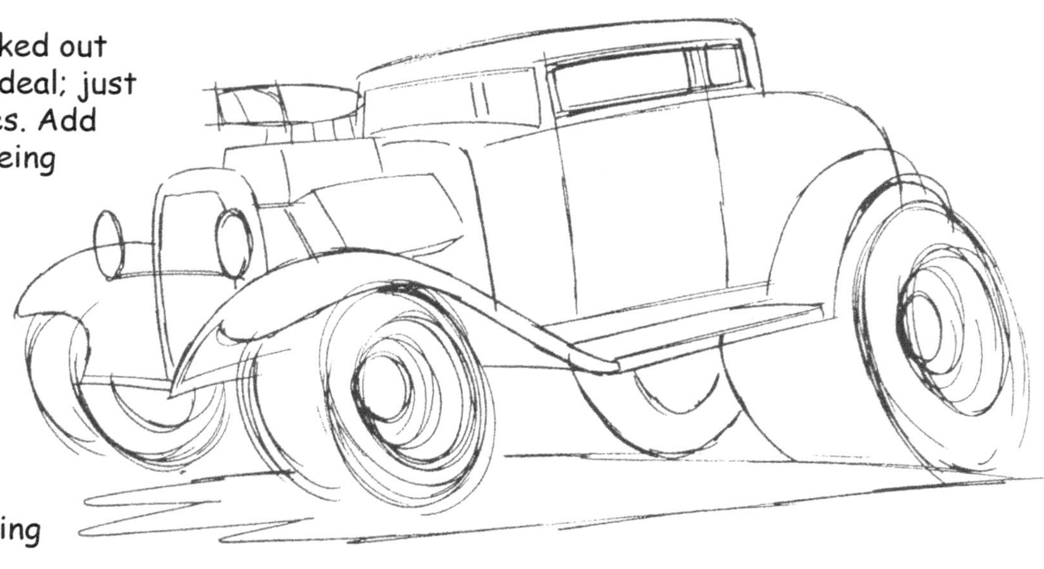

Notice how I've blocked out the engine. No big deal; just a few well-placed boxes. Add headlights and a bar being careful to get their placement right. Give the tires a bit more **contour**. I'm gonna' run chrome rims with baby moons on this one so I've roughed 'em in. Check over the fenders once more and add the running boards.

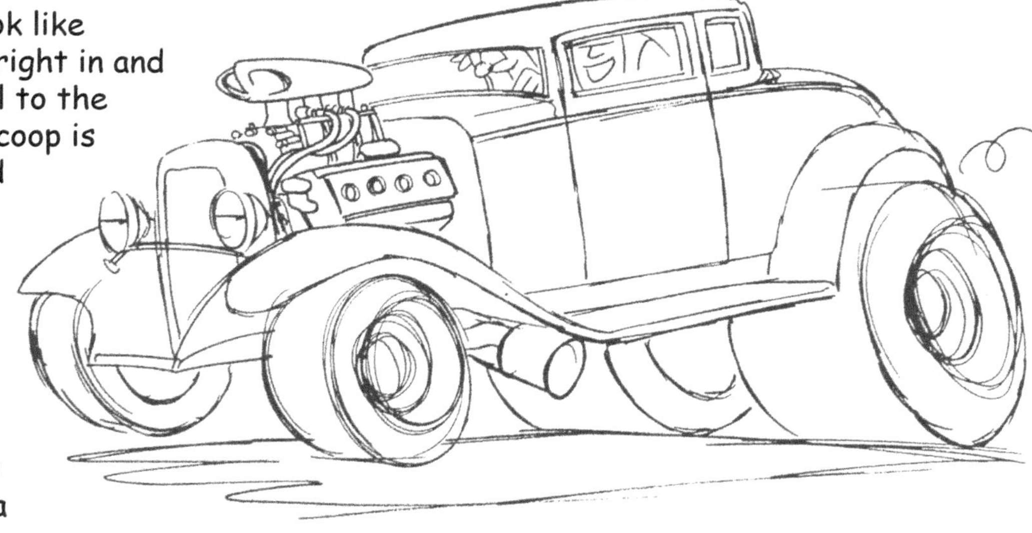

Now it's starting to look like something. Let's jump right in and add a little more detail to the Chrysler engine. The scoop is sculptured and you add fins and fuel lines to the blower. The valve cover bumps out in the middle for the plug holes. Give the headlights some buckets and innards. Rough in a set of **pipes** under the fender and a rodder to drive 'er.

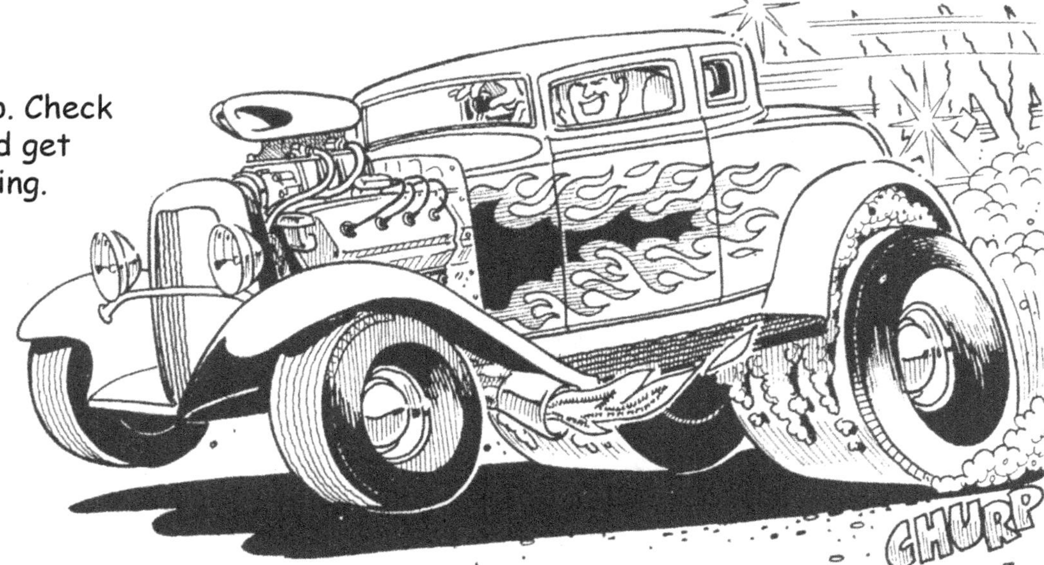

This is it: the final step. Check over all your details and get them just right for inking. Use a felt-tip or ball-point pen then erase all your pencil lines. Darks help add some definition. An early-Fifties flame job helps give your Deuce a traditional look. **Go!**

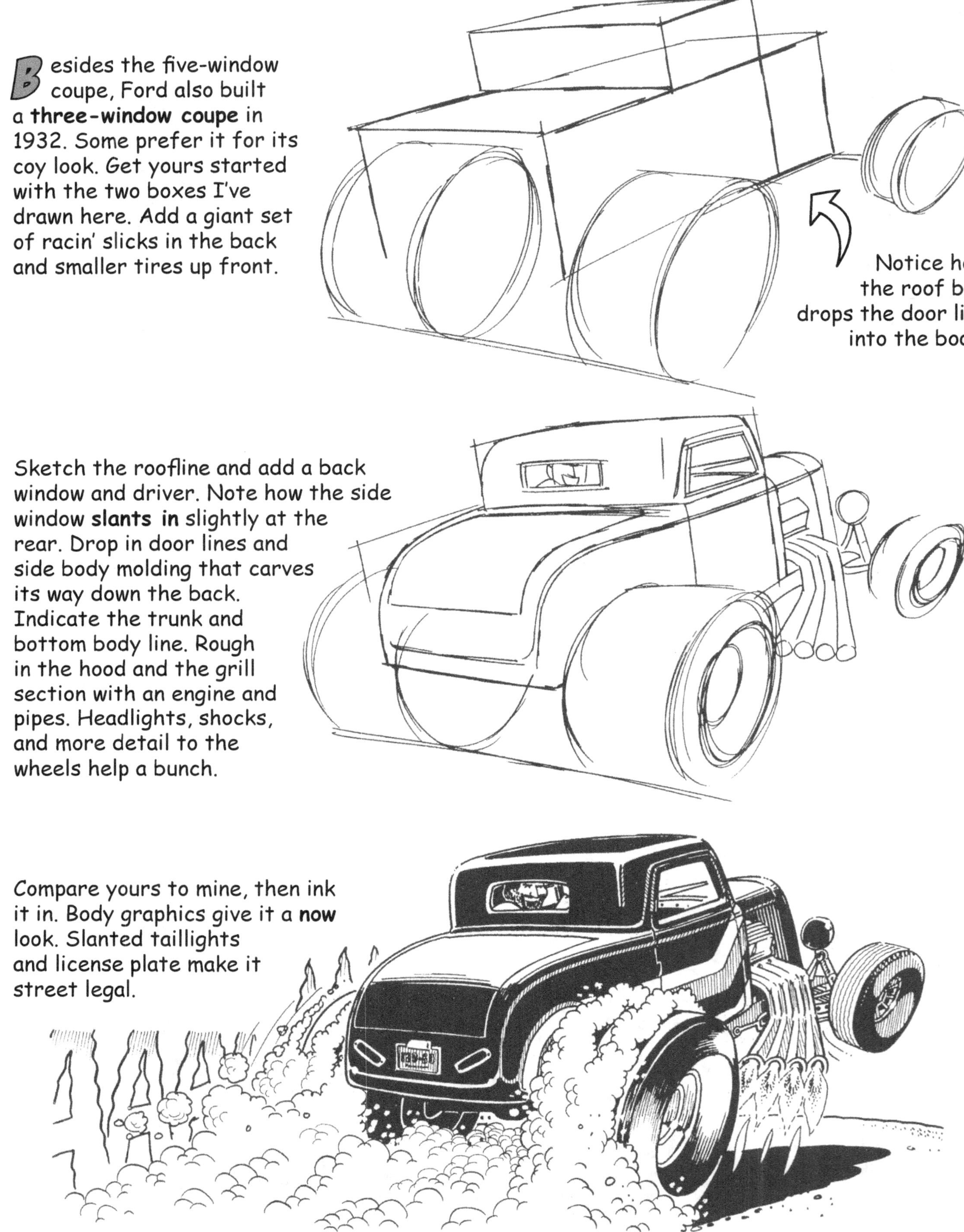

esides the five-window coupe, Ford also built a **three-window coupe** in 1932. Some prefer it for its coy look. Get yours started with the two boxes I've drawn here. Add a giant set of racin' slicks in the back and smaller tires up front.

Sketch the roofline and add a back window and driver. Note how the side window **slants in** slightly at the rear. Drop in door lines and side body molding that carves its way down the back. Indicate the trunk and bottom body line. Rough in the hood and the grill section with an engine and pipes. Headlights, shocks, and more detail to the wheels help a bunch.

Compare yours to mine, then ink it in. Body graphics give it a **now** look. Slanted taillights and license plate make it street legal.

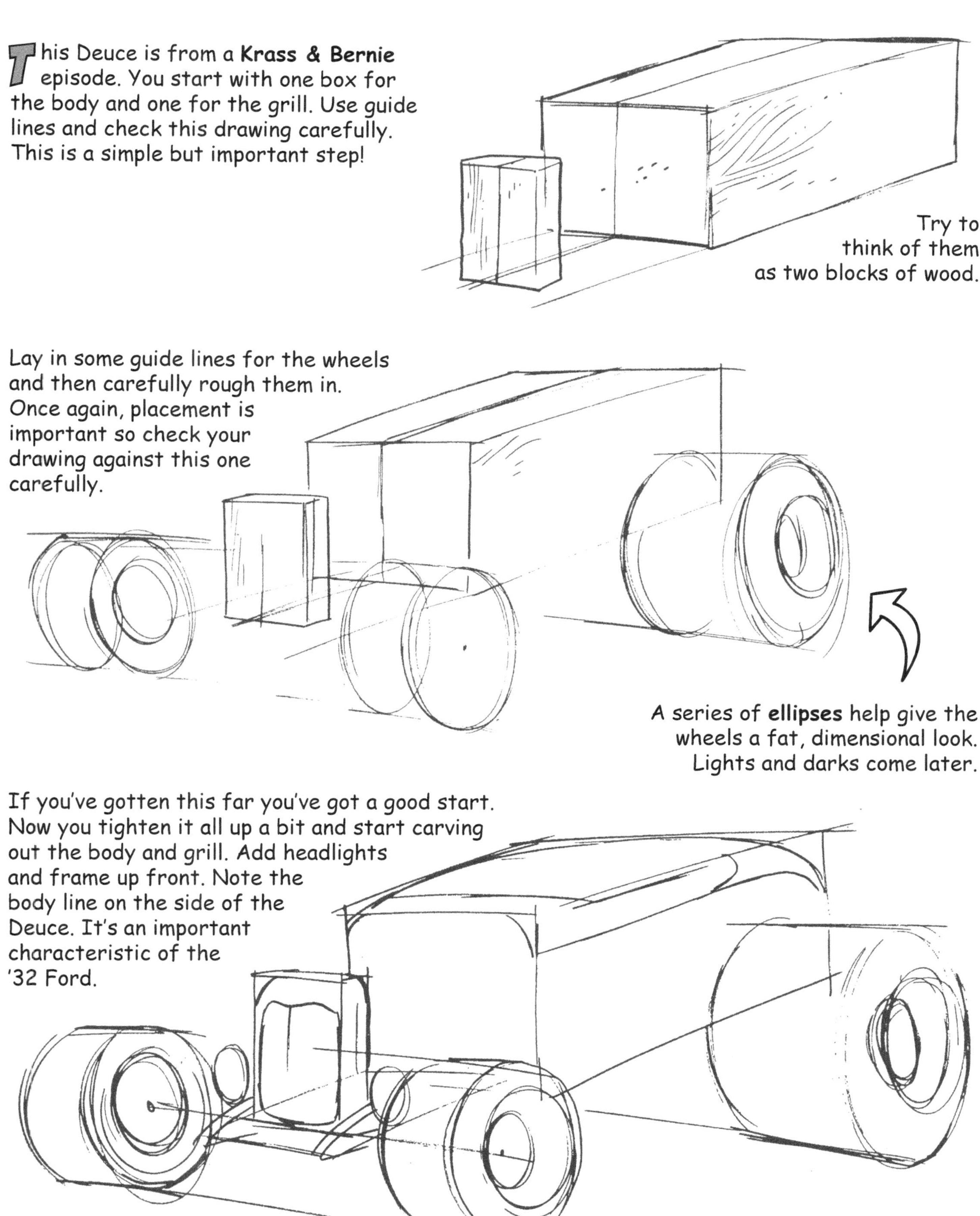

This Deuce is from a **Krass & Bernie** episode. You start with one box for the body and one for the grill. Use guide lines and check this drawing carefully. This is a simple but important step!

Try to think of them as two blocks of wood.

Lay in some guide lines for the wheels and then carefully rough them in. Once again, placement is important so check your drawing against this one carefully.

A series of **ellipses** help give the wheels a fat, dimensional look. Lights and darks come later.

If you've gotten this far you've got a good start. Now you tighten it all up a bit and start carving out the body and grill. Add headlights and frame up front. Note the body line on the side of the Deuce. It's an important characteristic of the '32 Ford.

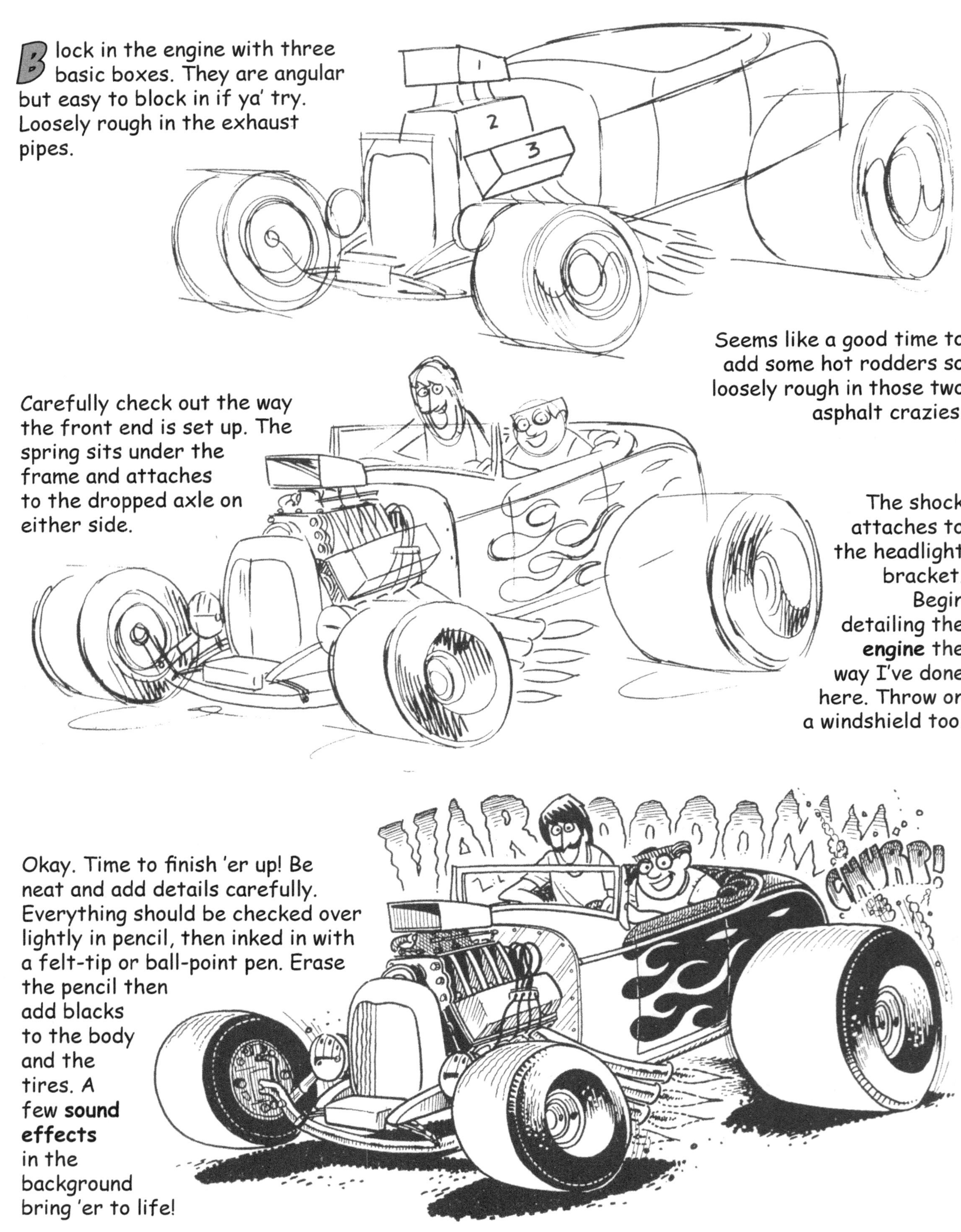

Block in the engine with three basic boxes. They are angular but easy to block in if ya' try. Loosely rough in the exhaust pipes.

Carefully check out the way the front end is set up. The spring sits under the frame and attaches to the dropped axle on either side.

Seems like a good time to add some hot rodders so loosely rough in those two asphalt crazies.

The shock attaches to the headlight bracket. Begin detailing the **engine** the way I've done here. Throw on a windshield too.

Okay. Time to finish 'er up! Be neat and add details carefully. Everything should be checked over lightly in pencil, then inked in with a felt-tip or ball-point pen. Erase the pencil then add blacks to the body and the tires. A few **sound effects** in the background bring 'er to life!

LEADSLEDS

Early customs were called leadsleds because of the large amounts of lead used in the customizing process. They are becoming popular again so let's try a real standard: the **'49 to '51 Merc!** Begin by laying out the two boxes shown here. Be careful to get your proportions right from the start!

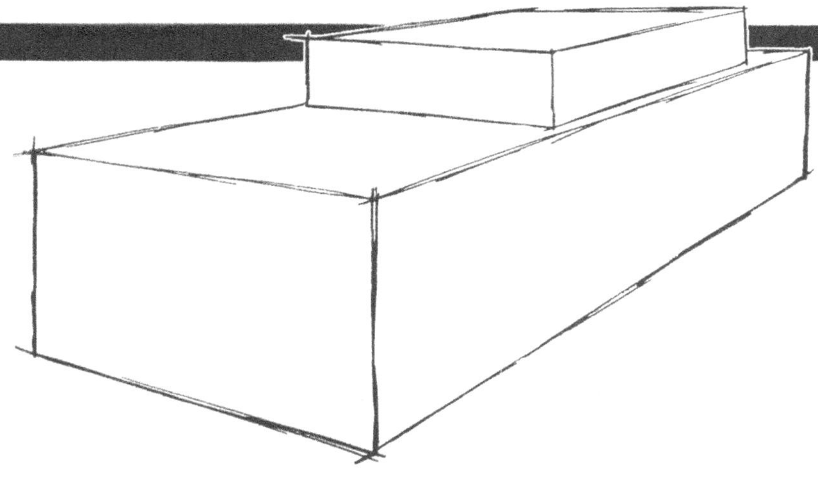

The Merc is boxy but very round and smooth. Keep this in mind while roughing in the roof, fenders, and hood line. Divide the front of the box in half then lay in the headlights with a pair of guide lines. Dropping a centerline down the middle of the car will help too.

Next, carve out the grill and front pan area angling off the centerline. Roll **the pan** around to the side and the back. Note the characteristic dip in the side body line. Add it carefully. Study how the hood lines follow the body contours then lay 'em in.

Now it's starting to look like **somethin'!** Continue working out the grill area following my sketch. Just around the side, add the front wheel well and basic tire shape. Placement is important. Rough in the side pipes along with the cruiser skirts. Carefully work out the side windows and windshield including the window sills.

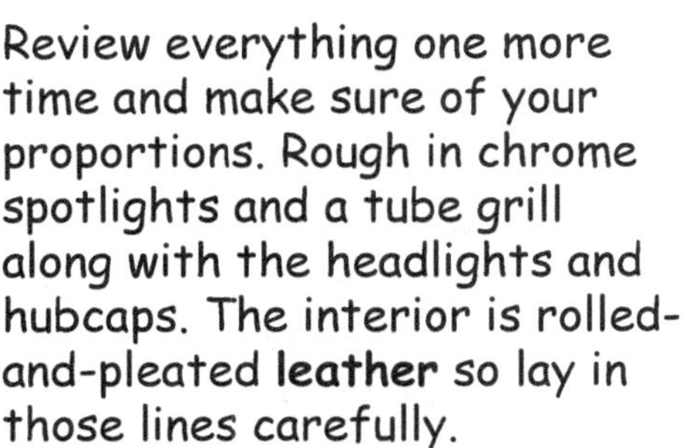

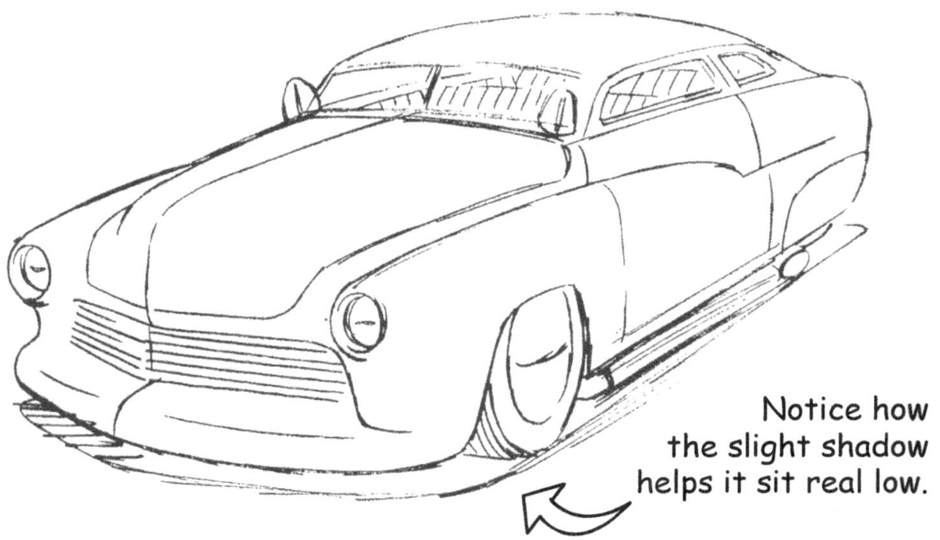

Review everything one more time and make sure of your proportions. Rough in chrome spotlights and a tube grill along with the headlights and hubcaps. The interior is rolled-and-pleated **leather** so lay in those lines carefully.

Notice how the slight shadow helps it sit real low.

If you've hung in this far you're all set for inking. Slowly outline everything adding darks to the chrome reflections. It's no secret that I'm a real flame job freak so **my** Merc will sport one. A ruler or any straight edge helps with the grill and side pipes. Use a felt-tip or ball-point pen to do the deed!

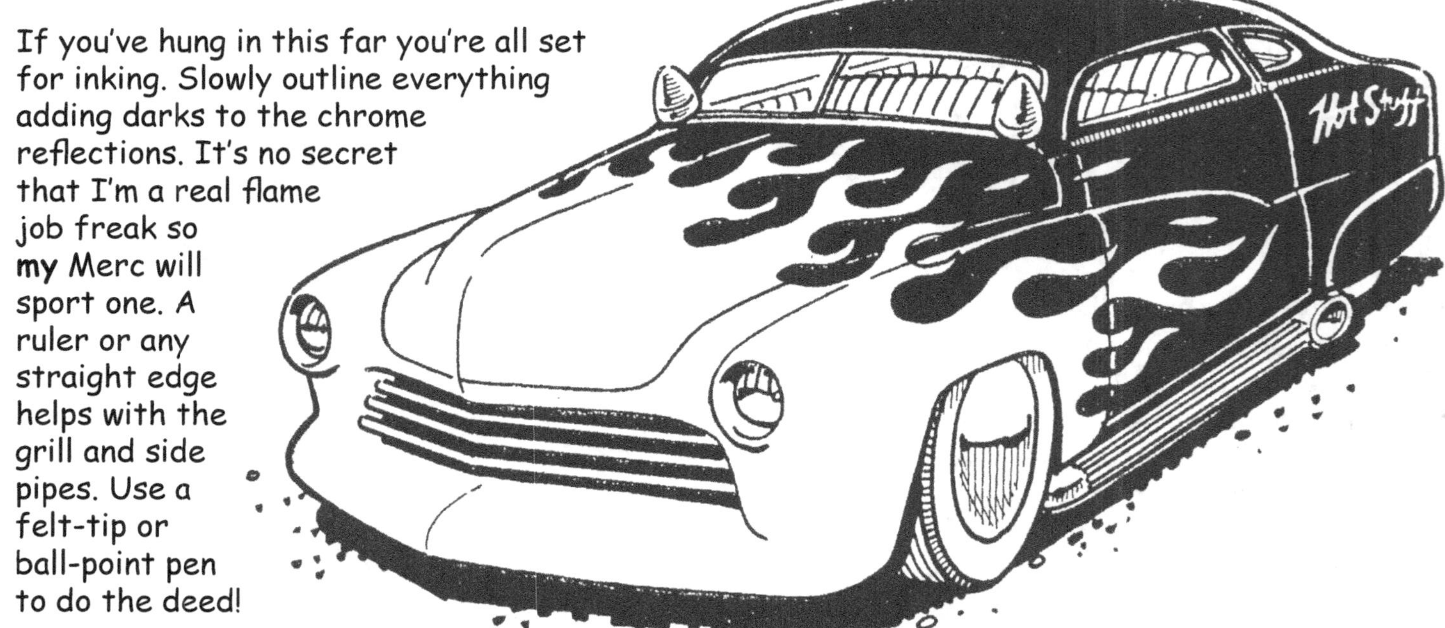

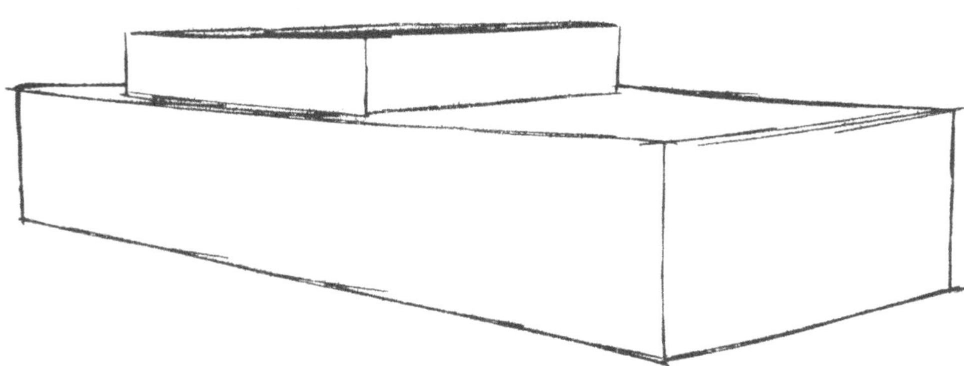

As the Fifties rolled on, later models became leadsleds. Here you get the chance to rework a **'55 Chevy** into something wild! Get the boxes here down on your paper.

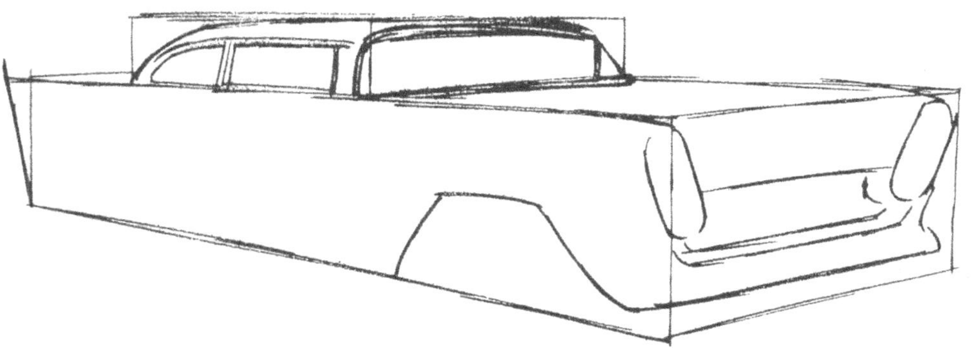

Rough out the roofline and window posts and then add the fin angle. Quad headlights sit at a slight angle helping to form the grill and bumper area. Add the front wheel well.

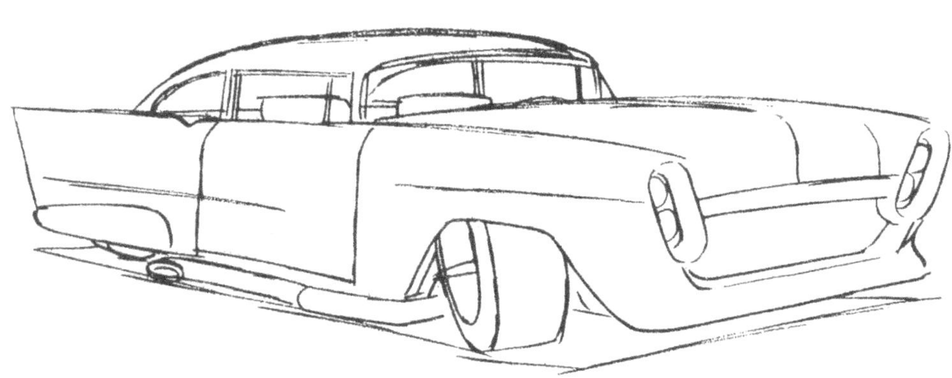

Work out the front end a bit more. Rough in both tires adding side pipes and skirts. Don't forget the fender dip at the rear side window. Loosely add the spots and the mirror.

Hokay . . . It's inkin' time again so put on your neatness hat and get goin'! It's scallops this time so lay 'em in so they flow with the natural body lines of the car. A shadow and highlights finish 'er up!

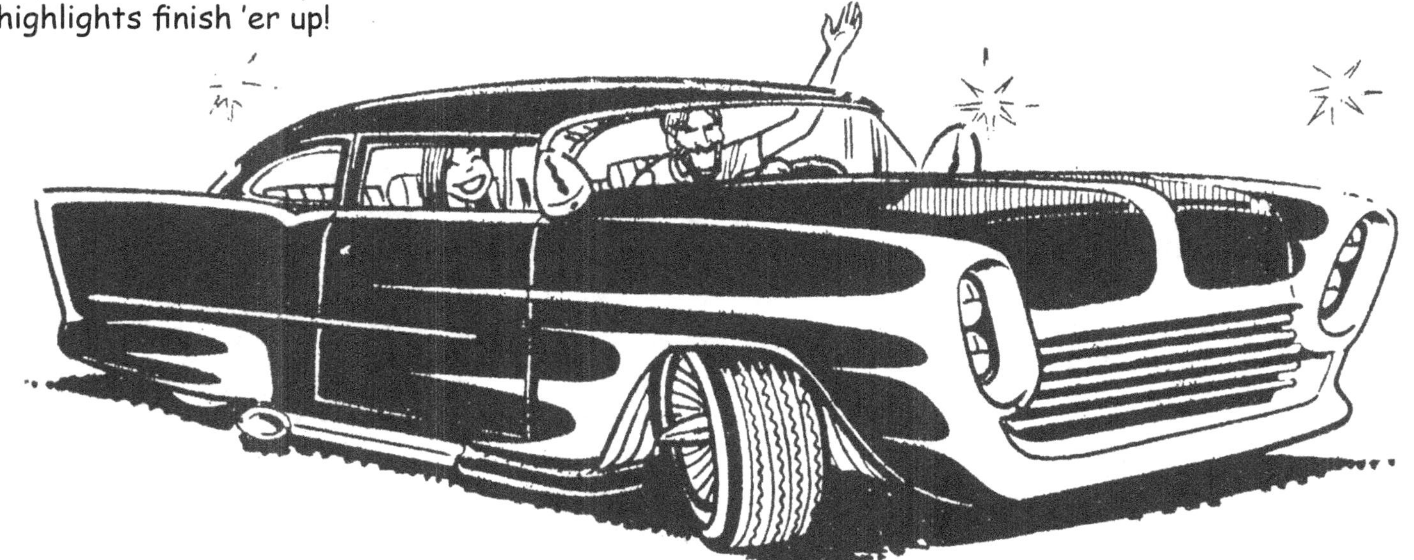

HOW TO DRAW
MUSCLE CARS

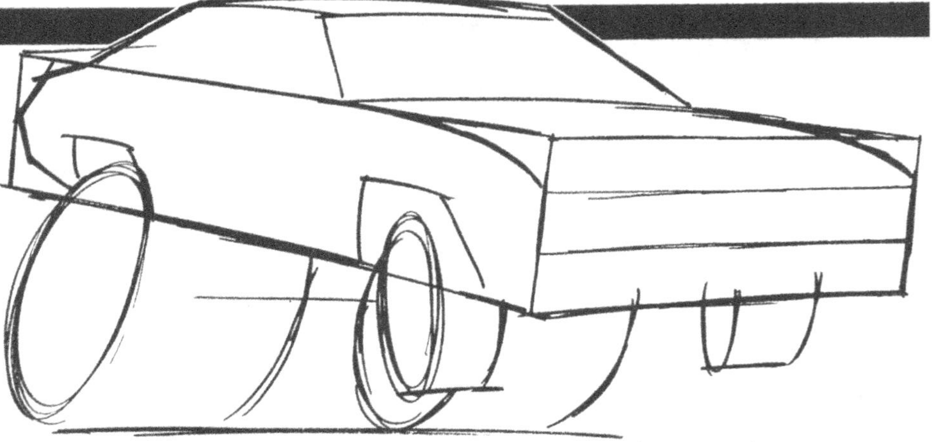

Muscle cars keep growing in popularity; and I mean other than Camaros and Mustangs. You start a 400-ci **'69 GTO** with the boxes you see here. Carefully curve the hood down to about a third of the front box and add a centerline. Carve out the rear fender and wheel wells then rough in the wheels.

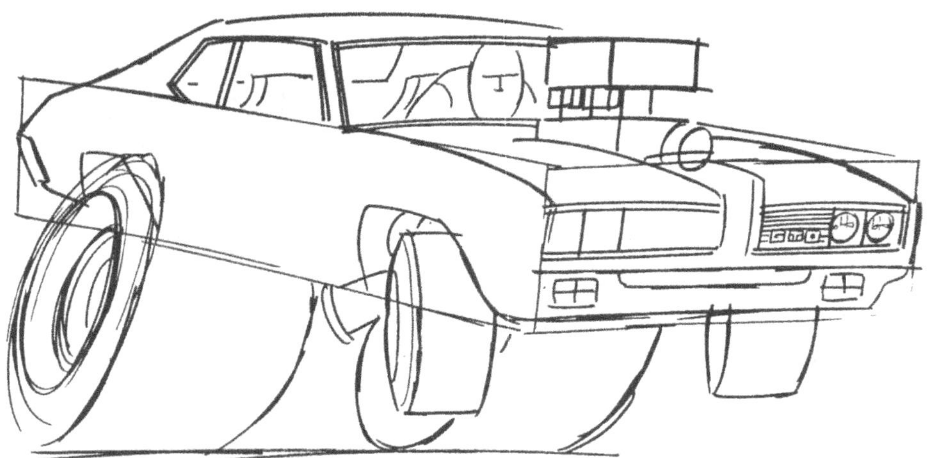

The next thing to do is open up the interior with windows an' a windshield and drop in a driver and seats. Box out the blower assembly adding the distinctive GTO nose up front. Block in headlights and grill trim then rough out the lower pan area. Give the tires some dimension and bolt in a set of tuned **headers**.

Check over what you've got adding details as you go such as flames, noise, blower parts, and license plate. Outline everything with a felt-tip or ball-point pen doing details with a finer line. Solid blacks help give the impression of paint an' gloss as well as helping light the tires from below.

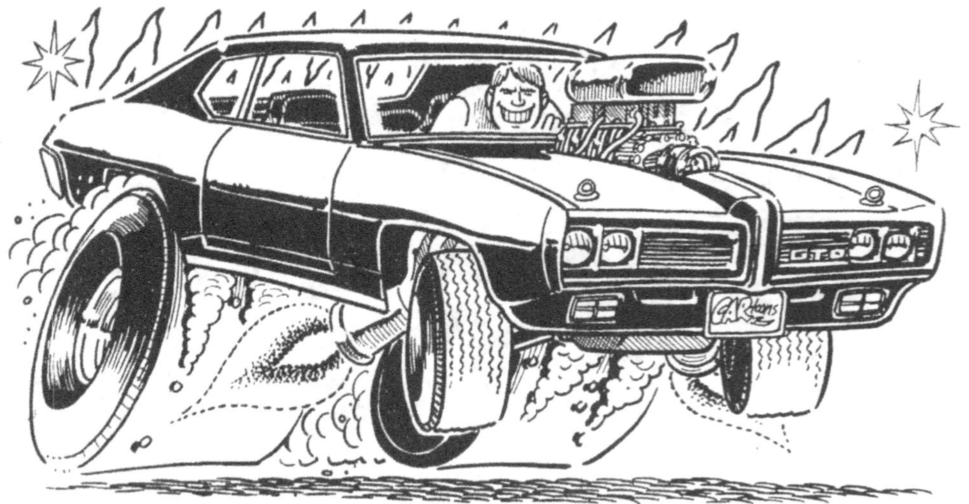

Another big non-Ford/Chevy muscle car is the **Dodge Challenger**! Start yours with two boxes. Bend the back fenders in a bit as shown here angling off the centerline. Cut out some wheel wells then rough in some giant tread in the back with some smaller tires up front. Carve the front fender down and back forming a new front hood line.

Tackle the rear section by first blocking in a spoiler then the taillights below it. The bumper falls below the centerline and has its own centerline. Bumperettes and license plate complete this step. Bump up the rear fenders and rough in some side sculpturing after adding wheel wells and tire detail. Block in the blower assembly as well as side and rear windows an' a roll bar.

Same deal as before. Check over all your details carefully adding a few last-minute things such as a wheelie bar and body graphics. Ink it in neatly utilizing some of the techniques you used on the GTO. Lights and darks help render chrome. **Fingers... do your stuff!**

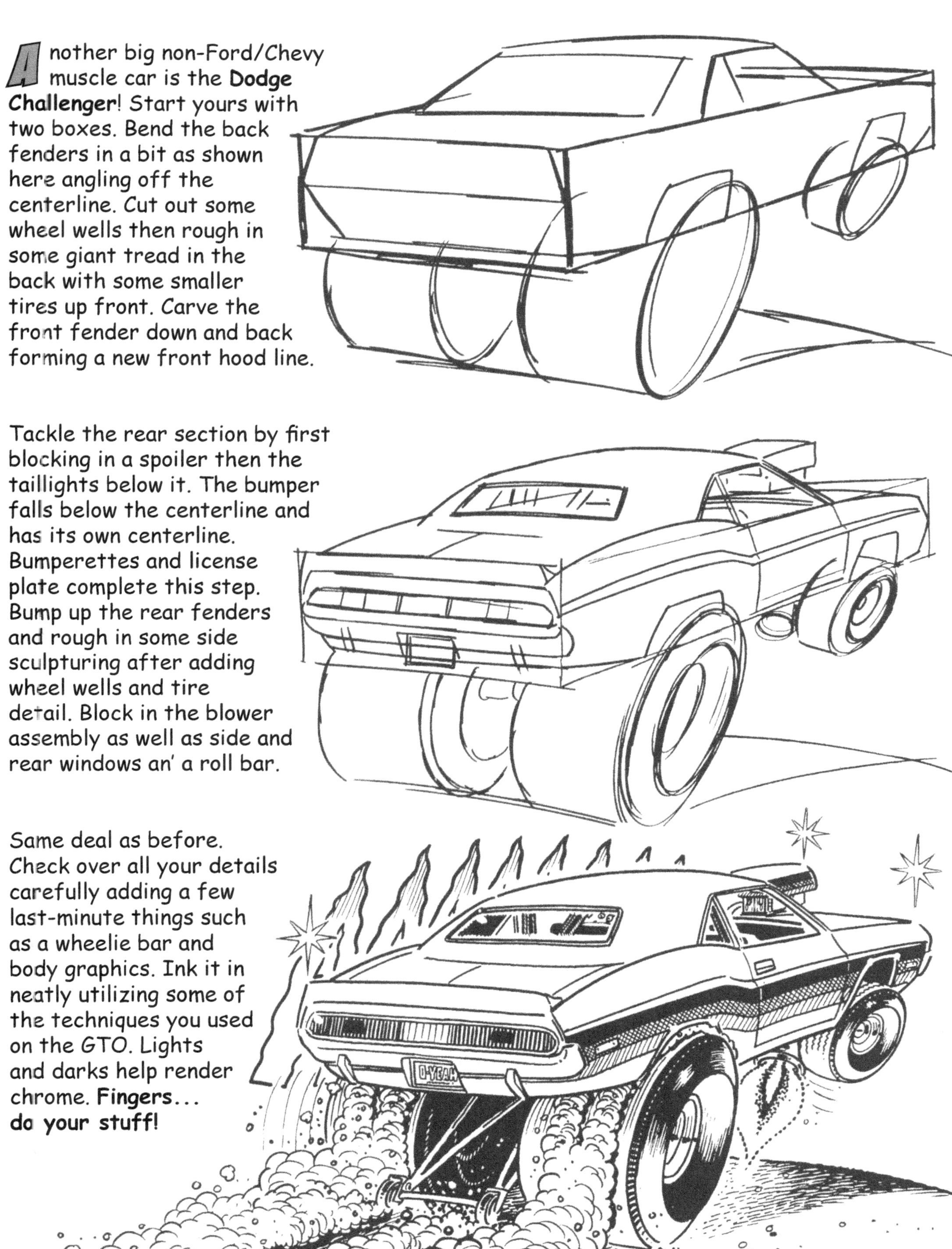

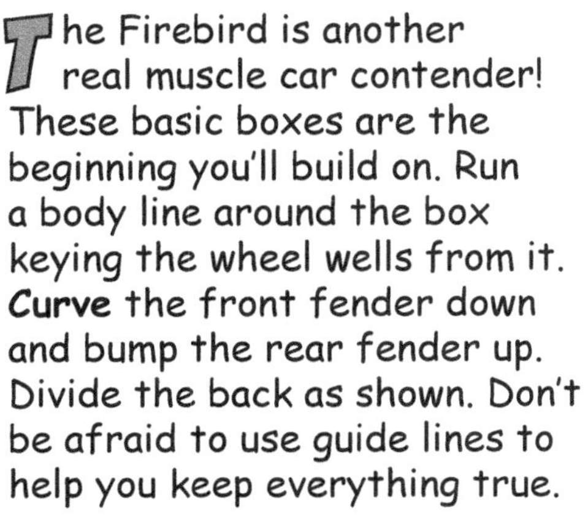

The Firebird is another real muscle car contender! These basic boxes are the beginning you'll build on. Run a body line around the box keying the wheel wells from it. **Curve** the front fender down and bump the rear fender up. Divide the back as shown. Don't be afraid to use guide lines to help you keep everything true.

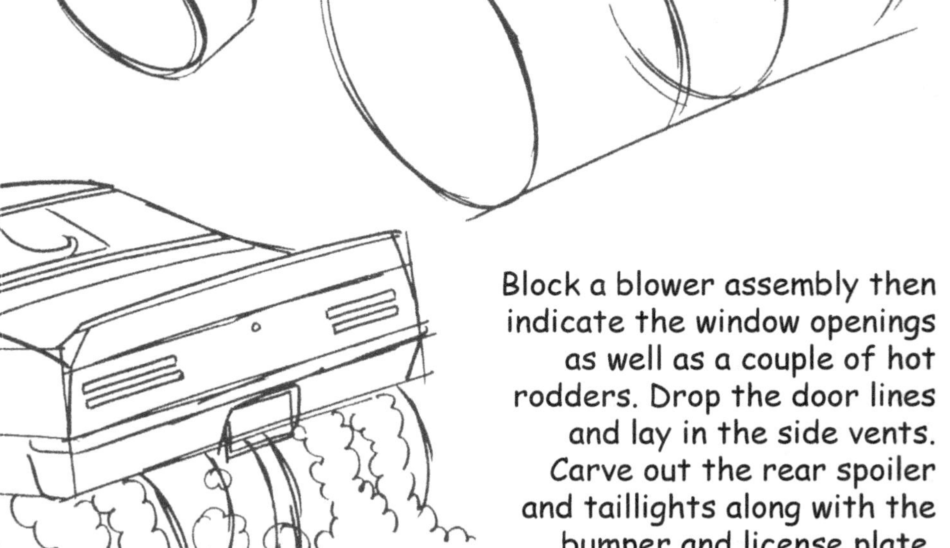

Block a blower assembly then indicate the window openings as well as a couple of hot rodders. Drop the door lines and lay in the side vents. Carve out the rear spoiler and taillights along with the bumper and license plate. Indicate headers and some dimension to the tires an' rims. Add smoke and shadow.

One more time, check over your work for problems then begin inking, doing major sections first then the finer details. **Go nuts** with some flames or other wild paint scheme. Smoke, noise, and exhaust fire always gets it up and movin' as does the body shadow and loose stones. Erase your pencil and enjoy!

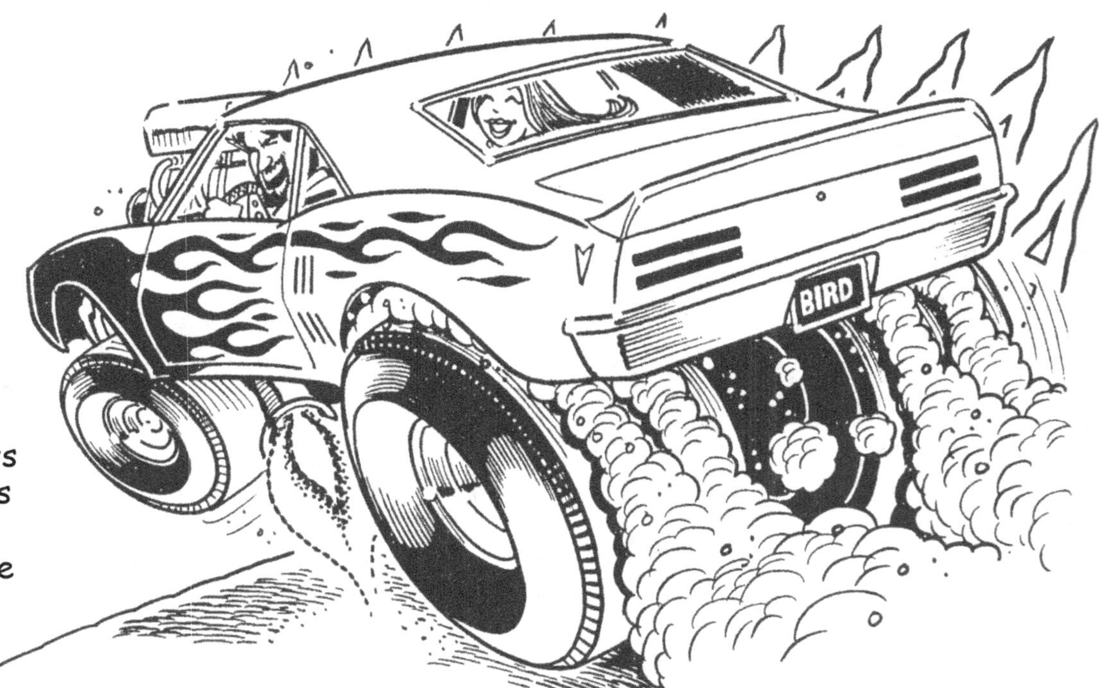

114

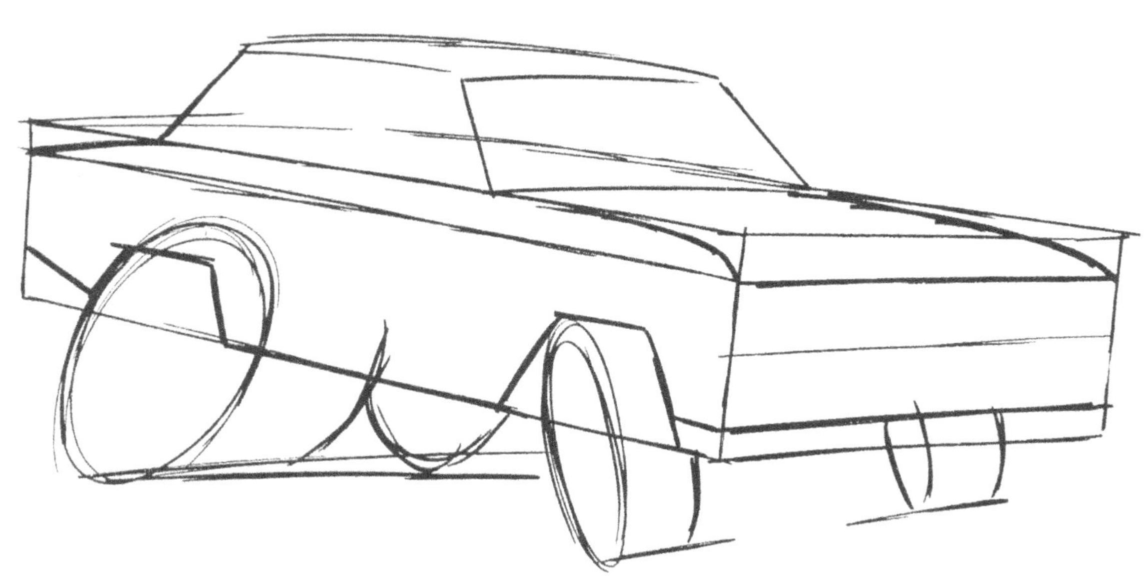

You can start a 427-ci '65 **Ford Fairlane** with two boxes. Taper the front and back fenders down to a side body line. Rough in tires and divide the front end as you see here.

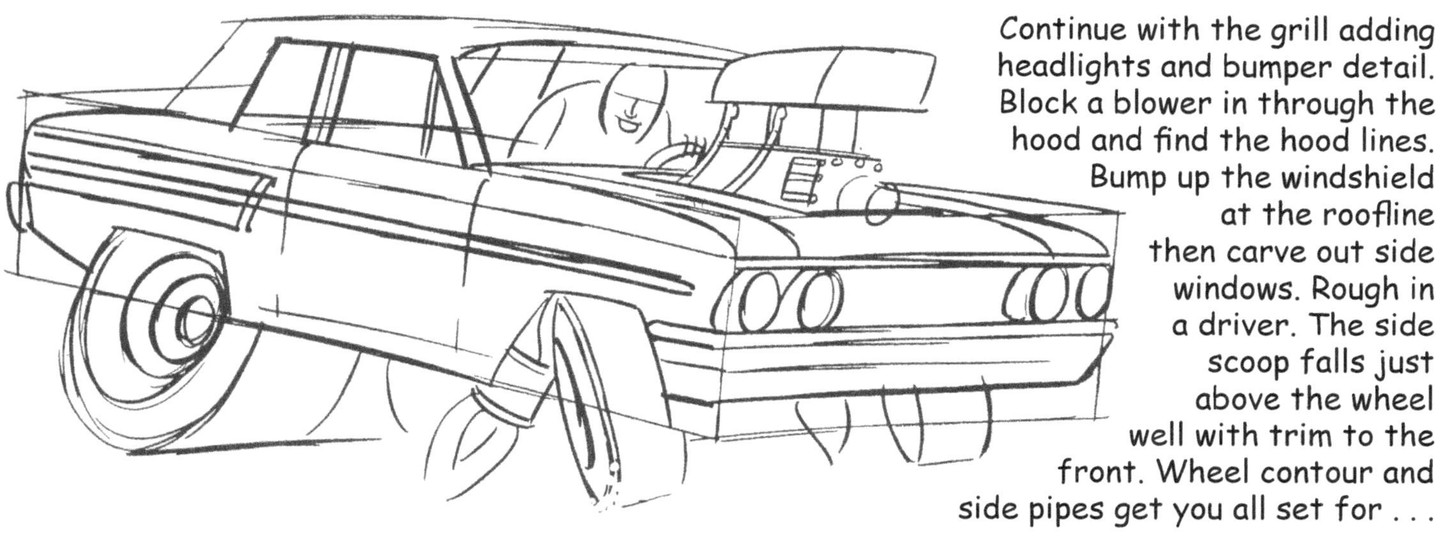

Continue with the grill adding headlights and bumper detail. Block a blower in through the hood and find the hood lines. Bump up the windshield at the roofline then carve out side windows. Rough in a driver. The side scoop falls just above the wheel well with trim to the front. Wheel contour and side pipes get you all set for . . .

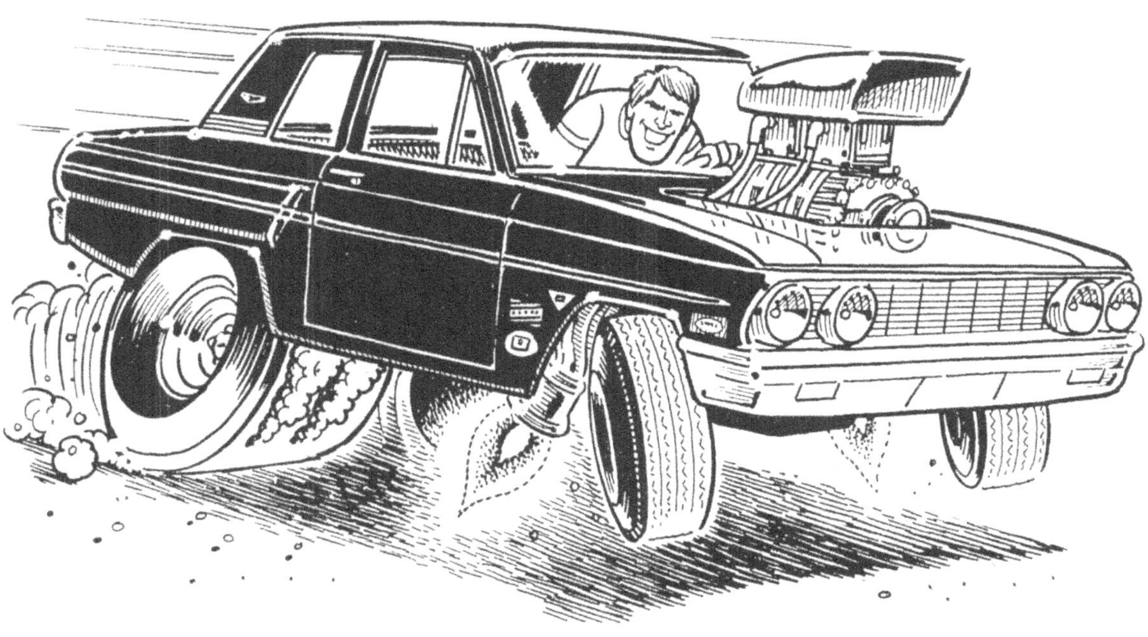

. . . Inking! Outline everything with a fairly thick line then add details with a finer line. Work out the grill in pencil then ink it with the help of a ruler. Solid blacks can help give the illusion of a **glossy** paint job. A shadow and tire lighting add some flash!

Oldsmobile sure put one together in 1970 with the 455-ci **W30 4-4-2**. These boxes help you get started. Divide up the front end as I've shown and bend the hood down. Cut out the wheel wells and rough in a set of small tires up front and biggies in back. Carve the fender up in back.

Divide the grill into two sections then box in the headlights. Loosely work out the bumper indicating lights, cutouts, and license plate. Hood scoops are next followed by the windshield and side windows. Add a driver then bump up the rear fender and lay in the side stripe. Pipes and tire detail help.

Make sure everything's right then crank up your pen and carefully ink it in bringing it to life with lots of noise, smoke, and some flame! Shadow and lighting push things along. Well-placed lights and darks give your drawing a real **professional** look.

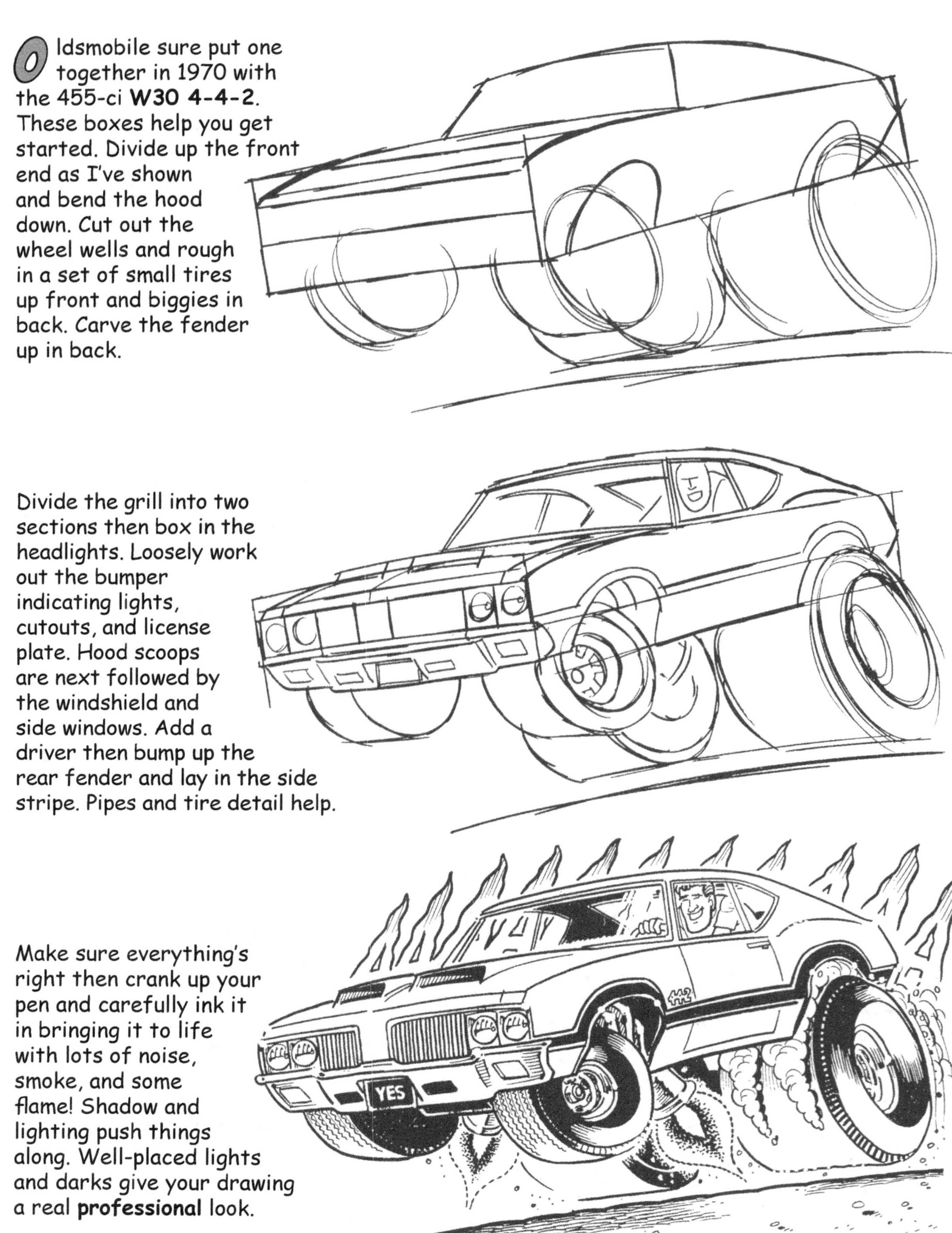

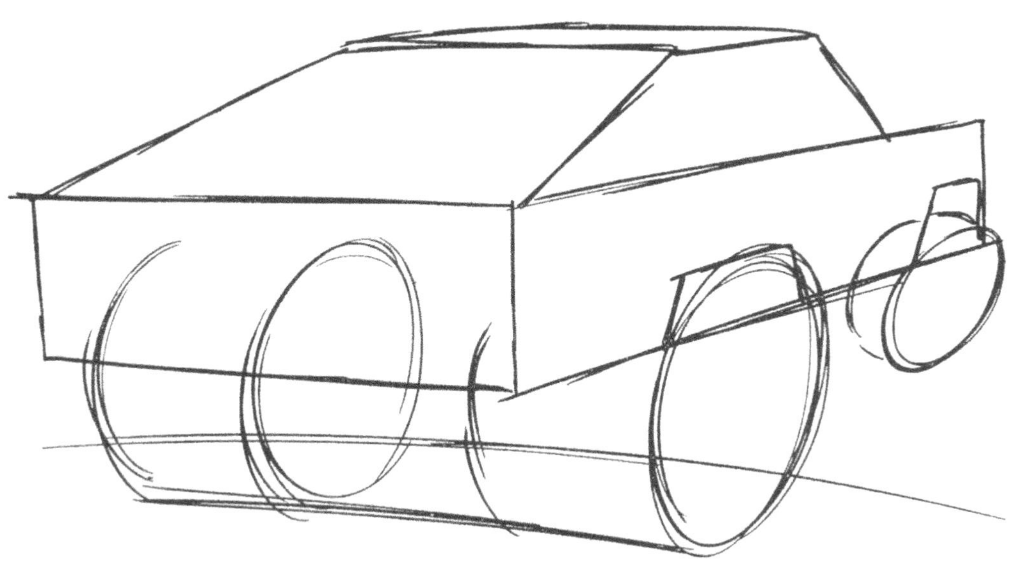

ere's one you've probably seen prowling the streets of your hometown: a '70 **Nova** with a 327-ci motor! Once again, copy these boxes as closely as you can. Rough in some wheel wells then loosely add some fat street slicks in back and a much calmer set of tread up front. Don't be afraid to use guide lines or draw right through things; it really helps!

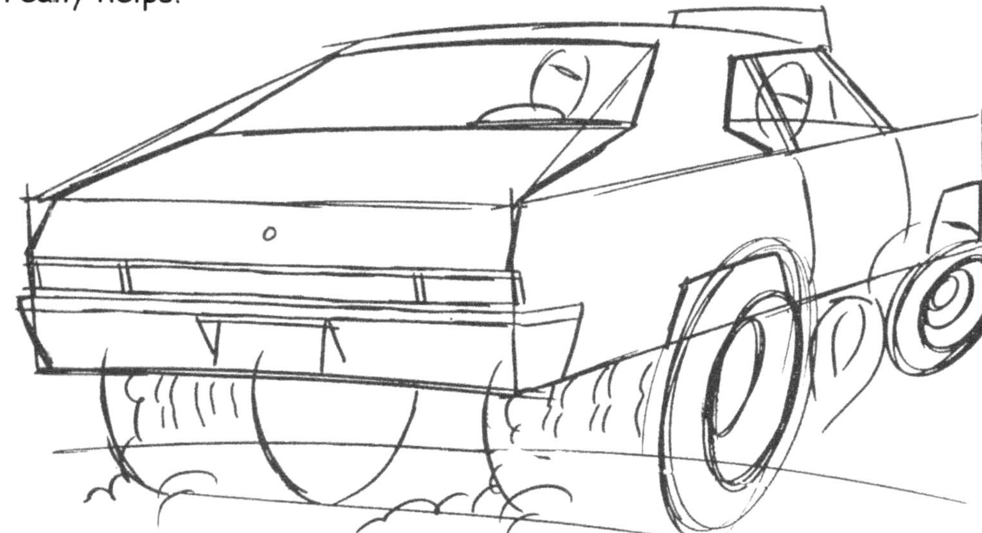

Next thing you're gonna' do is notch the rear roofline and carve out the back trunk line. Note how the rear section divides into the bumper and taillight areas. Get the basics then add detail. Rough in the side windows, dashboard, occupants, and blower assembly. Detail the tires adding some smoke an' cinders then **light a fire** in the headers!

Go over everything one more time adding rear bumper and taillight details as well as wheelie bars. Pencil in other details such as a roll cage and body graphics before inking with your favorite ball-point or felt-tip pen. Be neat!

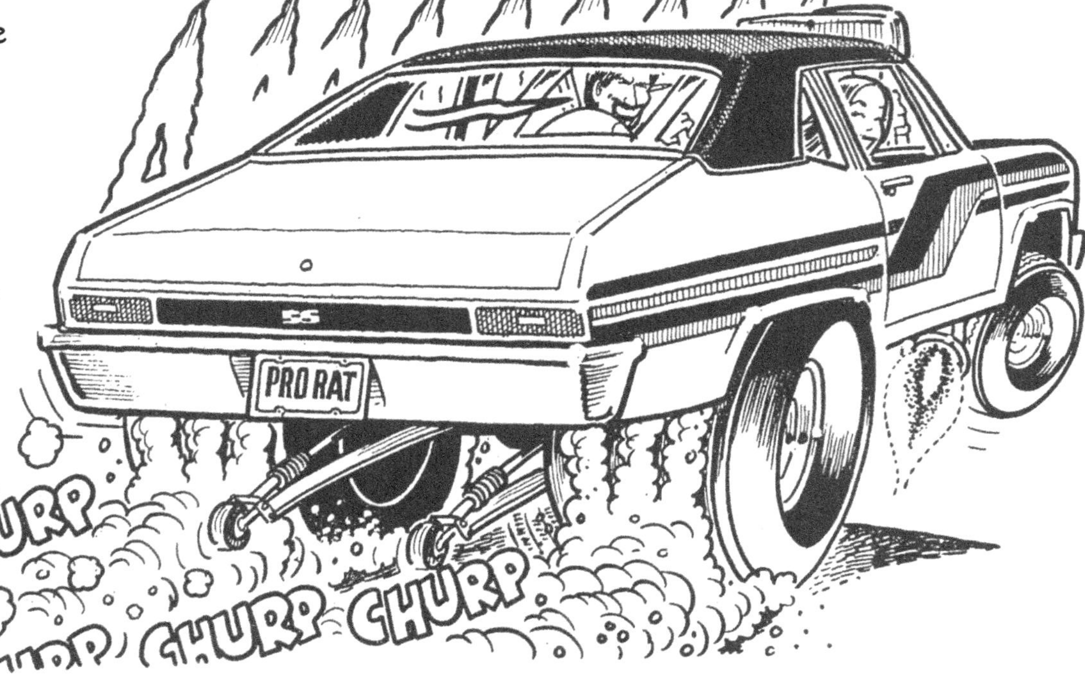

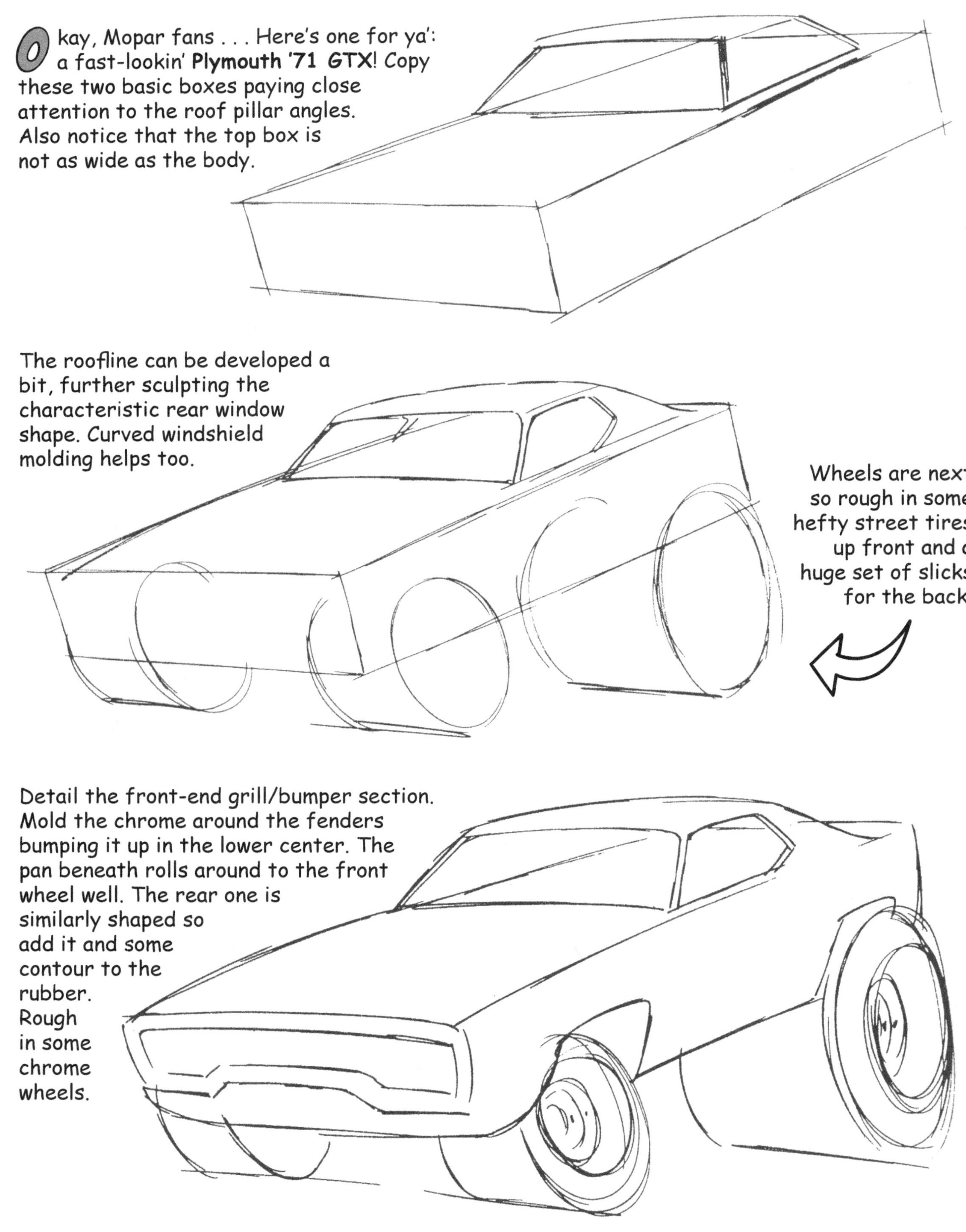

Okay, Mopar fans . . . Here's one for ya': a fast-lookin' **Plymouth '71 GTX!** Copy these two basic boxes paying close attention to the roof pillar angles. Also notice that the top box is not as wide as the body.

The roofline can be developed a bit, further sculpting the characteristic rear window shape. Curved windshield molding helps too.

Wheels are next so rough in some hefty street tires up front and a huge set of slicks for the back.

Detail the front-end grill/bumper section. Mold the chrome around the fenders bumping it up in the lower center. The pan beneath rolls around to the front wheel well. The rear one is similarly shaped so add it and some contour to the rubber. Rough in some chrome wheels.

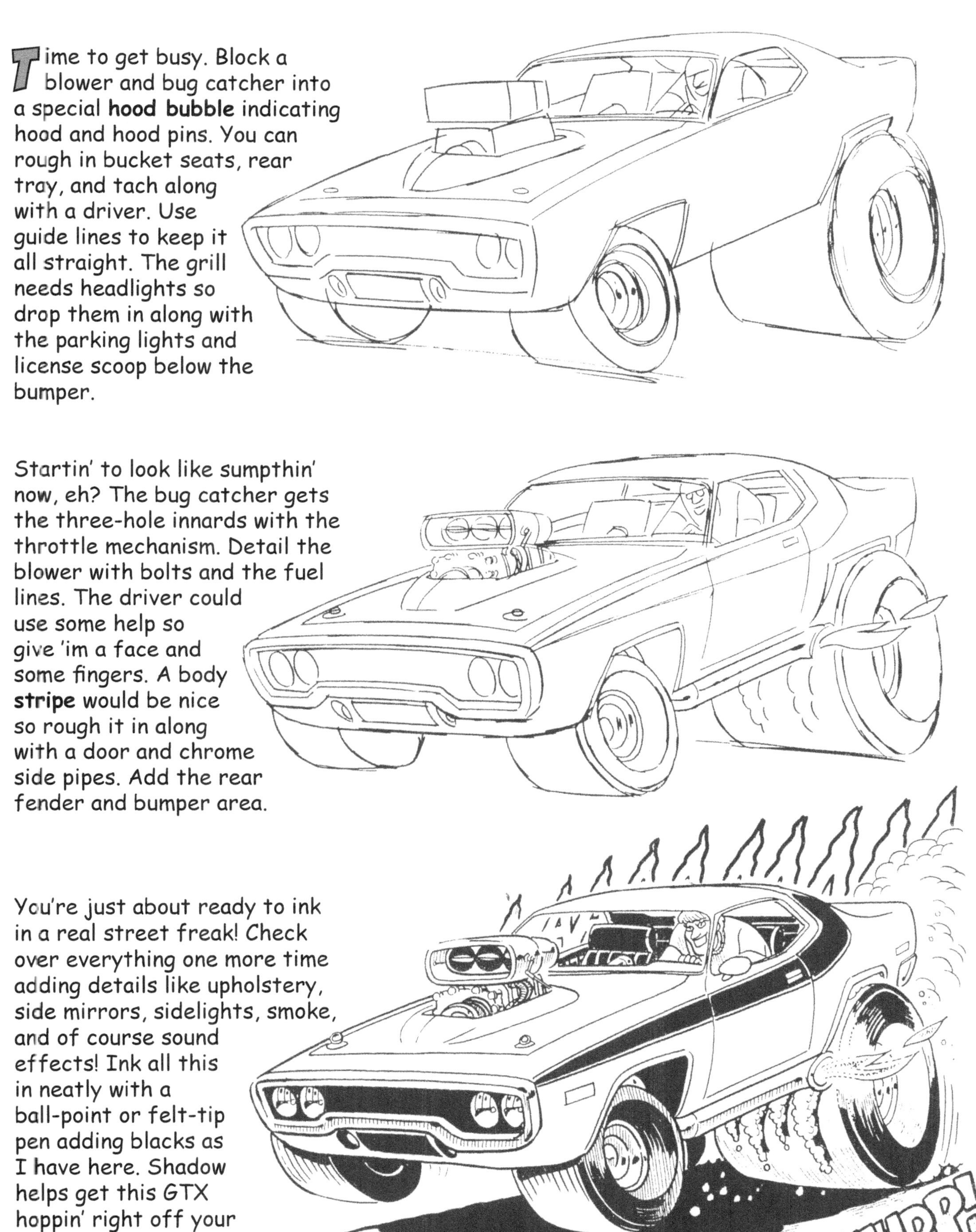

Time to get busy. Block a blower and bug catcher into a special **hood bubble** indicating hood and hood pins. You can rough in bucket seats, rear tray, and tach along with a driver. Use guide lines to keep it all straight. The grill needs headlights so drop them in along with the parking lights and license scoop below the bumper.

Startin' to look like sumphin' now, eh? The bug catcher gets the three-hole innards with the throttle mechanism. Detail the blower with bolts and the fuel lines. The driver could use some help so give 'im a face and some fingers. A body **stripe** would be nice so rough it in along with a door and chrome side pipes. Add the rear fender and bumper area.

You're just about ready to ink in a real street freak! Check over everything one more time adding details like upholstery, side mirrors, sidelights, smoke, and of course sound effects! Ink all this in neatly with a ball-point or felt-tip pen adding blacks as I have here. Shadow helps get this GTX hoppin' right off your paper.

One of the most popular sports cars around today is the Datsun **280ZX**. You can get one started with the two boxes shown here. Curve the body box a bit . . .

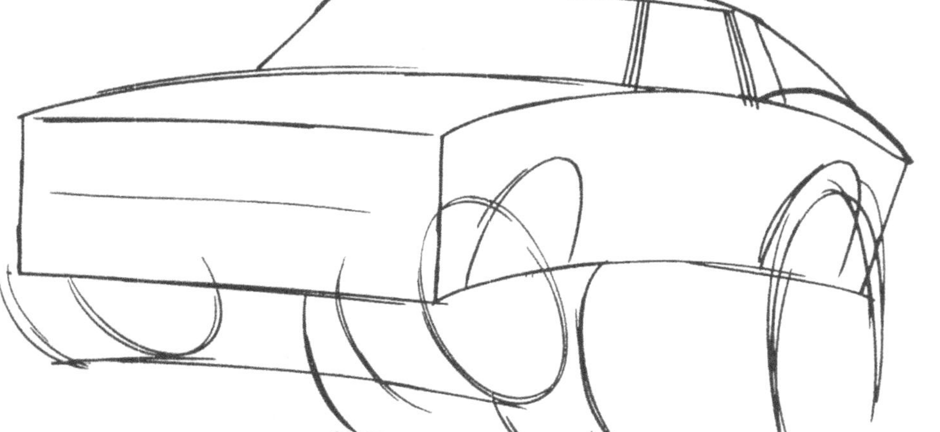

. . . Then add some side posts to the roofline and add the bump in the rear fender. Loosely rough in a set of street tires up front with a **giant** set of racing slicks out back. Then lay in a couple of wheel wells to match.

Rough in the headlight openings and headlights. Note that they line up with the hood lines. Add a bumper with parking lights using a few guide lines to help keep everything even. Key the side body line off that. Carve out a grill cavity and pan below. Add some contour to the wheels.

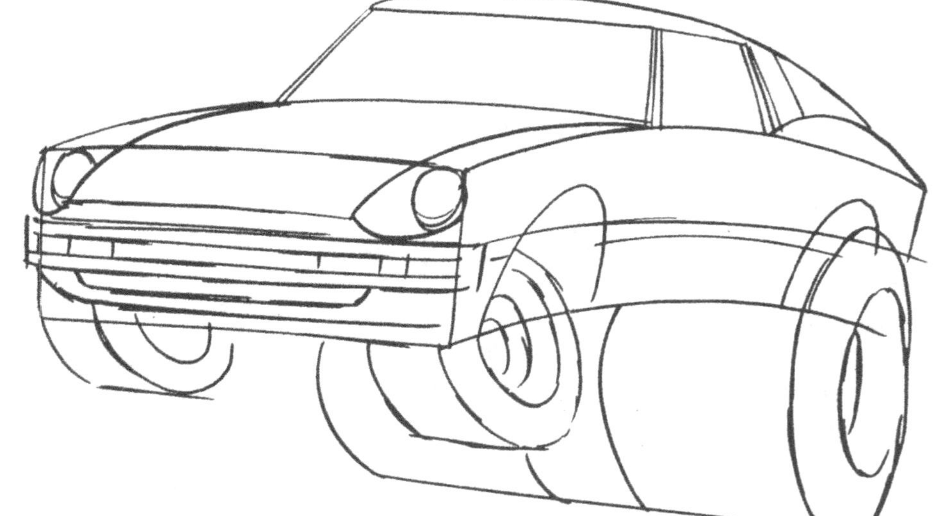

Clean up the front end a bit adding a hood bump and a bit of **attitude** to the headlights. Inside, rough in some seats and a driver. Outside, drop some door lines from the roof pillars then add some wheel well flares. The back bumper keys off the side body line.

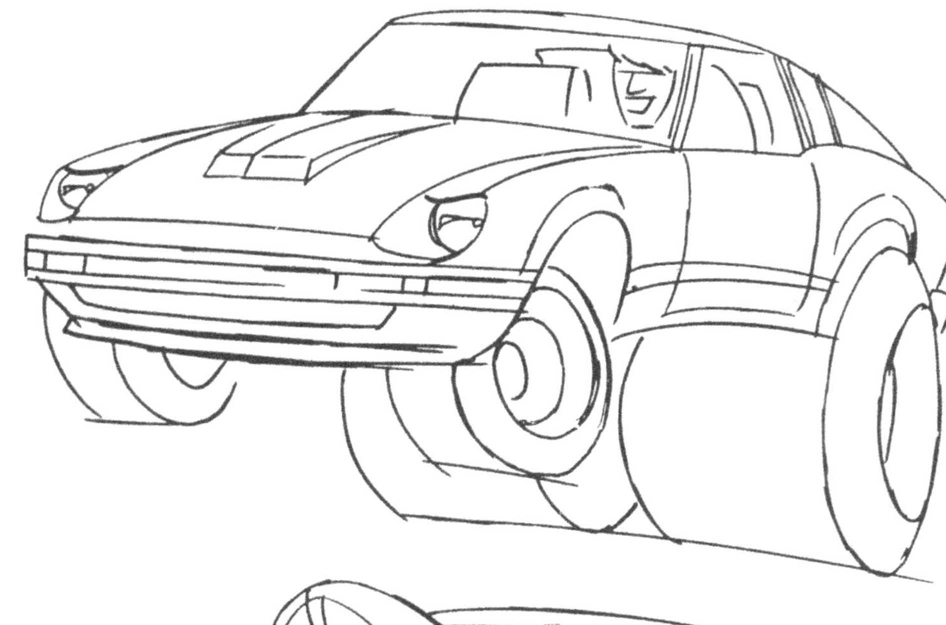

Now let's pop a big blower through the hood with a sculptured scoop on top. Detail the interior a bit more then add a giant set of pipes and flames. Smoke the rear tires and rough in a set of special rims. Give everything a final check.

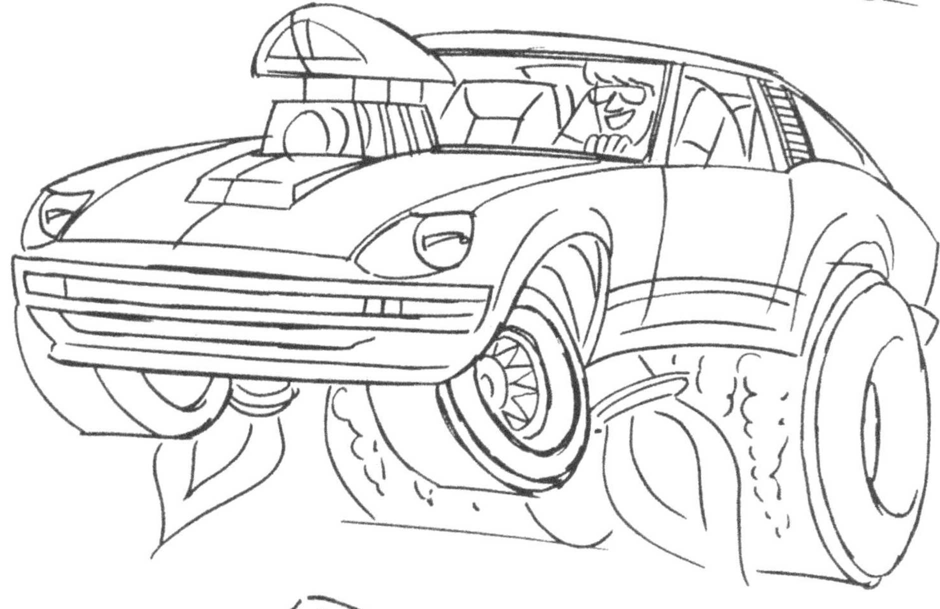

Give the blower assembly some final details. Add a side mirror and a flame job and you're all set for ink. Outline everything first, then show your special effects by finally adding some solid black. **Be neat!**

 more recent version of the ZX is the **300ZX**. Let's try one comin' right at you with two foreshortened boxes. Loosely rough in the street tread up front and huge slicks in the rear. Add wheel wells and flares along with a body line falling at the midpoint and wrapping around to the side.

Next, get busy shaping the hood down to the body line and roughing in the headlight areas. The bumper drops below that same body line followed by an opening and spoiler below it. Cut the hood for the blower and add an interior with a driver. Side mirrors, molding, oil pan, and pipes help to finish 'er.

Check over all you've got once more detailing things like blower assembly, headlights, and grill opening. A good photo **always** makes this step much easier. When you're satisfied, ink it all with your favorite felt-tip or ball-point pen. Then erase your pencil.

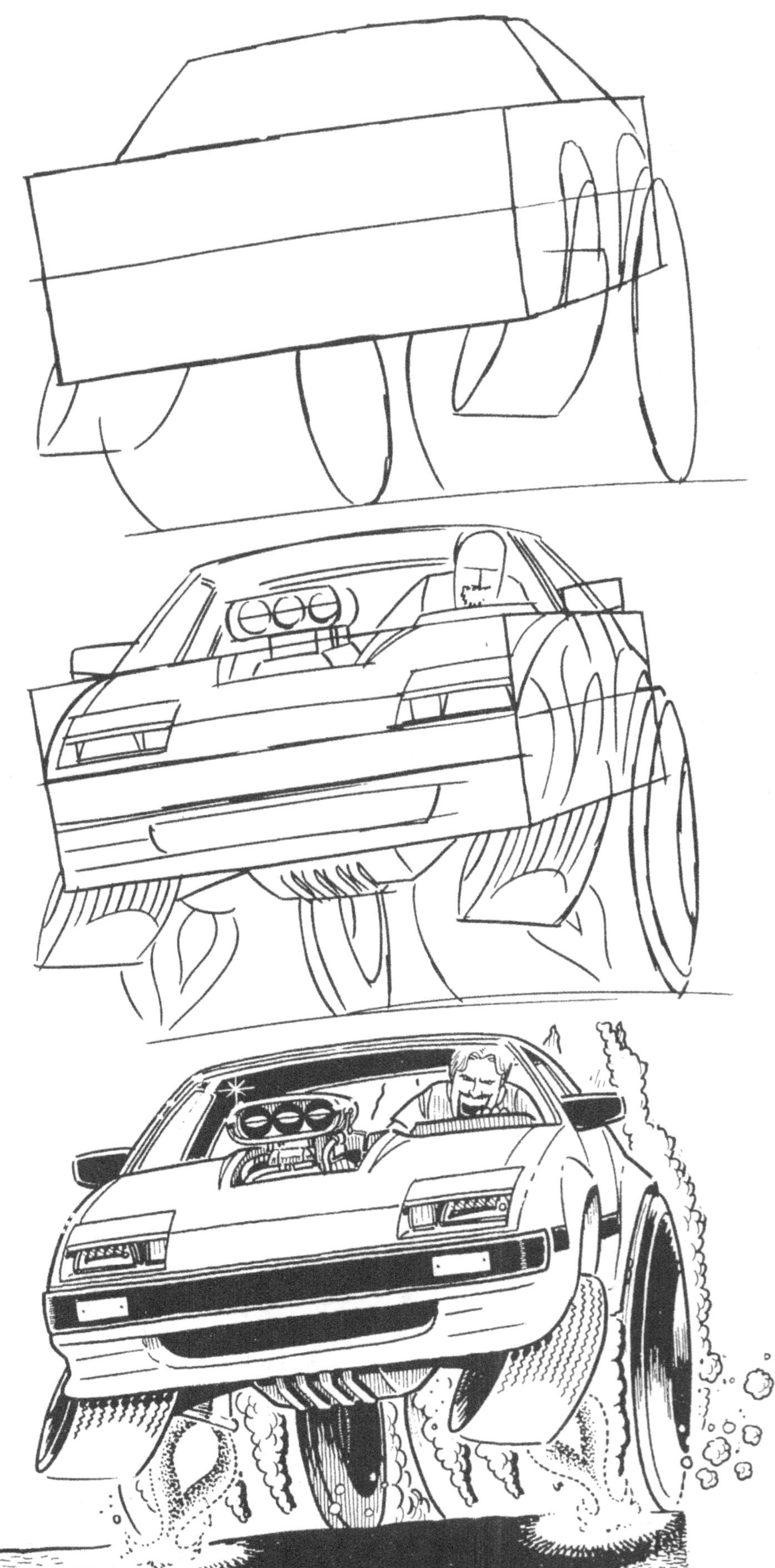

HOW TO DRAW
MERCEDES-BENZES

If you want a how-to on Mercedes-Benz you can start a **300SL-24** with these boxes. Copy them carefully. Lay in a wraparound body line then a set of tires. Rough in the hood line and front tilt using guide lines to keep it all true.

Once you've got the basics begin to rough in the windows adding door lines and a handle as you go. Spend some time on the grill area curving the bars and bumper lines slightly. Detail the tires a bit then add other goodies such as seats, mirrors, backlight, and bumper.

Go over everything again comparing yours to mine then drop in a driver and a full-body shadow. Ink it with a felt-tip or ball-point pen then add solid blacks as shown. A thick outline with finer lines for details will give your drawing a real pro look. Go magic fingers!

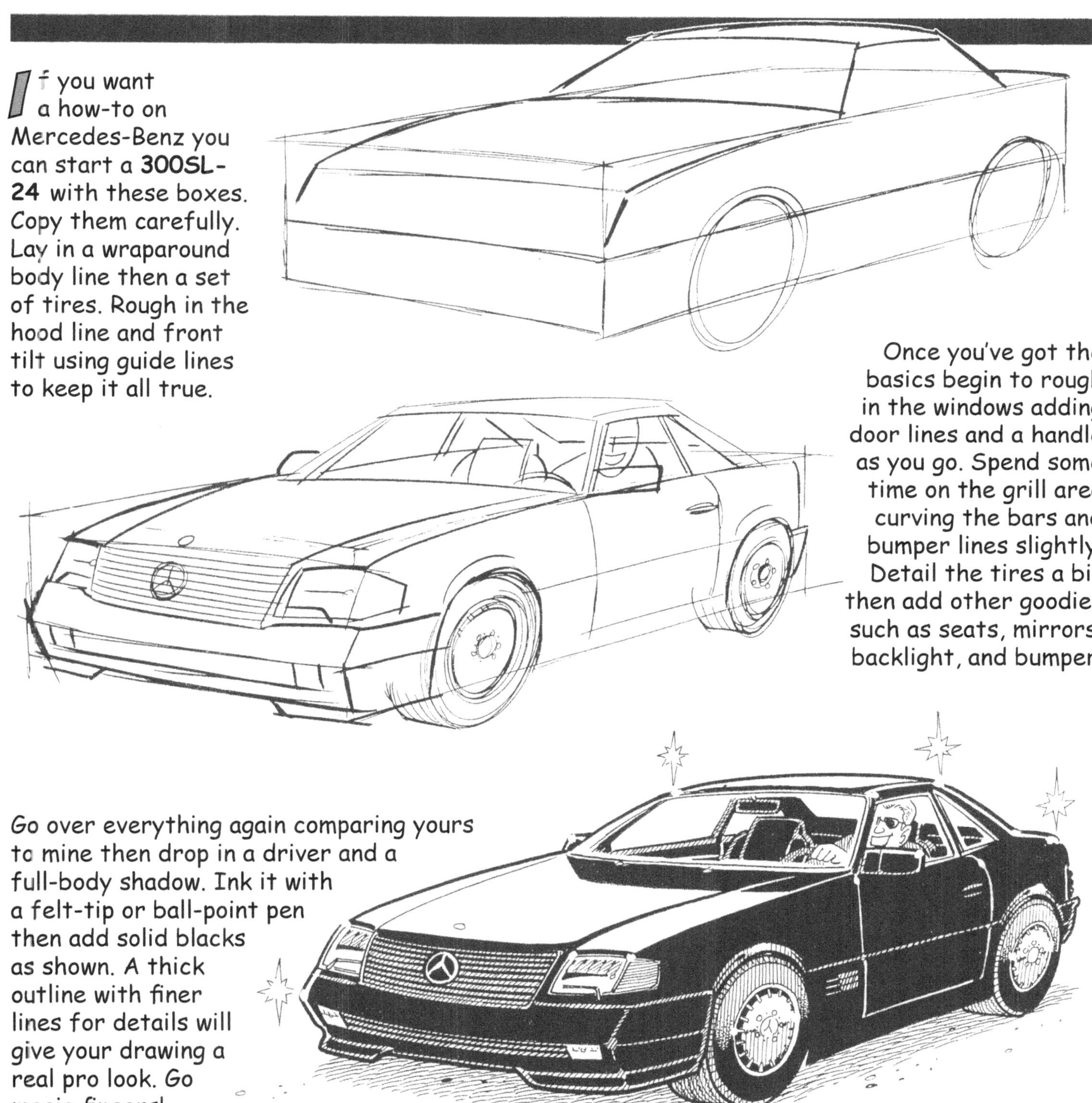

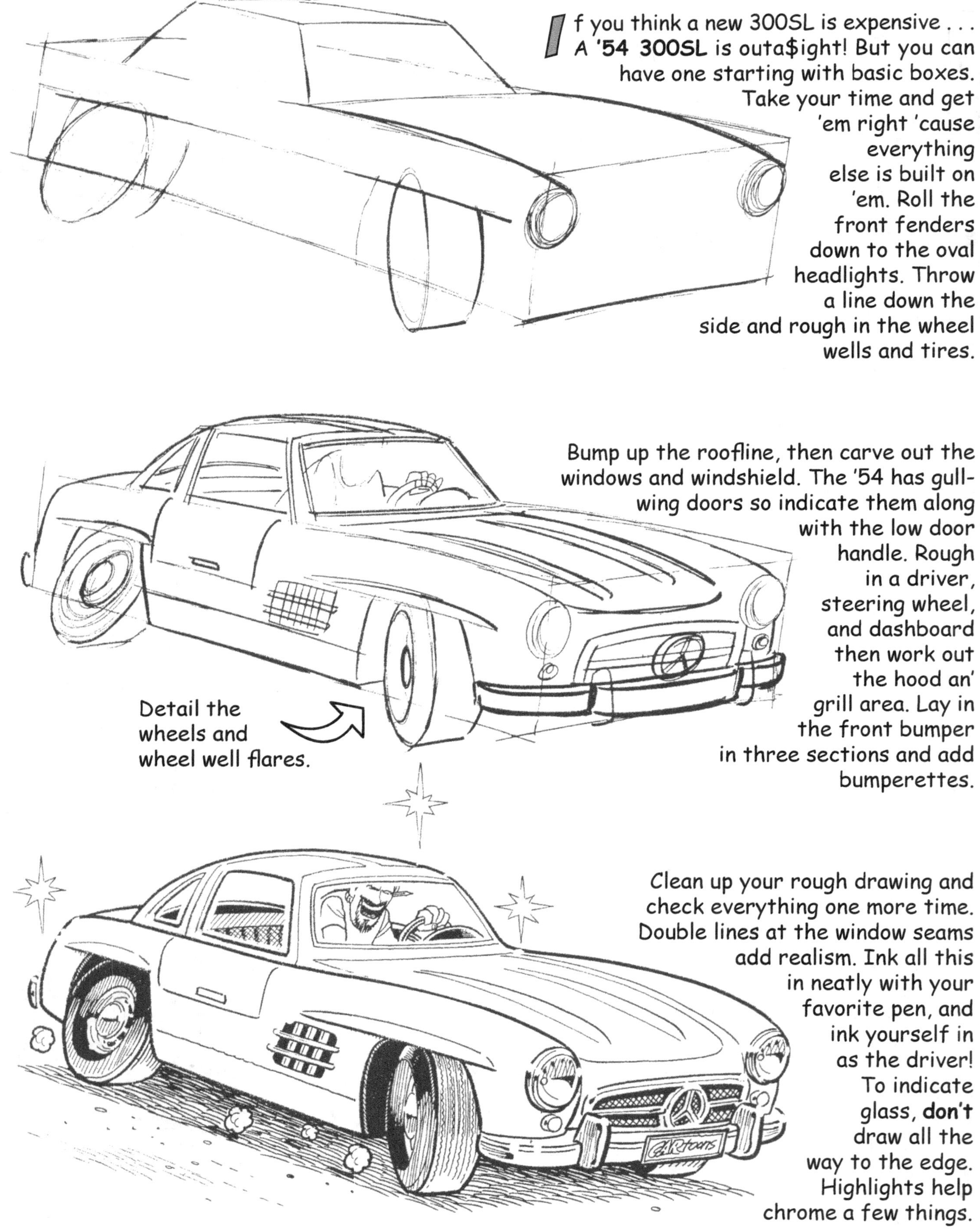

If you think a new 300SL is expensive . . . A '54 300SL is outa$ight! But you can have one starting with basic boxes. Take your time and get 'em right 'cause everything else is built on 'em. Roll the front fenders down to the oval headlights. Throw a line down the side and rough in the wheel wells and tires.

Bump up the roofline, then carve out the windows and windshield. The '54 has gull-wing doors so indicate them along with the low door handle. Rough in a driver, steering wheel, and dashboard then work out the hood an' grill area. Lay in the front bumper in three sections and add bumperettes.

Detail the wheels and wheel well flares.

Clean up your rough drawing and check everything one more time. Double lines at the window seams add realism. Ink all this in neatly with your favorite pen, and ink yourself in as the driver! To indicate glass, don't draw all the way to the edge. Highlights help chrome a few things.

CARtoons

HOW TO DRAW
LAMBORGHINIS

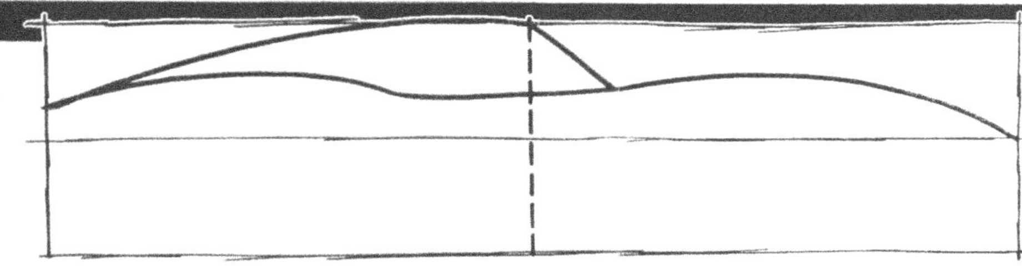

Here's the place to start: a '72 **Muira SV** in profile. Lay out the box as shown here dividing it into four equal parts. Graduate the roofline up to the midpoint and add the fender line below it.

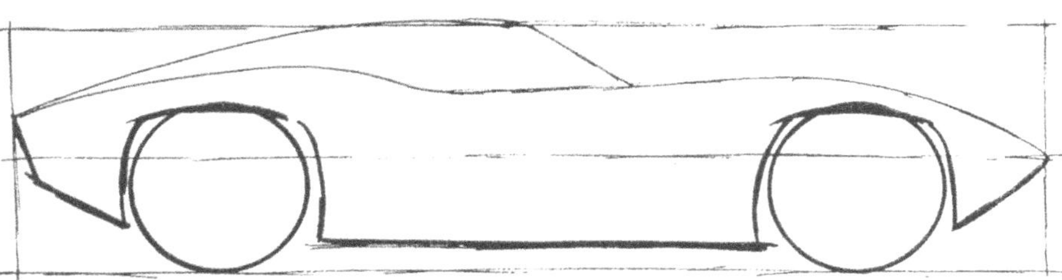

Next, rough in some wheel wells and tires. A compass or circular object helps here. Indicate the bottom of the body curving the front and back pans upward. Note how they hit the centerline.

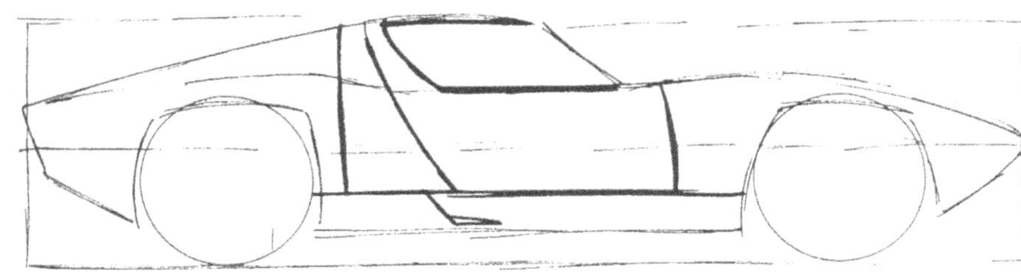

Carve out the side window and add some door/body lines carefully getting the curves right. Rough in a **scoop** below the bottom door line keeping its angle similar to the door line.

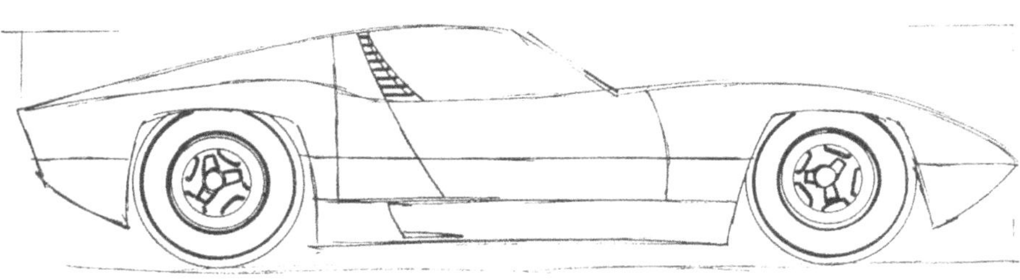

Now it's time to detail the wheels so let's add some slotted rims and knock offs. Also add the scoop area to the window frame. Check over all you've got once more . . .

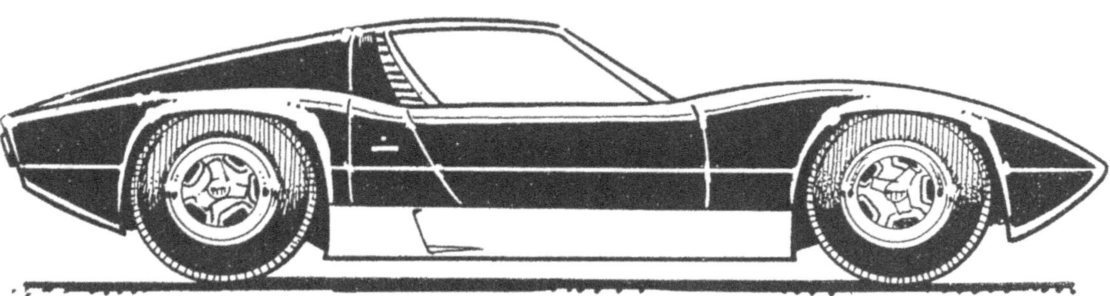

. . . 'Cause you're all set for inking! Use your favorite ball-point or felt-tip pen to outline all the basics then add detail. Flat-black areas finish 'er up!

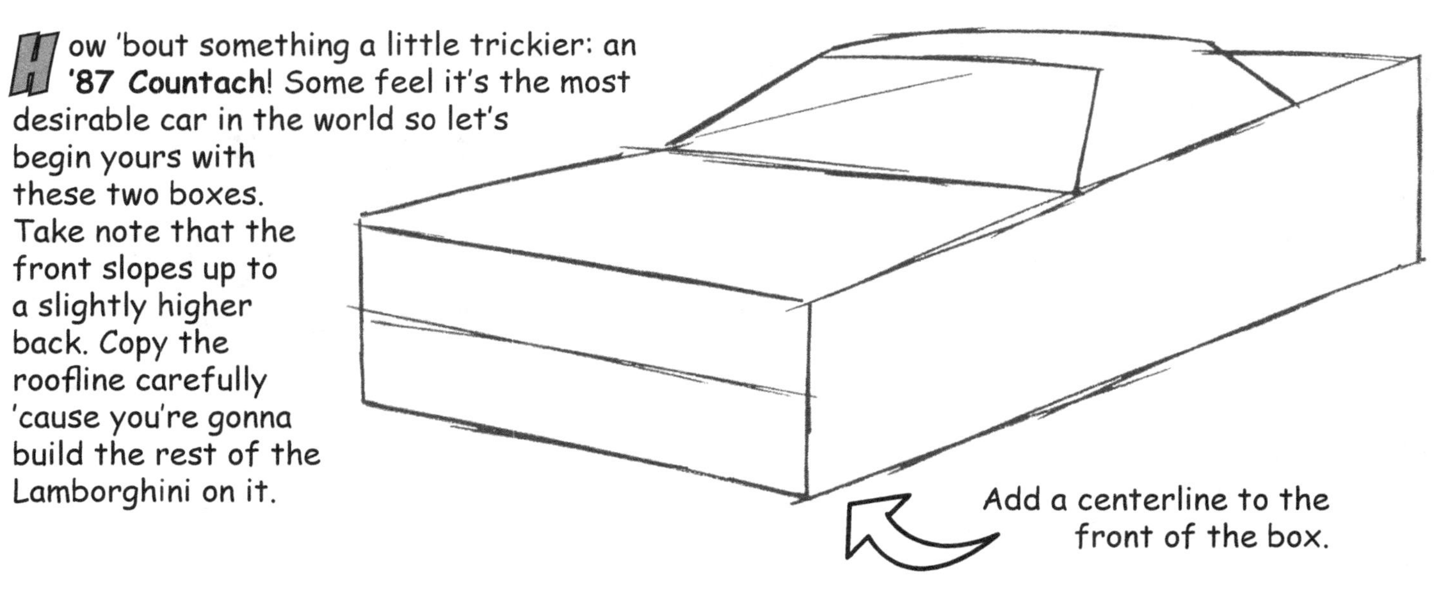

How 'bout something a little trickier: an **'87 Countach!** Some feel it's the most desirable car in the world so let's begin yours with these two boxes. Take note that the front slopes up to a slightly higher back. Copy the roofline carefully 'cause you're gonna build the rest of the Lamborghini on it.

Add a centerline to the front of the box.

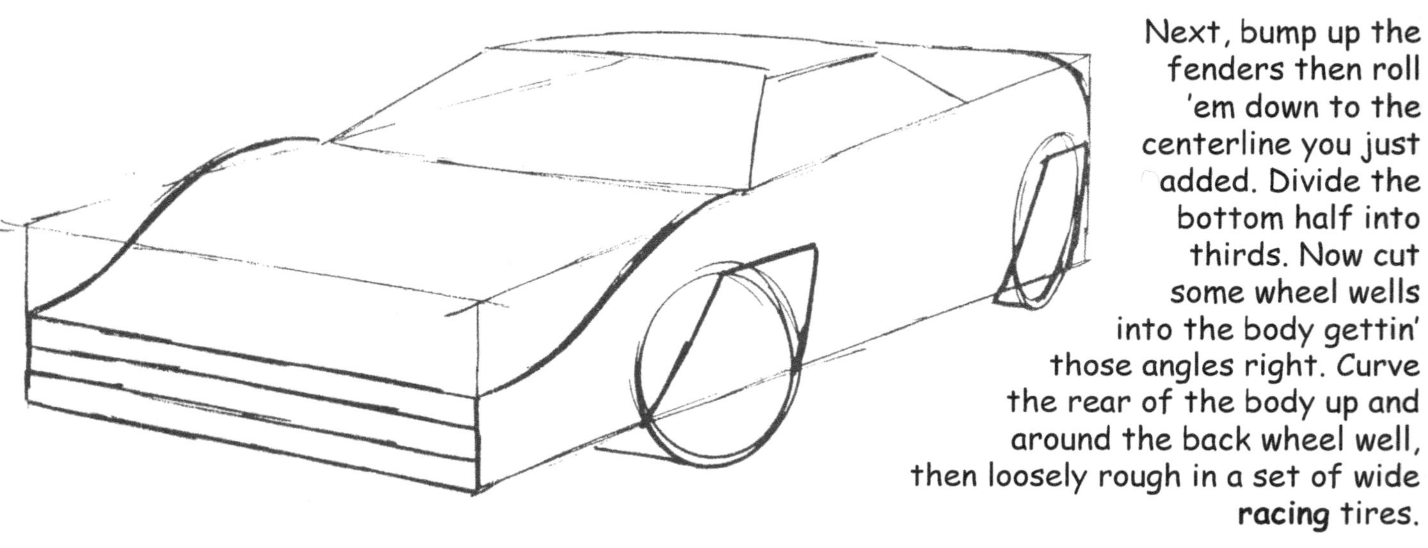

Next, bump up the fenders then roll 'em down to the centerline you just added. Divide the bottom half into thirds. Now cut some wheel wells into the body gettin' those angles right. Curve the rear of the body up and around the back wheel well, then loosely rough in a set of wide **racing** tires.

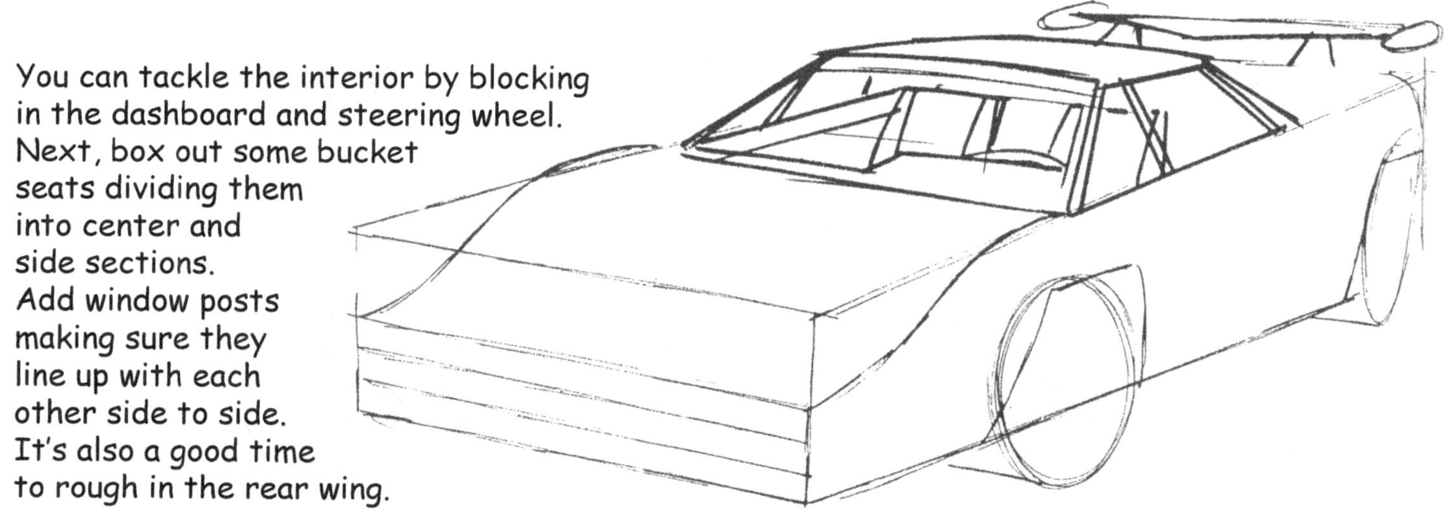

You can tackle the interior by blocking in the dashboard and steering wheel. Next, box out some bucket seats dividing them into center and side sections. Add window posts making sure they line up with each other side to side. It's also a good time to rough in the rear wing.

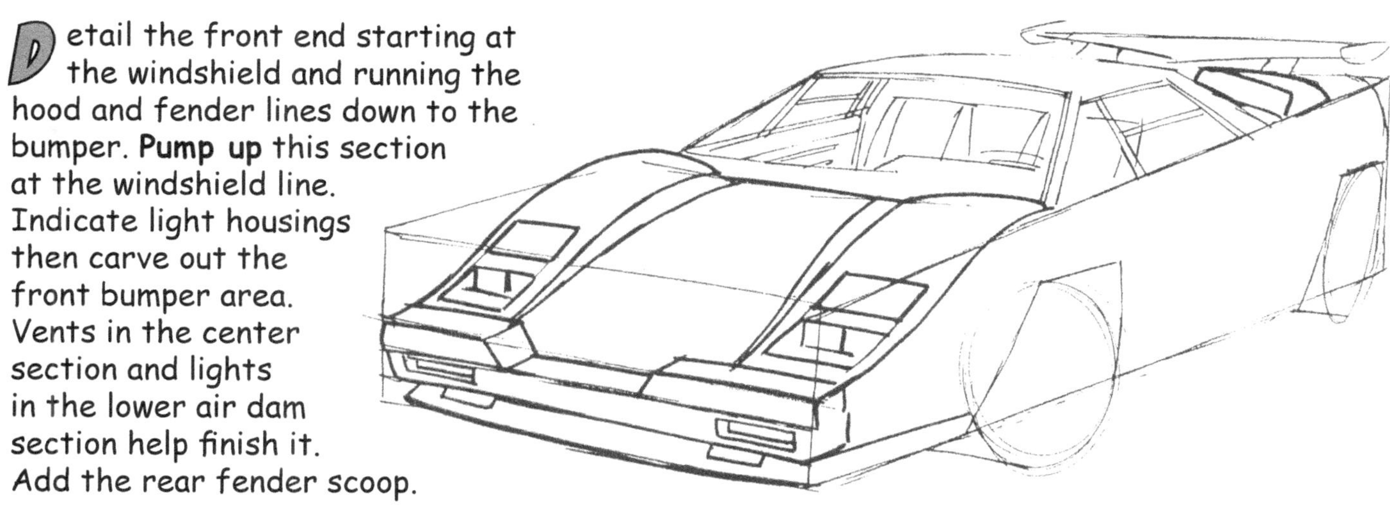

etail the front end starting at the windshield and running the hood and fender lines down to the bumper. **Pump up** this section at the windshield line. Indicate light housings then carve out the front bumper area. Vents in the center section and lights in the lower air dam section help finish it. Add the rear fender scoop.

Other details get you closer: side scoop, side lights, side mirrors, and hood logo. Carefully add flares to the wheel wells carving out a flat front edge. Take your time adding contour to the tires an' rims. Indicate tread too. Drop in a full body shadow and check everything twice.

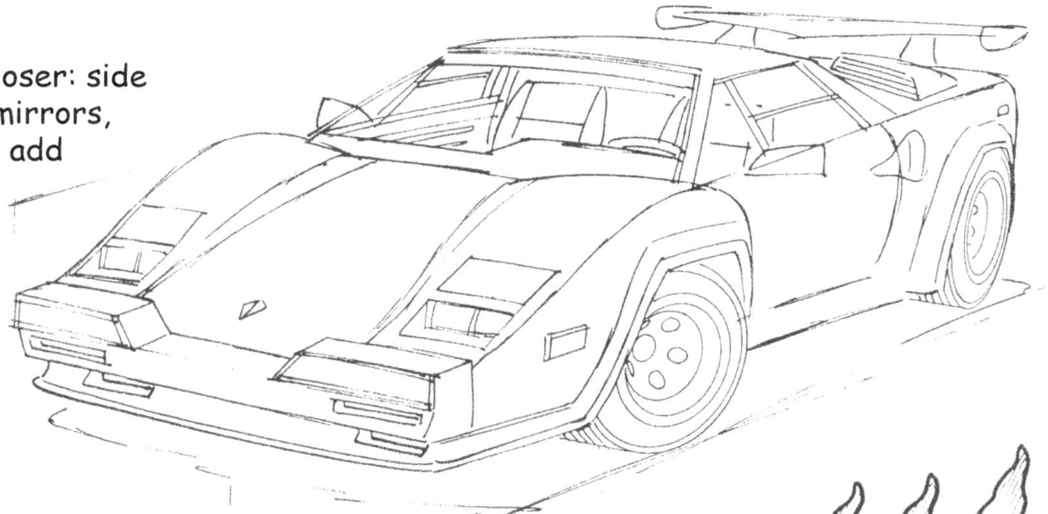

Get out your pen again and crank it up for the final step. It's important **where** you put ink but it's just as important where you **don't!** Small white areas and breaks in the line help give the illusion of gloss and shine. I add a lot of my highlights with white paint. Try it!

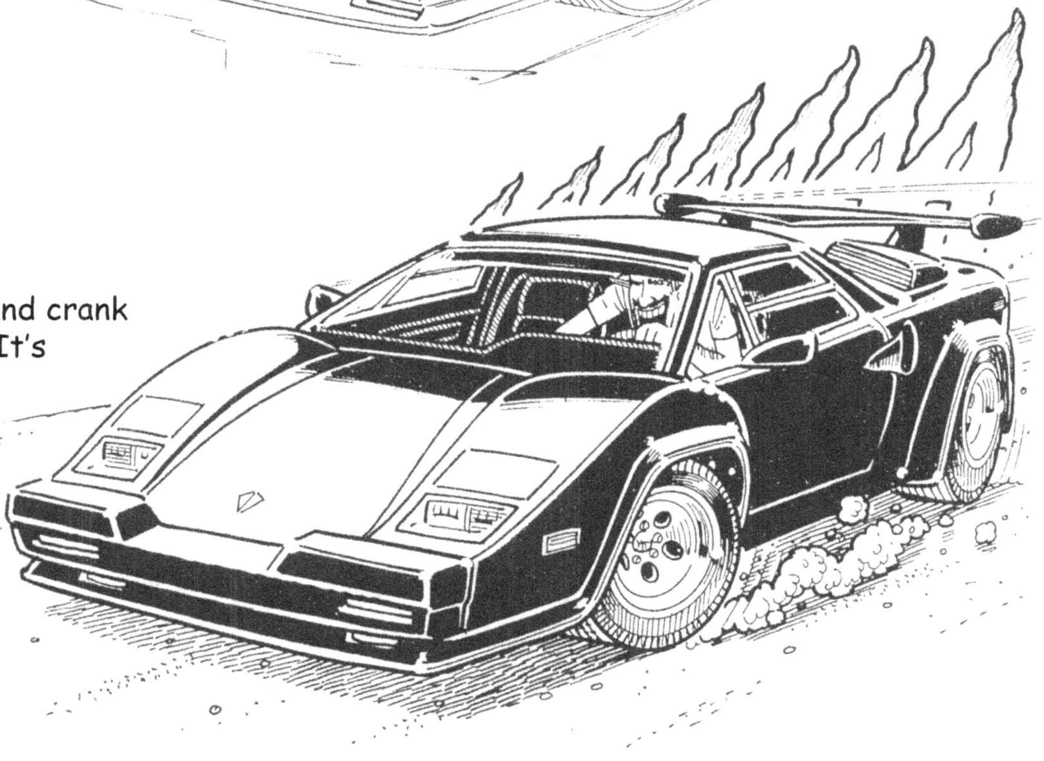

HOW TO DRAW PORSCHES

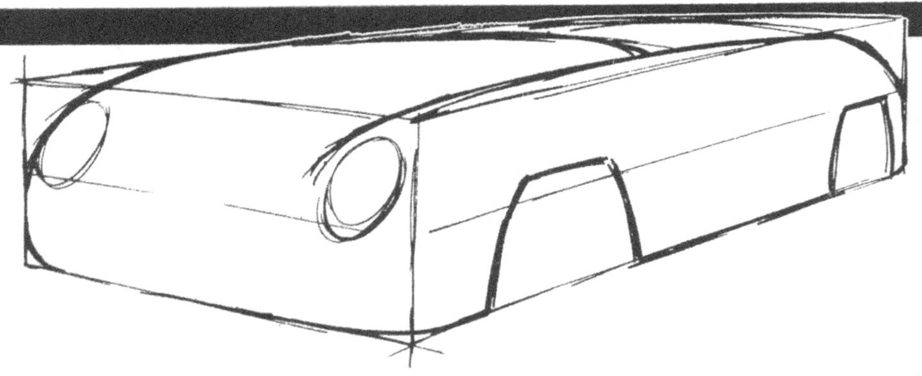

L et's start this section with the classic **1954–1959 Speedster** body style by roughing in a basic box. A centerline will help you position the headlights and wheel wells. Feel out the fenders and round the front corners.

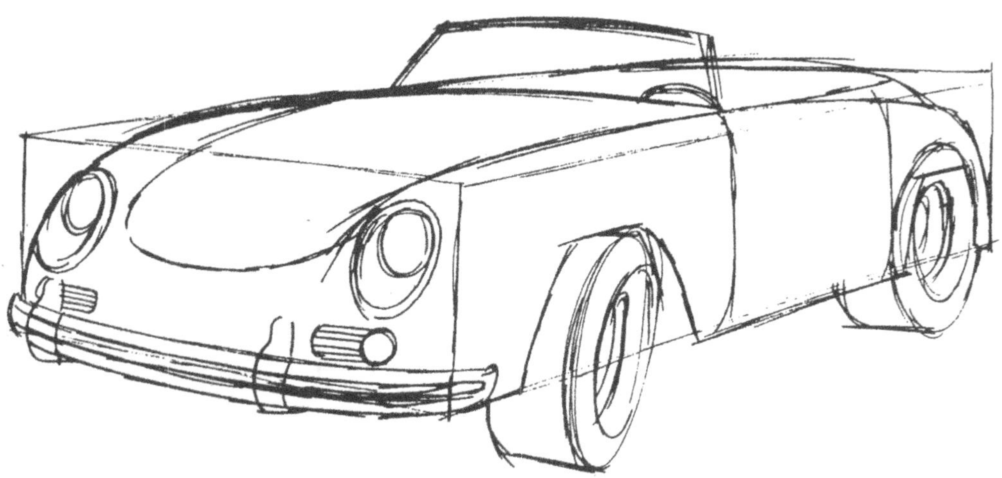

Position the windshield and front door seam about halfway back, flanked by twin mirrors. Indicate the steering wheel and convertible top cover. More detail to the headlights along with the vents and bumper improve the look. Tires improve the **stance**.

Add some body chrome, mirrors, and a hood ornament. Give a little more attention to the wheels. Take your time on the headlights indicating the glass covers. A beautiful driver lends an air of **class** as you ink all this in using a good pen. A dark body shadow gets it up and movin'!

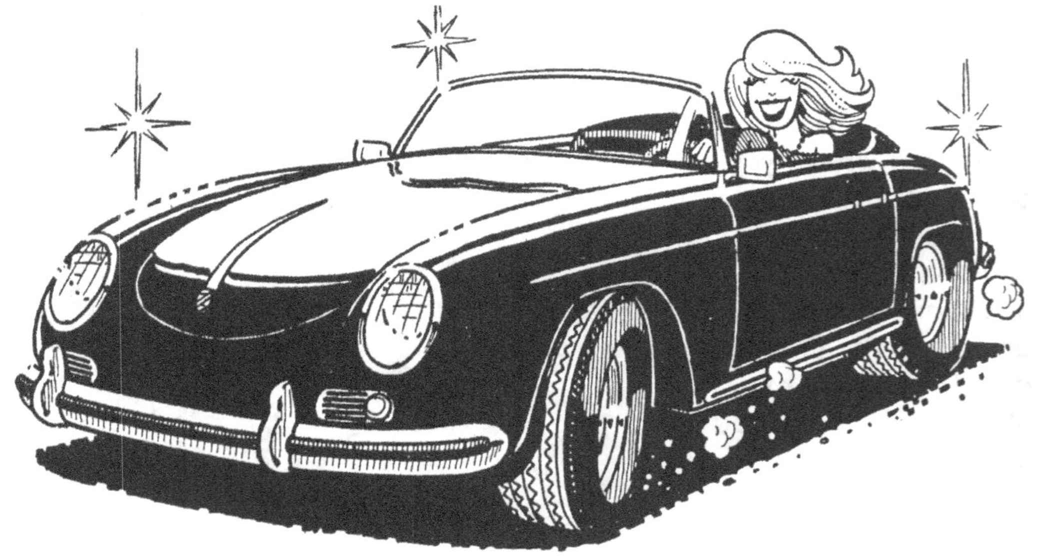

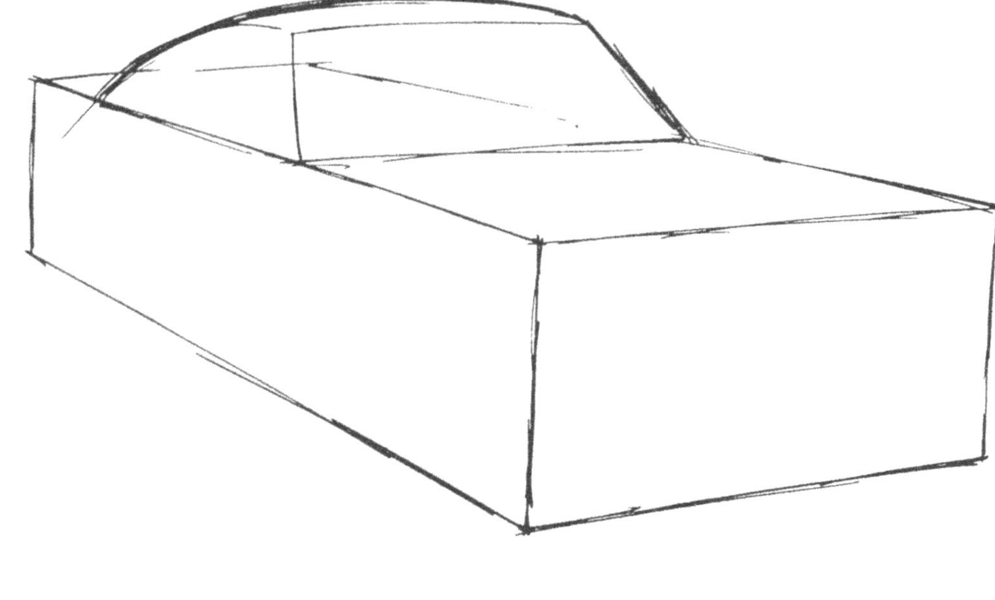

orsche dropped the Speedster "bath tub" design in 1966 and followed it with the 911 model. Later came this **930**. Start with two boxes and pay careful attention to the fastback roofline. Angle the windshield inward slightly. Make sure you get these proportions right.

Add some trim to the windshield slightly curving the top and bottom pieces. Position the headlights as I've done here. Notice how the fenders flow down to them. The top of the bumper starts midway down the front. Rough in some flared wheel wells. Then add tires in **motion**.

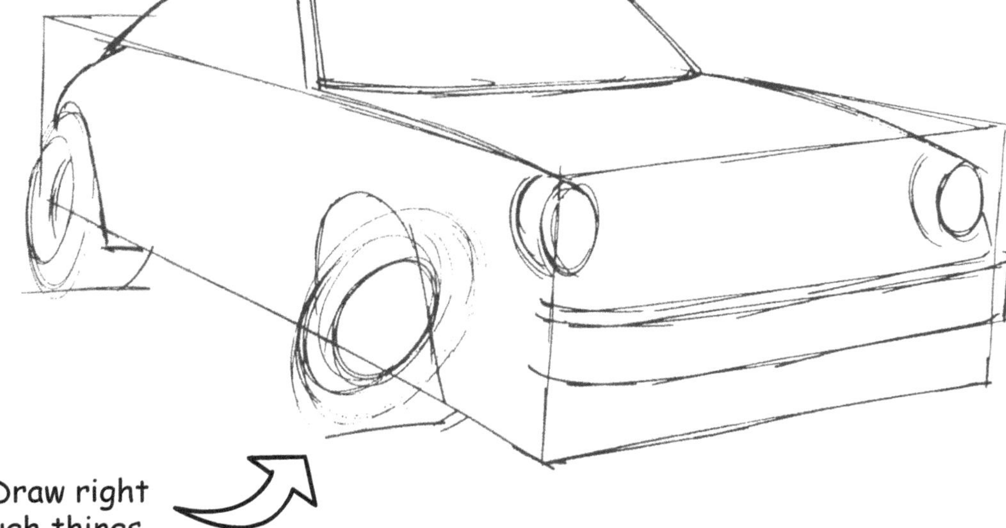

Now add some detail to the windows and rough in a dashboard an' steering wheel. Indicate a pair of mirrors along with the hood scoop. The hood seams angle down the hood to the bumper, which is a recoiling type, so you need to add a rubber shock absorber.

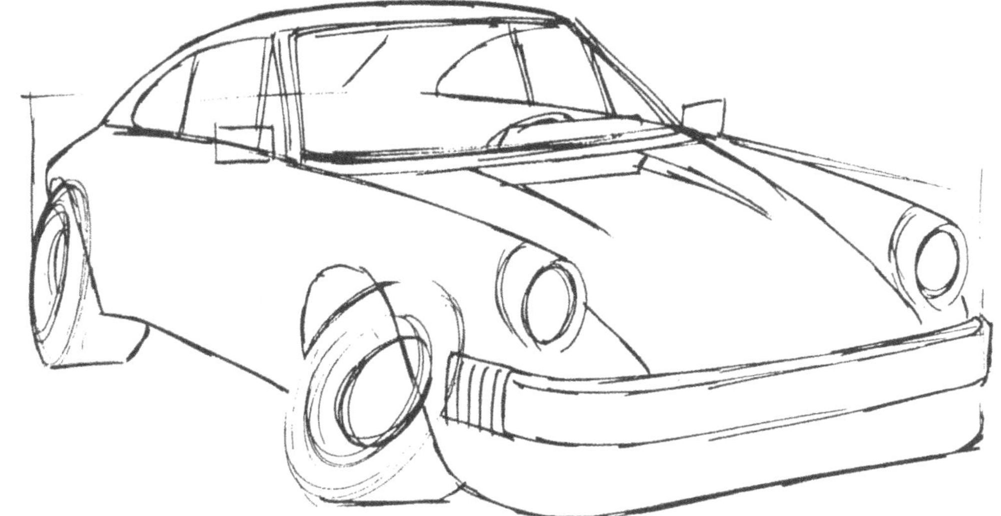

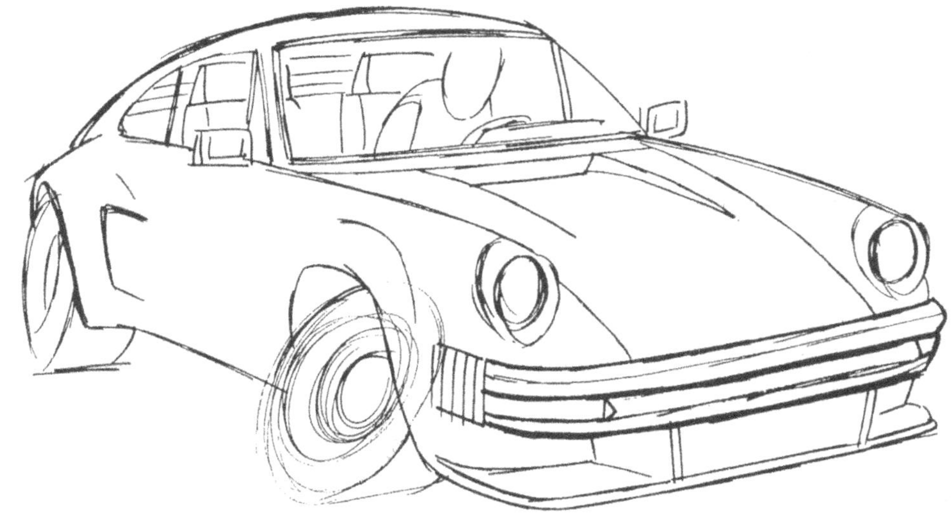

Time to start detailin' 'er out with a set of bucket seats for the interior along with a driver. The rear fender flare gets a scoop as does the front **spoiler**. Notice how the bottom flare wraps all the way around. Add front bumper detail by breakin' it down to the basics.

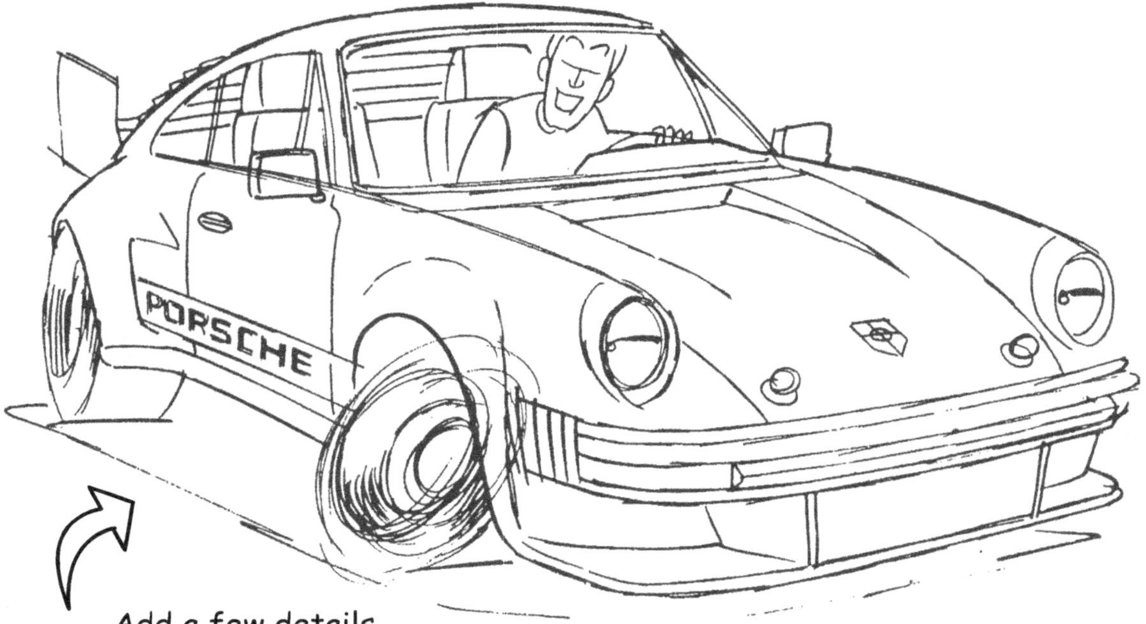

Wing and rear window vents help give your 930 a real competition look. Other details such as a Porsche stripe and hood pins push that same feeling.

Add a few details to the driver then drop in some rocker panel trim and a tight body shadow.

Go over all you've done one more time then get it ready for inking. Careful attention to wheels and chrome will help a bunch. Add darks to give the paint a **high-gloss** look. Smoke an' noise help bring 'er to life!

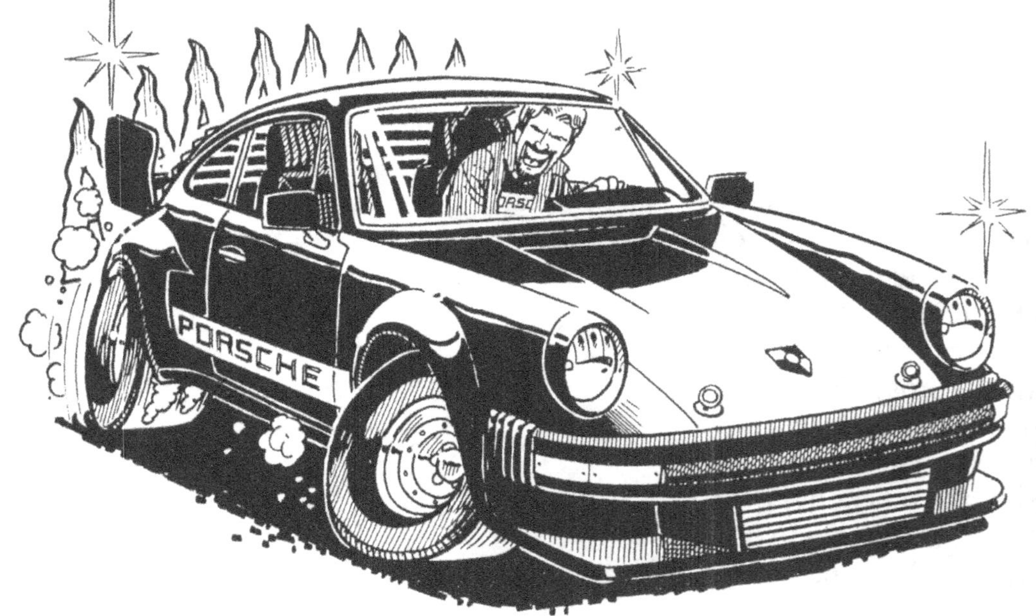

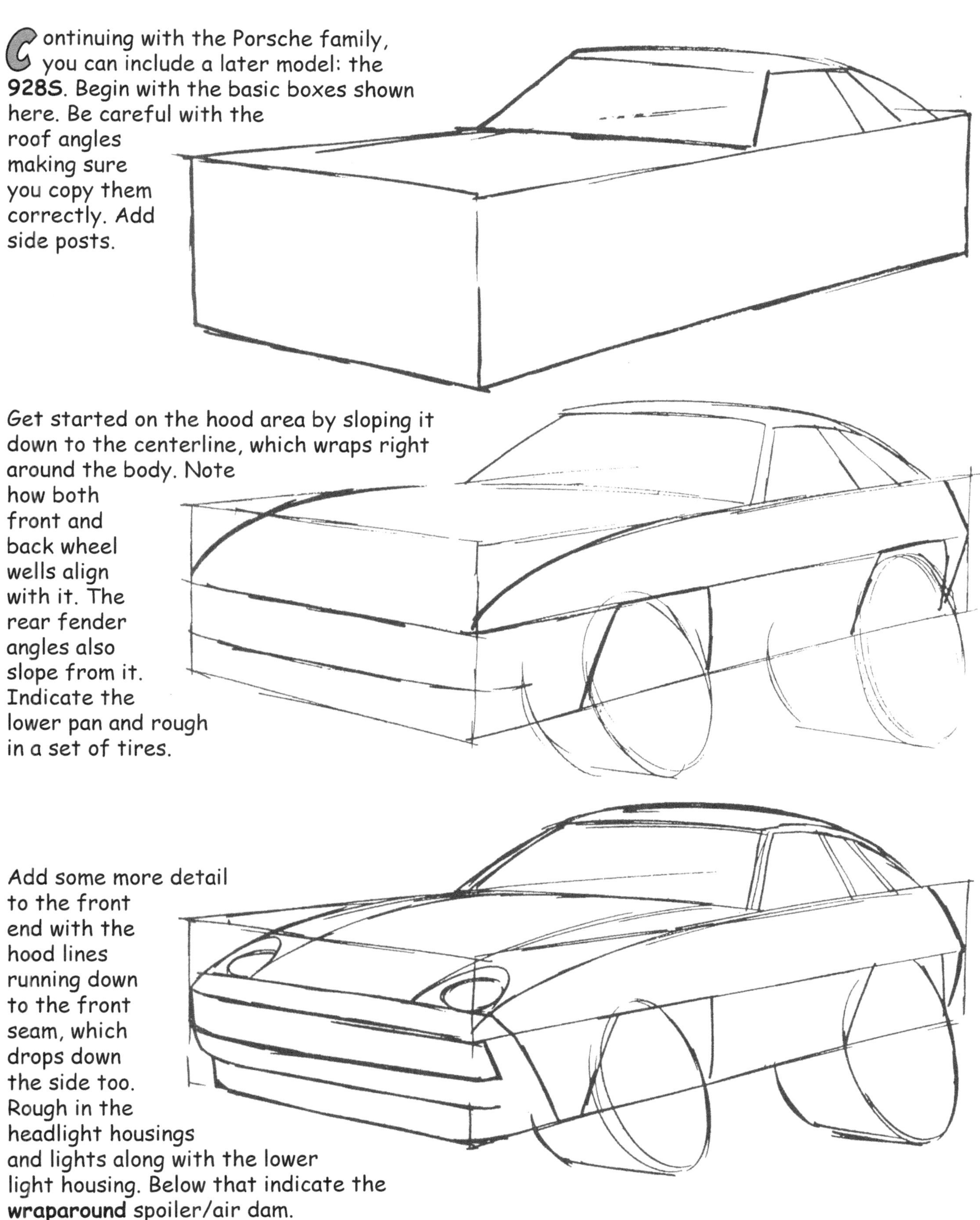

ontinuing with the Porsche family, you can include a later model: the **928S**. Begin with the basic boxes shown here. Be careful with the roof angles making sure you copy them correctly. Add side posts.

Get started on the hood area by sloping it down to the centerline, which wraps right around the body. Note how both front and back wheel wells align with it. The rear fender angles also slope from it. Indicate the lower pan and rough in a set of tires.

Add some more detail to the front end with the hood lines running down to the front seam, which drops down the side too. Rough in the headlight housings and lights along with the lower light housing. Below that indicate the **wraparound** spoiler/air dam.

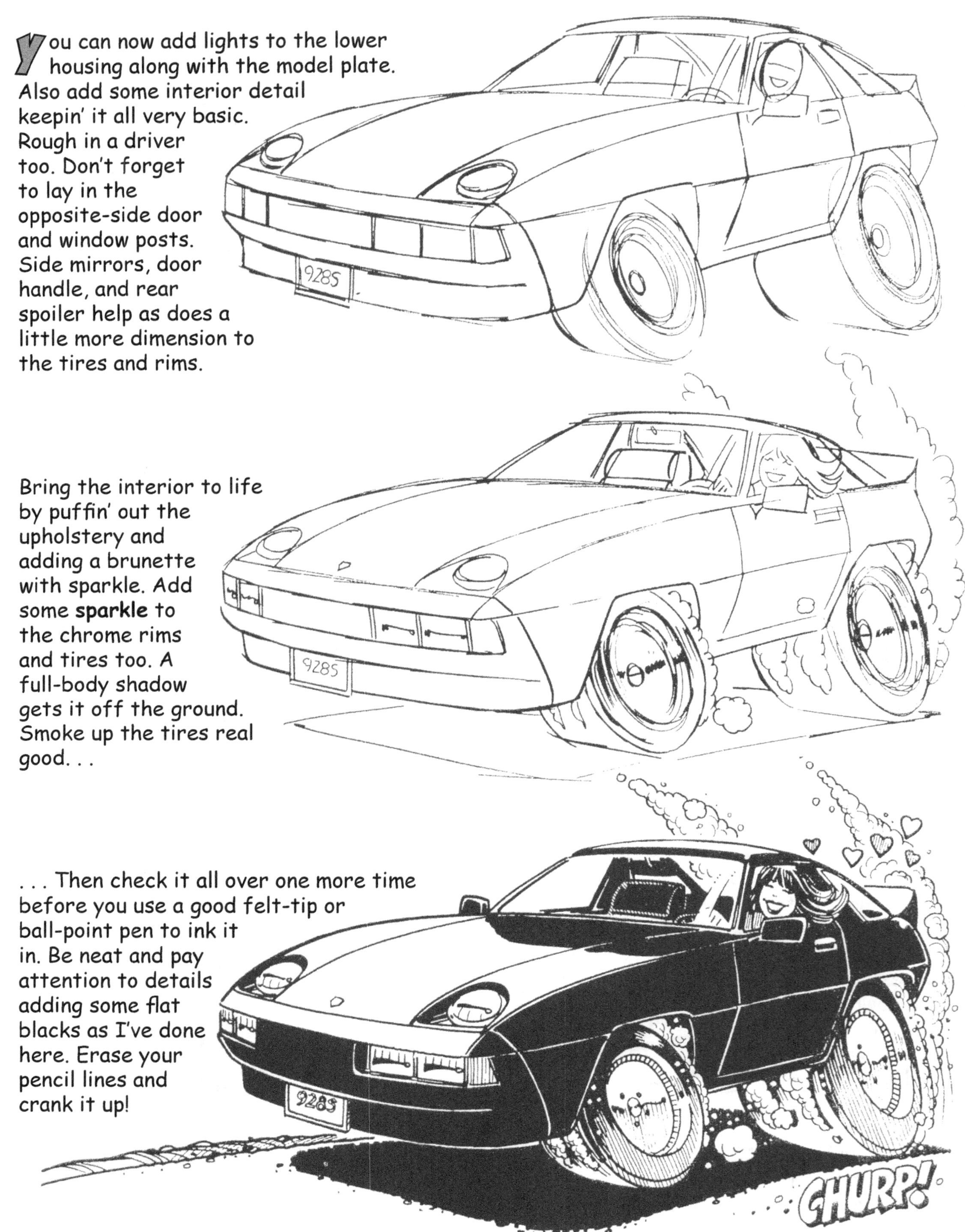

You can now add lights to the lower housing along with the model plate. Also add some interior detail keepin' it all very basic. Rough in a driver too. Don't forget to lay in the opposite-side door and window posts. Side mirrors, door handle, and rear spoiler help as does a little more dimension to the tires and rims.

Bring the interior to life by puffin' out the upholstery and adding a brunette with sparkle. Add some **sparkle** to the chrome rims and tires too. A full-body shadow gets it off the ground. Smoke up the tires real good. . .

. . . Then check it all over one more time before you use a good felt-tip or ball-point pen to ink it in. Be neat and pay attention to details adding some flat blacks as I've done here. Erase your pencil lines and crank it up!

Another family member is the Porsche **Super Carrera**. You begin it with (of course) two boxes. Be sure to get the curves down right. Then loosely add some wheels and wheel wells gettin' a little action into the runner. Lay some headlight openings into the curved front fenders keeping them lined up.

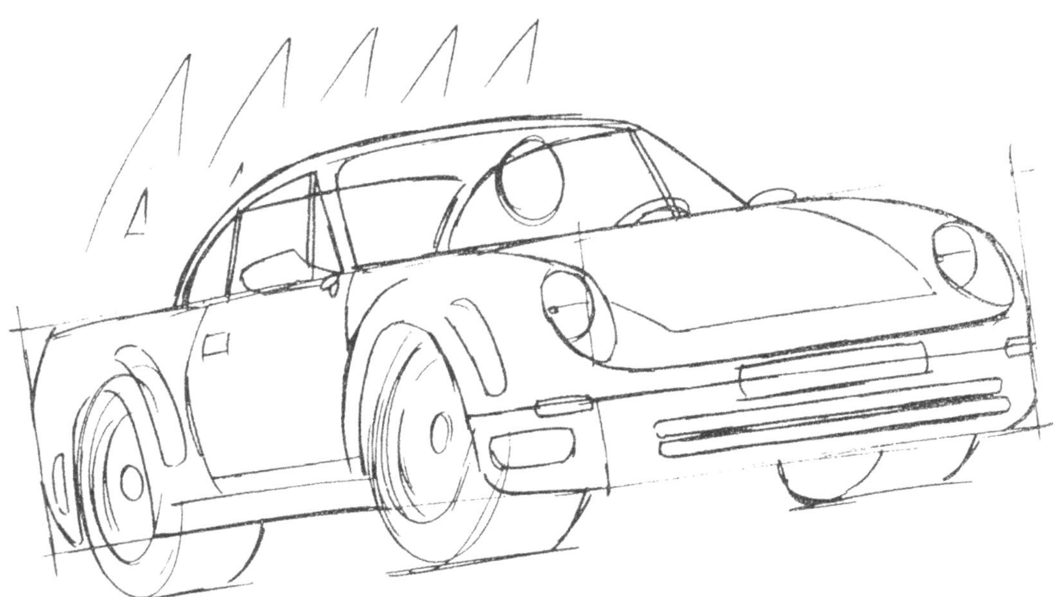

Some detail to the interior is next along with side window posts and mirrors. All fenders have air vents so you need to rough some in here. The front body line curves from the headlights with more vents below. Lay in the hood lines, door lines, and handle. Give the wheels a bit more detail and add some **sound**.

Check over everything one more time and give the vents some grill work. Indicate glass covers on the headlights and add gloss to the paint through the careful use of black. Get it up with a body shadow and smoke an' rollin' with well-lit tires. Ink it in, erase your pencil marks, and you've got yourself a $56,000 car!

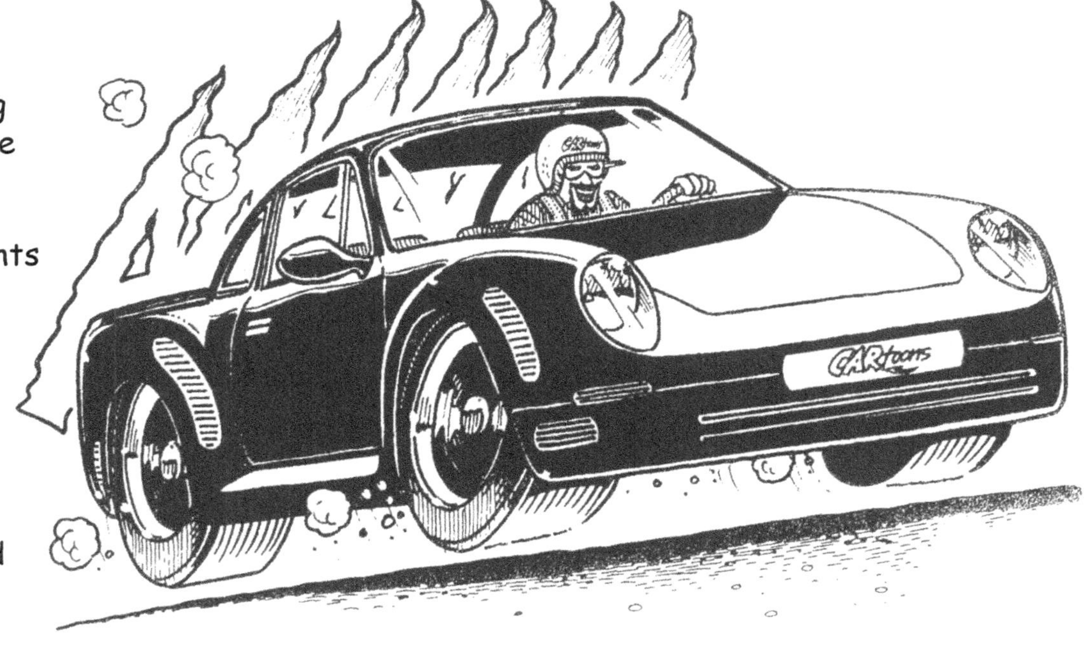

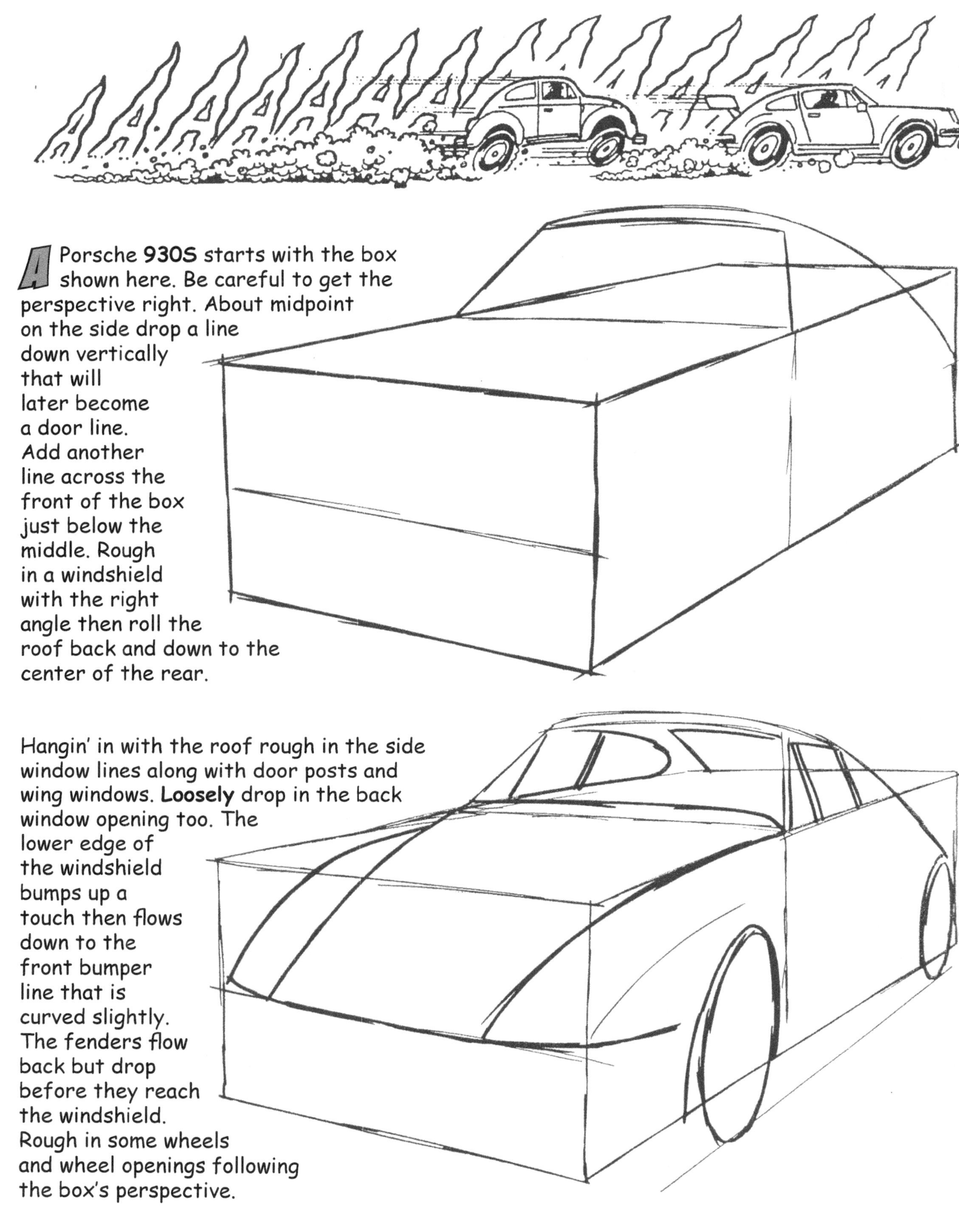

A Porsche **930S** starts with the box shown here. Be careful to get the perspective right. About midpoint on the side drop a line down vertically that will later become a door line. Add another line across the front of the box just below the middle. Rough in a windshield with the right angle then roll the roof back and down to the center of the rear.

Hangin' in with the roof rough in the side window lines along with door posts and wing windows. **Loosely** drop in the back window opening too. The lower edge of the windshield bumps up a touch then flows down to the front bumper line that is curved slightly. The fenders flow back but drop before they reach the windshield. Rough in some wheels and wheel openings following the box's perspective.

You can start the front end by first wrapping another line around it just below the earlier one then another one below that. The bottom edge of the air dam falls under it. Divide the bumper in half then drop in a parking light on each side. Continue the bottom air dam lines 'round the side, back to the rear fender. Add a hood scoop as shown.

Drop a couple of guide lines down the fender indicating the headlights and louvers then add fog lights and a grill area to the air dam. Bucket seats may now be roughed into the interior along with a steering wheel and side mirrors. Out back, rough in the rear spoiler, then cut an air scoop in the rear fender with **teeth**.

After you check it all over carefully, grab your favorite ball-point or felt-tip pen and ink 'er in! Begin by outlining large sections with a heavy line leaving details with a fine line for later. Add solid blacks and highlights as I've done here or create an original paint job of your own. A full-body shadow helps bring it to life!

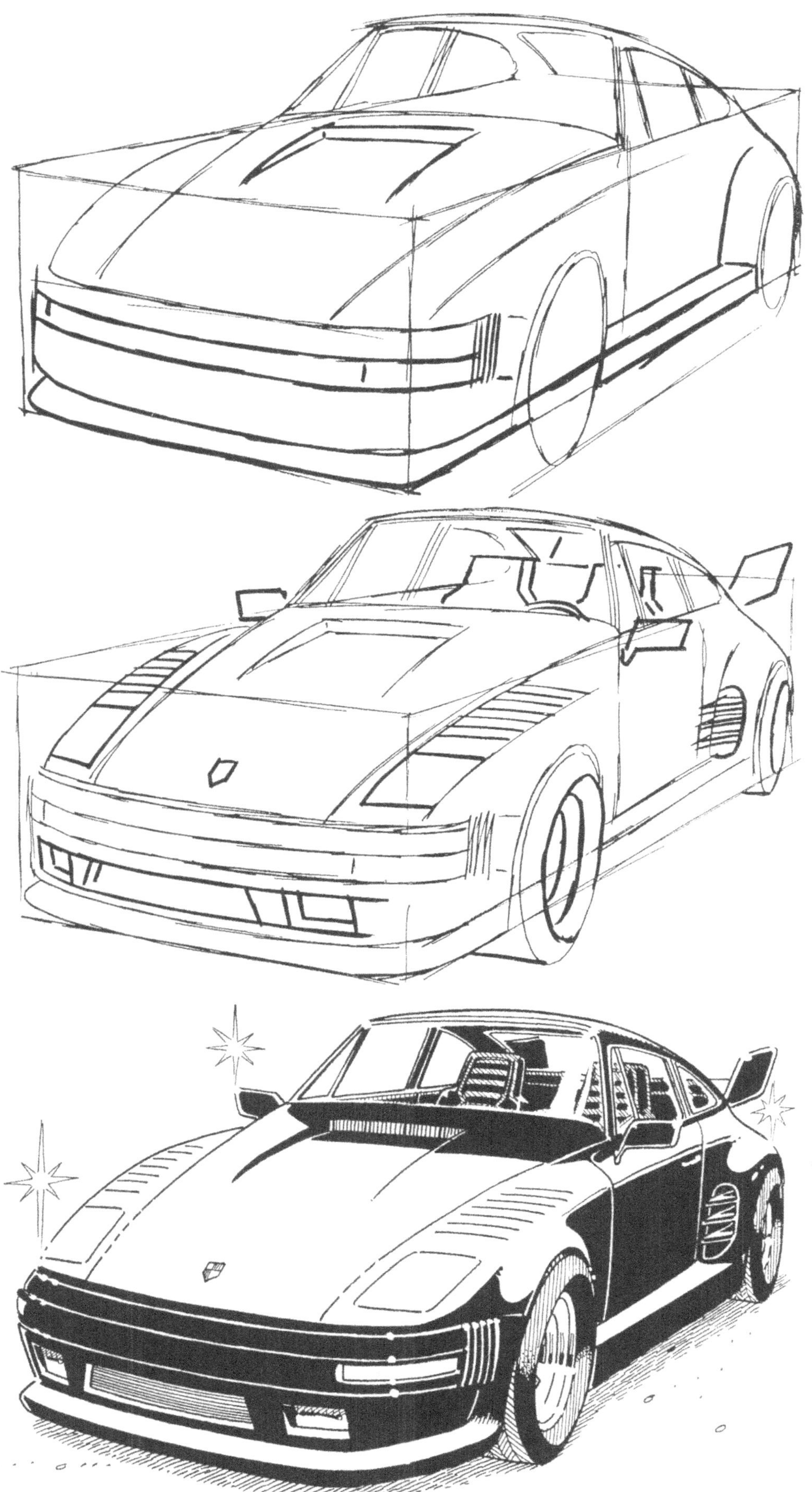

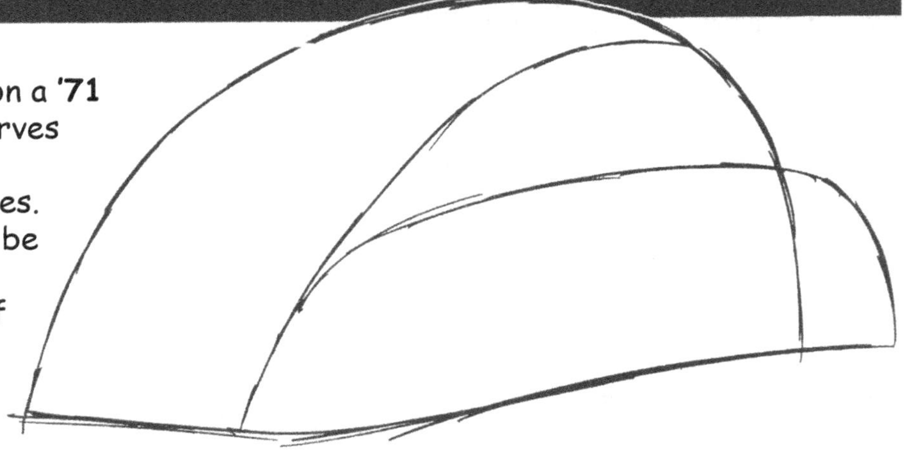

W hat better place to start than on a **'71 Bug Pro Streeter**? Copy the curves you see here very carefully, slightly bowing the bottom and side body lines. Everything you do from here on will be built on these basic shapes so take your time and try to feel the flow of the Bug's shape. You'll get it!

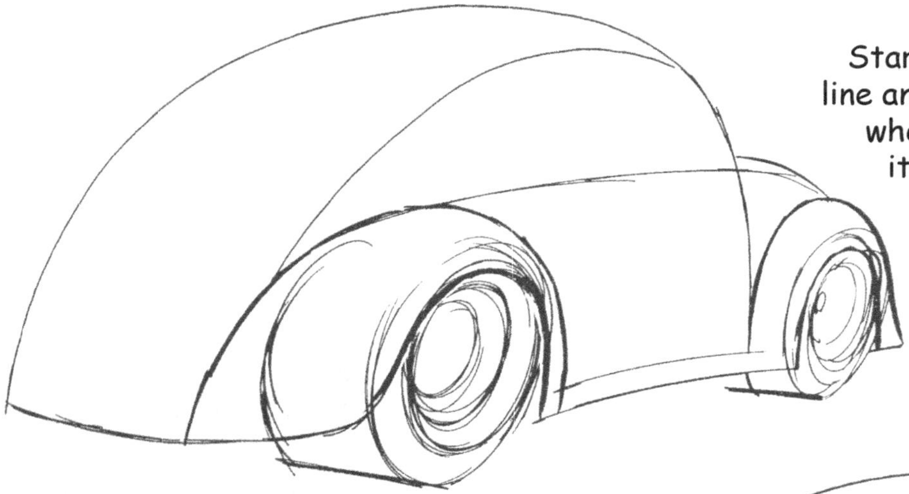

Start the rear fender at the side body line and follow it down to the bottom line where you add another line just above it to indicate the running board. The front fender rolls out beyond the front curve you indicated earlier. Now is also a good time to rough in some big n' little tires drawing right through things.

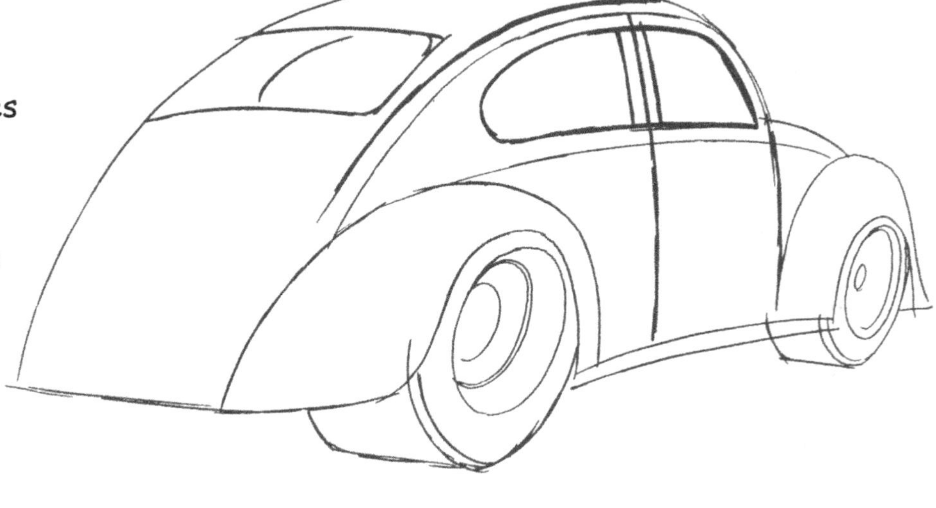

Time to think about some windows, dropping in the side ones by following the roof curve and the side body line. Split the side window in the middle with the door post then run a line through the middle of that to complete the door opening. The roof body line follows the **original** curve back to the rear window opening that keys off the side windows.

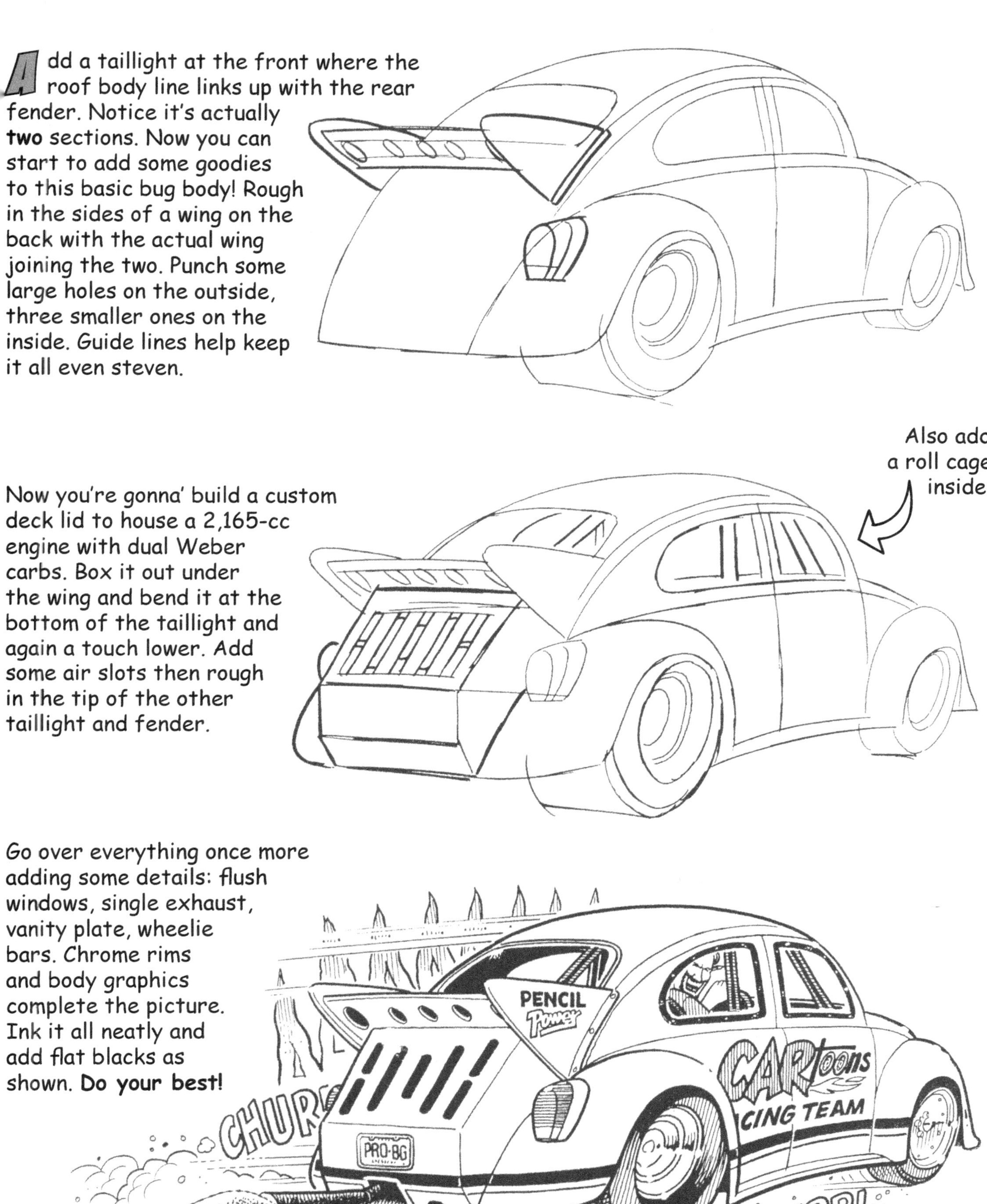

dd a taillight at the front where the roof body line links up with the rear fender. Notice it's actually **two** sections. Now you can start to add some goodies to this basic bug body! Rough in the sides of a wing on the back with the actual wing joining the two. Punch some large holes on the outside, three smaller ones on the inside. Guide lines help keep it all even steven.

Now you're gonna' build a custom deck lid to house a 2,165-cc engine with dual Weber carbs. Box it out under the wing and bend it at the bottom of the taillight and again a touch lower. Add some air slots then rough in the tip of the other taillight and fender.

Also add a roll cage inside.

Go over everything once more adding some details: flush windows, single exhaust, vanity plate, wheelie bars. Chrome rims and body graphics complete the picture. Ink it all neatly and add flat blacks as shown. **Do your best!**

PRO GASSERS

The looks of the drags are changing and a big part of that are the pro gassers! A good one to start with is this **Ford Fairmont**. Copy the boxes shown here being careful to get their proportions right. Rough in the wheel wells and indicate tire placement.

Note how high up in the well the tires sit.

Drop in the rear side window and add some window trim to the others. Block in the hood scoop in two sections, working your way down to the grill and headlight area. Notice how the hood line drops **toward** the front. Detail the grill pattern and wheels a bit.

Time to go over all you've done once more. Add a driver and inner roll cage. Hood scallops follow the centerline. Careful attention to the grill and headlights will give you a clean look. Ink all this neatly with a ball-point or felt-tip pen including some decals and numbers. Add blacks to the shadow and tires for contrast.

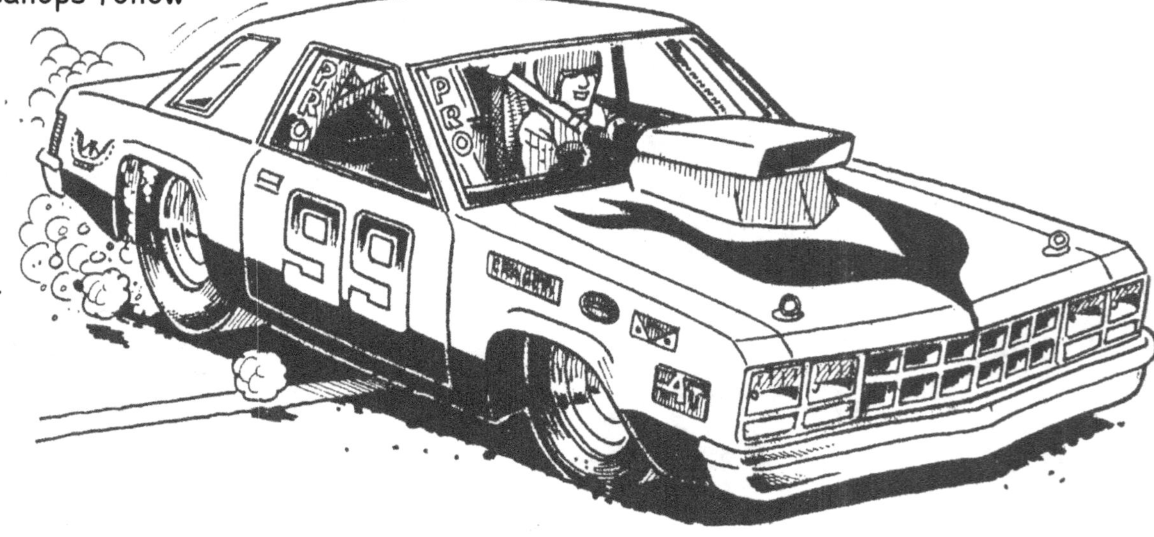

Smaller cars like this **Mustang** make great gassers. Start it with two basic boxes. Get 'em correct. **Everything** from here on will be built on 'em. Note the front fender dip an' grill angle. Place wheel wells as shown roughing in the smaller front and larger rear tires so that the body sits low and at a **slight** angle. With a centerline, pop a blower hole in the hood.

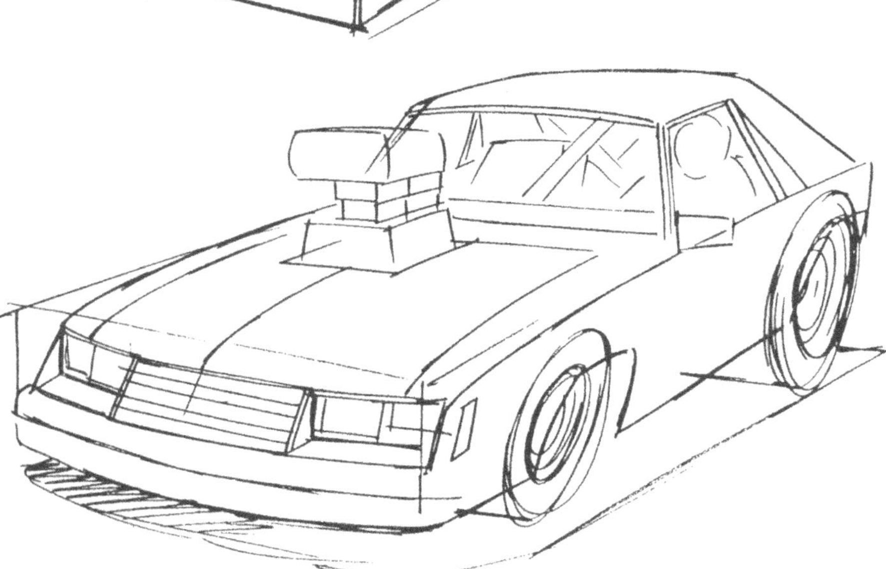

Let's start up front blocking in the grill area. First get that distinctive downward curve at both the hood an' bumper lines. In between add the headlight and grill areas. Plot the hood lines roughing in the blower and scoop. Loosely work in a driver with bucket seats, dash, and roll cage. Add the body shadow and some more detail to the wheels.

Check what you've done so far and don't be afraid to make some corrections here and there. Detail the blower system. Give more dimension to the grill area and headlight area as well as more definition to the front bumper. Note how it wraps around. Careful inking and the addition of body stripes help to finish 'er up. Don't forget to be neat!

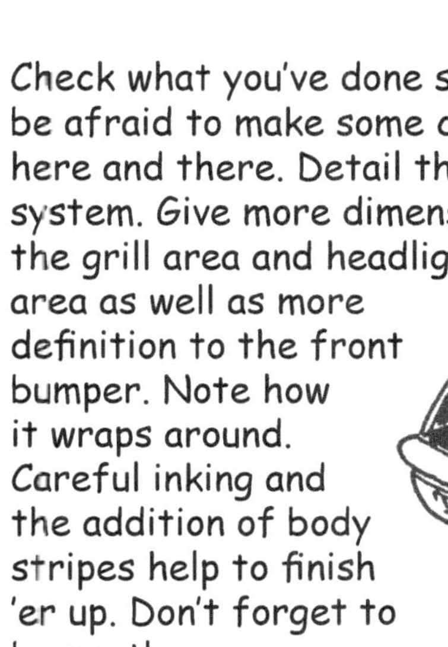

ot all pro gassers are new cars. Everyone's old favorite, the **'55 Chevy**, makes a great competitor. As always begin by constructing the two boxes shown here. Notice their upward tilt to give the Chevy some lift. Loosely rough in a small wheel well up front with a bigger one in back. Also rough in the front an' back bumpers and shadow.

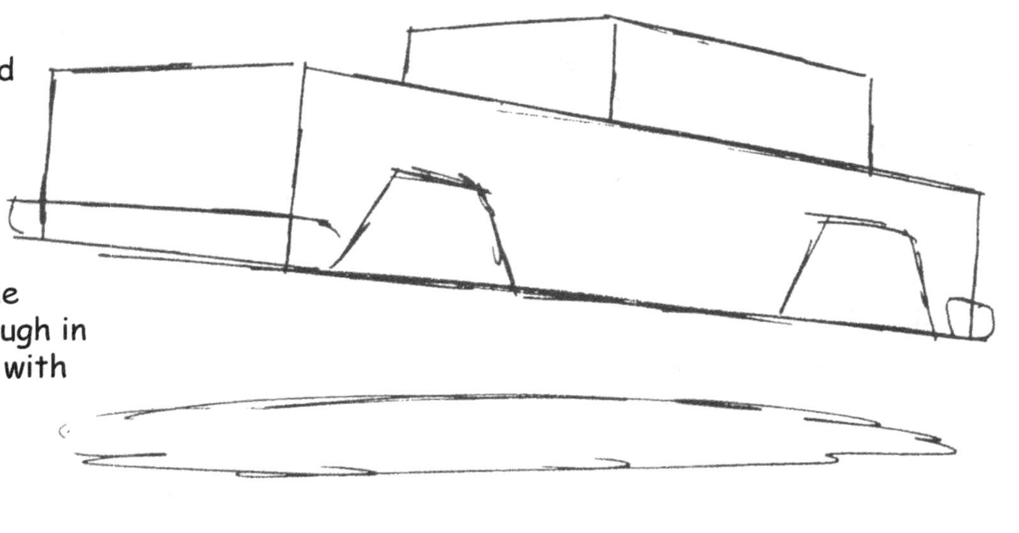

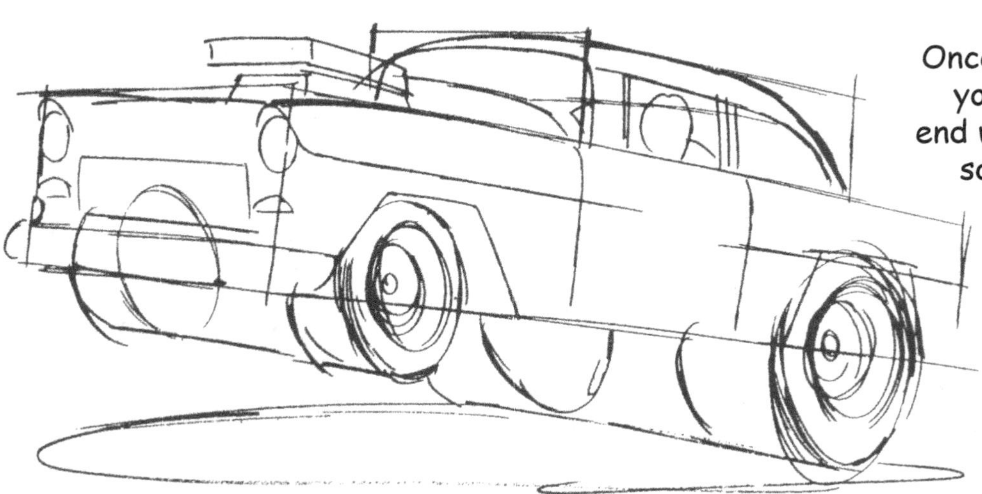

Once again you begin to build upon your two basic boxes. The front end will be fiberglass and seamless so lay in the headlights, parking lights, and the grill along with the hood scoop. Take note how the windshield and roofline are carved out of the top box. Add side posts and door lines. Rough in tires with **big** slicks in the rear and drop in a driver.

If you've got all the basics down so far, this last step of checking and cleaning up the Chevy for inking will be fun. A little more attention to the front end, wheels, and interior and you're ready to ink. Some lettering always helps a bunch. Neatly ink everything with your favorite pen, add some smoke and sounds, then erase all your pencil lines an' **crank 'er up**!

HOW TO DRAW DRAGSTERS

ragsters today sure are a lot different from when I was a kid but one thing's the same: They're all engine so let's start there.

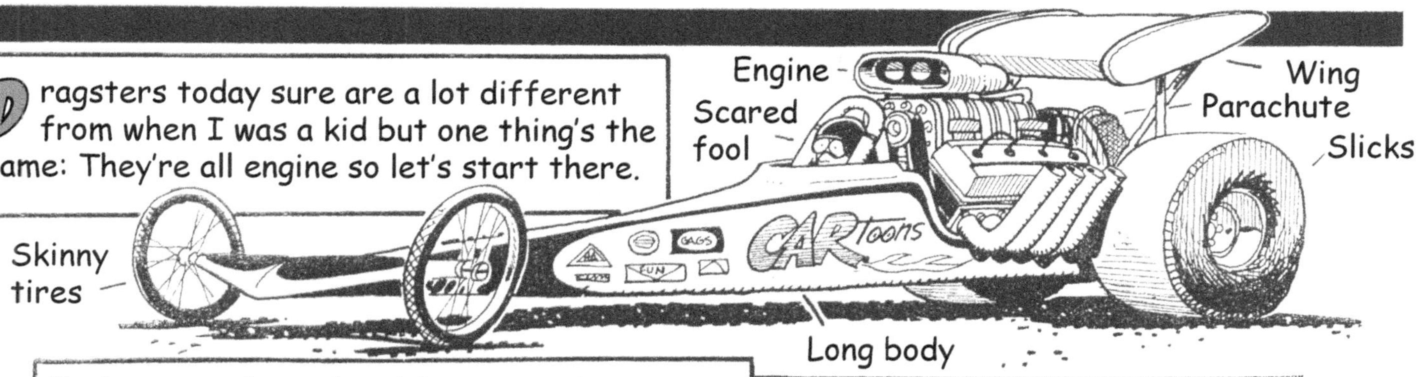

Engines are always hard for me to draw so I work from photos startin' with a rough sketch. Engines are fairly boxy so you break 'em down to their basics then build 'em up.

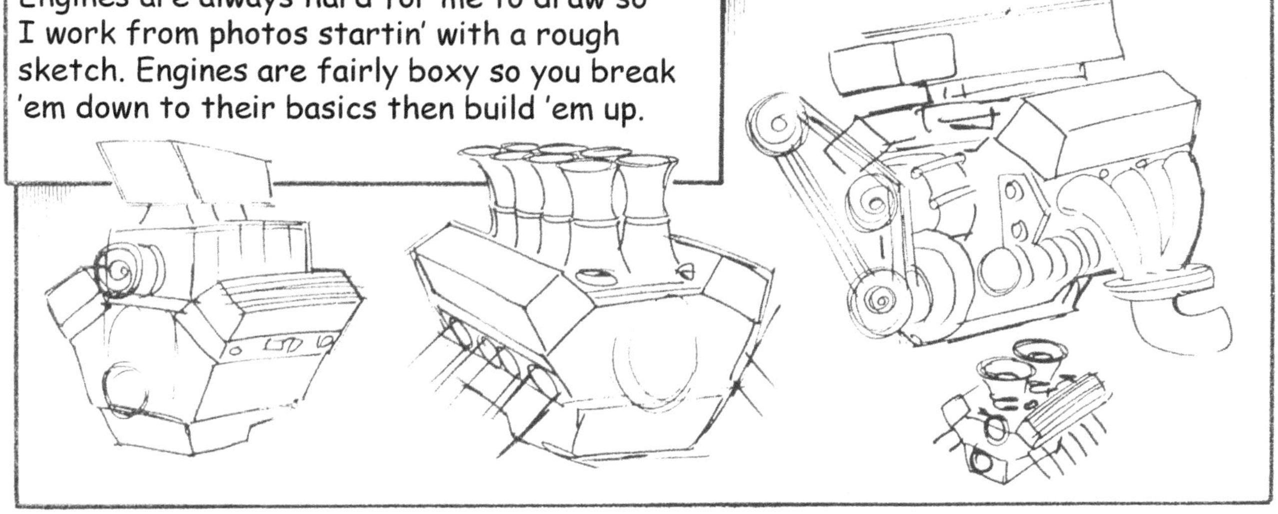

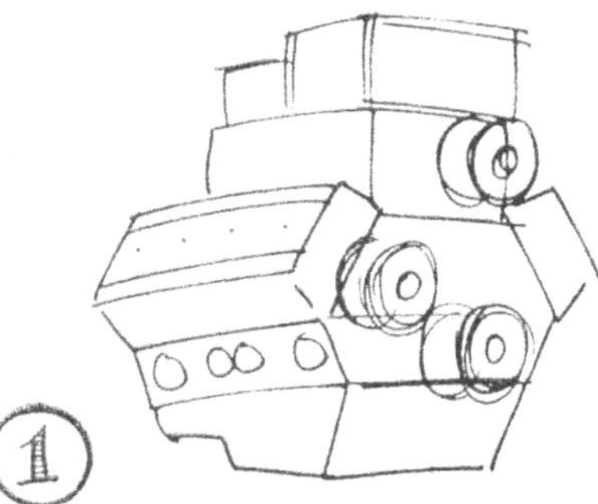

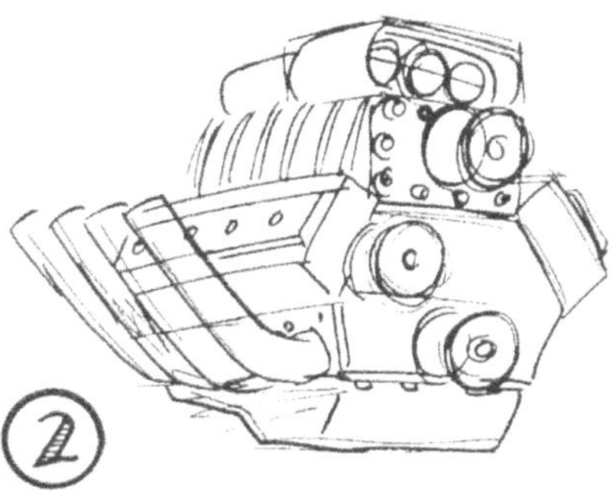

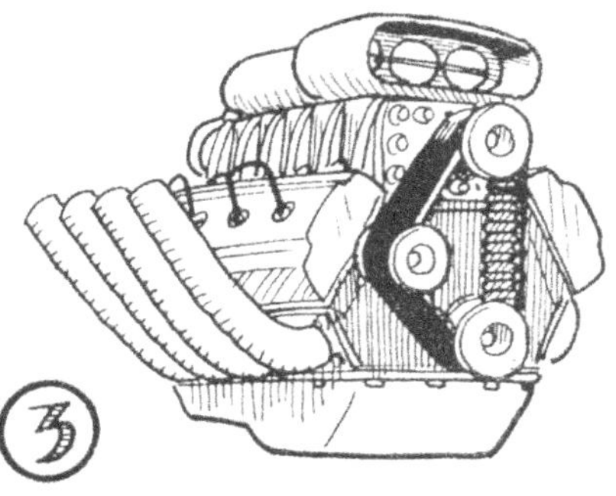

1 You start simple by boxing in the block, heads, blower, and scoop. Then add the pulleys.

2 Round the edges of the scoop. Add detail to the blower and valve covers and block in the tuned headers.

3 Detail all this a bit tighter and add the blower belt an' plug wires.

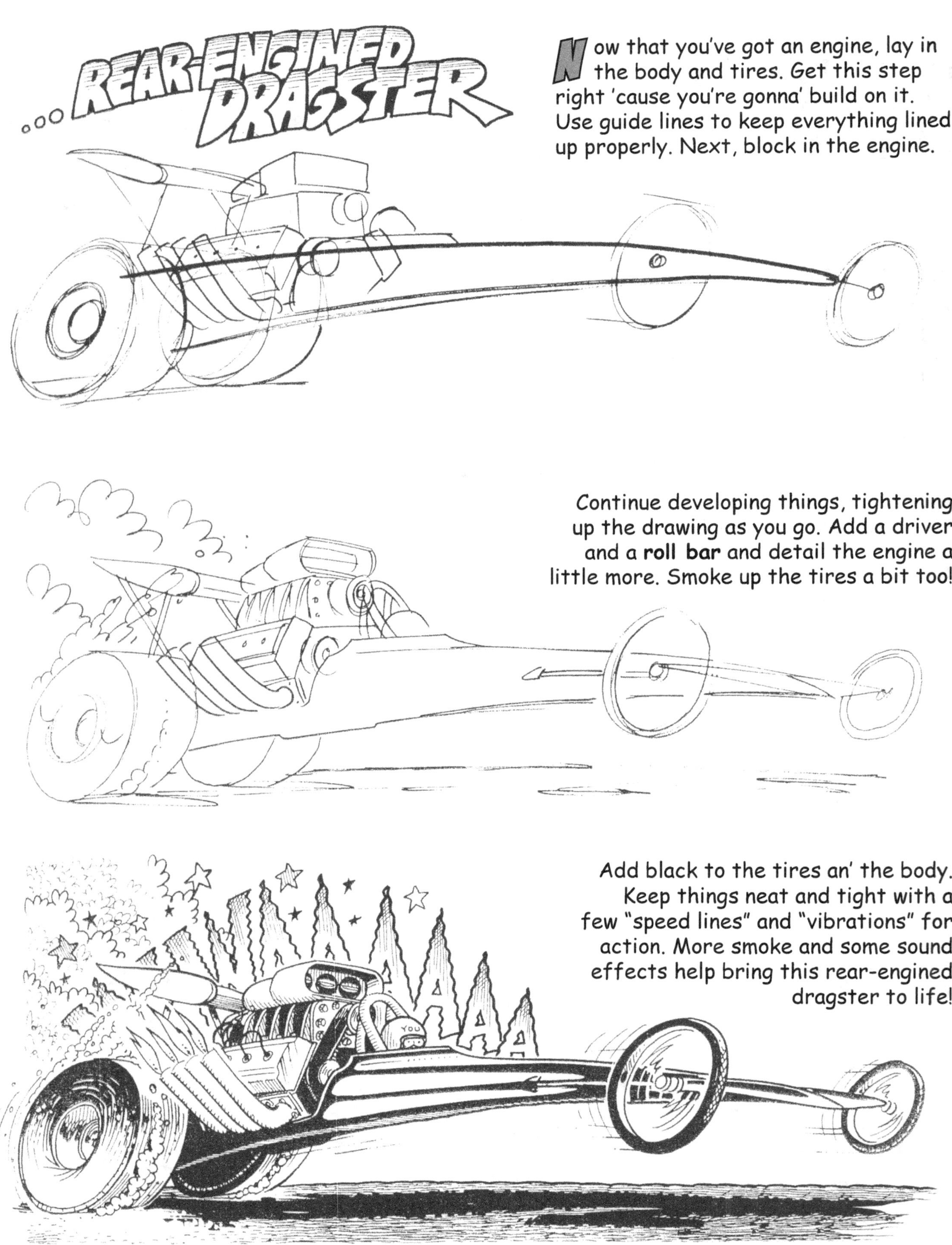

Now that you've got an engine, lay in the body and tires. Get this step right 'cause you're gonna' build on it. Use guide lines to keep everything lined up properly. Next, block in the engine.

Continue developing things, tightening up the drawing as you go. Add a driver and a **roll bar** and detail the engine a little more. Smoke up the tires a bit too!

Add black to the tires an' the body. Keep things neat and tight with a few "speed lines" and "vibrations" for action. More smoke and some sound effects help bring this rear-engined dragster to life!

HOW TO DRAW
INDY CARS

E veryone loves the Indy 500, and the cars are a lot of fun to draw! Start one with this box. Position the wheels as shown then rough in a bottom line.

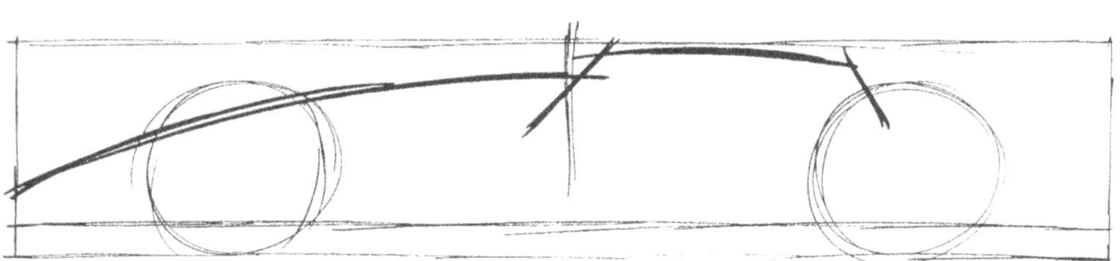

Loosely copy the body line noticing it cuts through the front wheel to the midpoint, bumps up and back, cutting down into the rear wheel.

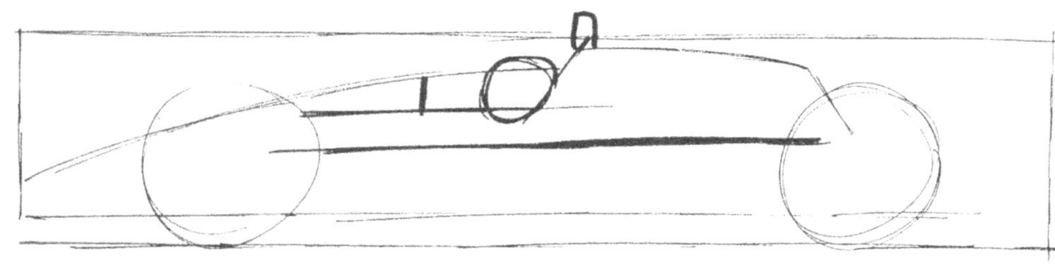

Divide the body in half then in half again to carve out the cockpit area. Rough in a driver and indicate a roll bar.

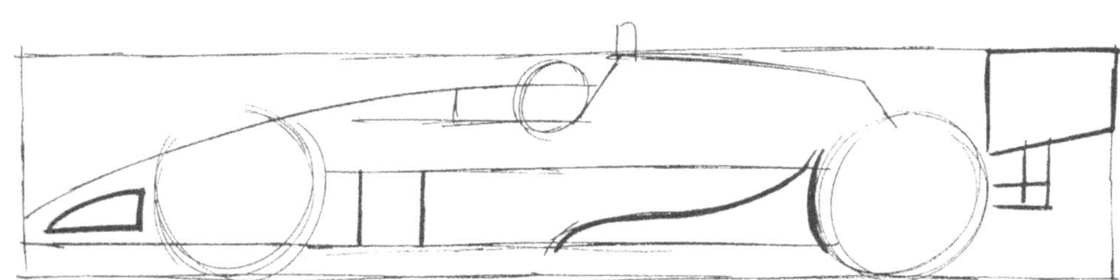

The lower part of the body gets a scoop and a rear wheel spoiler, a big spoiler out back, and a small spoiler up front.

More detail to the wheels and your **favorite** logo/graphics help it get ready for inking with a felt-tip or ball-point pen.

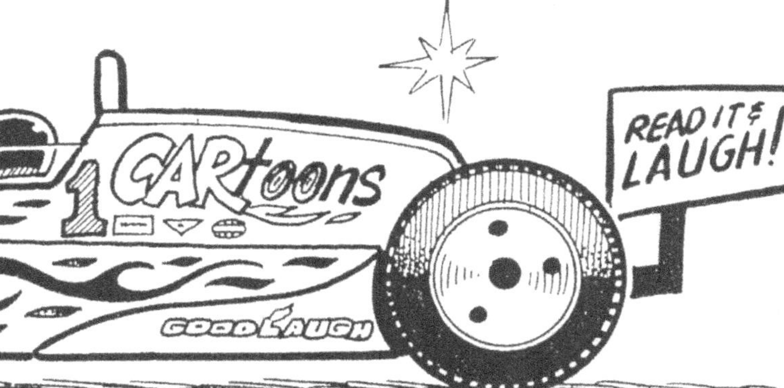

For a **three-quarter view** you start with a wedge and use guide lines to rough in some wide tires. Be careful to get the proper placement. Within the wedge, copy the curved outer shape of the body.

Everything will be built on this step so take your time. Do it right!

Add another top body line, which gives you the outline of the cockpit. Rough in the windshield and a helmet. Box in the scoop areas on the side. Air spoilers abound so get started roughing in the large rear one, the rear wheel wedge, and the full front one. Guide lines help you here too.

Time to letter some stuff on the side. Add some detail to the tires and suspension bars and you've got yourself an Indy racer! Carefully ink it all in using solid blacks as shown. Gentlemen . . . **Start your engines!**

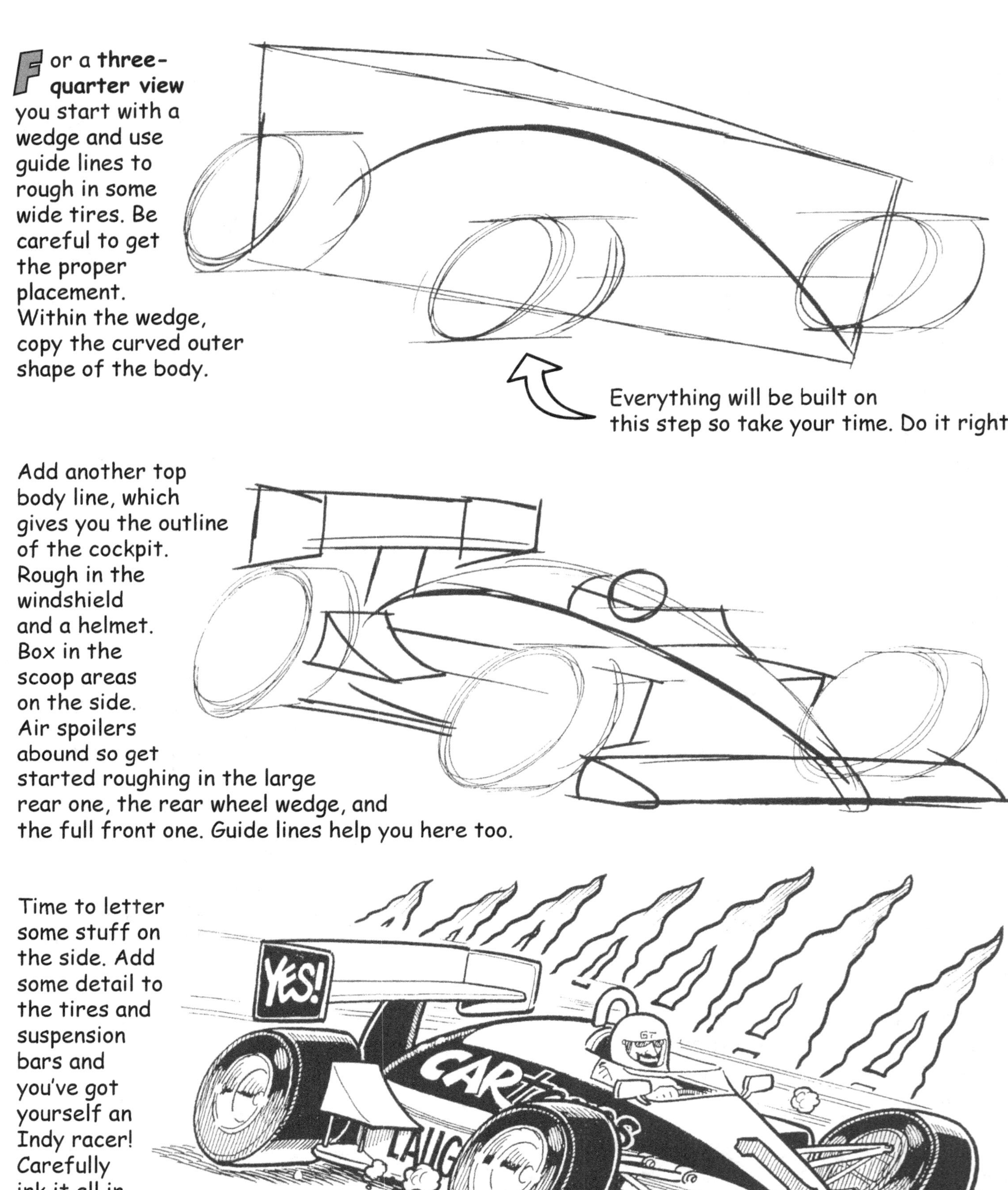